The problems of efficiently managing large enterprises are common to both the West and to the Soviet Union. The growth in management science in the West has been paralleled in the Soviet Union in the years since Khrushchev's fall. Professor Conyngham provides a comprehensive discussion of the efforts in the Soviet Union to develop techniques of scientific management that are consistent with the requirements of communist ideology and a planned economy.

The opening chapter outlines the reforms of Soviet industrial management during the post-Khrushchev era and, in particular, indicates the role that increased decentralization has played in the developing importance of management science. Conyngham then concentrates on the generation of management theory and its application to the existing economic system. Topics covered include the emergence of systems analysis as the basic approach to management reform, the application of mathematical models and computers to decision making, and the introduction of economic and behavioral methods of management control. The last part of the book deals with the impact of functional rationalization on the structure of the existing system and the ministerial reforms of the 1970s.

Conyngham concludes that the efforts to modernize Soviet industrial management under Brezhnev have been severely hampered by political, ideological, technical, and institutional constraints. The resolution of the problems of Soviet socioeconomic development remains a critical issue for the 1980s.

The Modernization of Soviet Industrial Management will interest specialists and students in Soviet politics, economics, and management and those concerned with organizational theory and management science.

THE MODERNIZATION OF
SOVIET INDUSTRIAL MANAGEMENT

SOVIET AND EAST EUROPEAN STUDIES

Editorial Board

The National Association for Soviet and East European Studies exists for the purpose of promoting study and research on the social sciences as they relate to the Soviet Union and the countries of Eastern Europe. The Monograph Series is intended to promote the publication of works presenting substantial and original research in the economics, politics, sociology, and modern history of the USSR and Eastern Europe.

SOVIET AND EAST EUROPEAN STUDIES

Books in the series

THE MODERNIZATION OF SOVIET INDUSTRIAL MANAGEMENT

SOCIOECONOMIC DEVELOPMENT AND THE SEARCH FOR VIABILITY

WILLIAM J. CONYNGHAM

CATHOLIC UNIVERSITY OF AMERICA
WASHINGTON, D.C.

CAMBRIDGE UNIVERSITY PRESS
CAMBRIDGE
LONDON   NEW YORK   NEW ROCHELLE
MELBOURNE   SYDNEY

CAMBRIDGE UNIVERSITY PRESS
Cambridge, New York, Melbourne, Madrid, Cape Town, Singapore, São Paulo

Cambridge University Press
The Edinburgh Building, Cambridge CB2 8RU, UK

Published in the United States of America by Cambridge University Press, New York

www.cambridge.org
Information on this title: www.cambridge.org/9780521243810

First published 1982
This digitally printed version 2008

A catalogue record for this publication is available from the British Library

Library of Congress Cataloguing in Publication data
Conyngham, William J.
The modernization of Soviet industrial
management.
(Soviet and East European studies)
Bibliography: p.
1.   Industrial management – Soviet Union.
I. Title.   II. Series.
HD70.S63C66   658'.00947   81–21630

ISBN 978-0-521-24381-0 hardback
ISBN 978-0-521-07026-3 paperback

For Margaret Frances

Contents

Contents

Preface

This study began in a deceptively simple way as an investigation of the impact of the 1965 economic reforms on industrial organization. In an earlier book, *Industrial Management in the Soviet Union*, my examination of the Communist Party's leading role in industrial decision making had raised several interesting questions that I hoped to pursue more systematically with respect to the reforms. These questions arose quite naturally from Khrushchev's repeated failures to revitalize industrial management in the late 1950s and early 1960s. During those turbulent years, it became strikingly clear that his striving to make the management system viable through the ideological and political mobilization of economic management was quite irrelevant under contemporary conditions. His trial-and-error approach, directed primarily at reorganizing the Party and state bureaucracies, failed to address the massive changes in the Soviet Union that had resulted from socioeconomic development. In a fundamental sense, Khrushchev's experience put into question whether any management system as big and complex as the existing Soviet system can, in fact, be rationally directed and controlled.

In the post-Khrushchev period, the continuing effort to create a modern management system has been simultaneously a reaction to the earlier period and a thrust to transcend it. The lessons of the political backlash that toppled Khrushchev have not been lost upon his successors, who have approached the problems of management cautiously. Nevertheless, there has been a gradually increasing awareness within the political leadership of the formidable challenges that a very complex socioeconomic system presents to a traditionally organized industrial system. Perhaps more acutely for Brezhnev than for Khrushchev, the central problem remains of how to increase the effectiveness of industrial management without simultaneously undermining the regime's political structure.

The genuinely new element in the search since 1964 for a modern industrial organization has been the complex and still not fully completed effort to develop a scientific theory of management as the starting point for rationalizing the management system. The assumption that social and economic processes can be consciously and rationally planned and controlled has been fundamental to Soviet Marxism. To define this issue in clear operational terms, however, has been extremely difficult for Soviet as well as Western specialists. At the beginning of the 1980s, there is still theoretical ambiguity as to whether a Soviet-type management system can direct a complex industrial economy with measurable efficiency. The experience of the past fifteen years strongly suggests that the organizational development of industrial management within the existing institutional framework remains an uncertain task.

The processes of rationalization have been centered on the resolution of two fundamental operational problems. The first encompasses those chronic problems of economic efficiency that have plagued the command economy since the early 1930s. The second, closely associated problem has been the expansion of organizational pluralism, which has been experienced as a growth in the role of the intermediate organs of management and as a suboptimization and corresponding loss of centralized direction and control. The twin objectives have been to improve both the efficiency of resource allocation and the integration and responsiveness of industrial organization.

The pursuit of these objectives over the past fifteen years has been a complicated process and has proceeded on a variety of levels under diverse circumstances. The most basic level, clearly, has been the quest for a theory of how to manage a complex industrial system. This search has, of course, been heavily conditioned by the complexity and institutional inertia characteristic of the present management system and by the paradigm of classical rationality that defines and legitimates it. In this respect, the central issue in management modernization has been whether an alternative model of management can be established under existing ideological and political constraints. This issue assumes importance insofar as the development of new management structures and methods have been logically derived from or related to a general model of how, ideally, the system should function.

The focus of this study is on the theories or conceptions of management that have evolved over the past two decades, how they have been applied, and what has resulted from them.

Chapter 1 outlines in broad strokes the structures, operational procedures, and context of reform of industrial management in the post-Khrushchev period. The remaining chapters center on the generation of theory and its application to the existing system. Chapter 2 examines the emergence of systems analysis as the basic approach to management reform. Chapters 3 and 4 investigate the application of mathematical models and computers to decision making and the introduction of economic and behavioral methods of management control. Chapter 5 reviews the impact of functional rationalization on the structures of the existing system. Chapter 6 discusses the ministerial reforms of the 1970s.

Over the course of several years of research, I have accumulated numerous debts, which I would like to acknowledge, if not repay. I am grateful to the Hoover Institution on War, Revolution and Peace for a grant and for valuable criticism on the first draft of the manuscript. I am also indebted to the Earhart Foundation for their financial assistance in preparing the manuscript. My family and I are especially grateful to the Warden and Fellows of St. Antony's College, Oxford, for their gracious hospitality to us during a year's stay in England.

I also owe a large debt to John P. Hardt of the Congressional Research Service, Donald Aufenkamp of the National Science Foundation, and Thomas West of Catholic University. Each made a significant contribution to the manuscript, without, of course, incurring any responsibility for it.

W.J.C.

Washington, D.C.

1

The context of management reform

In large part, the modernization of Soviet industrial management has assumed such exceptionally complex forms since 1965 because the system is conceived to be politically integrated and ideologically defined by the institutions of central planning and public ownership of productive property. Structurally, Soviet industrial management is a constituent element in the larger, highly differentiated, Party–state organizational complex. The dominant influences on industrial management are political.

In the division of labor between the bureaucracies of the Communist Party and the Soviet state, the state assumes formal responsibility for the determination of operational goals, allocation of authority and resources, selection and deployment of personnel, and coordination and control of the processes of implementation. Penetrating, overlapping, and controlling the state bureaucracy is the *apparat* of the Communist Party. Full-time Party officials routinely intervene in virtually every management function at every level of the hierarchy; the Party also has special responsibilities for mobilizing and integrating the system.[1] As T. H. Rigby has suggested, "The Soviet Union may be termed a mono-organizational society, since nearly all activities are run by hierarchies of appointed officials under the direction of a single overall command."[2]

The organization of Soviet industrial management is intricate. Its formal structure has close affinities with its classic counterpart in the West. It is defined by a hierarchical and pyramidal structure, specialization of function, explicitly fixed jurisdictions and performance criteria, and trained personnel. Formal authority flows from a single, if collective, source. The system has

1

assumed a technical and static form and encourages strict and authoritarian role playing.[3]

This mechanistic, determinate, and authoritarian model is, naturally, an ideal type. Soviet management institutions are more adequately conceived as a hybrid model of artificial and natural subsystems. In contrast to the explicit and rationalized artificial subsystem, the natural subsystem is the complex of cultural, social, psychological, and political relationships that develops around the artificial subsystem and that both supports and modifies it.[4] In Soviet practice, the function of the artificial system has been to shape and control the natural subsystem. Soviet management has traditionally placed a heavy stress on administrative discipline and political mobilization as primary devices for overcoming the risks of human variability, deviance, functional failure, and an excessive growth of affective relationships and suboptimization, or the execution of local, subsystemic goals at the expense of general organizational purposes. Without the natural subsystem, however, it is doubtful whether Soviet management could function.

Since the mid-1930s, management theory has played a minor role in the operation of industrial organization. Traditionally, the formal principles for distributing authority and function within the system have been described in both legal and managerial terms.

The public law tradition has emphasized three general principles. The most important has been democratic centralism, whereby centralized authority is combined with democratic participation and accountability. A second principle stresses the need to combine collective decision making with the responsibility of one-man management (*edinonachalie*). The principle of dual subordination has been the formal mode for integrating vertical and horizontal authority. Under this principle, an intermediate management unit is subordinate vertically to a superior organization and horizontally to a republican or local political authority.[5] Historically, Soviet management has been characterized by centralism, verticalism, and one-man management.

The current managerial concept for the distribution of authority is "limited functionalism." Toward the end of the 1920s, the functionalism of F. W. Taylor was introduced into Soviet industrial organization. The practice of each specialist issuing direct commands to line and staff subordinates, however, produced massive problems of coordination during the early 1930s. The complexity of the industrial economy was simply too great even in the mid-1930s to support a simple reversion to the line-staff structure. The compromise of limited functionalism permits staff or functional agencies to issue commands to subordinate organizations within the limits of their formal jurisdiction. In many respects, the compromise has led to serious indeterminacy in the management of the system.[6]

The management system

At the peak of the executive structure of the Soviet state is the USSR Council of Ministers, which has formal responsibility for setting industrial policy and directing the management system. Its formal structure is large and cumbersome (see Chart 1.1). In July 1974, for example, the Council was composed of a chairman, first deputy chairman, sixty-one ministers, thirteen chairmen of the most important state committees and, ex officio, the fifteen chairmen of the republican councils of ministers. Effective authority appears concentrated in the Presidium, an inner cabinet composed of the chairman and his deputies.

The Council of Ministers has comprehensive authority with respect to the planning, coordination, and control of the national economy. A stream of orders and decisions, frequently on highly limited and specific issues, is issued by the Council autonomously or in conjunction with the Central Committee of the Communist Party. Decision-making procedures and processes are carefully hidden from view. The size, structure, and functions of the administrative staff serving the Council are secret as well. Its administrative structure, however, probably resembles those of the union republican councils of ministers. The executive agency for the Russian Republic's Council of Ministers, for example, is the Administration of Affairs. It contains the secretariats of the chairman and his deputies and a series of branch and functional departments that parallel the republic's state committees and ministries. Each department coordinates and controls a related group of ministries or committees.[7]

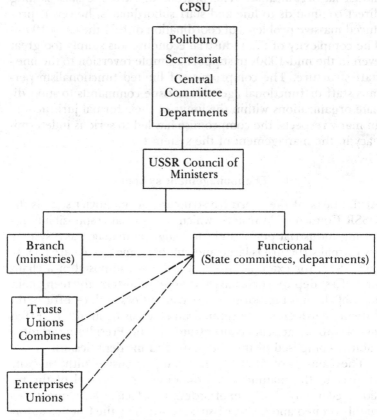

Chart 1.1. The general scheme of Soviet management. (Broken line denotes restricted communication linkages.)

The capacity of the Council of Ministers to coordinate and control the national economy directly is clearly limited. As the economy has grown more complex, the major burden of management has fallen increasingly on the agencies of the intermediate level, which are of two general types, the functional organs and branch ministries.

The functional organs

The most important state committees are those whose chairmen are simultaneously deputy chairmen of the Council of Ministers

Chart 1.2. *Major functional organs of economic management*

USSR Council of Ministers
USSR state committees and agencies

*State Planning Committee	*All-Union Farm Machinery Union
*State Committee of Material–Technical Supply	*Ministry of Finance
*State Committee for Science and Technology	*Central Statistical Administration
*State Committee for Construction Affairs	*USSR State Bank
State Committee of Prices	All-Union Bank for Financing Capital Construction
*State Committee for Questions of Labor and Wages	Committee of Inventions and Discoveries
*Committee of People's Control	*Committee on Printing
*State Committee on Professional and Technical Education	*Committee on Standards, Measures, and Measuring Instruments
State Committee of Procurements	Main Administration of the Microbiological Industry
*State Committee of Forestry	State Committee on Mineral Resources
*State Committee on Foreign Economic Relations	State Arbitration
	Chief Administration of State Material Reserves

*Members of Council of Ministers (July 1974).
Source: Pravda, July 27, 1974, pp. 1–2; G. Kh. Popov, ed., *Funktsii i struktura organov uprovleniia, ikh sovershenstvovanie*, Moscow, Ekonomika, 1973, ch. 4.

(see Chart 1.2). Legally, state committees are designated as all-union (report directly to Moscow) or union-republican (also report to a regional government agency). State committees are specialized by function but have fairly standardized formal structures. Authority is concentrated in a committee, board, or council. Larger committees normally have a smaller collegium composed of the chairman, his deputies, and heads of major departments. The critical functional agencies in industrial management have been those regulating inputs and outputs, the State Planning Committee and the State Committee for Material–Technical Supply. Since 1965, though, the roles of

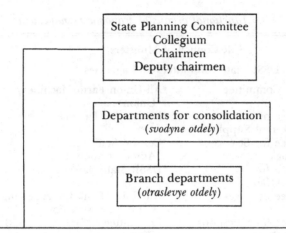

State Planning Committee
Collegium
Chairmen
Deputy chairmen

Departments for consolidation
(*svodyne otdely*)

Branch departments
(*otraslevye otdely*)

Organizations attached to Gosplan:
Scientific Research Economic Institute (NIEI), Council for the Study of Productive Forces (SOPS), Scientific Research Institute of Planning and Normatives, Institute of Integrated Transport Problems, Council of Gosplan, Interdepartmental Commission, Chief Computer Center

Chart 1.3. The structure of Gosplan. (Adapted from F. I. Kotov, *Organizatsiia planirovaniia narodnogo khoziaistvo SSR*, Moscow: Ekonomika, 1974, ch. III.)

other functional agencies have steadily expanded in response to the growing complexity of management.

The core functional agency is the State Planning Committee (Gosplan), which is responsible for formulating the national economic plans and coordinating their execution. The structure of Gosplan is very involved (see Chart 1.3). Gosplan has both a committee and collegium. At the bottom of the hierarchy are about forty branch departments, which negotiate and regulate the production plans of individual ministries. At the intermediate level are the consolidating departments (*svodnye otdely*) charged with balancing the ministries' plans with respect to such factors as capital investment, labor, finances, and region. At the top is the Department of the National Plan, which attempts to aggregate and integrate all dimensions of the national plan in conformity with the policy directives of the Communist Party leadership issued through the Council of Ministers.

The pressures of socioeconomic development have resulted in a continuous differentiation of structure. Since 1965, new departments have been formed for introducing new methods of planning and incentives, applying mathematical methods and computers in the national economy, and new developments in science and technology. In 1967, its Department of Prices became an independent state committee. A special department for coordinating the Soviet national economic plan with the Council for Mutual Economic Assistance (CMEA) has also been established. Among the many organizations attached to Gosplan, the Chief Computer Center has played a central role in the modernization of industrial organization.[8]

A fundamental institutional characteristic of Soviet management is the administrative allocation of supply through the State Committee for Material–Technical Supply, or Gossnab. Developed during the 1930s as a method for rationing scarce supplies to high-priority projects, the supply network has become firmly institutionalized in the general system of management controls. In 1973, Gossnab distributed about 60 percent of the working capital of industry.[9]

A union-republican agency with a ramified network of republican and territorial supply agencies, Gossnab, like Gosplan, has a full committee, a smaller collegium, and an administrative structure organized in branch, functional, and housekeeping departments. Of particular importance are the specialized chief administrations for the supply and sale of products (*soiuzglavsnabsbyty*) and for the sale of major construction projects (*soiuzglavkomplekty*). Because the planning and distribution of supply are shared with Gosplan and the ministries, the logistics of allocating inputs to industry have become massively difficult.[10]

Each of the state committees, like Gosplan and Gossnab, is a very large and complex organization. The State Bank, for example, which issues short- and long-term credit to industry and is responsible for the financial state of the enterprise, has twenty-two administrations and eight departments in its central *apparat* and has subordinate organizations in each republic province and major cities and districts. It manages 78,000 Soviet savings offices, handles the banking transactions for 570,000 Soviet enterprises of various types, and employs about 150,000.[11] The formal structures of the Central Statistical Administration and the Ministry of Finance are equally complicated.

Branch ministries

The core of industrial organization is the system of industrial ministries that were established in 1965 in essentially the form they had acquired in the 1930s and 1940s. As with the functional organs, the principal response of the industrial ministries to socioeconomic development has been differentiation of structure. Between 1966 and 1975, the number of all-union industrial ministries increased from sixteen to twenty-seven, although the number of union-republican ministries declined slightly (see Chart 1.4). As the industrial economy has matured, the ministerial system has exhibited an increasing diversity in size, products, production technologies, and management systems.

Some ministries are several times larger than General Motors. A ministry may control a few hundred enterprises or several thousand and employ as few as 500,000 or as many as 3.6 million. Production profiles may range from the relatively few products of the Ministry of the Coal Industry to the several thousand products of the Ministry of Chemical Industry. The mixture of production technologies also varies from custom production in the heavy machine-building ministries to continuous, highly mechanized production in some chemical and oil-refining plants.[12]

Traditionally, industrial ministries have been characterized by administrative designation (all-union or union-republican) or by type of output (extractive, heavy, or light industry). All-union ministries are primarily in heavy industry and defense. They have normally had higher levels of centralization, have managed fewer enterprises, and have less territorial dispersion and fewer hierarchical levels than do union-republican ministries. The latter, managing plants in the extractive and light industries, present significantly more involved problems of management.

The formal structure of the industrial ministry is also rela-

Chart 1.4. *Industrial ministries (July 1, 1974)*

All-union ministries	Council of Ministers Council of Ministers	Union–republican ministries
Aviation Industry	Machine Tool and Tool Industry	Geology
Automobile Industry	Shipbuilding Industry	Light Industry
Gas Industry	Tractor and Agricultural Machine	Lumber and Woodworking Industry
Machine Building	Building	Meat and Dairy Industry
Machine Building for Light and	Chemical and Oil Machine Building	Oil-Refining and Petrochemicals
Food Industry and Household	Chemical Industry	Industry
Goods	Cellulose–Paper Industry	Food Industry
Medical Industry	Electronics Industry	Industrial Construction Materials
Sea Fleet	Electrotechnical Industry	Fish Industry
Oil Industry	Machine Building for Animal Husbandry	Coal Industry
Defense Industry	and Fodder Production	Nonferrous Metallurgy
General Machine Building	Petroleum Industry	Ferrous Metallurgy
Instruments, Means of Automation,	Communications Equipment Industry	Energetics and Electrification
and Systems of Administration	Power Machine Building	Oil Extraction Industry
Radio Industry		
Medium Machine Building		
Heavy and Transport Machine		
Building		
Construction, Road Building, and		
Communal Economy Machine		
Building		

Source: Pravda, July 26, 1974, pp. 1–2; *Ekonomicheskaia gazeta,* no. 9 (1972): 11–12.

Chart 1.5. *Structure and functions of the functional chief administrations of a ministry*

Department	Functions
Planning–Economic	Current and long-term planning of the branch
Financial Administration	Forming consolidated branch financial balances and payments with the State Budget, banks, suppliers, and clients
Administration of Labor	Planning labor and scientific organization of labor
Organization and Wages	Organizing wage and bonus systems
Administration of Cadres and Educational Institutes	Supervising the preparation and repreparation of cadres and their use
Administration of Capital	Organizing the preparation and fulfillment of construction plans
Construction	Supervising construction
Administration of Equipment and Supply	Defining demand and distributing equipment and materials within the branch
Technical Administration	Preparing the planning and fulfillment of places for new technology and research and the development of new equipment and products
Production Administration	Chiefly engaged in the planning, specialization, loading of production capacity, and deliveries
Administration of the Chief Mechanic and Energy	Modernizing and repairing equipment and supplying heat and energy
Administration of Affairs–Chancery, Secretariat	Servicing the minister, deputy minister, and collegium of the ministry

Source: G. Kh. Popov, *Funktsii i structura, organov upravleniia, ikh sovershenstvovanie,* Moscow: Ekonomika, 1973, pp. 148–9.

tively standard. The basic structural division is between all-union and union-republican ministries. The union-republican ministry, prior to 1973, could have five or six hierarchical levels and a ministerial staff in each union-republic as well as in Moscow. In contrast, the all-union ministry was typically of three levels. At the top was the minister and five or six deputies, a consultative collegium, and a scientific-technical council. In 1970, the intermediate level of the ministry was composed of line agencies, the chief branch administration (*glavki*) responsible for production, and the functional agencies, the chief functional administrations. The number of *glavki* and chief functional administrations varied between twenty and thirty; the central staff averaged about one thousand.[13] Formal authority within the ministry is based upon *edinonachalie,* identifying the authority of the minister with the ministry. Formally, the chief production administration had direct operational control over the enterprise. It was the initial stage in planning, allocated supply and finances, disciplined enterprise management personnel, and could change or veto enterprise decisions. Functions for planning, supply, the administration of labor and training, finance, capital construction, and other functions were organized in the chief functional administrations. Because of their control of resources vital to the enterprise and the principle of limited functionalism, informal authority has tended to flow to the functional administrations (see Chart 1.5).

The industrial enterprise

In the 1970s, the role of the Soviet enterprise has become clouded by the rise of multiplant associations; at the end of the decade, however, the enterprise remained the principal structure for organizing production. Its formal organization reflects the organizational patterns of the ministries that plan and control its activities. Enterprise structure is conditioned by type of inputs, number of workers, extent of production specialization, types of production technologies, and degree to which the enterprise has a closed production cycle.[14]

The formal structure of the enterprise is usually standardized by the ministry. Within a ministry, enterprises are formally categorized by size, which is determined by the number of workers. Categories vary from seven in machine building to five in the chemical industry. The category of the plant determines the plant's departmentalization and the prestige and salaries of the director and other management personnel.

The basic administrative units of the enterprise are the plant leadership, the line production units, and the functional departments of the plant administration (see Chart 1.6). The number of vertical levels varies from two in small plants to four or five in larger enterprises. In the latter structure, hierarchy descends from the director to the head of production and then to the shop heads and first-line supervisors.

The enterprise director, like the minister, possesses comprehensive legal authority. Within the plant leadership, authority has been divided between the director and his first deputy, the chief engineer, who is normally responsible for maintaining the technologies of production and technical innovation. In smaller plants he may actually supervise production. With the increase in technological complexity and structural differentiation, deputy directors for economic questions and cadres have frequently been added.

The shop (*tsekh*) is the line organization responsible for the production process. Shops are divided into production shops and auxiliary shops for repair, instrument making, and other services for production. A plant may have as few as two or three shops or as many as twenty, as in the main plant of the Minsk Tractor Plant. Shops may employ from under one hundred to several thousand workers. The shop normally forms its own functional staff. The principle of limited functionalism does not apply in the enterprise.

The shop is usually divided into sectors, or *uchastki*. In shops with more than five hundred men, the sector is headed by a senior foreman. The smallest line unit of the plant is the brigade, which organizes ten to fifteen men.

Soviet management specialists agree that the formal organization of the enterprise tends toward excessive specialization. In one estimate, the Soviet enterprise averaged ten subdivisions in 1960. By 1965, this had more than doubled.[15] The reasons for this increase vary. In addition to environmental complexity, pressures are generated by the desire of smaller plants to duplicate the structures of larger plants in order to increase the number of higher-salaried and more prestigious jobs, to the neglect of informational technologies and to the bias for vertical line control. In 1971, plant directors, shop heads, and foremen comprised 43 percent of administrative personnel in Ukrainian industry.[16]

Management personnel

A central issue in the modernization of Soviet industrial management has been whether Soviet industrial managers have the vitality, flexibility, competence, and motivation required to operate the existing management system effectively. Unfortunately, information on the corps of managers is limited. As A. Levikov has pointed out, Soviet sociologists know almost everything about foremen, a little about plant managers, and virtually nothing about managers above the enterprise level.[17] Discussion here is limited to the enterprise level.

During the 1970s, a rough but realistic estimate is that administrative workers were 14 to 16 percent of total employment and 12 to 14 percent of enterprise workers. Growth in various categories of administrative personnel, however, has been uneven. Between 1957 and 1970, plant managers actually declined. In contrast, intermediate-level line and staff personnel increased by 340 percent. But employees performing clerical tasks (*sluzhashchie*) grew by only 134 percent, sliding from a low 7 percent in 1940 to a lower 3.5 percent of personnel in 1970.[18]

An important problem of Soviet industrial management is aging among Soviet managers. In 1963, Jerry Hough found 75 percent of plant directors of 170 large enterprises were over fifty.[19] David Granick has made a similar judgment.[20] In 1971, G. Kozlov of the Siberian Academy of Sciences estimated that 60 percent of Soviet managers were over fifty.[21] There may be variations among branches, though. A CPSU (Communist Party of the Soviet Union) study from the mid-1960s noted that 47 percent of the managers of the Ministry of the Automobile Industry and Ministry of Light Industry were over fifty; only 40 percent of the managers of a high-technology branch, Minpribor, however, were over fifty.[22]

By Soviet standards, Soviet managers are well educated. In 1970, about 75 percent of Soviet managers had higher educa-

Chart 1.6. *Typical structure of the administrative apparat of a chemical industrial enterprise*

Structural subdivisions and offices	Enterprises grouped according to wage fund				
	I	II	III	IV	V
I. Plant administration					
Director	+	+	+	+	+
Chief Engineer	+	+	+	+	–
Deputy Director for Commercial Questions	+	+	+	–	–
Assistant to the Director for Cadres	+	–	–	–	–
II. Departments and services					
Production–Technical	+	+	+	–	–
Central Plant Laboratory	+	+	+	+	–
Department of Technical Control	+	+	+	–	–
Department of Chief Mechanic	+	+	–	–	–
Department of Chief Power Engineer	+	+	–	–	–
Department of Chief Mechanic and Power Engineer	–	–	+	+	–
Department of Chief Surveyor in Mining-Chemical Enterprises	+	+	+	–	–
Department of Chief Geologist in Mining-Chemical Enterprises	+	+	–	–	–
Department of Chief Instrumentmaker	+	+	–	–	–

Department	1	2	3	4	5
Department of Equipment	+	+	+	—	—
Design Department	+	+	+	+	—
Department of Technical Security	+	+	—	—	—
Department of Scientific–Technical Information and Propaganda	+	+	+	—	—
Bureau of Scientific–Technical Information and Propaganda	—	+	—	+	+
Department of Technical Instruction	+	+	+	—	—
Planning Department	+	+	+	+	+
Planning–Production Department	—	+	—	+	+
Department of Labor and Wages	+	+	+	—	—
Research Laboratory for Economic Questions	+	+	—	—	—
Department (Laboratory or Bureau) of NOT	+	+	+	—	—
Department of Material–Technical Supply	+	+	+	—	—
Department of Sale	+	+	+	—	—
Department of Material–Technical Supply and Sale	—	+	—	+	+
III. *Bookkeeper*	+	+	+	+	+
Financial Department	+	+	+	—	—
Department of Cadres	+	+	+	—	—
Legal Bureau	+	+	—	—	—
Machine Accounting Bureau	+	+	+	—	—
Administrative Department	+	+	—	—	—

Source: S. Z. Pogostin, *Ekonomika i organizatsiia khimichesogo proizvodstva*, Moscow: Khimiia, 1971, pp. 24–5.

tion, but the overwhelming proportion were engineers with little formal management training. Educational levels, however, appear to vary sharply by branch. A survey in Gorkii revealed that 85.7 percent of managers in the chemical industry but only 26.2 percent in light industry had higher education.[23]

The formal training of low-level staff is less satisfactory. An official investigation in the late 1960s revealed that only one-third of trained engineers were working in their specialties and another one-third lacked diplomas.[24] Those with the least formal education were performing routine clerical and bookkeeping jobs. A survey in the Ukraine, for example, indicated that 18 percent of the economists, 25 percent of the norm setters, and 50 percent of the bookkeepers lacked any specialized training.[25] The quality of staff in these positions is mute testimony to their low priority.

Over the past two decades, recruitment and managerial development have become basic issues as the complexity of management has increased. Recruitment of high-quality personnel is relatively difficult. Soviet students have tended to perceive managerial work as bureaucratic, uncreative, and lacking professional definition.[26] This aversion extends to staff positions as well. Economists and accountants see work in the enterprise as highly routinized, poorly paid, and lacking social status. The result is poorly trained personnel and a heavy turnover of qualified personnel in these posts.[27]

Most managers are recruited internally, and self-selection is apparent. Few theoretically oriented engineers are attracted to line posts. "The reasons are well known," a shop chief has noted,

the manpower shortage, the high turnover, the difficulty of maintaining discipline because of prevalent drunkenness, plus the general difficulties of managing production at a time of increased demands, problems with supply and plan fulfillment, etc....That is why up to 80 percent of shop chiefs at some plants are practical workers who lack high school diplomas.[28]

Despite the problems of attracting high-quality personnel, a sense of blocked career mobility seems to be present in Soviet industry. As Levikov has noted, "The time of swift promotion has passed."[29] Opportunities for promotion are fewer in the most established industries and regions and somewhat greater in the growth industries and in the developing areas of Siberia and the Far East.

The factors that weight the opportunities for promotion to a directorship are numerous but vary in significance. In addition to higher education, membership in the Communist Party is virtually required for a directorship in heavy industry. Some type of voluntary public service or work in the Party *apparat* aids in promotion. To acquire and maintain Party membership, however, as David Granick has pointed out, is not very onerous.[30] Social class, prestige of educational institution attended, and theoretical level of training also appear to be minor factors.[31] Sex, however, is significant. In 1975, women made up only 9 percent of industrial managers, but 78 percent of all technologists, 75 percent of normers, and 86 percent of economists, planners, and statisticians in industry were women.[32] Their concentration in low-prestige jobs reflects not only traditional Russian social values but also the heavy burden placed on women by the dual responsibility of family and career.[33]

Just as professional education of managers has been absent, so also has been the concept of managerial development. Careers traditionally developed empirically. In the classic pattern, promotion occurred within a single enterprise. By the mid-1960s, this pattern clearly was changing. Of 109 managers' biographies collected by the writer, 65 percent had changed plants. Denisova's research indicates an even higher mobility: only 4 percent of managers in the Ministry of the Automobile Industry and 2.25 percent of those in light industry had careers solely within a single plant.[34]

In the normal pattern of promotion, a plant manager has been successively advanced to foreman, shop head, and chief engineer, a process that might consume twenty years. Traditionally, the move to a directorship is most easily achieved by the chief engineer. A study in one ministry noted that chief engineers won 72 percent of the directorship appointments. Advancement to chief engineer, however, was more open: Only one-third were deputy engineers; the rest were shop and department heads.[35] Informal, ascriptive factors play a large role in managerial appointments. Such factors, particularly previous career associations, are pervasive largely because of the marginal or illegal practices that a manager must adopt to survive. The *nomenklatura* system, a list of key managerial jobs requiring approval of the Communist Party apparatus, has been reasonably successful in establishing a corps of politically reliable and competent managers.[36] Control through application of administrative measures, however, has been less successful. For example, the ministries have stoutly resisted the policy of promoting personnel from previously approved lists of qualified candidates.

The motivations of Soviet managers, who function in difficult and stressful conditions, are undoubtedly as complex as they are for managers in other industrial systems. The process of self-selection clearly filters the excessively sensitive. Among the motives of managers, G. Kh. Popov and G. A. Dzhavadov have suggested, are money, prestige, challenging work, personal independence, and the desire to "rationalize economic activity."[37]

In the earlier phase of industrialization, economic self-interest was a basic motivator, and it still is important. The role of bonuses in explaining managerial choice is very familiar to Western scholars. In the economic model, the primary drive of the manager is to fulfill the production plan in ways that maximize the probabilities of receiving a bonus but do not jeopardize the fulfillment of future plans. The basic objective of securing a bonus explains the short time perspectives, extensive suboptimization, and marginal practices of the average manager. David Granick has persuasively argued that the goal of securing a bonus usually dominates managerial strategies in conditions of low career mobility and a heavy dependence on the bonus for total income.[38]

The manager's income is derived primarily from three sources. As a state official, the manager has access to a wide range of benefits, which may include a chauffered car, special housing, and the right to use restricted stores, medical facilities, and other services.

The second source is salary, the stable element in a manager's income. Salary is dependent upon the priority of the branch and the size of the enterprise. In 1971, Matthews estimated, the salary of a coal mine director was almost double that of a textile plant manager.[39] Salary differentials within a branch are also marked. Managers of the largest plants in the chemical industry were paid 2.5 times more than managers of the smallest plants.

The major reform of the salary structure in 1971, however, narrowed both branch differentials and the spread within the enterprise.[40]

Bonuses are the discretionary part of a manager's income. They are calculated as a percentage of salary and are awarded monthly or quarterly. The usual bonus scheme blends two elements: a bonus for the fulfillment of selected plan indicators and a bonus for completion of specific plan assignments. Legally, bonuses are limited to 60 percent of a director's salary; cases are occasionally reported of bonuses reaching 90 percent of a manager's salary.[41]

Processes of management

The processes of industrial management can be conceptualized in a variety of ways. In the classical model, the dynamics of management appear as a formally defined, highly integrated process directed from a single center and encompassing virtually every aspect of industrial activity. A more empirical view is to perceive Soviet managerial processes as a matrix of distinct, interdependent, and partially integrated activities defined by the boundaries of formal structure. The predominant flow of management activity has been vertical, and therefore an essential distinction is between macro- and micromanagement processes.

Over the past two decades, there has been a tendency among Soviet organizational specialists to distinguish the structural and functional aspects of management. As a process, macromanagement is conceived as an interrelated set of organized functions that includes planning, supply, information flows, finance, credit, capital construction, labor, technical innovation, and, most recently, social development and rationalization of management. The micro process is usually defined as the management of production. At both levels, each major function is divided into subsets of specific processes.

The functional framework for both macro and micro processes is the decision-making cycle, which is linear and sequential. The cycle is conceived as an input–output model in which the process is defined by stages: goalsetting, preparatory management (forecasting and planning), operational management (direction, coordination, and motivation), and reporting and control. Each specific management function has an organizational technology defined as the actions, operations, and procedures performed by the manager to accomplish a given task.[42] In order to simplify the discussion here, the processes are designated as planning, coordination, and control.

The key decision-making function has been planning, which is a primary instrument for the execution of economic policy as well as the integrator of management activity. Although important, coordination and control have traditionally been subsidiary. Decision-making procedures and organizational technologies have been shaped by both the imperatives of the traditional strategy of economic growth and the limitations of management. The planning process, for example, has been highly constrained; it has been effectively limited to a year and confined to a limited range of products. The amount of information required to make choices was reduced by considering only a single variant of the plan, planning from existing levels, and stressing incremental change. Planning procedures were directed primarily to expanding output within established proportions and priorities and to eliminating bottlenecks. The objective of economic planning was to increase productive resources rather than final product. It has, therefore, been conservative.

Even within a simplified framework, however, the processes of the central planning system have been complex. Procedures organizing the process are familiar and need only be sketched here. Planning procedures have developed as a staged and linear process along predominantly vertical lines. In the first stage, the Communist Party leadership defines the most important directions, priorities, and tasks of the plan. In the next phase, Gosplan translates these political directives into control figures or general production targets, which serve as benchmarks for compiling the operational plans of the ministries and enterprises. In the third phase, the plan is negotiated among different levels within the ministry and then between the ministry and the appropriate department within Gosplan. The departments for consolidation within Gosplan then attempt to balance and integrate the production, financial, labor, and other elements of the plan into a coherent whole. In the next stage the Council of Ministers and the Politburo correct and approve the plan. In the final phase the plan is disaggregated and distributed to the ministries and enterprises.[43]

The most cumbersome and information-intensive aspect of the planning process has been the centralized administrative allocation of supply. The basic responsibility for balancing inputs and outputs is Gosplan's. This function, however, is shared with Gossnab and the ministries. The enterprise initiates the process of forming the supply plan by applying for specific quantities of resources. Depending upon the resource's priority, the supply administration of the ministry negotiates the order with the relevant Gosplan or Gossnab department or agency.

The supply agency then issues specific authorization orders, or *nariady*, which permit a producing and client enterprise to negotiate the production of a fixed amount of goods within established limits for quality, assortment, and delivery dates. The supply agency also issues general allocation orders, or *fondy*, which authorize the holders to obtain a given quantity of rationed resources. The primary allocation of *fondy* is to about a hundred ministries, departments, and agencies. Each primary holder then disaggregates and distributes resources to enterprises and other users. Actual control over the physical movement of goods, however, remains the responsibility of Gossnab.[44]

The basic computational instrument for balancing inputs and outputs is the material balance, shown in Chart 1.7. The material balance is a matrix in which inventories of a raw material or product are matched against the planned needs of the economy for a given period. Balances are formulated in both physical and monetary indicators. On the distributional side of the balance, the most important demands have been for production and construction. On the planning side, demand is calculated as the coefficient of direct expenditures required to produce a given product times the total number of products or amount of materials required for a given period. Theoretically, in a comprehensively planned economy a balance should be computed for each product and then aggregated into a single global balance. Quite clearly, informational and computational constraints have made this impossible to do. Balances are struck only for the most important products in Gosplan, Gossnab, and the ministries.

The central organizational problem of industrial management has been coordination. Soviet administrative specialists identify two basic types of coordination, vertical and horizontal. Formal procedures for coordination are surprisingly limited and am-

Chart 1.7. *General form of the material balance*

Resources	Distribution
Production	Production needs
Import	Capital construction
Other sources	Export
Stocks at beginning of the planning period:	Market fund
At producers	Other expenditures (additions to state reserves and other)
At users	Stocks at the end of the planning period:
	At producers
	At users
All stock	All stock
All resources	All distribution

Source: N. S. Koval, *Planirovanie narodnogo khoziaistva SSSR,* 3rd ed., Moscow: Vysshaia shkola, 1973, p. 57.

biguously defined. In the postwar period, there has been no special organization for general coordination and control of economic processes. The function of general coordination within the state apparatus has been centered in the national and republican councils of ministers. Formal authority for the coordination of planning and plan implementation rests with Gosplan.

Special coordinational functions are performed by departments of the councils of ministers, state committees, and a maze of special councils, committees, and joint commissions designed to coordinate interministerial and complex regional tasks or projects. A common approach for coordinating larger-scale interbranch projects has been to designate one of the executive ministries or departments formal coordinator. Within the ministry, the collegium has formal responsibility for coordinating policy. Operational coordination usually devolves to the planning–economic administration or production administration of the ministry.[45]

Coordination and control are closely associated. Designed to secure "precise and undeviating execution" of plans and established rules,[46] control is usually defined in both narrow and broad terms. The narrow definition of control is defined as *re-viziia*, or inspection. *Reviziia* is conceived as a systematic but limited investigation of a given function by an authorized agency in accordance with defined rules and procedures.

The broader type of control is associated with political or mass control. *Proverka* is projected "first of all to uncover the shortcomings, to expose illegal actions, to aid the honest worker, to punish the incorrigibles, and to attain execution of the decision."[47] A growing use of the concept of control is to signify the regulation of a process. As a planning specialist has noted, the task of control is "to uncover and prevent disproportions in the development of different branches and economic regions and in the development of the economy as a whole."[48]

The organization of political and administrative controls over the industrial economy is more complex and decentralized than the procedures for either planning or coordination. The proliferation of bureaucratic and mass control agencies since Stalin has made the coordination of control a major issue of industrial organization.

Political control has been exercised by the Communist Party apparatus and the *soviets*, the Committee of People's Control, and the Procuracy, court system, and Ministry of Internal Affairs. Among the state committees and departments, special control responsibilities have been exercised by Gosplan, Gossnab, the Ministry of Finance, and the State Bank. Of special importance is the State Arbitration Commission, an institution attached to the USSR Council of Ministers that arbitrates economic conflicts.[49] Finally, within each industrial ministry, arbitration and special inspection offices reinforce the control activities of the *glavki* and chief functional administrations.

Problems of management

The central functional problem of the Soviet economy is its lack of balance and the costs that flow from this condition. Pressures to modernize industrial management occur within a context of conflicting forces. The system of industrial management over the past half-century has become deeply institutionalized. The new environment to emerge with socioeconomic development, however, has produced severe pressures to adapt the system.

It is evident that the existing system of management enjoys

broad legitimacy and exhibits a tenacious institutional inertia. This situation applies equally to the goals defined by the traditional strategy of growth and to the ideological premises that are the keystones of the system. Normatively, the classic model of industrial organization precedes the revolution and was given political and ideological sanction by Lenin.[50] The existing system is socially supported by millions of industrial officials and workers who have a material and psychological stake in the status quo; without this support, of course, the system would cease to exist.

The historically sanctioned model of management has been sharply challenged by socioeconomic and cultural development, though. The new environment has had the dual effect of intensifying the chronic problems of management and creating a host of new ones. The pressures generated by the inefficiencies of the existing system and the need to develop a new strategy of growth provide the political motivation to modernize the system of management. The pressures of development are manifest in five major ways.

Despite the massive resource endowment of the Soviet Union, reserves of cheap minerals and fossil fuels are declining as ecological costs rise. Moreover, the country is using natural resources at an exponential rate.[51] Huge developmental costs are projected for maintaining the natural environment and developing new energy and mineral resources in Siberia and the Far East.

Second, the Soviet economy is experiencing a labor shortage. In the 1970s, about 90 percent of the working-age population in the Russian Republic was employed. Through the late 1970s and into the 1980s, annual increments to the labor force are expected to be less than 1 percent.[52]

Third, there is pressure stemming from the slowdown in economic growth and rise in capital–output ratios. Labor productivity, output quality, and technical progress have all been lagging behind Soviet needs. Abram Bergson has noted that, after 1957, factor productivity dropped below the break-even point. To sustain earlier growth rates, increasing amounts of capital stock will be necessary, a policy in direct conflict with investment required to meet other social and economic needs.[53]

Fourth, development has produced an extremely intricate

economic and organizational environment. The industrial economy produces more than ten million products in almost three hundred branches of the economy. Prior to the reforms of the 1970s, Moscow managed almost fifty thousand enterprises. The challenge to administrative rationality is clearly severe.

Finally, there is evidence of serious social and cultural strain in Soviet society. By 1976, the birth rate had dropped to 18.2 per thousand, a drop attributed to the housing shortage, demand for higher living standards, and employment and changing role of women in Soviet society.[54] Divorce is increasing; socialization of youth has become more difficult; and such forms of social disorganization as alcoholism have become pervasive social problems. V. G. Treml has estimated that Soviet alcohol consumption carries annual social costs of 7.3 percent of national income as well as incalculable human costs.[55] Under conditions of rising demand and shrinking resources, the need to construct a more rational and flexible management system has assumed major importance.

Issues of macromanagement

The problems of the existing management system are deeply rooted and intertwined. The convergence of a long-term trend toward structural and functional diversity with chronic deficiencies of management function has produced the most serious problems of organizational effectiveness and integration.

Pressures on the integrity of the formal structure stem most immediately from the number and complexity of organizational relationships. The patterns of organizational cooperation and conflict have been also influenced by the impact of limited functionalism. Vertically, there has been a gradual diffusion of authority from the top to the intermediate levels of management, and, horizontally, a steady shift of authority from line to staff personnel. A paradoxical result has been to stimulate the growth of organizational pluralism while simultaneously increasing structural rigidity.

Restricted functionalism as a doctrine for allocating authority has the advantages of speeding up decision making and reducing the load on the competence of managers. This division of authority, however, is also responsible in part for the indeterminacy, jurisdictional conflict, loose coordination, and suboptimization of decision making. The strong role of functional agencies in planning and management is also linked with the flow of authority away from the line managers. The danger of turning the line offical into a broker of organizational relationships has been clearly stated by G. Kh. Popov:

In conditions of numerous functional agencies, the rights of which are guaranteed, the leader actually loses part of his independence; his initiative is restricted, and he ceases to be a moving force. He begins to balance among the orders of numerous higher agencies and maneuvers among the points of view of subordinate functional services.[56]

The vertical diffusion of authority has reduced the level of structural integration without increasing flexibility or decreasing institutional inertia. Although the Council of Ministers can establish basic policy, its staff is clearly inadequate for giving operational direction to an economy of this size and complexity. At the intermediate level, Gosplan's authority and resources are equally constrained.

Organizational relationships among the functional agencies, ministries, and enterprises therefore produce contradictory results. Direction of the ministries is highly centralized but poorly coordinated. Competition among state committees places heavy reporting requirements on the ministries and enterprises; each ministry, in turn, is bombarded by a flow of inconsistent commands and instructions. This condition is complicated by the high concentration of authority within each functional agency. Operational decision making, therefore, tends to be slow and ineffective. This pattern of vertical coordination tends to be repeated in simpler forms in the ministry.[57]

Perhaps the most complex problem confronting the modernization of the management system is intellectual, a central issue in a system whose norms stress the superiority of explicit and rational management procedures. There is little doubt that cumulative experience gives the Soviet manager an adequate intuitive model of the way the system actually functions. Whether these models are useful for decision making in a complex and dynamic environment has, of course, been questioned. Central planners and ministerial officials make decisions with only hazy notions of production capacity, required capital investment, true loads on equipment, production reserves, and existing levels of technology at any given time.[58] The severe structural and cognitive limitations of the existing management system have clearly contributed to the economic and organizational disequilibrium characteristic of the existing system. These limitations are particularly evident in the vertical coordination of planning. Using traditional planning instruments and techniques, Soviet planners have chronically failed to achieve balanced plans. Michael Ellman has quite rightly insisted that Gosplan officials cannot make 1 percent of the calculations needed to balance the plan.[59] Computing the plan has become a highly developed art in which the skills and intuition of the planner are crucial. The major part of the data is not fixed, and the overwhelming number of specific planning procedures is not standardized.[60]

A key computational weakness of planning is the inadequacy of the material balance. It cannot produce a balanced plan because the "balances are not complete, nor universal, nor integrated into a system, and technology does not correspond to the technological assumptions."[61] The balances do not include more than 60 percent of production, are built only for a single commodity, and are calculated on the basis of direct rather than full inputs. Norms and coefficients used in computing balances are generally weighted in favor of the more efficient producers, are subject to errors of aggregation and averaging, and may be inaccurate or obsolete.[62]

Imbalance in the plan also reflected an indifference to economic criteria in decision making. Prior to the 1965 reforms, economic transactions carried a predominantly administrative character. Money fulfilled essentially accounting and control functions. There was no charge for capital investment or payment for natural resources, primarily for ideological reasons. Prices were set administratively, were infrequently reformed, and reflected political priorities. Wholesale prices, based upon average production costs, had little informational value to the planners because they failed to incorporate either relative scarcities or consumer preferences.

Among the most enduring problems of planning and management have been the virtually inseparable issues of measuring the economic efficiency of enterprise performance and motivating efficient managerial decision making. The focus of this problem over the past twenty-five years has been the familiar one of "success indicators." Planning and bonus indicators have notably failed to stimulate the satisfaction of consumer demand or encourage technical innovation or risk. Low-quality output, irrational production mixes, and inefficient use of labor, equipment, and materials have been among the results attributed to deficient planning indicators. The basic problem, as Alec Nove has indicated, is that rewarding plan fulfillment for intermediate goods and services (rather than final product) encourages waste and inefficiency.[63]

Organizational factors have also played a significant role in producing unbalanced plans. The process of balancing and integrating the plan has involved compromising numerous conflicts of interest at each level of the hierarchy. Under political pressure to maximize growth, central planners have had a strategy of extracting the largest possible output from the ministries and enterprises with the least possible inputs. The latter, in contrast, have had a major stake in securing a plan with operating reserves. Due to the fact that the planners at each level lack comprehensive and accurate knowledge, the planning process has been one of negotiation at each level of the hierarchy, combining command and bargaining. The result has been to produce plans with sufficient realism to be operational but with insufficient balance for efficient execution. The frequently intense conflicts of interest, however, thwart a purely technical approach to planning: "The search for technically precise planning solutions," a central planner has noted, "continually runs up against the flow of opinions, interests, positions – in the first instance between the ministries and Gosplan departments."[64]

Unbalanced plans have also resulted from the lack of coordination between production and supply plans, which has numerous causes. Supply planning procedures are complex. The supply plan itself is a compromise of conflicting organizational interests, normally negotiated before an enterprise knows its final output bill. In order to overcome an initial overcommitment of resources, supply officials will occasionally assign inputs from plants that are under construction, lack the necessary technology, use obsolescent or arbitrary norms, or are seriously overloaded.[65] Planning and supply agencies may also issue conflicting production assignments. Gosplan delivers the plant's production program in aggregate figures; the operational production schedule, however, is formed on a quarterly basis using allocation orders distributed by the supply agencies.

In the existing system, processes of planning and management have involved almost exclusively questions of centralization of authority and vertical coordination. Socioeconomic development, however, has raised some very large-scale problems connected with technical innovation and regional development. Organization of these projects involves relationships that do not fall within a single chain of command.

The most familiar problem of horizontal coordination has been the chronic failure of enterprises of one ministry to meet contractual obligations for the supply of another ministry. In general, the ministries have struggled to maintain maximum control over their operating environments. Their interest in stable production technologies and minimum innovation has, therefore, been strong. This fundamental interest in maintaining an independent and autonomous production complex naturally results in a tenacious institutional inertia. The use of formal coordinating mechanisms like joint commissions and councils to regulate relations among ministries has usually failed because these mechanisms normally require voluntary cooperation. Even relatively minor matters such as standardizing axles in motor vehicles may take years of bargaining among ministries to resolve.[66]

Among the most intransigent problems of horizontal coordination has been the integration of branch and regional development. A chronic issue historically, the emergence of massive projects of resource development in Siberia in the past two decades has given this problem critical importance. Effective mechanisms have become vital for coordinating such decisions as the siting of new plants, production and distribution of consumer goods, responsibility for environmental quality and pollution controls, and development of social infrastructures.[67] Except for the brief period between 1957 and 1965, ministerial interests and "departmentalism" have dominated this relationship, mute testimony to the weakness of organizational controls.

In both its broad and narrow definitions, management control has been shaped by chronic operational problems of planning and coordination. Regulation by the ministries and functional agencies has been geared toward correcting operational deficiencies that emerge during the production process. The prevention of deviation from centrally determined norms and goals alternatively has been the responsibility of the political and specialized control agencies using various forms of bureaucratic and mass controls. Both have concentrated on problems of vertical coordination without conspicuous success.

Operational regulation of enterprise production is primarily a responsibility of the ministerial *apparat*. The degree of centralized control, however, is conditioned by structural factors. Enterprises of an all-union ministry are usually more tightly controlled from Moscow than enterprises of union-republican ministries. Within all-union ministries, enterprises that use complex technologies or produce large and complex products are less closely supervised than plants using mass production technologies. Large and prestigious plants normally have fewer routine controls and preferred access to resources. In general, the intensity of direct ministerial controls is conditioned by the volume and diversity of information to be processed and the degree of coordination required within the *apparat* itself.

Limited managerial capabilities naturally force the establishment of priorities. Regulation by the ministries has been tighter over planning, supply, and investment than over labor safety or technical innovation. External constraints on the actual authority of the plant manager have, therefore, varied. The amount and productivity of equipment is fixed, but other decisions on the use of supply, transport, labor, quality of production, and loading of equipment are under the control of the enterprise manager. In one estimate, 5 percent to 30 percent of decisions made on repair, production scheduling, and product mix selection are the plant manager's.[68] Failure to meet production quotas, however, invites rapid intervention from the Party as well as the ministry.

The traditional instruments and methods used by the ministry to regulate the production process are crude and frequently counterproductive. The ministry can reduce the pressures of disequilibrium in a plant in a variety of ways. It may accept an understated plan or reduce output targets, redistribute production quotas among plants, juggle delivery dates or production schedules, or transfer supply, investment, or labor from a plant with reserves to one under stress. A frequent device is to divert production destined for a "foreign ministry" to one of its own plants, thereby setting up a chain reaction within the industrial economy.[69]

Ministries also contribute to the imbalance. Like the planning and supply agencies, ministries may issue late plans, order unauthorized production, arbitrarily increase above-plan output, or change production plans without changing other plan indicators, particularly for supply. Because regulation by the ministries may create imbalances in other sectors, Gosplan or Gossnab may be forced to intervene, but usually with minimal effect. Actions of these and other functional agencies are usually slow and laced with jurisdictional conflict. In any case, the administrative costs of coordination are high. During the first half of 1973, for example, 840,000 officials made the trip to Moscow for these purposes.[70]

The traditional response of plant management to the structural and decision-making problems of macromanagement are familiar. Their practices, in aggregate, constitute the informal system of management. Plant managers attempt to buffer an uncertain and risky environment by searching for loose plans and large inventories and by hoarding labor. They may also use illegal supply agents, or *tolkachi*, to maintain the flow of inputs. Managers may also resort to gray or black markets to buy or exchange scarce commodities, manipulate prices, or use questionable accounting methods to meet success or other plan indicators. Reports to the ministry or to a functional agency may be distorted or, more rarely, falsified.[71] Bureaucratic controls developed to prevent or to uncover managerial deviance have traditionally been weak, largely because the informal system is part of the regulation process. There is little surprise therefore that check-ups and audits by the ministries' special control departments have been criticized as irregular and conducted by small and poorly trained staffs. The ministry, moreover, seldom takes action on reported violations, either simply noting them or even dismissing them.[72]

Although the state committees and specialized control agencies naturally have a stronger interest in controlling suboptimization, they also normally choose regulation over the prevention of deviation. The criticism of supradepartmental controls, however, has been so trenchant that some Soviet specialists believe this phase of control should be abolished. Like the controllers of the ministry, they are also overloaded, and poorly trained and produce questionable results. A particular weakness of supradepartmental control has been the overlap and duplication among control agencies due to lack of coordination.[73]

The ineffectiveness of administrative methods of managerial control is also evident in the effects of judicial and economic sanctions. The Soviet press will occasionally report the sentencing of enterprise managers for up to two years for low-quality production or delivery of substandard supply. Criminal sanctions for report padding, however, are seldom invoked.[74]

Economic sanctions also have had a marginal impact on managerial behavior. Sanctions for shoddy work, legally quite heavy, are seldom enforced.[75] Fines have been singularly ineffective because they have virtually no influence on the financial position of the enterprise. Fines levied by the State Arbitration Commission normally are less than 1 percent of profits and are not included in the calculation of bonuses and other enterprise funds.[76] Mass control has been equally problematical, particularly with respect to the competence and objectivity of volunteer controllers.[77]

Enterprise decision making

Management within the enterprise has been decisively shaped by unbalanced plans, poor coordination, and inadequate regulatory mechanisms. Structurally, high levels of contingency and urgency in the processes of micromanagement have strengthened the role of informal structure at the expense of formal organization. Soviet managers have traditionally set up tight informal decision-making groups, or "family circles," for defense purposes. They have also been reluctant to delegate authority and traditionally have been indifferent to formal rules and procedures. Soviet managers have institutionalized a crisis style of management with authoritarian overtones. Substantively, studies have shown that as much as 87 percent of a manager's time has been spent on operational problems, 50 percent on questions of supply.[78]

The intense involvement of Soviet managers in operations is a direct consequence of a continuous threat to the breakdown of production technologies. Traditionally, this threat has carried high economic and social costs. One of the most serious consequences of uneven supply, for example, is "storming," an unbalanced production cycle in which two-thirds of the monthly plan is fulfilled in the last ten days. The stress is usually severe; among its costs are a hoarding of labor, rises in production costs, lower quality, disruptions of deliveries to other plants, and a sharp rise in social and psychological tensions.[79]

It has been evident for many years that operational strategies developed by Soviet managers to fulfill the quantitative indexes of the plan in order to receive a bonus have been a primary source of waste and inefficiency. The principal dimensions of this strategy have been several: production of material-intensive products, which results in a chronic overexpenditure of resources; maintenance of a reserve of fixed machinery, labor, and other resources; indifference to quality; and resistance to changes in production technologies or output.[80]

The traditionally low priority of technical innovation for Soviet managers is clearly a serious constraint on socioeconomic development. The earlier noted source of resistance is rooted in a complex of economic and organizational conditions and indicates the depth of the problem of reorienting managerial behavior. Soviet planning policy has traditionally allowed very little slack for innovation. Financial allowances have seldom covered research and developmental costs; prices do not provide the necessary incentives for innovation; new or untested technologies may not work or may disrupt existing technologies to the detriment of plan fulfillment. The introduction of new products or technologies may also create new costs and risks in the retraining of workers, the acquisition of new equipment and raw materials, and the refashioning of the network of suppliers and customers.[81]

Managerial resistance to technical innovation and other entrenched practices clearly come into basic conflict with the core of the new growth strategy: a rise in labor productivity through technical progress. In the Ninth and Tenth Five-Year Plans, 90 percent of economic growth has been planned from this factor. Although rates of growth in labor productivity vary, a long-term slide has been unmistakable. This is reflected in the 50 percent cut in the projected growth rate of labor productivity in the Tenth Five-Year Plan over 1971-5 rates.[82]

The slowdown in the growth of labor productivity is attributable to the policies of full employment as well as labor hoarding and slow technical innovation. It also reflects the fact that enterprise auxiliary functions such as transportation or maintenance are manned by manual workers at levels from 1.5 to 3 times higher than capitalist enterprises of comparable size. At the management level, this is compounded by the irrational use of engineering and technical personnel. An estimated 70 percent of Soviet engineers perform some nonengineering functions, including a large number of routine technical and clerical tasks.[83]

A principal consequence of socioeconomic development has been the rise in importance of the human factor in management. The primary instrument for social control in Soviet industry has been the political and social mobilization of the work force by the Communist Party, trade unions, and other social organizations. Although these agencies continue to work intensively, problems of job dissatisfaction, labor turnover, and alcoholism seriously reduce labor productivity.

It is not clear, of course, that satisfied workers are more productive. Most studies show, not unexpectedly, a relatively high level of job satisfaction, in some cases reaching 90 percent.[84] Labor turnover, however, is considered a serious problem. Total annual turnover in Soviet industry is about 30 percent. Only 20 percent of this is *tekuchest,* usually defined as an unplanned and spontaneous exit from a plant by a worker on his own volition. It also includes the relatively few workers who are fired.[85] On the whole, the Soviet worker is fairly mobile. He changes his job, enterprise, or branch every four years, his specialty every six, and his residence every twelve. Turnover tends to be higher in the less-industrialized regions and larger industrial cities; it is also higher in smaller plants and low-priority industries.[86]

The conclusions of sociological research on the causes of turnover are not fully consistent, reflecting diverse research strategies as well as differing situations. Generally, job dissatisfaction is linked with poor working conditions and income and is reinforced by rising expectations and still inadequate supplies of consumer goods, housing, and social services.

Most studies show a strong correlation between job satisfaction and poor organization of production and harmful or unpleasant working conditions. Turnover, for example, is 50 percent higher than average in "storming" plants. It is also higher in mass production industries and plants with three shifts. Extreme noise and vibration, extremes of temperature, poor sanitary conditions, and inadequate social facilities are also important.[87] Income as source of motivation and job satisfaction has high salience, although its rank order varies.

Except for younger workers, social factors still appear to be secondary to production and economic factors as a cause of turnover. Social conflict, particularly with management, also appears to have minor importance. For evident reasons, however, this may be a "hidden" factor. In Ufa, for example, 45 percent of workers quitting their jobs expressed dissatisfaction with the management of the plant; but only 13.3 percent who had positive evaluations of management wanted to leave.[88]

In the 1970s, the most sensitive sphere of management–labor relations has been. the employment of youth and women. Their role in the work force has become decisive. Youth now supply 90 percent of additions to the work force, and women make up about half of the labor force.

The problem of turnover in Soviet industry is essentially a youth problem. In the Russian Republic, two-thirds of all turnover occurs among workers under thirty. In profile, the young male or female worker who leaves a job has an incomplete or general secondary education, has been in the plant for less than three years, is unskilled, and suffers from poor social adaptation.[89]

The problem of adapting to working-class roles is most acute among graduates of academic programs, which have produced about 80 percent of secondary school graduates. The traditionally strong bias of these graduates against low-prestige occupations is a major motive in turnover. Noting that 70 to 90 percent of secondary school graduates continue to strive for higher education, two Soviet authors have pointed out the essential dilemma, which stems from the fact that the demand for specialists with higher education is only 25 percent of secondary school graduates: "Therefore, with each year, the problem of the gap between the personal ambitions of youth and the needs of the national economy sharpens."[90]

Perhaps the most serious social issue in industry is the employment of women. Social research of working women in industry singles out three special and interrelated problems that have importance for Soviet economic and social development: combining marriage and career; vulnerability to the physical environment of the work place; and status and role in the work force.

The most intense issue is undoubtedly the severe stress that arises from women's dual roles as workers and mothers. Almost 87 percent of women in the prime child-bearing years of twenty to twenty-nine are employed in the economy, and 80 percent are married.[91] The major strain is found in the crushing burden of work. In addition to the standard 41-hour week, women work an additional 3 to 3.5 hours per day at home.[92] The social consequences of a 60- to 70-hour work week for the Soviet family are evident.

Social responsibilities as well as working conditions strongly influence the turnover of women. Distance from the plant, availability of plant housing and child-care facilities, and work on the night shift all have a major influence on turnover. Heavy physical labor as well as poor organization of labor can also stimulate turnover. Wages generally play a less important role in turnover among women than among men.[93] Their concentration at the bottom of the wage and skill hierarchies, however, constitutes a growing social issue. For industry as a whole, women are ranked from 0.6 to 1.4 grades below men.[94] In Belorussia, for example, 78 percent of women with comparable education and experience were in the bottom two ranks, in contrast to 42.9 percent of men.[95] The reasons are complex, but the results are clear. Women have reduced career perspectives and are pessimistic about promotion.[96]

Among the more pervasive behavioral problems in industry are labor discipline and alcoholism. Questions of labor discipline include absenteeism, coming to work late or leaving early, unauthorized absences from the work place, insubordination, and drunkenness on the job. The extent of violations of labor discipline is unknown because reporting is unsystematic and distorted and not published.

Although absenteeism is linked with a variety of factors, one of its principal causes is drunkenness. A study of the Western

Siberian and Kuznetsk Metallurgical Combines showed that 85.8 percent of all violations of labor discipline and 90 percent of all absenteeism were related to drunkenness.[97] The sharpest drops in labor productivity, similar to the American experience, come on Mondays and on the day after holidays and paydays, when attendance drops 20 to 30 percent.[98]

Traditional methods of social control vary. The worker may be fired, given a warning, deprived of his bonuses, reduced in rank, censured by his work group, or sent to a comrade's court. Few of these traditional sanctions appear to be very effective.

The sense in a decline of managerial control over labor is heavily conditioned by the shortage of manpower and the sharp competition among managers for labor. This tendency has been strengthened by the provisions of the 1965 reform, which made every worker on the books an asset. If he is fired from one plant, he is usually quickly hired by another.[99]

The manager usually punishes the majority of labor discipline violations by issuing a warning or strict warning; more rarely does he deprive the worker of his bonus or fire him. Although enterprise policies naturally differ, one investigation revealed that 64.8 percent were given a warning or strict warning; 11.1 percent were transferred to lower-paid work; and only 6.6 percent lost their bonuses.[100] Between 1966 and 1969, labor discipline appeared to deteriorate even in leading plants like the Svetlana Association, which significantly strengthened administrative sanctions.[101] In response to declining social control, Brezhnev in 1970 initiated a national campaign to increase labor discipline and counter drunkenness.[102]

The search for management theory

Perhaps the primary drive to create a modern theory of industrial management has been the repeated failures under Stalin and particularly under Khrushchev to improve the efficiency of management through traditional means. With failure has come intellectualization as the problems of management have taken more complex contours. The intellectualization of management reform has occurred on two levels. Initially, there has been an effort to redefine and relate the problems of management to the larger economic, social, and cultural changes that have accompanied socioeconomic development. On a second level there has been a sustained effort to devise operational theories, structures, and technologies of management appropriate to the new environment and effective in countering organizational pluralism and a wasteful allocation of resources. Theory at both levels has drawn heavily from Western scientific and social thought.

The scientific–technical revolution and management

The sustained effort to develop a global theory of societal change in the 1960s and 1970s has diverse roots. Challenged by Marxist revisionism in Eastern Europe and domestic political dissent, the Soviet political leadership has felt a pressing need to defend Soviet institutions as well as to develop an empirical theory of social change. The task, in F. Burlatskii's view, has been to define the massive changes in Soviet society using Marxist categories of development.[103] Instrumentally, a theory of social development should provide empirical descriptions of social change as the first step toward the rational evaluation and management of developmental tasks.

The redefinition of the contemporary Soviet environment has proceeded under the dual rubric of the "developed socialist society" and the "scientific–technical revolution," or STR. Both concepts reflect Western theories of industrial and postindustrial society and are frequently used interchangeably. There are, however, some conceptual differences.

The developed socialist society is more orthodox ideologically. It defines Soviet society as a limited stage in a continuous line of historical development. It is urban and industrial, and enjoys a growing standard of living and increasing social consciousness.[104] In contrast, the STR incorporates elements of postindustrialism and is future oriented. It primary focus is on the revolutionary impact of science and technology on human society in the last half of the twentieth century.[105] The stress on the centrality of science and technology for further socioeconomic development implies potentially far greater institutional change because the tasks of development differ significantly from those of the more conservative concept of the developed socialist society.

There is no full agreement among Soviet scholars on either

the nature or long-term social and economic consequences of the STR. Its key assumption is that scientific knowledge is the basic force in economic and social development. Fundamental advances in science will lead to radically new technologies and revolutionize the economic basis of Soviet society, turning "science into a direct productive force." Rapid development of such disciplines as nuclear and low-temperature physics, molecular chemistry, electronics, and dozens of other fields leads directly to such technologies as fast breeder reactors, synthetic fibers, computers, and hundreds of other technologies with military or economic applications.[106]

Although Soviet writers are optimistic about the impact of technology on industrial productivity, their assessment of the social and institutional consequences of the STR has been more ambivalent. Its impact on industrial labor is evaluated positively because automation will end the division of labor introduced during the first industrial revolution. Labor becomes intellectualized and highly skilled, with subsequent shifts in the occupational structure and reduction in class differences.[107]

The STR is also expected to create problems. Ecological damage produced by industrial pollution and the chemicalization of agriculture will rise. Greater social equality and participation will increase conflict as social interests expand and diversify. The dynamism of social change will also produce a severe challenge to human health and adaptability. Life styles will become more diverse as channels for informal social communication and participation multiply. Looming ahead is the development of mass societies and cultures.[108]

This ambivalence also extends to the impact of the STR on traditional institutions. The increased dynamism and complexity of social processes intensify existing pressures on institutional integration. According to one major statement, the STR will lead to new political institutions that permit open discussion required for innovation, political competition, and the end of political repression.[109] The spector of technocracy also arises. The philosopher Pavel Fedoseev warned that, as the specialization and skills of the manager increase, the power of executive agencies also increases, leading to "bureaucratic and technocratic" distortions that could threaten the role of the Party.[110]

The STR also raises fundamental questions for social and industrial management. There is a sharp distinction between those who would use science and technology to strengthen existing institutions and those who argue that dynamism and complexity require new organizational forms. Complexity, the sociologist D. A. Kerimov has insisted, effectively prevents comprehensive social programming. Only a few key relationships can be administratively controlled. The remaining require internalized norms and values to harmonize conflicting social interests with regime goals.[111] For the same reasons, the value of mass coercion as an instrument of social control is reduced.

The future of a mechanistic and bureaucratic approach to management is also an issue for industrial organization. Here as well, application of science and technology reinforced the classical conceptions of conservatives. For others, however, the STR implied a fundamental reorientation. A joint Soviet–Czech report noted: "It is impossible to manage contemporary production complexes as a machine or complex of machines operating according to the mechanical laws of Laplace. Any attempt in this direction turns striving to manage into powerlessness and self-deception; for it leads planned goals into contrary results."[112] To overcome the limits of bureaucratic management requires a statistical rather than determinate approach and the use of indirect regulators in place of direct administrative controls.

Whether the STR will promote industrial democracy or technocracy is a central issue for Marxist social theory. Academician V. Glushkov has asserted, for example, that a broad network of computer centers can extend rather than restrict participation. A competition of ideas rather than actions can occur through a continuous popular referendum in an "electronic forum." In a Rousseauesque vision, Glushkov can predict the end of professionalism and stereotyped social behavior as human creativity advances.[113]

His optimism, however, appears to be a minority position. Burlatskii, for example, considers the twin thrusts toward increased mass participation and the professionalization of management to be "one of the more sharply living contradictions born of the scientific–technical revolution."[114] The weight of opinion appears tilted against the growth of industrial democracy. G. Kh. Popov, for example, believes that a highly qualified leadership will continue as a vital need of industrial management. The alienation (*otchuzhdenie*) created by a hierarchy of power will characterize industrial management for a long time. In contrast to Glushkov's optimism, Popov predicts that computerization will increase the concentration of power.[115] At best, industrial democracy will be confined to the election of first-line supervisors and be limited to a narrow range of secondary issues.

Some sources of theory

The search for a modern theory of industrial management has been motivated by the same complex of conditions and needs that have influenced the Soviet political leadership to support the development of the social sciences as a whole. The quest for a theory of management shares with the social sciences generally a common heritage, purpose, and developmental experience.

Their common heritage springs from the virtual destruction of the empirical social sciences under Stalin and their slow and ambivalent restoration under Khrushchev and his successors. Their common purpose has been to serve as policy sciences. Under existing conditions of uncertainty and risk, even a conservative ideologist like V. Kelle could note in the early 1970s: "Social science becomes a mandatory component in the functioning of the social system at all levels, a necessary instrument for the solution of social problems and a tool of management science."[116]

The slow development of the social sciences to professional maturity has stemmed, in part, from the resistance of strongly entrenched academic disciplines, which have strongly opposed establishing such fields as demography and sociology as autonomous disciplines. They have also braked the formation of professional journals, the training of researchers, and other aspects of professional development.[117]

Technical and methodological conflicts have been intense among proponents of behavioralism and traditionalism in all of the social sciences. The most serious constraint on the development of the social sciences, however, has been opposition of the professional ideologists, whose fears of ideological relativism and pluralism were neatly summarized by a conservative reviewer of *Leninism and the Administration of Social Processes*. The empirical social sciences, the critic charged, produced serious ideological distortions. They substitute apolitical concepts of the natural sciences for sociopolitical categories. Their stress on analytical methodologies is ahistorical. The empirical social sciences, moreover, present concrete social research without reference to general ideological concepts. Behavioral models, in addition, reject the use of such philosophical categories as "essence," thereby "depoliticizing" social reality. Finally, the social sciences have failed to develop a research style based upon the objective laws of social development as these are defined by Marxism-Leninism.[118] Despite the inertia produced by academic resistance, methodological complexity, and ideological anxiety, however, the urgency of contemporary problems has pushed the social sciences, and the search for modern management theory, forward.

The development of a theory of management has had three basic objectives. The first has been to construct more useful general models of how the system does or should work. A second more practical objective has been to prescribe concrete measures to increase organizational integration and a more efficient processing of resources. Finally, management theory has been confronted with the task of management development and education.

Like the other social sciences, management theory has been seriously hampered by the vacuum left by Stalin's ruthless repression of management science in the 1930s. For almost thirty years, writers followed an axiomatic and deductive approach to industrial organization, stressing fixed, permanent principles and relationships of administrative subordination and control. Management research was confined to the enterprise or the branch. Any attempt to approach management problems beyond the branch was repressed as a deviation toward the "organizational sciences of Bogdanov."[119]

In order to fill the vacuum in management theory, Soviet scholars over the past twenty years have turned to a variety of sources. The most important efforts have been to incorporate their own experience with large-scale development into the management of the civilian economy; to return to the classical management science of NEP (New Economic Policy), and to survey management theory and practice in the advanced industrial societies of the West.

The experience gained in the management of large-scale military and space programs is undoubtedly important as a source of theory but difficult to evaluate. Robert Campbell has persuasively argued that some of the major advocates of a cybernetic approach to management – Academicians Glushkov, Sobelev, and Dorodnitsyn, among them – were deeply involved in military research.[120] They have also forcefully advocated the modernization of industrial management. The tight security surrounding Soviet military and space research, however, makes uncertain this source's contribution to theory.

Soviet interest in reviving the management thought of NEP has been limited. Although the movement for the scientific organization of labor (NOT) is playing a prominent role in rationalization on the micro level, there has been a consensus that classical management theory is intellectually too limited to deal with contemporary problems.[121] A more interesting contribution to a modern theory of management from NEP was made by A. A. Bogdanov (1878–1928), a physician and revolutionary best known for his philosophical disputes with Lenin on Mach and Avenarius.

Bogdanov's influence lies in his theory of *tektologiia,* a science of universal organization that anticipates many of the concepts of cybernetics. In developing his themes of organizational harmony and social equilibrium, Bogdanov used such concepts as feedback, entropy, negative and positive selection, and morphogenesis. He also advanced the notion that growth of a system depends upon its capacity to assimilate variety and to increase its complexity.[122] Branded a "reactionary" and close to Taylorism, Bogdanov shared with Bukharin, Stephen Cohen has suggested, an attraction to the language of modern social theory, an emphasis upon social equilibrium, and a pluralist approach to historical materialism.[123]

The major external source for developing a modern theory of management has been the advanced industrial societies, particularly the United States. Direct interest in U.S. industrial organization dates from the late 1950s and has included virtually every aspect of management. Primary attention, however, has naturally centered on those theories and practices most relevant to Soviet problems. Although behavioral theory has not been neglected, principal interest has centered on advanced technical and organizational developments in heavy industry.

Substantive focus has been on management theory, new structural forms, the development of computer-based informational systems, advances in decision theory and management development, and education. A major channel for the collection and analysis of information has been the Institute of the USA and Canada, a research institute of the Academy of Sciences formed in 1960. This has been supplemented by broad programs of exchange initiated under détente as well as extensive translation of Western management literature.

Soviet students of American management like D. M. Gvishiani and Boris Milner have been thoroughly aware, of course, of the technical limitations and institutional inertia that have characterized applications of American management science; moreover, the scale and complexity of the problems of centralized planning are much greater than those addressed by American management science. The attraction, nonetheless, was strong in the 1960s and early 1970s.

Soviet scholars have given the closest attention to systems analysis and quantitative methods of decision making. Gvishiani, a major force in the development of a Soviet management science, gives detailed treatment in his comprehensive study of American management thought to the use of mathematical models, systems of optimal decision making, econometrics, scientific forecasting, and the development of PPB (plan-program–budget) systems in the federal government. He and others have had a particular interest in the use of systems analysis for organization of the firm and of research and development. The incorporation of such techniques as building trees of goals, the use of cost–benefit analysis, CPM (critical path methods) and PERT (program evaluation and review techniques), and other quantitative methods has been an important contribution to Soviet management theory.[124]

Western advances in the technology of information processing have been viewed as a revolutionary development in organizational decision making and control. Their interest has naturally focused on very large, computer-based systems for information retrieval and planning and control. Special attention has been devoted to such large systems as Medlar of the National Institutes of Health and the management information systems of NASA and the Department of Defense. Such large-scale time-sharing systems as Cybernet and Arpanet have attracted the closest scrutiny because their scale fits Soviet needs.[125]

Soviet management specialists, particularly Boris Milner, have also carefully examined the types of adaptations made by American corporate structures to complex and uncertain environments. They have noted trends toward multiplant operations and conflicting patterns in the delegation of authority; the substitution of committees for one-man management; and the proliferation of staff groups for such functions as long-term planning, data processing, and technical innovation. Of particular interest has been the growth in the role of consultants.[126]

Modern forms of project management have generated a great deal of enthusiasm. The creation of temporary project groups to coordinate a project from design to completion has been seized upon as a solution to the problem of departmental barriers that plague existing Soviet methods of management. American experience with matrix structure – the integration of project with line – staff structure – has also been studied for Soviet application.[127]

The modernization of Soviet management clearly requires a system of management development and education. Virtually all of the problems of management personnel found in the West are perceived to apply in Soviet industry as well. Soviet specialists have studied the curricula of the major American undergraduate and graduate schools of business as well as a wide variety of in-service training facilities. Of particular interest has been the redirection of business education away from classical theory toward behavioral science and quantitative methods of decision making.[128]

Some theoretical and research directions

Through the 1970s, no theoretical consensus emerged on how to modernize the system of industrial management. Theoretical development was slow. Like the social sciences generally, construction of a viable theory was complicated by institutional inertia, the extreme analytical difficulties of the problems of management, the opposition of conservative managers and ideologists, and the struggle of different theoretical tendencies and groups to control its development. The close association of modern management theory with contemporary Western culture presented a particularly powerful obstacle.

The threat perceived in Western theory is, of course, deeply rooted in Russian culture. The admission of a Soviet lag in theory clearly damages national self-esteem. The political and ideological consequences, however, are viewed more seriously. The overevaluation of Western theory, Gvishiani has warned, leads to a discrediting of the Soviet system. Western managment theory is a "Tower of Babel" of competing schools immersed in positivism, empiricism, and existentialism.[129] To reduce the corrosive effects of ideological pluralism and relativism, there has been a systematic effort to follow Lenin's injunction to separate the scientific and technical core of Western theory from its social and cultural foundations. As social theory, Western management thought is ritually castigated as a clever but futile effort to harmonize the contradictions of capitalism and to forge new methods of class exploitation. Particular attention has been devoted to the "unmasking" of human relations theory, which is charged with reducing management theory to psychology and creating illusions that are manipulated to reduce the intensity of the class struggle.[130]

The penetration of Western management science among Soviet specialists, however, has been extensive. By 1974, the exposure of the "reactionary essence" of Western theory has become, in Gvishiani's view, an urgent issue: "Its urgency is determined by, along with other reasons, the fact that the scientific, technical, and economic ties between the socialist and capitalist states have expanded substantially in the last few years."[131] In 1978, Gvishiani repeated his warning against the ideologically subversive effects of Western theory while simultaneously endorsing those aspects useful to the Soviet system.[132]

The fragmented state of Soviet management theory has many causes, its struggle for legitimacy among them. It is also attributable to numerous unresolved substantive problems. Four issues have been particularly controversial: the autonomy of management science; its scope; the methodological basis of theory; and, finally, the relationship of management theory to Marxism-Leninism.

On the issue of the formal status of management theory there has been a continuing effort to find the middle ground among competing positions that management science should be fully autonomous or an offshoot of one of the established disciplines. A similar effort is evident in locating the scope of management theory between confining theory to micromanagement or expanding it to encompass the economy as a whole.[133]

These issues have been closely related to questions of the structure of theory and its methodology. The initial thrust was to create a comprehensive and detailed theoretical structure. This resulted in an excess of "scholastic theorizing," which has tended to trivialize theoretical development.[134] Both Popov and Gvishiani have argued that a meaningful theory cannot assume a classical and deductive form. Popov, in particular, has been sharply critical of the Taylorists, or "NOT enthusiasts," who want to create a theory of universal management principles or "recipes" that can be applied mechanically to given situations.[135] Indeed, some theorists, noting the high level of contingency that empirical theory must incorporate, simply deny the possibility of creating a finished theory.[136] For them, management theory is a hybrid of science and art, thus preserving a role for managerial experience and intuition. The latter structure, not coincidentally, preserves a role for the leading role of the Communist Party and blunts the largely symbolic threat of managerial technocracy.

Methodological controversies on the degree to which any complex system can be quantitatively described have been prominent in the development of all the social sciences. The central role assigned to quantitative methods of decision making in management reform, however, has given this issue a sharp edge. Few scholars totally reject quantitative methods. Equally, only a minority would endorse the position of L. I. Evenko of the Institute of the USA and Canada that management cannot be improved unless all of its aspects are described by mathematical models.[137] The most widespread view is that, however useful, extreme complexity prevents a full mathematical formalization of decision making.[138]

Ideological opposition to an uncritical absorption of Western theory has already been noted. A second basic objective has been to prevent the rise of an autonomous theory outside of ideological control. Ideological opposition is dramatically illustrated in the case of cybernetics.

The rise of cybernetics as the new general theory of scientific management in the 1960s was rapid. At the 1966 Moscow conference on industrial management, Gvishiani stressed the necessity for the most rapid development of the mathematical and technical dimensions of management theory. Priority was to be given to the growth of cybernetics, theories of information, mathematical methods of decision making, and computerization.[139] But by 1972 this support for cybernetics as the new general theory of management had faded sharply.

Under pressure from ideological opposition and technical complexity, Gvishiani rejected the legitimacy of a purely technical or cybernetic approach. Management theory was, he declared, above all economic and sociological. The ideological primacy of the political economy of socialism was assured in his affirmation that management theory must have a concrete historical, rather than abstract, analytical basis.[140] The reason was clear. If the theory of management is exclusively technical, D. Pravdin pointed out in another context, then there is no difference between a capitalist and socialist regime.[141]

As Soviet management theory enters the 1980s, what has developed as a general theory of management is a loose hybrid of quasi-autonomous disciplines that have unevenly developed approaches and methodologies. The most important of these disciplines in the 1970s has been economic cybernetics. Despite conservative opposition, cybernetics has dominated management research, education, and rationalization. Economic cybernetics, however, has not swept the field totally. The movement for the scientific organization of labor, traditional economic research and the foundations of a sociology and psychology of management as well as labor have also developed in the 1960s and 1970s.

An important aspect of theoretical development has been the organization of research. Generally, research has proceeded in a decentralized and uncoordinated fashion, characterized by local initiative, duplication of effort, and continuing jurisdictional conflicts among competing research organizations. One important consequence has been to release a flood of low-quality research, which has contributed to the relatively low prestige among managers of management science.

Limited and tentative efforts were made in the early 1960s to coordinate management research. The rapid and uncontrolled expansion of research in the mid-1960s, however, created a minor crisis. The 1966 all-union conference was convened in large measure to curb the "shop approach" to theory construction and bring it under control. To create order in the search for management theory, the conference proposed the formation of a new management research institute in the Academy of Sciences, the establishment of a learned journal, and the founding of a national training institute for managers.[142]

A national institute for management training was formed in 1971, but an authoritative learned journal has not yet appeared; nor has a major research institute. The establishment of a series of research institutes with a cybernetic and management thrust in the middle and late 1970s, however, may evolve into functional equivalents of such an institute.

Without centralized planning and direction, the loose organization of research has given it a strong entrepreneurial flavor. Generally, a traditional division of labor has prevailed. Theoretical research has been centered in the institutes of the Academy of Sciences; branch institutes attached to state committees and ministries tend to greater specialization and applied research. Much of management research is contract research and has been conducted in hundreds of small departments, laboratories, and sections of plants, administrative organs, and educational institutions. For many, such research is a secondary activity.[143]

A full description of the management research complex is beyond the scope of this book. Notice should be taken, however, of several outstanding institutes that have made major contributions to the cybernetic approach to management. Within the national Academy of Sciences are the Central Economico-Mathematical Institute, the Institute of Problems of Administration, and the Siberian Division's Institute of Mathematics and Institute of the Economics and Organization of Industrial Production. In the Ukraine, the Institute of Cybernetics in Kiev has played an outstanding role in developing managerial technologies. In 1972, the Soviet Union was a founding member of the twelve-nation International Institute for Applied Systems Research established outside of Vienna.

The dominance of the cybernetic approach to management theory has resulted in the formation of several major new institutes in the 1970s. An All-Union Institute of Cybernetics for agricultural research has been formed. In 1976, an Institute of Systems Research, headed by Gvishiani and his deputy Boris Milner, was created under the joint control of the State Committee for Science and Technology and the Academy of Sciences. Two institutes for CMEA and international management have also been formed. Among the most important developments was the establishment under Academician N. V. Melnikov in 1978 of a new Academy of the National Economy, which will have research and training functions.[144]

Systematic research into organizational behavior has been more restricted. For research centers like the Academy of Sciences' Institute of Social Research, Institute of Psychology, and Institute of State and Law, management research has had secondary importance. The development of industrial sociology, however, has made important contributions to understanding behavior in the enterprises.

The educational establishment has played an increasingly important role in developing management theory. The model facility has been Moscow University's Center of Problems of Administration of Social Production, formed and headed by G. Kh. Popov. Since the early 1960s, the center has functioned according to Popov's conception of theory development, combining speculation with teaching and rationalization. The center's demonstration effect, however, has been disappointing.[145]

As part of the larger policy of economic integration with CMEA, cooperative management research with Eastern Europe has expanded. Eastern European research is more advanced and experimental than Soviet research, in part because of some members' association with International Labor Organization programs. As a result of this interchange, Soviet specialists have gained access to a large, interesting, and sometimes disturbing literature.[146]

2

The systems approach to management reform

The massive surge of enthusiasm among Soviet natural and social scientists in the 1960s for the application of cybernetic concepts to economic processes was rooted in the judgment that the
economy had escaped control by traditional methods. As Loren
Graham has noted, cybernetics rekindled the hope that these
processes could be brought under rational control.[1] By the end
of the decade, there was a good deal of truth to the view that
"cybernetics as a science, a methodology, a class of machines,
and perhaps as magic word, has been the object of particular
reverence and hope in the Soviet Union."[2] Through the 1970s,
the cumulative costs of implementing a cybernetic approach to
the rationalization of management has undoubtedly tempered
this enthusiasm. The long-term consequences of the cybernetic
approach, nonetheless, may have critical significance for the
shape of industrial management because it has resulted in an
intellectual as well as a technical revolution.

Systems as a logic of management

The value of the systems approach for the rationalization of
management has been constrained to some degree by ideological
pressure and serious methodological problems that have
emerged with the development of the discipline. A central issue
that has gripped Soviet as well as Western specialists has been to
achieve a consensual definition of what constitutes the systems
approach. For many, the large number of conflicting conceptions grouped under the label of systems analysis constitutes a
methodological crisis of the first order,[3] a crisis that arose ini-

51

tially in the problem of distinguishing general systems theory from cybernetics.

General systems theory, whose principal research center is the Academy of Sciences' Institute of the History of Science and Technology, has had as a major interest the formulation of a general methodology of science, or, in the obscure phrase of a leading group of theorists, a general systems "ontology."[4] The institute's intellectual orientation has been deeply influenced by a wide range of Soviet and Western theorists, including A. A. Bogdanov, Ludwig von Bertalanffy, Kenneth Boulding, and M. Mesarovich. Of these, the major figure has been von Bertalanffy.[5] Output in Soviet systems research has clearly been prodigious. I. V. Blauberg and others have estimated the publication of more than one thousand books between 1958 and 1976.[6]

Systems theory and cybernetics are frequently used interchangeably, although their relationship has become a serious theoretical issue. N. G. Gaaze-Rapoport, a senior researcher in the Institute of the History of Science and Technology, has given a useful initial analysis of their relationship. In his view, general systems theory and cybernetics share a focus on the properties of the total system; each concentrates on a system's structure and functions; each investigates only the most general features of a system; and each views the dynamics of a system from a behavioral perspective.[7]

There are also significant differences. General systems theory investigates both logical and real systems; cybernetics concentrates only on the behavior of real systems. Their origins are also different. Cybernetics originated in the theory of automatic regulation of relatively simple, closed-loop systems, gradually expanding its technical approach to more complex systems.[8] In contrast, general systems theory developed from the study of biological systems. The distinction becomes significant insofar as social organization is conceived in predominantly mechanistic or organic terms. The bias toward a mechanistic and closed model of organization is clearly more congruent with the classic conception of management. The distinction between mechanistic and organic models is, of course, conditional because formal organization necessarily combines both.

Through the 1970s, cybernetics has been the dominant approach to the modernization of industrial management. General systems theory is viewed as too diffuse and abstract to have major payoffs. The assumption has been that cybernetics, using an input–output model, has a more powerful set of concepts and methodologies for understanding and controlling complex management systems.[9]

There is evident caution, nonetheless, in applying a cybernetic approach to management. The political and ideological threat is obvious. Secondly, cybernetics is only in an initial stage of development. Like general systems theory, it operates at a high level of generality, answering questions of how rather than what. It must draw from other disciplines substantive empirical recommendations. Finally, cybernetics is theoretically unfinished. As a leading Soviet economic cybernetician has noted, a "language" for economic cybernetics has yet to be developed. "It has not even framed those hypotheses that would explain from a single point of view the sum of problems that stand before the discipline."[10]

Soviet cybernetics has been heavily influenced by Western thought. The most important Western sources have been Norbert Weiner and Ross Ashby, whose major books were translated in 1958, and Sir Stafford Beer, whose book appeared in Russian in 1965. The concept of cybernetics accepted by most Soviet scientists is that it is a discipline, based upon mathematical methods and computers, that focuses on the research of management control processes in complex, dynamic systems.

Virtually all Soviet specialists assume that management is a process of communication and control that counteracts systemic disorganization or entropy and has the task of establishing a dynamic balance between a system and its environment. Management structure is a hierarchy of controlling and controlled subsystems and is functionally defined as an input–output model. Scientific management of complex systems is achieved through modeling informational processes using such disciplines as information theory, mathematical logic, linear and dynamic programming, game theory, and research operations.[11]

The core concept of cybernetics is information. Informational processes are assumed to be universal and, in the view of B. V. Biriukov, to play the same role in cybernetics that energy plays in physics.[12] Communication forms the relationships that define structure; it also provides the basis upon which a system functions. Information is defined as the knowledge of an environment's state or an organization's internal condition. In this perspective processing of information is the major function of management. Although management cannot be reduced only to informational relationships (a popular position among some Marxist revisionists), it is inseparable from it.[13]

Western approaches to information theory have not been absorbed without ideological stress and modification. The dilemma appears in a variety of contexts. A statistical approach to information theory is essential to an effective transmission and processing of very large amounts of information. The acceptance of Claude Shannon's conception of the statistical nature of information and his functional definition of information as the reduction of indefinitiveness raised serious ideological issues. An unqualified assumption of indeterminacy would separate Soviet Marxism from cybernetics because all forms of predeterminism would become illegitimate, thereby justifying an open or pluralistic Marxism. To avoid this, Academician A. Kolmogorov has developed an "algorithmic" approach combining deterministic and stochastic approaches.[14]

There can be little surprise that, as members of an applied discipline, cyberneticians were divided sharply into three distinct, if overlapping schools. The broadest view was that cybernetics, with qualifications, was the contemporary general theory of management. A narrower interpretation was that it was essentially concerned with the management of informational processes. In the most conservative definition, cybernetics was a purely auxiliary science derived from the theory of automatic control and limited to the quantifiable aspects of management.[15] Most tension has arisen between the first and second positions.

The first position was forcefully advocated by A. I. Berg, a leading radio engineer and first chairman of the Cybernetics Council of the Academy of Sciences. Defining cybernetics as a "universal science of complex systems or processes," Berg defined management as the optimal control of a system's transition from one state to another.[16] In contrast, V. M. Glushkov held that cybernetics examines systems as informational flows through input–output channels. Management in these terms is a control process that transforms information for the purpose of exerting influence on a managed subsystem to achieve a projected goal. Information, rather than resources, is optimized.[17] The central problem of a cybernetic approach to management reform lies in the limits of a technological model for controlling a complex social system. The possibility of building a rigorously quantified model of social relationships is usually discounted because the total amount of information is too large to be processed fully and social relationships are ambiguous and nonlinear in their causal dependencies.[18] Organic and social systems, V. A. Lektorskii and V. S. Shvyrov have insisted, require as assumptions that purely mechanical explanations are inadequate for explaining a system's origins and behavior and that such systems are self-organizing.[19] Both the nature of social systems and the complexity of the environment reduce the capacity of management to achieve comprehensive social programming.

Toward a theory of managerial control

The rise of the social sciences has had as goals not only an increased understanding of complex social processes but also the prescription of specific policies for increasing social integration and the efficiency of resource allocation. Through the 1970s, the social sciences operated primarily within a cybernetic framework of organizational control.

In the broad conception of cybernetics, the scope of the discipline includes the study of methods that can alter behavioral processes in the guidance of a system's transition from one state to another.[20] The conception of regulating a complex system's behavior through feedback assumes a reduction of administrative and other direct social controls. These should be replaced by indirect determinants that steer social processes and maintain systemic equilibrium. The problem of developing regulators of organizational behavior has been a central issue of management reform over the past two decades.

The contributions of cybernetics are primarily methodological and technological, and therefore the development of behavioral regulators has been the work of economists, sociologists, social psychologists, and other specialists. In the most rigorously technical system, these mechanisms should regulate the economy automatically. Such a mechanistic approach to social control is clearly congruent with a high level of centralized programming. This essentially conservative approach appears to have guided the thinking of the more moderate economists on the 1965 reforms. An excellent example was A. M. Birman's explanation of the reform's basic mechanisms. Rationalization of economic management, he argued, required replacing administrative methods with effective economic and social regulators. These regulators, in the form of interest rates, norms of profitability, a reformed price structure, and broader use of the market would aid in the coordination of macro- and microeconomies. Such mechanisms would provide the enterprise managers with the information required to react effectively to complex and rapidly changing conditions. To secure reliable behavioral responses to these signals, Birman linked performance with economic incentives and sanctions. Incentives directly dependent upon efficient utilization of resources would force managers to observe all plan parameters and stimulate the fulfillment of planned goals. Among its advantages would be a reduction of information and stereotyped decisions.[21]

The still close association of Soviet economists with Taylorism has made economic incentives the primary factor in the search for regulators of behavior. The low effectiveness of these methods, combined with a need to incorporate more organic approaches to organizational control, has stimulated an interest in Western theories of social control. Through the 1970s, however, the development of a new Soviet theory of social action or human relations, remained in an initial stage of development.

The views of Marxists toward the functional analysis of social relationships clearly differ. The Polish sociologist Piotr Sztempka has observed that functionalism has a "fundamental affinity" with Marxism, based upon common conceptual models.[22] The Soviet approach to Parsons and social systems theory, however, has been more ambivalent ideologically. Parsons has been attacked as a defender of capitalism and pluralism and for using an ahistorical, evolutionary, and antidialectical methodology. But his analysis of complex social systems holds an attraction because it offers a possible route to a formalization of social knowledge and therefore to social forecasting and planning.[23]

The substantive aspects of Parsons' thought of greatest interest to Soviet sociologists are related to his theory of social action. Parsons offers an organic approach that avoids biological determinism and focuses on what Silverman has described as the Hobbesian question of social order.[24] The integration of a social system through the creation of roles based upon stable expectations derived from a universal and shared value system expresses an orientation that is clearly compatible with Soviet culture and institutions.

A similar congruity is evident in the assumption that organizations are internally integrated through goals that reflect the values of the larger social system. The stress by Parsons on functional imperatives (adaptation, integration, goal achievement, and the management of social conflict) as well as the importance of communication and decision making for social integration clearly meet some of the genuine Soviet needs for a macro theory of social control. Finally, the primacy of political institutions in the hierarchy of control structures and the use of an input–output decision model are fully congruent with existing methods of control.[25]

The Parsonian emphasis upon the value of culture and social norms in integrating Soviet society and a principal reliance on socialization for behavioral control has been described as useful but insufficient. On the philosophical plane, Soviet social psychologists object to the view that human experience has value insofar as it has meaning because this creates serious epistemological problems. In addition, the principal practical problem lies in an acknowledged gap between official norms of the regime and the far greater number of diverse, implicit, and informal norms that arise outside of official norms and are not influenced by formal sanctions.[26]

A Marxist theory of social change begins, I. M. Popova has suggested, with changes in the material environment. The divergence in values, which is the source of social tension, arises from rates of change that are more rapid in the material environment than in the formal norms defining social behavior. To maintain social equilibrium through a strategy of rational control involves manipulating the system's parameters, which are the social and material environment, informational flows, group norms and values, and social sanctions. Within this context sociology has the dual function of describing the social and economic environment in operationally relevant terms and prescribing those influences designed to structure behavior in desired directions.[27]

The search for effective methods of social regulation implies a theory of motivation. In their quest for methods that promote social harmony and organizational responsiveness, Soviet sociologists and social psychologists have challenged the traditional Taylorist view of the primacy of economic incentives and sanctions in motivating behavior within organizations. Borrowing heavily from human relations theory, the Ukrainian psychologist S. G. Moskivich has noted the theoretical approaches of Maslow, Herzburg, and Likert on the satisfaction of human needs within organizations.[28]

Although a theory of motivation based upon such concepts as self-actualization is a minor theme in the rationalization of management methods, there are implications for the traditional organization of the Soviet enterprise and for alienation in socialist societies. Some of these implications have been spelled out by the eminent management specialist Iurii Cherniak. In his view, the basic question is how a worker in administration can be motivated to give his full knowledge and commitment to the organization. The army of workers in Soviet management, he has argued, are not abstractions but living people who are very different and have their own personal goals and interests. Citing Douglas McGregor's *Human Side of Enterprise,* Cherniak believes a Theory X approach to management, which attempts to regulate behavior through money and petty administrative controls, is simply too primitive in contemporary circumstances.[29]

On the whole, it is evident that the conceptualization of industrial organization as a functional system has had interesting results. The depth of the intellectual challenge of cybernetics has been extraordinary. Cybernetics has defined the fundamental problems of organization in genuinely new ways and has offered new approaches and methods for resolving the problems of very complex organizations that function in dynamic and uncertain environments. Cybernetics and the systems approach, however, have a general orientation and unresolved problems. A cybernetic approach has therefore had serious ideological and technical problems in translating theory into a coherent program of rationalization that reflects a consensus. This condition, in turn, has influenced its specific direction.

Systems and the management paradigm

Perhaps the most fundamental issue to arise in connection with the application of the systems approach to the modernization of management is the continuing relevance of the classical mechanistic model of industrial management institutionalized during the early stages of industrialization. Prior to the introduction of systems analysis and cybernetics as a scientific methodology, classic rationalism as the model of rationalization was virtually unchallenged. This is no longer true. The systems approach has spawned a number of diverse and competing models that carry diverse implications for the reform of the management system.

It is clear that some conservative scholars have borrowed from the language of systems analysis to reinforce the classical model. Iurii Kozlov, a legal specialist, for example, warned that cybernetic concepts could be "overrated." As a system, the structures and functions of management are defined through administrative law. Authority is monocratic and hierarchical; the autonomy of any subsystem is therefore conditional. Management control is a function of the command authority, which each organ receives as an element in the formal system of state administration.[30]

A cybernetic model offers a different perspective. Two distinct models, each with a large number of concrete variations, emerge. The shape of the model depends initially upon the definition of cybernetics adopted. In the narrower definition, technology is dominant and industrial management is structurally defined as a computer-based information system. This conception, expressing an engineering approach, produces a clearly mechanistic and deterministic model. The more complex management models are those developed on the assumption that economic decision making occurs within a complex socioeconomic system whose processes are stochastic.

The technological model of the management system is primarily defined by the capabilities of mathematical modeling and computers. The initial reaction of conservatives to the computer

technology that emerged in the 1950s was a rekindling of hope
that the classical administrative model could be strengthened
and expanded. In what L. Leontiev has called "the childish dis-
ease of computerism" (*detskaia bolezn kompiuterizma*), conservatives argued that the chronic lack of balance in the economy was
caused by the restricted scope of administrative planning. The
vastly increased capacities for information processing and computation of the new technology held out the hope for a fully
centralized planning system in which production and exchange
could be controlled "down to the last nail."[31] Such a fully determined system would eliminate the need for any redistribution of
authority or indirect stimulation of choice in desired directions.
In its most abstract form, the computer-based model not only
appeared as a panacea for the existing system but, with development, promised an unalloyed automated system of decision making.

The cybernetic model of the economy sketched by Academician Glushkov does not exhibit the same degree of technological
determinism as the earlier expectations. Nonetheless, he views
the economy as a closed-loop system. In his model, the economy
is conceptualized as a set of relationships established by a
nationwide network of computer centers located in the major
Soviet industrial centers. Through the network would flow the
information required to plan and manage the economy. Operational management would be the responsibility of a central dispatcher for the economy as a whole, who would establish production priorities and direct the flow of orders and tasks to the
various production units. In this system, industrial management
takes the form of a fully centralized man–machine dialog.

In Glushkov's model, the primacy of the technological factor
does not exclude economic and social factors, but it does reduce
them to a secondary and dependent role. He accepts, for example, the necessity of a marketlike mechanism as the source of
feedback in the management of a large and complex economic
system. He rejects, however, a traditional "socioeconomic market," which links producers and consumers on the basis of economic interest. It will eventually be replaced by the computer
network that functions as an electronic market: "The EVM (electronic computing machine) will eventually play the role that
commodity–monetary relations play at the present time." Even

in acknowledging the necessity of economic criteria and stimulation, Glushkov has contested the view of Birman and other economists that these can "automatically" solve the problems of the system. Technology is the primary factor in management rationalization.[32]

A more complex cybernetic model is constructed by economists like N. Ia. Petrakov and V. Nemchinov, who stress the priority of economic and social factors in industrial management. Their initial assumption is that the economy is a very complex system with numerous subsystems. The system is characterized by stochastic processes that cannot be fully formalized and therefore fully programmed. Under this model, both the mechanistic paradigm and the traditional methods of planning and control are subject to fundamental redefinition.

The model of Petrakov, a deputy director of CEMI, is a deliberate attempt to unify Norbert Weiner's emphasis on the system–environment relationship with Stafford Beer's concentration on internal structural relationships and processes.[33] The socialist economy is conceived as a "self-conscious" system that lacks complete self-knowledge. Indeterminacy in the economy does not result from restrictions of human knowledge, which, theoretically at least, could be corrected by increasing the amounts of information and the speed of processing. Rather, indeterminacy is the inescapable result of the objective impossibility of describing a system in a single language.

The lack of full knowledge of the specific dynamics of the system requires the notion of the black or gray box. To make inferences on the nature of processes within the box requires an observation of the relationship between inputs and outputs of the system. Rational control of a system of this size and complexity is achievable only through the manipulation of inputs and the extrapolation of internal processes and outputs into the future. Both internal processes and outputs, by definition, are statistically defined, that is, have a contingent and probabilistic behavioral pattern.

Petrakov assumes that, if the pool of knowledge about the system's behavior increases, the level of determination also increases, and the size of the black box decreases. But a fully determined and risk-free system cannot be constructed because empirical knowledge of any dynamic system interacting with an environment is inexhaustible. The relativity of human knowledge, in his view, has been demonstrated by modern genetic theory and Heisenberg's principle of indeterminacy. Two immediate consequences may be drawn for a theory of management. Although management is a conscious and purposeful activity, Petrakov denies teleology to objective social processes. Secondly, a variety of languages must be used for decision making. The system is, to this extent, pluralist.

To reform the economy defined as a large and complex system, a new rationality for economic management and a new language of economic planning must be developed. The older, mechanistic rationality of viewing management as the conscious and purposeful predefinition and control of all processes within the system must be rejected. From the strategic and developmental perspective, rational management can no longer be perceived as achieving a fixed and precisely determined set of goals through the least expenditure of time and resources but must be seen as a flexible process of continuous search and correction through feedback of the goals of development.[34]

The importance of this particular variation on the cybernetic conception of the national economy for the redefinition of the Leninist model of the economy and for traditional decision-making procedures is clear. In a lengthy article in *Novyi mir* published in 1970, Petrakov noted that the paradigm of the economy as a single, large machine was no longer viable. If the mechanistic model were true, all economic goals and relationships would be clear. Management would simply consist of constructing a plan to connect needs with resources. But, citing indeterminacy and the perceptions of Kurt Vonnegut's novel *Utopia-14*, Petrakov concludes that man cannot be programmed.[35]

These particular assumptions were clearly those displayed in the cybernetic critique and model of the economy defined by Academician Nemchinov in a controversial and still influential article published in 1964.[36] The moving force behind the establishment of the Central Economico–Mathematical Institute, Nemchinov argued that the principal problems of economic management stemmed from the central planners' lack of knowledge about resources and the lack of feedback. He considered it mandatory that the simplistic conceptions of the traditional system be jettisoned.

Dividing the economy hierarchically into global and local subsystems, Nemchinov declared, "A primitive view of the interrelations between large and small economic systems can only create the type of ossified, mechanistic system in which all parameters of operation are set in advance and the whole system run by quotas from top to bottom on every given point."[37] Eventually, he predicted, the system would simply crack under the pressure. Reform of the management structure, at its base, had two objectives: to assume the priority of systemic goals; and to ensure the continuous functioning of the feedback mechanism.

To achieve this, Nemchinov proposed, as Stanley Cohn has noted, dismantling the system of microeconomic planning by reducing direct administrative relationships and expanding the role of the market in planning and control of Soviet industry.[38] Influenced by the model of Oscar Lange and the Yugoslavian experience, Nemchinov proposed an extensive change in distribution of authority and the procedures for planning industrial outputs and supply.

A central concern for Nemchinov was the evident conflict of economic and social interests, which was an acknowledged source of the extensive suboptimization and lack of balance in the economy. To align global and local interests he proposed a new system of planning through the expansion of the traditional principle of *khozraschet,* or economic accountability. Enterprise plans were to be established as plan contracts negotiated on the basis of mutual economic advantage by the central planners and the enterprises. In his model, the enterprise only signed contracts for production whose prices covered costs and acceptable profit levels. To make the pricing system serve not only accounting but also incentive and allocative functions, Nemchinov proposed a radical reorganization in the planning of prices. Fixed prices were to be limited to a small list of key products. He consigned the great bulk of goods to a decentralized market mechanism governed by a system of price controls.

Perhaps the most fundamental of Nemchinov's proposals was his determination to eliminate the centralized allocation of supply, which he believed should be replaced by wholesale trade in the means of production.

To regulate plan fulfillment, he relied upon an incentive system based upon profitability and manipulated to adjust production to changes in demand. Comparing the system of economic regulators, such as a fixed charge on capital, with the Watts governor, he argued for a set of economic and financial levers that operated in such a way that the enterprise had a strong interest in executing the plan. The plan, in turn, was a map for directing and coordinating economic management rather than a blueprint. A strong and early advocate of the use of economic models and computers in management, Nemchinov nonetheless clearly perceived their limitations as management techniques. In contrast to Glushkov, he felt technology would play an important but secondary role. The computer-based information system was primarily limited to operational control.[39]

The development of a cybernetic model of social management that would redistribute authority within the political system in a shape similar to the Petrakov and Nemchinov models of the economy has yet to be constructed. The widely publicized model of social management developed by V. G. Afanasev in the *Scientific Management of Society* adopts a general cybernetic framework and terminology. Cybernetic theory, however, plays an auxiliary role. A prominent ideologist who has specialized and written extensively on scientific communism, Afanasev uses Marxist-Leninist categories of social analysis and presents a basic defense of traditional institutional arrangements of authority and function.[40]

Although the model of social management developed by Afanasev is clearly an effort to legitimate the established political and administrative role of the Communist Party and the Soviet state, it is also a model for the reform of the structures of decision making and control in limited and incremental but quite definite ways. In Afanasev's model, the core relationship is between Soviet political institutions and the larger society. These structural relationships are institutionally defined by public ownership and a conscious planning of societal processes. Afanasev supports the traditional Marxist view that the transition from spontaneously regulated social processes to planned social control is a principal advantage of socialism. Afanasev admits that a range of social and demographic processes are stochastic and therefore can only be partially regulated through the planning system. These processes, however, are of secondary importance and do not challenge the rationality of the traditional planning system.[41]

Whereas the models of Petrakov and Nemchinov are clearly open or adaptive systems, the model of Afanasev is similar to those of Kozlov and Glushkov in being relatively closed. The central source of authority in forming the plans and programs that manage Soviet society is the subsystem for control, or "subject of control," the complex of political, administrative, and social institutions headed by the Communist Party. Afanasev assumes this authority over Soviet society to be formally unrestricted. The "competence of the Soviet state as a subject of control extends to direct scientific guidance of all social processes, economic, sociopolitical and to the country's relations with the external environment."[42] Within this complex, the most important policy task for the Communist Party is to exercise the "scientific control of Soviet society."

The model of the Soviet administrative system, drawn by Afanasev along traditional institutional lines, clearly falls within the mechanistic paradigm. A classical administrative rationality is revealed in his view that a rational administrative structure is one in which functions are clearly defined, precisely specialized, and closely coordinated. Afanasev, however, does not absolutize the administrative factor or advocate the full centralization of administrative power.[43]

Scientific Management of Society and other books by Afanasev are extended monographs on the rationalization of economic and social methods of management within the constraints of the existing ideological and institutional structures of Soviet society. Numerous economic, sociopsychological, ethical, and aesthetic processes are assumed to be beyond the direct control of the formalized administrative structure. To maintain and expand political control over Soviet society in its present complex phase of development, the role of indirect economic and social methods should be increased and feedback and decision-making procedures improved. Afanasev has also been a forceful advocate of the need to incorporate the methodologies and results of social research and computer-based technologies into the decision-making process.[44] Whether the traditional political structure he defends and proposes to expand is compatible with the extensive functional rationalization he advocates is obviously debatable.

The surge of empirical social research developed over the past two decades is evidently becoming an important source of descriptive information on the enterprise. Theoretical analysis of this material from the point of view of management, as the work of Popova and others illustrates, however, is only in an initial stage. A recent effort to develop a general model of the enterprise as a social system, however, has been outlined by A. I. Prigozhin.

Prigozhin defines the social structure of the enterprise as the interaction of two key sets of relationships: factors (age, sex, ethnicity, profession, and other psychological and sociological variables) that relate the organization to the larger social system; and, secondly, internal relationships that constitute the three subsystems of the enterprise structure. The latter are the technical system; the sociotechnical system, which relates men and technology; and, finally, the administrative system, which is constructed on the basis of the sociotechnical system.[45]

As a sociologist of organization, Prigozhin has a primary interest in the impact of technology on the social organization of the enterprise. He analyzes, for example, the levels of freedom a bench worker who participates in the various social systems enjoys. In the sociotechnical system, technology determines human behavior and prescribes choice. The formal organization also constrains choice, although less rigorously, administrative relationships having an inherent degree of ambiguity. Only in the informal group created independently of the formalized structure does the worker have automony because he is free to choose his associates and norms of behavior. In the sociotechnical system, the worker is a productive force; in the informal group, he is a person.[46]

SOFE as a policy paradigm

The most significant of the efforts to create a comprehensive alternative paradigm of economic decision making to emerge in the Brezhnev era is SOFE, or the system of optimal functioning of the economy. Optimal planning has been closely associated with Vasilii Nemchinov and his followers, who have steadily pressed the potentials of economic modeling and computer-based informational systems for a central planning system. Through such major research institutes of the Academy of Sciences as the Central Economico–Mathematical Institute, the

Siberian Division's Institute of Mathematics and Institute of Economics and Organization of Industrial Production, and Gosplan's Scientific Research Institute of Economics, research on a broad front of problems related to the introduction of mathematical methods and computers into planning has been carried on since the late 1950s. Dozens of other branch and republican institutes have been involved in the application of systems theory to economic decision making as well.[47]

The SOFE conception has a dual significance. It is important initially as a theoretical statement of the possible applications of modern technologies to the decision-making system. SOFE is also important, however, for its impact on the new strategy of rationalization that arose in the late 1960s as the extension and modification of the economic reforms undertaken in 1965.

Theoretically, SOFE presents primarily a functional approach to the reform of the decision-making system based on models and computers with an extensive reorganization of the formal structures for planning and control. In addition, SOFE presents an effort to reform management methods in line with its basic conceptions of functional optimization and structural reorganization. The theory of optimal decision making, it should be pointed out, is far from complete, and a number of its basic propositions are bitterly challenged.[48] The specific proposals for procedural and organizational reform of the planning organs have been solidly resisted. Significantly, SOFE has also raised a number of basic questions related to the political economy of socialism.

The paradigm of optimal planning and management developed in SOFE should be placed squarely within the revisionist tradition. In the form presented by its principal spokesman and promoter, N. F. Fedorenko, SOFE is a response of the scientific-technical revolution to the problems of the modern Soviet economy.[49] Fedorenko, the protégé of Nemchinov and director of CEMI, has argued that the assumptions of the classical model that describes the economy as a "gigantic organism, all elements of which receive commands from a single center and mechanically fulfill them" are "naive and oversimplified."[50] The economy, in his view, should be approached as "a highly intricate system to be optimized, a system consisting of a multiplicity of subsystems and operating under incomplete information."[51]

Fedorenko and his colleagues have focused particularly on the traditional system of planning. The existing system has been oriented traditionally to satisfying constraints and achieving internal balance rather than to an efficient response to changing social needs. In the traditional system, described by the SOFE advocates as a "resource–branch" system, plan targets and resource allocations have been determined by administrative methods and by the institutionalized procedures and structures of the planning bureaucracy. Such a system precludes the solution of interbranch and systemic problems of development because the existing system of planning is inherently restricted to the reproduction of resources on a branch or territorial basis.[52]

A principal criticism of traditional planning has been its methods of computation. The matching of production needs with resources through the calculation of thousands of specific material balances has been dismissed as simply inadequate. The construction and coordination of these balances requires huge expenditures of time and resources, and, in the final analysis, they are incomplete. Such a method of computation cannot lead to either balanced or optimized plans.[53]

In approaching the rationalization of the planning and management system, the paradigm has clearly been defined by cybernetics. Throughout its development, the technological dimension has been primary. Fedorenko had been an early proponent of a purely quantitative approach to economic science, going so far as to press for a new political economy of socialism. In the 1970s, however, under pressure from conservative political economists, Fedorenko has tended to redefine the description of the basic paradigm. He has emphasized that the economic system cannot be adequately described as a man–machine system but is primarily a social system. Mathematics, he has noted, cannot serve as the master key to decision making because analytical methods derived from the physical sciences are not completely applicable to more complex social processes.[54] The ideological orthodoxy evident in the more recent pronouncements of the proponents of SOFE, however, appears to have had little impact on the practical proposals for the functional rationalization of economic decision making.

The distinctive feature of SOFE is its specific objective of developing an optimized decision-making system – the construction of rules of rational economic choice under conditions of constraint.[55] Organizationally, this involves building a "goal-resource" system in place of the existing "resource-branch" system. Initially, this requires a fundamental shift of focus from the routinized increase of resources characteristic of the traditional system to one of planning from final goals. The concept of "resources" is defined to include not only labor and material resources but also social and technical resources. SOFE assumes that at any given moment the total resources of a society are limited in relation to social demand and are interchangeable.[56] Given these assumptions, the problem for SOFE is to create a decision-making system that optimizes resource allocation or, more specifically, to construct a system that can reliably produce the mixture of goals and resources that best meets long-term developmental objectives.

The rationalization of the existing system of planning and plan implementation requires a process that Fedorenko has described as "metaplanning."[57] Metaplanning has the specific objective of producing a synthesis of mathematical models and computer technology with the procedures and organization of planning. The planning function is conceived as an integration of the two subsystems. It is simultaneously part of the supersystem of economic administration as well as a distinct, relatively autonomous subsystem defined structurally by informational flows. The integration of the planning system initially requires the definition and coordination of two distinct sets of criteria: criteria established by the supersystem that constitute the parameters of the plan; and internal criteria that specify the procedures whereby the planning system transforms information relevant to the plan's parameters.[58]

Fedorenko and his colleagues have adopted Ashby's concept of diversity (*raznobrazie*) as the formal principle for the integration of the subsystems. Ideally, there should be some rational correspondence between the number of possible states of the economy and the number of internal states that can be reproduced within the system of planning. Because the number of potential economic states is continually growing, metaplanning has the complex task of increasing the capabilities of the planning system to reproduce the diversity of the environment and to select a future optimal state and trajectory.[59]

The SOFE approach to the rationalization of planning and

management appears to be governed by two primary methodological assumptions. The first is clearly that the full diversity of the economy cannot be formally reproduced within the planning system, and thus, as noted previously, the classical paradigm of a rational and consciously controlled system of comprehensive planning is chimerical. The other methodological assumption is historical and in some respects contrary to the first. The existing system has inertial properties that prevent short-range deviation from established patterns. To overcome the limitations of complexity and institutional inertia, the proponents of SOFE have advocated a fundamental revision of the functions and structures of management.

The complex of measures for the rationalization of the planning system have been assembled by CEMI scholars under the rubric of the system of integrated planning, or SKP.[60] SKP is designed to align goals with resources, to coordinate plans of different time lengths, as well as to integrate planning methods, organizational structure, informational flows, and computers. The principal methodological change is the adoption of the program-goal (*programmno-tselevoi*) approach, which integrates the goals of development with an optimal allocation of resources. Specific long-term goals are formulated, integrated, and ranked in a tree of goals, which describes developmental priorities. The tree of goals, in turn, is based on a general forecast of social, political, economic, and technological developments over a fifteen- or twenty-year period.[61]

As the principal planning document, the long-term or general plan is an aggregate of the specific programs that specify and relate the allocation of resources in time to one or more of the several goals of the general plan. In this conception, programs not only serve as instruments for the distribution of resources but also function as a method of administration. Five-year and annual plans become organically subordinate to the general plan and its specific programs and should be organically integrated with them.[62]

The technological core of SKP is the interrelated network of models and computers that define and service the computational and informational aspects of the new planning system. The system assumes the operation of a broad group of economic and social models in the construction of national and branch plans of different time lengths. The production models include long-term forecasts of consolidated indicators of economic growth; interbranch planning models, principally the interbranch balance; and optimized models of the development and distribution of single- and multiproduct complexes and branch optimization models. Among the social models are welfare models (primarily of income and consumption); demographic models; and models of labor migration on a territorial, branch, and occupational basis.[63] Network models, using PERT or some variation of it, presumably would control the development of the programs that constitute the core of the general plan. All planning and control models would, in turn, be integrated into a computer-based information system. In the early 1970s SKP was advanced by CEMI as the planning methodology for the automated system of plan calculation (ASPR), which is discussed later in this chapter.[64]

The functional rationalization of economic decision making assumes the necessity of an extensive reorganization of the structure of the planning system. In line with the description of the economy as a very complex system, the economy's structure is projected as a network of decision-making blocks whose processes are both formalized and unformalized. These processes are intimately intertwined with the necessary informational and organizational structures. From the perspective of the rationalization of management structure, SOFE addresses two basic problems: the allocation of authority within the formal structure; and the methods whereby the distinctive interests of the various subsystems are to be harmonized.[65]

Although there is no fully developed concept of management structure associated with SOFE, "structurization" of the hierarchical system clearly follows the lines of functional analysis of the production process. The basic methodology for developing the structure, Fedorenko suggested in 1968, should encompass the entire social production cycle from the extraction of raw materials to the production of finished goods. The process should be decomposed into a series of processing stages. Within each stage the management structure is to be formalized according to the informational flows and needs characteristic of this phase of the process. Each of the major stages can be broken down into substages whose management structure is also defined by internal informational flows. The process of decomposition can continue until the stage of physical production is reached.[66]

Theoretically, the adaptation of the formal structure of management should also flow from the functional demands created by the introduction of economic models and the computer network. From the functional perspective, SOFE has been described as a multistaged, interbranch, and interregional scheme for iterative optimization that encompasses all the basic sectors of the economy.[67] To reduce the informational stress of a complex decision-making system, the SOFE design for structural rationalization envisages a basic three-tiered hierarchy of national, branch, and production organs of management. At the national level, the principal additions to the existing structures should be the program–goal complexes, which are interbranch and administered from a single center. Branch organs remain dominant at the intermediate level. Within the individual ministry, Fedorenko and his colleagues have argued for the development of large-scale, multiplant management structures in the form of production unions and scientific-production unions.[68]

The proposals of SOFE for the redistribution of authority within the management structure are complex. On the whole, the strategy has been to modify rather than to alter radically the command economy.[69] The approach is the traditional one of concentrating the decision-making focus of the central planners on long-term problems of development and delegating operational decision making to the intermediate and production levels of the hierarchy. Specific demarcation of clear lines of authority, however, has been and remains difficult.

The authority structure of optimal functioning can function, in the abstract, as V. F. Pugachev pointed out, either as a regime of absolute planning or as a system composed of independent and self-learning subsystems.[70] The reconciliation of contradictory trends is, of course, difficult. On the one hand, introduction of mathematical models and computers supports the traditional centralization of planning and management controls. The definition of the economy as a very complex system and the necessity of establishing a division of decision-making labor, however, alternatively suggests the need for decentralization, or, more precisely, the delegation of decision-making authority. Although committed to the second view, Fedorenko, unlike Nemchinov, has not rejected the use of direct administrative methods but has proposed to blend direct and indirect controls as a means of coordinating the macro- and microeconomies. If there was a discernible trend in the 1970s concerning the emphasis placed on the most desirable mixture of the two approaches, it appears to have been in the direction of strengthening administrative controls.

The basic thrust of SOFE, emphasizing the primacy of inter-branch relationships and a single, integrated, computer-based informational system, has been to increase the primacy of global goals and the control of the central planners over systemic development. Each subsystem, however, requires simultaneously what Fedorenko has described as "degrees of freedom" (*stepeni svobody*).[71] He has been a particulary strong advocate of what may be labeled a parametric approach to the distribution of decision-making authority. In its simplest form, the central planners set directive plans that establish in aggregated indicators the inputs and outputs of the plan. Within these boundaries and subject to evaluation by the higher management agencies, the production association or enterprise enjoys operational independence.[72]

This effort to find an optimal mixture of centralized and decentralized controls is evident in SOFE's proposals for the reallocation of authority within the politically sensitive supply and pricing mechanisms.[73] Although CEMI has been a leader in developing models for the optimal distribution of key products such as steel, cement, and chemicals, its senior economists have also argued for the decentralization of supply through the development of wholesale trade in the means of production. Fedorenko has been sharply critical of the failure of Gosplan and Gossnab to implement more rapidly this provision of the 1965 economic reform.[74]

Whether Fedorenko initially shared Nemchinov's view that the entire system of central rationing should be abolished is unclear. In the 1970s, however, he explicitly and repeatedly declared that scarce and strategic resources should be administratively allocated to the most important developmental programs.[75] Nonetheless, the expanded use of contracts, freely negotiated within centrally determined boundaries by cooperating plants, has remained a basic tenet for the structural reorganization of horizontal relationships.

The SOFE proposal to establish a parametric approach to

price fixing is closely associated with the delegation of authority over other planning and managerial functions. The details of what constitutes an optimal mixture of model-based and negotiated prices, however, have not been made explicit. On this, as on other major aspects of the SOFE proposal, CEMI scholars have not always held a consensus. There seems to be general agreement that shadow prices derived from the optimal plan and functionally related to the goals of development should have a dominant role.[76] Such a system of optimal pricing is necessarily selective and confined to key products.

Fedorenko has been particularly critical of the inflexible and highly detailed regulation of prices from the center that has survived since 1965.[77] As part of the broader policy of decentralization, he has argued for a pricing procedure in which the central planners set the price limits for aggregated groups of products within which producers and consumers have the right to contract specific prices along with technical and other specifications. The stress on a flexible price-fixing authority has been particularly focused on retail trade, where rapid feedback is important to the satisfaction of social demand.[78]

The logic of a controlled delegation of operational decision-making authority has naturally raised the importance of economic methods as the instrument of indirect control. In ordering the unformalized component in the system of optimal functioning, economic methods and *khozraschet* have a double purpose. At one level, economic methods have the function of reducing systemic imbalance by harmonizing global and local economic interests. In addition, economic levers should promote an optimal allocation of resources with respect to long-term goals.[79] Fedorenko has been a major critic of the efficacy of the 1965 reforms in promoting either goal.

This criticism has been directed initially to the two success indicators adopted in September 1965: the amount of products sold and profitability. Since the mid-1960s, CEMI economists have been pressing for "net profit" as the sole indicator for evaluating and stimulating the production unit as well as for serving as the local criterion of optimality.[80] The insistence on the use of a single success indicator has been partially a response to the mathematical demands for solving extremal tasks. The use of a single indicator, rather than multiple indicators, however, has also been justified as a means of reducing the "games" played by the enterprise managers among different incentive-forming indicators. Specifically, it is assumed that net profit would reduce managers' indifference to the cost of production. It would permit the number of centrally planned indicators to be cut. Most importantly, the indicator would make the evaluation of the enterprise dependent upon the final results of its activity.[81]

To ensure an accurate weighing of policy alternatives and the full evaluation of the final activity of the enterprise, CEMI economists have noted the necessity for a complete economic evaluation of the factors of production. This has necessitated pushing this aspect of the 1965 reforms much further than those actually adopted or implemented.[82] Fedorenko has pressed for realistic charges for the use of all natural resources, including ecological costs, and for a full charge on labor costs. Among other advantages, a labor tax would help to correct the traditional bias toward capital intensity as well as reduce the practice of hoarding labor.[83] The SOFE scheme also includes measures for a more effective use of financial and credit levers. These include an equalization of interest rates and capital charges and a sharp reduction in the amount of investment financing through the budget.[84] In one proposal, Fedorenko has advocated restricting budget financing to research and development and the introduction of new technology.[85]

The core of the SOFE strategy for balancing macro- and microeconomics as well as achieving an optimal allocation of resources has been the pricing mechanism. The system of prices serves as the principal lever for orienting the relatively autonomous production unit toward the national economic optimum as well as for stimulating production efficiency and technical innovation.[86] To be effective, the proponents of SOFE have argued, the pricing system should be flexible and capable of responding to changes in production and distribution. For this reason, Fedorenko and others have rejected average branch costs, the current basis for price formation, as adequate for an optimal system of decision making.[87]

The development of a system of optimal prices clearly has the potential for a revolutionary impact on the procedures of economic planning and control. Two opposing schemes of planning have arisen within the ranks of the optimal planners on the cardinal question of how to integrate local and global interests. In the purely normative model, the subsystems communicate to the center the parameters of their own models of production capacity. The central planners optimize the tasks and send them directly to the production subsystems.[88]

In the second scheme, the central planners calculate a plan based on the parameters submitted by the production subsystem but communicate optimal criteria. The criteria are communicated in terms of their coefficients – prices, which are maximized by the production units.[89] As Robert Campbell has noted, if shadow prices can be found, the plans and commands of the administrative model can be eliminated. "It will be enough to announce the shadow prices and tell everyone to do his best to increase the value of the output and cut costs in the light of the prices."[90] What happens if the production unit should choose to maximize criteria other than those transmitted from the center, however, remains unresolved.

Although the employment of economic models and computers in planning and management has been significantly developed since the Twenty-fourth Congress in 1971, the specific proposals for an optimized decision-making system have been deeply controversial, particularly at the national level. The primary opponents of SOFE have been the conservative political economists, economists, and central planners who perceive and resist the impact of SOFE on traditional concepts and practices of planning and management. In this perspective, ideological, theoretical, and organizational questions have tended to merge in the discussions on SOFE that have been held over the past decade.

The complex problem of implementing a system of optimal functioning should not, however, be attributed solely to a politicized opposition. As will be indicated, the construction of a set of hierarchically integrated and optimized models linked with a computer system in a complex economy is a formidable technical task. Moreover, it is evident that the nature of both the issues and the opposition have shifted perceptibly over time.

As E. I. Maiminas has noted in his thoughtful essay on the development of the Soviet school of mathematical economics, the focus of discussion during the 1960s centered on problems related to the solution of extremal tasks and to the criterion of optimality.[92] In the 1970s a new and more practical stage centering on the application of the systems approach to specific aspects of planning and management emerged. The new tasks are predominantly linked with the building of OGAS (All-State System for the Collection and Processing of Information for Reporting, Planning, and Management of the Economy), and more generally ASUs (automated systems of administration) at all levels.[93] The shift from a predominantly theoretical to an applied set of concerns has naturally engaged a distinct set of interests, specifically those operating officials most directly influenced by the introduction and implementation of the systems approach. It is, nonetheless, characteristic of the contemporary phase of adaptation that the unresolved theoretical issues of the earlier period have remained a vital, if subsidiary, set of concerns.

The theoretical cleavages that have emerged with respect to SOFE have been an integral part of the larger issue of the relationship of cybernetics and the traditional political economy of socialism.[94] In many respects, the core issue of this debate has been the definition of the global criterion of optimality, the yardstick used at the national level to measure and compare the utilities present in different variations of the national plan. The problem of finding an acceptable criterion of optimality may be resolved into two questions, which are not easily distinguishable: the criteria used to select and order several competing goals; and the most effective allocation of resources in relation to a given set of goals.

The issues of how the goals of development are to be formulated and selected and what the impact will be of a regime of optimal functioning on the distribution of political authority and the finality of planners' preferences remain unresolved, but are evidently sensitive. The optimal planners have been extremely wary of selecting the specific developmental goals of Soviet society; they have also failed to assert that any configuration of resource allocation defined by an optimality criterion necessarily must be accepted by political authority.[95] The adoption of an optimal decision-making system does, however, imply a significant reduction in "voluntaristic" or "intuitive" decision making but leaves unclear what aspects of the planning system's functions should be transferred to the machine.

What has been explicitly asserted is the view that the political, economic, and social aspects of policy should be grounded in economic constraints. Fedorenko has been intensely critical of those house economists who have provided the technical justification for economic policies adopted without consideration of the economic dimension.[96] As part of his effort to redirect the development of Soviet economics, he has argued that economics is a policy science whose function is to ensure that the "leading organs... know the economic cost of not taking optimal decisions."[97]

The development of a global production function of the economy clearly acts as a constraint on political choice in another way. As part of the general strategy of shifting planning to final goals rather than to the reproduction of resources, the CEMI group has advocated social consumption, the maximum satisfaction of social demand, as the global criterion of optimality.[98] What constitutes social demand, however, is ambiguous and subject to varying interpretations. It may be broadly defined to include societal demands such as defense and administration or more narrowly as personal and social consumption. Fedorenko has used the broad interpretation of social demand at widely differing times.[99] There is reason to believe, however, that Fedorenko and his colleagues have had a stronger preference for defining social demand as welfare. In constructing the plan, Fedorenko has argued, available resources must be allocated in such a way that, for any given planning period, the goal should be the maximum growth in living standards.[100]

This stress is not arbitrary, being derived from a more basic perception of the nature of social development in the Soviet Union. Under conditions of the scientific–technical revolution, the satisfaction of increasing social demand is grounded in the prerequisites of economic growth and the strategies of macro-social control. Social demand must be satisfied as a stimulus for those specialized and skilled workers who operate complex production technologies. In addition, the satisfaction of social demand is related to the ineffectiveness of administrative controls to direct large-scale stochastic social processes. Differentiated incentives and wage policies, Fedorenko has suggested, are necessary for indirect leverage over demographic processes and labor migration. Finally, welfare is considered to be vital in the promotion of social equality and the reduction of social privilege.[101] The stress on maximizing social welfare has naturally raised the objection that this criterion reverses the relationship between heavy and light industry and, in fact, fixes global priorities of development.[102]

The construction of a methodology for the optimal allocation of resources to a given set of goals has proven equally problematical. Discussing the problem in respect to the 1965 economic reforms, Fedorenko noted:

The commensurability of social utilities of particular commodities and resources is a basic assumption in the theory of optimal planning. The theory assumes that the utility corresponding with the highest possible level of satisfaction can be realistically evaluated. Utility is expressed in terms of price resulting from the optimal plan. In economic terms, the price of a commodity (resource) corresponds to the money contribution made by the increase of the given item to the attainment of the good. The main difficulty lies in finding the ways for an individual enterprise to harmonize the conflicting trends in the growth of output and the changing structure of its costs in order to balance the interests of the enterprise and those of society.[103]

Part of the difficulty clearly has been the complexity of the problem of measuring social utility either normatively or statistically, a topic that is discussed in Chapter 3.[104] Critics of the normative approach, for example, have ridiculed the deductive approach by asking whether ten bicycles can be equated with one motorcycle.[105]

More generally, critics of SOFE have challenged the feasibility of a single criterion of global optimality. Among the barriers to the construction of such an optimizing mechanism has been the problem of the massively complex system and huge number of indicators that the extension of optimization to all economic and noneconomic processes necessarily entails. Moreover, developing a production function for consumption has been complicated by the problem of measuring social demand because this involves highly sophisticated social research into the demands of highly differentiated social groups and into changes in living standards. The construction of a mathematical statement of the optimum has not been resolved in large part because it involves the reconciliation of a large number of demands within the framework of a single criterion.[106] The severe problem of using a single criterion of optimality has led Petrakov, among others, to espouse a multicriterial approach employing vector optimization and the Pareto optimum as a means of avoiding conflict among goals.[107] In general, however, there appears to be little agreement on the key issues of how to proceed from the abstract definition of social utility to its specific formulation.

In general there has been a lack of consensus among the optimal planners on what should constitute the specific measure of social utility. Among the leading proposals has been the maximization of costs.[108] The necessity of decomposing the optimum into a hierarchy of global and local criteria has been an additional complication. Net profit, advanced as the local criterion, for ideological reasons cannot serve as the global criterion. The integration of national and local criteria through the instrument of optimal prices clearly requires the prior solution of the extremal problem, which, in turn, is influenced by the global criterion selected. Finally, it is evident that if the problem is one of comparing social, rather than economic utilities, the solution is in part "qualitative" and thus, as the SOFE critics have suggested, cannot be fully resolved within the terms advanced by this mathematical solution of extremal tasks.[109]

Among the most controversial propositions of SOFE is the use of marginal utility and cost-benefit analysis as the methodology behind optimal allocation of resources.[110] The introduction of such a criterion, Fedorenko has noted, "gives the possibility of measuring the national economic effect received from the use of additional units of resources in all variants of the plan."[111] The proposed introduction of marginalist theory into Soviet planning is undoubtedly of revolutionary significance, its operational premise being that economic value is formed as the result of a multiplicity of factors, including scarcity and opportunity costs, and thus coming into conflict with the labor theory of value.[112] Although it can be reasonably argued that the labor theory of value has had little practical significance as a guide to economic decision making, the legitimacy accorded to a multifactor theory of value clearly undercuts the theoretical basis of Marx's critique of capitalism.

The technical difficulty of defining social utility or measuring social demand has been intimately linked with questions of the reformulation of the traditional political economy of socialism.

Fedorenko raised the question of a modified political economy during the 1966 discussions of optimal planning, and the issue has continued without resolution into the 1970s.[113] Charging the traditional political economy with being exclusively "descriptive" and "qualitative," lacking explanatory power, and useless as an analytical instrument, Fedorenko proposed the creation of an economic science capable of offering "constructive" advice to policy makers on concrete issues.[114] A quantitative approach to economic decision making, he asserted, would limit the role of intuition in decision making and the huge economic losses that result from it.[115] The incorporation of the "constructivist" approach to political economy, however, has had little success. In 1976 Fedorenko complained that a new political economy had still not been developed and that the political economists delayed year after year in issuing a new textbook.[116]

There is little doubt that the reluctance to provide full ideological legitimacy to SOFE's approach to the rationalization of planning and management has been rooted in the threat to the values and interests of those economic theorists, planners, and managers who are required to accept and implement it. The ideological opponents of SOFE have been clearly disturbed by the ahistorical character of the use of mathematical logic, despite the assurance of Fedorenko, among others, that the mathematical school is rooted in Soviet experience.[117] Ia. Kronrod, for example, has charged the optimal planners with the introduction of a neopositivistic methodology into Soviet economic science which challenges the objectivity of economic laws.[118] This criticism is closely linked with the belief that SOFE, principally by adopting social utility and marginalism, will legitimate subjective, essentially psychological criteria as the bases for decision making.[119]

The entrance of Soviet economic science into the mainstream of world economics has been particularly objectionable to conservative critics such as S. Strumilin.[120] A. Eremin and L. Nikoforov have charged Fedorenko with an attempt to develop a theory of optimal economic behavior, bypassing the traditional Marxist approach of investigating production relations. In their view, the functionalism underlying the theory of optimal functioning is inevitably apolitical.[121] In this vein, Kronrod has termed the axiomatic approach of SOFE an eclectic mixture of incompatible components derived from the traditional political economy and Western utility theory.[122] In reply, Fedorenko has charged a number of political economists with a determinism so complete that it virtually excludes the influence of human choice on events.[123]

The political economists have been joined in their criticism of SOFE by the central planners, who have been strongly opposed to the adoption of SKP as the future planning methodology. Strumilin, in response to the 1966 discussions, launched a sharp attack on the basic components of the new system in a 1967 article in *Voprosy ekonomiki*. He appeared to be particularly disturbed by the view of the CEMI "mathematicians" of the economy as an "inertial system."[124] In 1968, he continued the attack on the notion of long-term planning, scientific forecasting, interbranch balances, and programming, declaring that there was nothing new in the theory of optimal planning.[125]

The formal adoption of the new strategy of rationalization at the Twenty-fourth Congress, however, has activated the open opposition of the central planners. Their hostility became clear in a conference convened in 1973 on the adoption of SKP as the new "technology" of planning in conjunction with the development of APSR. Although SKP had been approved with mild criticism by N. P. Lebedinskii, who is the head of Gosplan's Computer Center, and other Gosplan officials in October 1972, in the Division of Economy of the Academy of Sciences,[126] their opposition rapidly mounted. In 1973 Lebedinskii accused the supporters of SOFE of intending to replace directive planning with forecasting, of eliminating the balance method of planning, and of ignoring annual planning.[127] His Gosplan colleague, Iurii Balik, expressed some anxiety that the directive quality of planning would dissolve into informational processes; in addition, Balik feared that the implementation of a system of statewide forecasting would bypass the state planning organs.[128]

In 1975 Lebedinskii again voiced the fear that a reorganization of methods and procedures in the traditional planning system would reduce the status and role of the central planners. SKP could not be used as the planning methodology for the computer-based planning system. The employment of a gigantic tree of goals, he predicted, would disrupt the entire system of planning. He attacked what he termed the exaggerated roles assigned to programming and forecasting under the new methodology and complained again that the primary reliance on the interbranch balance would reduce the role of planning balances in computing the plan.[129]

Despite the often intense ideological and bureaucratic opposition to SOFE, however, Fedorenko's model has served as the basis for the cybernetic reform of the management system.

3

Developing a technology of management

During the Brezhnev era, the drive to modernize industrial management has developed in two distinct, but overlapping phases. In both phases, technical and economic factors have prevailed over social concerns in the rationalization of the management system. From 1965 through 1969, the economic reforms gave priority to changing structural relationships and motivation. Its apparent failure to improve significantly the efficiency of industrial organization resulted in a shift of priorities. Brezhnev announced the turn to a scientific and technological strategy of rationalization at the December 1969 Plenum of the Central Committee. He declared, "We are giving great significance to speeding up the tempo of development of systems of administration, information, and electronic technology."[1] The technological thrust maintained dominance through the mid-1970s, when it, too, became caught up in the familiar cycle of excessive expectations and rapid disillusionment.

The shift to a scientific–technical strategy of rationalization coincided with a broader reassessment of Soviet economic development and international political status. A basic economic factor was the recognition that a declining growth rate and capital–output ratio and a threatening labor shortage required a new strategy of economic development. Technological progress, Brezhnev announced in 1969, had become the core of a new growth strategy replacing the older "extensive" growth based upon high capital investment and large increments to the labor force.[2]

The turn to a technical strategy also appears to have been influenced by domestic and foreign political considerations. Suboptimization of decision making and expansion of the political role of the intermediate management levels increased under the economic reforms. The introduction of modern management methods, Paul Cocks has argued, was designed to counteract this slippage of power.[3] Foreign policy considerations were equally important. The rapid development of the concepts of the scientific–technical revolution in Eastern Europe and the West presented a fundamental ideological challenge to the leading role of Soviet Marxism. The lag in technological innovation clearly carried a threat other than the loss of political prestige. The impressive growth of the Western European economies, Brezhnev observed in 1968, was producing resources which were actively implementing their foreign policies.[4] Finally, in the wake of the Czech invasion, joint projects of scientific and technical development opened new avenues for implementing a policy of political and economic integration within the Soviet bloc.

Brezhnev summarized many of these considerations in his report to the Twenty-fourth Congress in 1971. It was necessary, he noted, to come to grips with the challenges presented by the environment of the "developed socialist society." The solution to such problems as economic growth and efficiency, structural complexity, multiplying demands on scarce resources, and the political aspects of the scientific–technical revolution required that technology serve as "the main lever in the creation of the material–technical base of communism."[5] Within this framework, Brezhnev continued to identify the rationalization of planning and management as a priority political objective.[6]

The Twenty-fourth Congress legislated a broad program of rationalization which the Twenty-fifth Congress largely continued. The Congress authorized an expanded development and use of mathematical methods of decision making and the construction of a national automated management system (OGAS). The Congress also ordered an extensive reorganization of the ministerial system with a heavy emphasis upon the creation of large multiplant industrial and production associations. Finally, it intensified the stress on managerial development and training.[7] Policies for social planning and development, although important, remained secondary.

Conceptually, the structural and functional aspects of modernization were to form a single, integrated approach to reform. The lack of unified theory and effective organization, however, has resulted in a decentralized and fragmented process in which technical, economic, and behavioral approaches have taken independent and often conflicting paths. To improve coordination, a special division for rationalization was added to the Tenth Five-Year Plan. The plan, however, has been criticized as methodologically weak, incomplete, and lacking in detail; moreover, no special controls were provided for implementation.[8]

Following the general outlines of the SOFE model, the central focus for technological rationalization has been the planning system. Policies have included planning from final rather than intermediate results, the development of a fifteen-year plan, and the use of program-goal techniques. The two basic components of the project were an extensive application of mathematical methods and the construction of computer-based information systems. Analytically distinct, the two elements became inextricably linked in the creation of an optimal system of planning and management.

A question of modeling

Over the past two decades, the cybernetics boom has fueled the development of mathematical models for a wide range of decision-making tasks. In economic decision making, hundreds of models have been constructed and tested on numerous specialized problems at every level of the hierarchy. In the present decade, however, the linking of mathematical models with computers has given modeling of economic processes a more specific direction.

There is no unified or officially accepted classification of economic models. A variety of categories are used to classify the models used in Soviet planning and management. They are distinguished according to scope and level (macro and micro), time frames (static and dynamic), the function modeled (planning or control), and whether a principle of optimization is used.[9]

From the perspective of ideological and structural change in management, an important distinction is between statistical and analytical models. Statistical models assume stochastic processes and are built according to "black box" principles, using information from time series and sample surveys. Although statistical models provide more complete descriptions of economic and social phenomena, their informational base and potential for comprehensive and centralized controls are less. The Soviet tradition clearly gives precedence to analytic models which are determinate and offer greater control over the socioeconomic system.[10]

Over the past decade, primary Soviet interest has been in building macromodels of the planning system. These models have concentrated in the first instance on the solution of those very large developmental problems envisioned in a long-term optimal plan. The principal mathematical technique for optimizing planning decisions has been linear programming. In this respect, the Soviet Union can rightly claim to be a pioneer through the work of the distinguished mathematician and economist, L. V. Kantorovich, whose seminal study appeared in 1939.[11] Equally valuable has been the contribution of L. S. Pontriagin to the theory of dynamic programming.[12]

The application of linear programming for solving extremal economic and management problems has the practical value of producing an optimal and determinate plan which also has a system of planning indicators coordinated with the plan. Properly executed, optimal decisions cannot only allocate resources more efficiently but also increase the system's balance.

On the national, branch, and regional levels, optimizing techniques can be applied to a broad range of planning and control problems. They can be used to allocate investment and locate new plants, to distribute production orders and supply, to allocate energy or transportation, to specialize production, and to link producers and consumers, and these are but a few of a host of applications.[13] Within the enterprise, linear programming can be useful for optimizing technical–economic planning, production scheduling, equipment loading, selecting production mixes, inventory control, and other standard operations research problems.

The value of linear programming for rationalizing decision making, however, is restricted to a limited class of problems that meet defined conditions and assumptions. An effective linear model presumes, as Kantorovich has emphasized, that the ingredients of the model are homogeneous, linear (vary uniformly over a given range of values), and well structured (full, accurate, and complete information can be assured). The model should also contain a clear and undisputed criterion of optimality.[14] These conditions are difficult to fulfill for most planning problems.

The more serious of Soviet developmental problems are dynamic and weakly structured. The number of unknowns is extremely large; and the values and algorithms or decision rules are ambiguous. Many economic and social processes are stochastic and nonlinear. Decision making under conditions of risk and uncertainty is the rule rather than the exception.

It is precisely in relation to these conditions that systems analysis has created such strong Soviet interest in Western management science. Although such methods as simulation, decision-tree analysis, networking, game and waiting line theory, and various methods of nonlinear programming produce only "satisficing" solutions, they can sharpen and orient the planner's judgment.[15] Soviet employment of these techniques, however, has been selective.

The concept of the long-term plan

Perhaps the most intellectually arduous as well as controversial aspect of the reform of planning in the 1970s has been the construction of an optimal long-term plan for the period 1976–90. Initially, the structure of the plan was conceived as an integrated global plan developed in great detail. The complexity and informational problems of such an approach, however, forced the realization that the direct and centralized computation of such a plan exceeded Soviet capabilities.

For evident reasons, the execution of an integrated, optimal, fifteen-year plan has proven difficult. The long-term plan, worked out by the Chief Computer Center of Gosplan and CEMI, has been conceived structurally as an interrelated set of parameters or indicators derived from final goals and broken down into three five-year plans.[16] The plan has assumed as the global criterion of optimality the maximization of national income in 1990 in terms of an unstated ratio between investment and consumption. The local criterion of optimality was that normally used in optimal branch planning; the minimization of production and transportation costs.[17]

In the initial attempt to construct an optimal long-term plan, seven macromodels, or classes of models, were used to compute the plan. They included a model of population growth and the balance of the labor force and a model of growth and allocation of national income, presumably calculated for the final year of the plan. A core set of models were those used to calculate the structure of social demand. Other models used in computation were an interbranch balance of production and distribution, optimized branch models of development and distribution, and optimal multibranch models. In aggregate, these models serve as the foundation for an integrated optimal model.[18]

Methodologically, the actual construction of the plan was conceived as the sequential integration of formalized informational blocks. The basic task in the plan's construction was to define its social goals. The social goals, in turn, determined the amount and material substance of the final product. The demographic forecasting model clearly played a key role: Not only was it basic to the definition of social demand, but it also defined the supply of labor as a constraint.[19]

Defining the future

The complex of models which support the calculation of the long-term plan can conveniently be divided into preplan and planning models. The preplanning phase of the planning process has naturally grown in importance as the length and complexity of the plan has been extended. In large part, the extraordinary demands for information to set goals and determine probable resource needs has been the function of long- and medium-term forecasting.

An early effort in the post-Stalin period to forecast socioeconomic development appeared in the 1961 Party Program. Essentially a political and ideological document designed to mobilize Soviet society, the program was unrealistic and quickly abandoned after Khrushchev's fall.[20] The turn to analytic methods of long-term forecasting began in 1966. The objective has been to develop an integrated forecast of the needs and trends of development of Soviet society up to the year 2000.

Formally, the global forecast should integrate six specialized forecasts of the environment in which Soviet society will function, including demographic, resource and ecological, and military and foreign policy forecasts. The global forecast should also include forecasts of scientific and technical progress, social demand, and economic development.[21] In the economic forecasts, which contain both branch and regional projections, noneconomic factors are calculated as constraints on growth.[22]

Soviet forecasting techniques are those familiar in the West. Informal as well as formalized techniques are used to build forecasting models. Perhaps the most influential informal method is scanning developments in the advanced industrial societies for comparative purposes. This procedure is closely associated with such procedures as expert evaluation through such techniques as Delphi.

The two leading analytical approaches are to construct statistical models based upon time series and to use extrapolation and factor analysis. The alternative set of procedures are grouped under the rubric of "normative" forecasting.

Normative forecasting methods are considered desirable in the search for optimal goals when several variants are present. The task of normative forecasting is to build a model suitable for planning by including in it fixed numerical values (normatives) for projected goals of the plan. In the arsenal of techniques for normative forecasting are constructing scenarios, using game theory, building a "tree of goals," matrix methods, network analysis, and simulation.[23]

The preferred technique for blending various techniques into an integrated forecast is PATTERN. PATTERN, developed in the early 1960s for technical forecasting by Honeywell, employs a matrix to compare results with criteria. The procedure, however, has been judged too demanding for Soviet adoption. It requires dozens of man-years to construct and too heavy an investment in scarce, highly skilled manpower.[24]

Forecasting Soviet socioeconomic development not only involves uncertainty but also arouses political and ideological anxieties. The tension is evident in the methodological conflict over the approach to forecasting consumer demand, one of the final goals of the long-term plan. One method is to use statistical models. The second is normative, defined in this case as the use of fixed coefficients of rational consumption. The latter approach is preferred because it produces a determinate model and is consistent with an authoritatively controlled "model of life."

The utility of the normative approach, however, is sharply limited. Such data as assortment, for example, are ignored. The research institute of the Ministry of Trade restricts the range of products to thirty or forty in its forecasts, whereas more than double that figure is needed. The norms of rational consumption themselves are questionable. Only a few have been calculated precisely, and, as they are fixed, they do not accurately reflect changes in demand over time. The Ministry of Trade, nonetheless, has resisted the use of statistical models.[25]

The results of forecasting consumer demand by using the normative method, not surprisingly, have been unreliable for planning purposes. A short-term forecast made in 1971 for the 1973 annual plan deviated from results by 15–20 percent. Forecasts for longer periods presumably would deviate by wider margins. The application of factor analysis, however, confronts serious informational problems. Trade turnover and family budget statistics, in Levin's view, understate unsatisfied demand by as much as 30 to 40 percent.[26]

The quality of Soviet forecasting clearly requires the closest scrutiny by Western analysis because it may provide significant clues to projected Soviet domestic and foreign policy. Some of the initial demographic, natural resource, ecological, and other materials used in this study clearly are derived from initial Soviet forecasts. Military and foreign policy forecasts evidently have greater political sensitivity and have been less publicized. Among the reported forecasts of international relations conducted between 1971 and 1975 was one of the course of socialist integration into CMEA and one of Chinese development. The Institute of World Economy and International Relations prepared the forecasts of the development of the economies, science and technology, and social processes of the advanced capitalist countries, with particular attention to the political significance of the energy and resource crises.[27]

The interbranch balance

Of the hundreds of models constructed over the past two decades for improving plan computation, the most important have been the interbranch balance models. Although they are not optimal models, they can be optimized. The use of input–output analysis provides for the possible calculation of both indirect and direct inputs, which is necessary to correct the imbalances produced by traditional balancing methods. The fundamental significance of the interbranch balance for the long-term plan is that it could enable the central planners to move from the planning of intermediate to final production goals.[28]

The interbranch balance can serve as a synthetic table for the economy. As an input–output planning model, the balance could coordinate and balance output and investment parameters and regulate interbranch flows. Interbranch balances can be built for the economy as a whole or in regional and branch blocks. The models may be static or dynamic and constructed in terms of past (ex post) economic behavior or for future (ex ante) economic behavior. An important distinction lies in the unit of measurement used in the matrix. Interbranch balances have been constructed using both physical and monetary units.

The Soviet effort in this area has been intensive. Between 1960 and 1972, thirteen national and forty regional tables had been completed or were nearing completion. Among the more important of these models have been those developed by the Central Statistical Administration. In the early 1960s, Soviet statisticians completed for the 1959 planning year the first large-scale ex post model for the national economy and subsequently developed larger models for 1966 and 1972.[29] More recent models are also under construction.

Ex post tables have been constructed in product as well as monetary form. The 1959 physical table was constructed as a matrix of balances for 157 industrial commodities. The 1959 value table was designed as a "traditional, Leontiev-type, static, open input–output table showing 83 sectors." The value tables for 1966 and 1972 were expanded to 110 sectors. In form, the 1966 ex post model is a flow table of three quadrants. The first quadrant is a square matrix of interindustry transactions. The second quadrant indicates the distribution of the output of the producing sectors among the final users. The third quadrant is the value-added quadrant, which shows depreciation and factor payments originating in each of the producing sectors. In addition, there are two square (110×110) tables which supplement the flow tables and provide data on direct and full input coefficients.[30]

The construction of an ex ante or planning interbranch balance capable of direct application to the planning process has proven to be a difficult and controversial exercise. Since 1962 the Economics Institute of Gosplan (NIEI) and the Chief Computer Center of Gosplan have been working, respectively, on separate value and physical planning tables. The Central Economico-Mathematical Institute has been active in this area as well. At the branch level, NIEI has been working with more than two hundred branch research and design institutes to develop a consistent system of indicators for measuring direct expenditures.[31] Through 1973, a static, ex ante interbranch balance composed of sixteen branches for 260 products had been constructed. A model developed in monetary terms, however, could not be built, largely due to informational problems.[32] In 1976 the director of NIEI announced that NIEI had worked out and tested a dynamic interbranch balance for the long term.[33] Details on the structure and quality of this model, however, are scarce.

The methodological basis for the construction of the planning interbranch balance has been the information derived from the ex post models. The central problem in the construction of the balance has been the definition of technical coefficients, which are based upon forecasts of technical progress in the various branches of industry and which include both direct and full expenditures. To be fully useful, the normative base of the interbranch model should embody the basic tendencies of technological development, changes in the structure of demand for raw materials and energy, as well as changes in the organization of production. With accurately constructed normatives for each final product in the balance, the planner could then define the value of the product, the amount of interbranch deliveries, and (in a dynamic model) the amount of capital investment and labor. The specific uses of the ex ante model are clearly very large, particularly for the coordination of the output and supply plans.[34]

From the point of view of the economic information revealed by Soviet input–output analysis, the work done on ex post models is considered to be "superior to most tables produced by other countries." The ex post models contain information on the number employed in each sector, working capital in each sector, and data on fixed capital stocks by sector according to some twenty-five categories of assets. Soviet tables also contain more detailed data on the value-added and final quadrants. The major weakness of the ex post table lies in the fact that the distribution of a commodity is measured differently in value and physical terms and that, in the model described in value terms, the data is given in producer prices.[35]

The value of ex ante interbranch balances for planning purposes has been relatively marginal. Paradoxically, the ex post models have been more extensively used than the planning interbranch balances. The reasons for the relative failure to use the interbranch balance in planning have been expressed by two leading figures in the development of Soviet econometrics, Albina Tretyakova and Igor Birman. Among the reasons they offer are (1) the conservative nature of the planning apparatus; (2) serious difficulties in the aggregation of data; (3) discrepancies between the table, which is product-oriented, and planning practice, which is institutionally oriented; (4) the unreliability of direct input coefficients, principally with respect to future technical progress: (5) present planning practice, in which deliberate distortions in information are introduced; (6) the inability of the Chief Computing Center of Gosplan to recalculate the input-output tables rapidly enough to meet changing conditions. In their assessment, input-output analysis will play no significant role in future Soviet planning.[36]

The limited development of the interbranch balance has confined its use to preplan calculations and as a check upon plans constructed by other methods. As V. Vorobev, a deputy chairman of Gosplan, has complained, existing models have been inadequate for solving such planning problems as linking the production plan with the plan for capital investment or for relating the balances of production capacity and output with financial indicators. The utility of the model has been restricted because it is static and treats capital investment as part of the final product rather than as a resource.[37]

The application of the interbranch balance even in limited areas, moreover, has had ambiguous value. Vorobev cites the experience of using the model in the preliminary stages of preparing the 1973 and 1974 plans. In 1974 the plan for aluminum production was reduced. Using the balance, the planners calculated the amount of caustic soda required for aluminum production. According to the model, the cut in the production of caustic soda should have been 5,000 tons. Due to changes in technology and the norms of direct expenditures, however, the demand for caustic soda actually rose by 35,000 tons. Other serious discrepancies were also observed, in large part because of inadequate technological coefficients of direct expenditures.[38] To increase the applicability of the interbranch balance, particularly for long-term planning, it is clear that intensive research is required. Among the demands placed on the model are that it be dynamic, integrate material and value indicators, and be capable of optimization. A primary requirement for use in a program-goal strategy of planning is a model that includes capital investment lags and can aid in relating investment programs with branch development plans. A particular need is for a model which can aid in the calculation of the financial resources for programs at the time the program is formulated. Among the growing demands for an improved interbranch balance is the need to integrate the national plans of the CMEA countries with the plan of the Soviet Union.[39]

On the whole, it appears clear that the decision to build a directive optimal long-term plan presented such severe problems that it could not be completed for the Tenth Five-Year Plan. The task of working out and integrating more than one hundred optimal branch plans proved to be too complex. The reliability of the plan's calculations became suspect with the recognition that the eighteen-branch ex ante planning interbranch model could not be used.[40] The declaration by Brezhnev in 1976 that the long-term plan would have an indicative rather than directive character reflects the technical as well as political problems encountered in the initial stage of its construction.[41]

Intermediate developmental models

The lack of a global and optimal "trajectory" for guiding Soviet socioeconomic development clearly determines the optimality of the intermediate-level planning models constructed over the past twenty years. In theory, national and intermediate models should form an integrated complex of models. Through the 1970s this was not achieved. The program-goal, multibranch, regional and branch models that constitute this class should therefore be considered suboptimal and structurally isolated.

The modeling of large-scale programs

The principal innovation in the adaptation of Soviet planning and management to deal with the problems of development and the scientific–technical revolution has been the introduction of programming methods associated with PPB. Programming for developmental purposes has been traditional in Soviet planning practice. Large interbranch or regional programs are usually formulated by government decree, often in detail. The decree normally indicates the goals, time periods for execution, chief executants, and the responsible agencies (usually a head ministry) for coordination of the program. Resources for the specific program are allocated through the production plan. High-priority military and space projects are usually managed through special management organs with their own authority and resources.[42]

Goal-oriented programs are the principal methods for planning from final results. The individual program should define the whole complex of work from its initiation to its completion, integrating planning and control in a single process. The programs should be directly connected with the other divisions of the plan, particularly production, supply, and capital construction.[43]

Program-goal methods can be applied to developmental projects of any complexity or level of the hierarchy. Soviet interest, however, has focused on big-system projects. The Tenth Five-Year Plan formally replaced the traditional system of "coordinational plans" with two hundred goal-programs, the large majority of which are for scientific and technical development. Among the major programs are those for introducing computers into the economy and for NOT.[44]

In the late 1960s and early 1970s, proponents of optimal planning viewed the long-term plan as the aggregate of goal-programs whose completion required more than five years. The concentrated opposition of the central planners forced a modification of this conception in a more traditional direction. Although Fedorenko has apparently accepted this redefinition, he continues to hold that the complex of goal-oriented programs is the most important component of the long-term plan.[45]

The principal management technique for building goal-programs is the "tree of goals," the *karkas* of the long-term plan.[46] The tree of goals is a matrix which defines the hierarchy of goals, broken down into blocks or subsystems, that must be completed to achieve the final goals of the project. The method recommended for coordinating and controlling the program is network analysis (SPU).[47] The scope and complexity of the project naturally determines the type of analytical technique employed. Relatively small construction or research and development problems can use determinate models built by critical path methods and optimized through linear programming. Larger developmental projects, however, involving tens of thousands of events, require PERT.[48]

There can be little surprise in the relatively minimal global impact of programming on Soviet management through the 1970s. The application of network methods has been decentralized and uncoordinated. There have been fairly extensive applications at the branch level. The Ministry of Ferrous Metallurgy, for example, reported using network models for over two hundred projects.[49] In the automobile industry, network models have also been used in the Togliatti, Kama River, and Gorkii construction projects.[50] A tree of goals and networks have also been applied to the pilot project in Latvia for coordinating eleven distinct programs.[51]

Since the late 1960s, program-goal methods have been formally adopted for joint USSR–Eastern European projects. Programs involve cooperation in forecasting, planning, and coordination of developmental projects in the most important branches of industry. In 1976 five critical areas were selected for integrated development: energy and raw materials, machine building, food, consumer goods, and transportation. Top priority has been given to energy.[52]

Within the Soviet Union, the shift to a strategy of long-term programming is still largely nominal. The designation of large projects as programs is mainly a cover for a group of isolated programs which lack central direction or integration.[53] The reasons for this insufficiency are closely related to the problems of developing the long-term plan as well as introducing the programs into practice.

In a summary report to the 1977 conference on program-goal methods, Fedorenko noted that, despite the publicity, relatively little progress in applying the new methods had been made. There had been no consensus on the premises for constructing an integrated tree of goals. There also had been no agreement on the role and place of programs in planning; no single concept of utility; and no agreed measure for evaluating final results.[54] Without the long-term plan, an integrated complex of programs lacks definition.

It is also clear that the technical problems of constructing models for large developmental projects are severe. One of the most serious is developing criteria for establishing the rank, order, and sequence of goals and attaching quantitative values to them.[55] Secondly, the models present very difficult informational problems. Among the most challenging problems is the question of "languages." The determination of final goals, the allocation of resources, and the distribution of operational tasks are distinct analytical phases of model building. They require different techniques for translating decision trees into coherent plan-programs.[56]

The major operational problem for introducing the programs into practice has been the allocation of resources. The lack of a method for integrating programs with plans of production and distribution is critical in this respect. The goal-programs of the Tenth Five-Year Plan stand outside of the plan. As a result, the goals of the Latvian program were short of supply and had to be corrected. Some of the interbranch research and development programs have failed and will fail because the ministries do not provide for them.[57] These methodological and resource problems apply particularly to the programs of management rationalization. After viewing the 1976–80 plan, Popov concluded simply that the plan should be reworked.[58]

Multibranch and regional models

It is in this context that the ongoing effort to model multibranch and regional complexes should be judged. The modeling of interbranch complexes is evidently part of the larger effort to come to grips with interdependency, a primary source of the chronic imbalance of the existing system.

Multibranch models are part of the complex of models of the long-term plan. The principle for creating a multibranch system is the contribution which a branch makes to final demand as this is defined by a long-term goal-program. The models are designed to solve two interrelated tasks: determination of the optimal development of interdependent production branches; and definition of the level of demand for these products by other branches. Basically, the objective is to optimize the development of vertically integrated branches.[59]

Models of multibranch complexes have been built for the wood and wood procurement industries, for the drilling and refining of oil, for agrarian–industrial complexes, and for the oil and chemical industries.[60] The most advanced of the multibranch models is the optimal fuel and energy balance. The development of these branches is conceived primarily as an allocation problem. The modelers used linear programming and a local criterion of minimal projected expenditures. The national fuel–energy balance is broken down into twenty-seven regional subbranches. With them, plan computations can be made for such specific decisions as locating atomic power plants.

This model, however, is an exception. Multibranch modeling is in an initial stage of development. Coordinating national demand with the development of multibranch complexes requires further development of the dynamic interbranch balance and goal programs. It also requires the creation of special computational techniques to solve the very complex problems involved.[61]

Multibranch models can be conceived as primarily a regional type of planning problem. Over the past decade regional planning has assumed a central role in the reform of central planning because it is the key to the solution of several critical social and economic problems.

The goal of the regional modelers has been to build an optimal interbranch–interregional model, work on which began in 1962 in the Institute of Economics and Organization of Industrial Production. In the view of three leading specialists in the field, the possibility is remote of developing an "adequately optimized" model of this scale because of the extremely large number of stochastic processes which must be included in the model.[62]

The working concept of regional modeling to emerge over the past decade has been the production complex, a system which integrates the industry, agriculture, natural resources and energy, and infrastructure of a defined territorial division.[63] The larger production complex is the regional system, such as Western Siberia or Kazakhstan, which is too large for a single model. The operational planning concept is a subsystem of the regional system, the territorial-production complex (TPK), such as the Saian energy complex or the Abakan industrial center. In addition, several of the largest cities, including Moscow and Leningrad, have been designated as TPKs.[64] Because each TPK itself is a very large system, it is conceived as a complex of hierarchically organized subsystems.

The goal in developing models of the TPK is to avoid some of the familiar and extremely expensive mistakes which have been chronic in Soviet construction. Although a number of models of TPKs have been built since 1964 and tested experimentally, regional planning models have not been used in actual planning practice.[65] Moreover, the progress of regional modeling has been slowed by a number of serious problems, which include a lack of official support.

The intellectual difficulties have been inordinate. Regional models, as Bandman has pointed out, have been poor because of "the complexity of structure, diversity of relationships, the open, dynamic and stochastic character of functioning, the probabilistic character of the initial information, the nonlinearity of many dependencies, and the indivisibility of many of its constituent elements."[66] Of critical importance is the severe demand for information which even relatively small territorial complexes place on the model. The result is that no general scheme of development for a TPK has yet been constructed.[67]

Optimal branch planning

The most successful development of optimal planning models has been for the branch. As early as 1961, Nemchinov suggested that the cement industry begin work on an optimal plan of development and distribution. Since 1966, Gosplan has regularly instructed the ministries to prepare optimal five-year plans. In 1971, 32 ministries and 150 research institutes submitted seventy plans.[68] By 1976, virtually all ministries had submitted optimal plans for the Tenth Five-Year Plan.

In conjunction with the construction of branch automated systems of administration (OASUs), the broad objective has been to create a full complex of branch models. Minimally, this complex should include forecasting models, models of long-term development and distribution, current planning models, and models for reporting and operational control. Modeling at the branch level, however, has developed unevenly.

Priority has been given to construction of five-year plans. The specific objective has been to make more efficient investment decisions on such problems as the long-term structure of production, location of new enterprises and definition of their optimal size, and specialization and level of automation.[69]

Two basic types of optimal plans of development and distribution have emerged. The most successful models are single-commodity models for the determination of future production capacities and location of new plants. More complex and difficult to construct are multicommodity models, which may involve interrelated decisions on hundreds of plants.

Branches are by definition very complex systems. Even relatively simple models involve hundreds of equations, thousands of variables, and tens of thousands of indicators. In the main, optimal branch models are determinate and two-staged. They are semidynamic; that is, the indicators are fixed for the end of the planning period. Fully dynamic models, which can optimize each year of the plan, have not been built. The usual methods of optimization are linear and whole-number programming. The normal criterion of optimality is minimal production and transportation costs.[70]

Despite the heavy investment in optimization, the return has been modest through the 1970s. No fully optimal branch plans have been developed. Optimal plans have been limited to specific products or subbranches.[71] The most successful use of models has been in ministries with a small nomenclature of products and specialized equipment. Optimal plans with a broad nomenclature and universal equipment have not been developed.[72] The most effective models are those for the development and distribution of plastics, cement, fertilizers, synthetic fibers, cable, and fuel and energy. Where these methods have been used, there has been an increase in the use of production capacity of 3–4 percent and a savings in transport costs of 5–6 percent.[73]

Branch planners have devoted relatively less attention to constructing models for current planning or operational control. An exception has been their use by Gossnab and selected ministries to allocate production and supply. In 1976 the allocation of ferrous and nonferrous metals, wood and wood products, chemicals and cellulose, and oil and oil refining produced estimated savings of 20 billion ton-miles and 86,000 tons of rolled iron.[74] The Ministry of the Chemical Industry has produced a consolidated balance of 800 products with 100 types of raw materials.[75] This type of model, however, appears to be exceptional. Models are used primarily to check and correct plans calculated by more traditional methods.

The least developed aspect of branch modeling is operational control. The technical problems of producing determinate control models under conditions of great diversity and rapid change are severe, the critical control problem being supply. The application of statistical analysis to forecast bottlenecks or of network analysis offers potential approaches to the problem. The Ministry of the Electrotechnical Industry reportedly can exercise operational control over 20,000 products for domestic consumers and 750 products for export.[76] This type of model also appears to be rare.

In the scheme of branch optimization, branch indicators should form the basic parameters for the developmental and production programs of the operating units. This level of vertical integration has not been achieved. With the development of automated systems of administration at the enterprise level, the potential for optimization has risen dramatically. The application of linear programming and other scientific methods of management, nonetheless, has been slow. Through 1976, only 5 percent of enterprise planning tasks had been optimized.[77]

Priorities for optimal planning have developed in a distinct pattern. Unlike the branch, in the enterprise there is little concern with optimization of long-term planning. In conformity with traditional practice, emphasis has been on current planning. The usual application is the solution of such extremal tasks as the loading and use of equipment within the shop or brigade.[78] Optimization of the general production program is seldom attempted. For reasons even more pressing than in the branch, few control models of plan fulfillment have been built.

As Soviet industrial management enters the 1980s, the direct impact of optimal methods of decision making has been limited. The most successful applications have been in branch planning, where dramatic improvements in the efficiency of resource allocation have been visible for a restricted class of applications. The major models of SOFE, however, have been only partially developed, and their feasibility is in doubt. The computational and informational problems experienced in the intensive effort to develop a complex of decision-making models infused Kantorovich's 1975 Nobel Prize with a note of pessimism. Soviet modeling, he declared, suffered from *shablon*, or stereotyping. Creative new approaches were necessary to advance beyond the limits reached in the mid-1970s.[79] These limits have naturally proven to be serious constraints on the role of computers.

Computers and decision making

The introduction of computers on a mass scale into industrial decision making in the 1970s was the second important application of science and technology to management. The basic goal of computerization has been to provide decision makers with relevant data in the most useful form at the time it is needed. Since 1970 the principal focus has been on developing informational processing systems with retrieval, inquiry, and analytic functions.

The advance to a total systems approach in the application of computers in the 1970s has been controversial. Underlying the conflict have been two sharply differing perceptions of the potential value of computers to decision making. Both conceptions have supported the notion of an integrated, decision-oriented, computer-based informational processing network.[80] The more restricted notion defined the system as an automated data-processing system (ASOD), which lacked an analytic function.

The more ambitious concept, pressed by the optimal planners, conceived the system as an automated system of management (ASU). The model of the ASU is a man–machine decision-making system in which some formerly human decisions are transferred to the machine and in which all planning and operational management processes are optimized.[81] The *idealnaia* (ideal) ASU at the enterprise level, for example, is highly mechanistic. All management functions should be fully modeled. The system should have a completed technological base, automate all production processes, and use a single man-machine language.[82]

This highly mechanized conception of ASUs clearly conforms to the classical paradigm of management structure. It has served as the general model for the construction of a massive national automated system of management. In many respects, it has been the embodiment of the scientific–technical revolution.

The concept of OGAS

The operational concept of a national automated management system announced at the Twenty-fourth Congress in 1971 was the All-State System for the Collection and Processing of Information for Reporting, Planning, and Management of the National Economy. The system is usually referred to by the acronym OGAS. OGAS is conceived as a total informational processing system with an analytic function. As a comprehensive man–machine decision-making system, OGAS should ultimately include all phases of planning, reporting, and controlling of plan implementation. The analytic functions of the system are initially defined by the quality of the mathematical models incorporated into the system.[83]

Structurally, OGAS has been projected as a hierarchy of informational flows, technically modeled on the analogy of an integrated power grid. OGAS is linked with two primary subsystems: the state network of computer centers (SNCC); and the all-state system for data transmission (OGSPD). OGSPD, in turn, is a subsystem of a larger single automated network of communications.[84]

A final detailed structure has not been officially announced. In 1975 D. G. Zhimerin, director of OGAS since 1971, declared the system to be a four-level hierarchy of interactive ASUs. At the top were the informational subsystems of each ministry and state committee, including the KGB. A second level would be the fifteen republican systems (RASUs). The project included about 200 regional time-sharing computer centers. The base would include about 25,000 ASUs of economic enterprises and production associations.[85] As part of the grand design of socialist integration, OGAS would eventually be integrated with the national informational systems of CMEA.

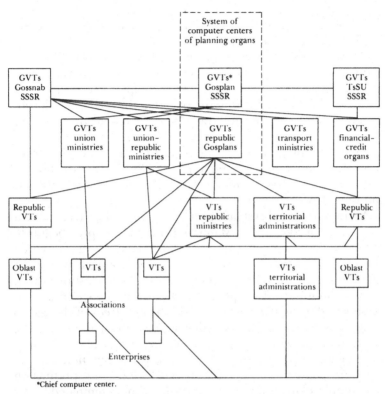

*Chief computer center.

Chart 3.1. The structure of OGAS. (Source: Iu. P. Lapshin, *Razvitie avtomatizirovannykh sistem upravleniia v promyshlennosti,* Moscow: Ekonomika, 1977, pp. 148-9.)

An alternate and perhaps earlier version of OGAS has been outlined by Iurii Lapshin of Gosplan. This model closely resembles the structural priorities of SOFE: the dominant function is planning and is clearly an overlay of the existing system of management. The key system is Gosplan's automated system of plan calculation (ASPR), which is horizontally integrated with the systems of the State Committee for Material-Technical Supply and of the Central Statistical Administration. A second level includes the other departmental and ministerial systems. Republican and territorial computer centers are on the third level. At the base are the ASUs of local territorial organs, enterprises, and production associations. (See Chart 3.1.)

At all levels, individual ASUs are clearly very complex systems.

Functionally, they are conceived as input–output systems which will process data into optimal decisions. Their design, however, has followed classical lines.

Gosplan's ASPR, for example, has followed the formal organization of Gosplan.[86] It has been designed as a four-level hierarchy of decision-making blocks. At the top is the complex of subsystems for consolidating the plan. On the second level, subsystems will perform the traditional planning functions of balancing resources with end uses. The third level is new: subsystems for integrating and coordinating associated branches (fuel and energy, machine building). At the base are the branch informational subsystems connected with republican and ministerial ASUs.

An important subsystem of OGAS is ASU–MTS (Automated Management System for Material Technical Supply), begun in 1966 and designed by CEMI and more than sixty other research institutes. It is also an overlay of Gossnab's existing structure. In its final form, the system will connect 130,000 consumers with tens of thousands of suppliers. By increasing the speed of processing and using normative models, the hundreds of thousands of personnel currently processing supply information could be relieved of the tedious labor of compiling supply plans. Because only new information will be processed, computations can be simplified and the time gap between forming the production and supply plans dramatically reduced, if not eliminated.[87]

A similar gain in speed and accuracy of decision making is expected from the management information systems of the other state committees. The goal of the State Price Committee's ASOItsen is to maintain centralized control of administrative pricing under conditions of rapid growth in price data. To achieve this, ASOItsen will have three subsystems for forecasting prices, for the automated calculation of price lists, and for price control.[88]

The ASUs of the ministries and enterprises follow the general design of the departmental systems. The ministerial system (OASU) is the operational network, integrating the chief functional administrations, *glavki*, production associations, and enterprises into a unified decision-making system. An integrated approach to the development of OASU, however, has been a goal frustrated by the wide diversity in the size, production technologies, product mix, and operating conditions of the ministries.[89] The design of OASU and of the lower systems, nevertheless, has a common general structure. Each system has a complex of functional and support systems adapted to the individual ministry's or enterprise's needs.

Among the industrial ministries, the flagship OASU is clearly the system of the Ministry of Instruments, Means of Automation, and Systems of Administration (Minpribor). Minpribor, a high-technology branch, plays a major role in the military as well as civilian economies. Unlike the OASU of many other ministries, ASU–Pribor has been under intensive development from the mid-1960s as a demonstration project.

The structure of the network is hierarchical and based upon the ministry's organizational structure, which was extensively rationalized in the late 1960s. The system has sixteen, rather than the standard twelve, functional subsystems. These serve seventeen chief functional administrations and twelve all-union industrial unions. The number of computer-based decisional tasks has gradually risen from 70 in 1970 to 280 in 1975. The most important functional subsystem within ASU–Pribor is the planning subsystem. It should be pointed out that OASUs of other ministries are considerably less developed.[90] No other system, for example, has reached the recommended number of subsystems by 1975.

The level and quality of development of automated systems for the management of the enterprise (ASUPs) vary widely. As a matter of policy, the construction of ASUPs has been limited to plants with over three thousand workers. Smaller plants which are not absorbed into production associations are to be grouped into territorial computer centers. The most effective of the ASUPs are those systems, like ASU–Pribor, which serve as demonstration systems.

Two types of ASUP, for continuous and discrete technologies, are being constructed. The latter creates subsystems for each production task and uses local parameters for each of the network's functional subsystems. Demonstration projects for the machine-building, electrotechnical, and instrument industries have had wide publicity.[91]

The ASUP of the Barnaul Radio Plant was begun in 1964 under the direction of Academician Marchuk and the Siberian Division of the Academy of Sciences. In 1967 Barnaul was selected as a typical ASUP and is the model for fifty-one enter-

Table 3.1. *Growth of ASUs in Soviet management (1966–78) in numbers*

	1966–70	1971–75	1976–78	1966–78
ASU enterprises	151	838	210	1,199
ASU technological processes	170	564	590	1,324
ASU territorial organs	61	631	180	872
ASU ministries and departments	19	168	45	232
ASOI[a]	13	108	55	176
Total	414	2,309	1,080	3,804

[a]Information processing systems.
Source: *SSR v tsifrakh v 1978 godu*, Moscow: Statistika, 1978, p. 76.

prises throughout the Soviet Union. A primary subsystem for the management of basic production will include subsystems for planning of production, technical–economic planning, book-keeping, economic analysis, and several other functions. A second major subsystem will be constructed for the preparation of production.[92] ASU–Barnaul, however, is still incomplete.

An important demonstration ASUP has been the system designed by Glushkov's Institute of Cybernetics for the Lvov Television Plant. It was specifically designed to meet the needs of a plant producing a single technologically advanced product using a mass production technology. In operation since 1967, Lvov has focused on operational planning and control. Subsystems for these functions have the task of stabilizing the flow of more than twenty thousand parts and components to the assembly lines. In line with the interest of Glushkov in technical cybernetics, Lvov uses machine registration of data and computer printouts to reduce documentation.[93]

Breaking the informational barrier

The decade between 1965 and 1975 was a turbulent period in the application of computers to management. At the beginning of the 1980s, there is still no clear indication that a program for building a mass computer system can be implemented successfully. High-quality ASUs have undoubtedly been produced, but as a whole the program has been seriously flawed. By the mid-

1970s, serious disillusionment had developed with respect to computers. A fundamental problem was in the strategy of implementation. As Table 3.1 indicates, a crash program for constructing OGAS increased the number of ASUs five to ten times between 1971 and 1975. The crash program inaugurated in 1971 offers a convincing case study of the minimal value of traditional Soviet mobilizational methods of development for building intricate, high-technology projects such as OGAS. Beyond strategy, however, have been unresolved policy issues as well as questions of the availability of the technical, economic, organizational, and human resources required to implement a program of this scope and complexity.

Some policy issues

The policy of computerization has stimulated a wide range of issues of varying importance over the past two decades. Among the major issues have been the specific functions that computers should perform, a system's configuration and core functions, and the order, sequence, and priorities that should prevail. Among the most bitterly controversial questions has been which bureaucracy should supervise the construction and operation of the computer network.

Many of these conflicts of structure and purpose were evident in the scarcely concealed rivalry between Fedorenko and Glushkov on the conception of the system and the struggle between Gosplan and the Central Statistical Administration for control over it. Like other large interbranch developmental projects, OGAS has suffered from rampant suboptimization.[94]

The depth of cleavage between Fedorenko and Glushkov can easily be exaggerated. Both have agreed that the system should be multifunctional and goal-oriented; that the formal structure should be thoroughly reorganized for maximum effect; and that the system should develop under unified direction and control. As primary bridges between the political and scientific communities, moreover, their positions have naturally been somewhat flexible on controversial issues.[95]

Their differences, though, have been substantial and have decisively influenced the system's development. In part, their disagreements stem from their academic specialties and the functional responsibilities of CEMI and the Institute of Cybernetics in the system's construction. Fedorenko and his institute have been deeply involved in the complexities of economic and informational modeling. He has increasingly interpreted cybernetics from a complex systems approach. Glushkov, on the other hand, as a mathematician and engineer, has had a primary, if not exclusive interest in technology. His view of cybernetics and the model of management derived from it, noted in Chapter 2, is more mechanistic and technical.

Although relative, their differences became operational in defining the structure of OGAS. In SOFE, Fedorenko has consistently stressed the priority of the planning function and optimization. As a consequence, the State Planning Committee and ASPR should be the core of the system, and its direct linkages with the ministries and republican planning committees the primary set of relationships. Aware of the constraints of complexity on economic and informational modeling, Fedorenko has insisted on a degree of subsystem autonomy.[96]

The contrasting position of Glushkov has emphasized the functions of operational management and control, a greater concentration of authority, the necessity of a "bottoms up" approach to the system's construction, and the creation of an independent national computer center to integrate the network and serve as "super dispatcher."[97] These contrasting views have been summarized and reflected to a large extent in their conception of the ideal structure of the system.

Fedorenko has consistently advocated a two-level, planning–production hierarchy. The operating level is OASU, which integrates the ASUP of the branch into a single system. The superstructure, in his view, should be a territorial–branch system integrated primarily through Gosplan. Glushkov, in contrast, has conceived OGAS as a three-tiered system based upon ASUP. The intermediate level, however, should be territorial rather than branch and composed of horizontally connected regional centers. At the central level would be the All-State Computer Center, which includes Gosplan as one subsystem.[98] If SOFE provided the general outline of the system adopted in 1971, the tilt toward time sharing in the mid-1970s has given Glushkov's views new vitality.

A central policy issue in the development of a national information system has been the bureaucratic struggle for control over the project's implementation. From the early 1960s, it was clear that the project's integrity was threatened by departmentalism, a scattering of scarce resources, and the emergence of incompatible information systems. From 1963 to 1971, control over OGAS's predecessor, the State Network of Computer Centers, alternated between Gosplan and the Central Statistical Administration; neither agency possessed the authority or the resources to curb organizational pluralism or an exponential rise in costs of construction.[99]

The decision in 1971 to construct OGAS as a system integrating SNCC with the concepts of SOFE generated political conflict at the highest levels. The decision may have been delayed until a month before the Congress. On January 21, 1971, Fedorenko publicly complained that no mention was made of long-term planning and forecasting in the Draft Directives of the Ninth Five-Year Plan. He advocated a policy commitment to a long-term plan of ten to fifteen years based upon twenty- to twenty-five-year forecasts.[100] This was subsequently included in the directives of April 9, 1971.

The Congress ordered the most rapid development of OGAS. Soviet industry was required to increase the output of computers by a factor of 2.4 and of central processors by a factor of 2.6. All ministries were ordered to complete the first stage of OASU by 1975 and to increase the number of ASUP by a factor of 7.[101] The human factor in management receded to a secondary plane.

The management of OGAS also underwent extensive reorganization. The new organization was not announced at the Congress and did not emerge publicly until December 1971, although Theodore Shabad of the *New York Times* identified D. G. Zhimerin with the computer program in June of that year.[102]

The State Committee for Science and Technology assumed administrative control of the project. An interdepartmental council was formed to coordinate policy under the chairman of the committee. A new agency for operational management of OGAS was placed under the control of Zhimerin, a power engineer, who was also appointed a first deputy chairman of the committee.[103]

The new management structure, Zhimerin declared in an initial statement, was to serve as a "general staff" for OGAS.[104] Its functions were to integrate policy, research, and development and, presumably, coordinate construction. The new agency's authority, however, was restricted. It lacked control over the production of computer hardware; moreover, space, military, educational, and medical programs were outside of its jurisdiction.[105]

The building of OGAS on a crash basis reduced the capacity of the new agency to direct rationally the development of the project. The decentralized and pluralistic tendencies of the earlier period continued and probably increased. There is considerable support for the observation of Glushkov in 1976 that OASU still had uncoordinated designs, placed excessive stress on vertical relations, produced hardware at odds with the needs of the system, and continued to have a chaotic organization of documentation.[106] To counteract the disorganization, Glushkov argued in 1974 that Zhimerin's agency should serve as the general contractor of OGAS in order to exercise operational authority over its development, a function which it was not performing.[107]

Technical development has raised new policy issues. In 1973, the introduction of third-generation computers and supporting software introduced the technical possibility of on-line, multiprogram processing. Adoption of time sharing based upon a regional network of computer centers offered to centralize data processing and unified the system from its inception. Time sharing also offered economies of scale. In one estimate, time sharing would save 20 to 25 billion rubles in investment and 4 to 5 billion in maintenance costs.[108]

The shift to time sharing on an experimental basis occurred in 1973. Gosplan and the Interdepartmental Council set up time-sharing centers in Minsk, Tula, Tallin, and Tomsk. These centers perform data processing for all enterprises in the region, including those of all-union ministries with fewer than two thousand employees. Each center services thirty to forty users, has a central data bank, and offers both batch and on-line processing. Some users will have a "dialog" capacity and others a query capability.[109] Production difficulties with the ES-1040 and ES-1050 central processors has slowed time sharing's development.[110] The Twenty-fifth Congress, nonetheless, decreed that up to 80 percent of new computer capacity will be in this mode.[111]

The policy of time sharing has revitalized familiar lines of cleavage between proponents of territorial and branch systems. The Central Statistical Administration has made an expected claim for control of it. Both Gosplan and the ministries clearly oppose it, fearing a loss of control over information. Gosplan continues to press forward with ASPR.[112] Brezhnev's speech to the Twenty-fifth Congress, moreover, continued to stress significant elements of SOFE: long-term planning; incorporation of mathematical models and ASU; evaluation by final results; program-goal methods for large developmental projects; and organization of management by groups of related branches.[113] Whether time sharing and SOFE are compatible is not clear.

OGAS as a developmental project

The construction of a project of the size, complexity, and interdependence of OGAS has placed severe demands upon the technical, economic, and organizational resources of Soviet management. The combination of fundamental policy conflicts, intense mobilization, complex technical demands, and inadequate resources has resulted in indeterminacy, waste, and inefficiency. One consequence has been growing skepticism about ASU's value. Although visible progress has been made, serious problems remain for the 1980s.

Design and the rationalization of information

The cybernetic approach to modernization of management has raised the task of rationalizing information for decision making to first priority. The objective of designing a management information system has been to maximize the value of a minimal flow of information. This has meant a determination of information utilities, investigation of informational processes, and the building of an appropriate technological base.

Achieving greater utility at less cost is an enormous problem. Socioeconomic development has simultaneously created a need for more diverse and complex data as the amount of data to be processed has grown. In the early 1970s, an estimated 120 to 170 billion indicators circulated annually in the economy (up to 70 percent in the supply system); planning alone processed 2.7 to 3.6 billion indicators. The great bulk of data, however, is processed in the ministries and enterprises,[114] which handle about 90 percent of all data. The utility of this information is low. The data is characterized as excessive, inaccurate, and duplicative; moreover, the system is heavily overloaded, processing only a small amount of data. The value of information is further reduced by bureaucratic distortions and social psychological factors.[115]

The approach to the design of ASU has been functional. System designers normally model informational flows within an organization.[116] This effort to build comprehensive empirical models proved to be extremely difficult. As Glushkov has noted, the design of an ASU is several hundred times more complex than the design of a space project.[117] Fedorenko has estimated that an annual plan of a *glavk* in a machine-building ministry has five hundred to six hundred constraints and as many as five thousand variables. Models can construct only several dozen of the most important.[118]

The complexity is evident in an attempt by Gosplan RSFSR (the full acronym for the Russian Republic) to build a network model of the planning process for ASPR. With this model, central planners could intervene in the planning process at any point in the plan's composition. Gosplan RSFSR was presumably chosen to construct the model because its planning process approaches the complexity of that of Gosplan USSR. It compiles a plan for 59 ministries and departments, 73 provinces, and 10 large regions. A previous modeling attempt in the mid-1960s failed, largely because of complexity. Gosplan RSFSR has 40 departments and 156 branch and consolidation sections. Over three thousand forms and tables are used in compiling the plan. The final planning document runs to more than twelve thousand pages.

The network is consequently very complex. More than twenty thousand events are built into the model. The primary sector networks have thirty to forty events and three hundred to four hundred events are scheduled for departments like capital construction.[119] Although published information is indefinite, the model is presumably too complex to be determinate and thus to strengthen centralized control.

The rationalization of the informational system is conceptually closely related to modeling of informational flows; the model should provide the basis for analysis and subsequent reduction and unification of indicators and information-processing procedures. A closely related aspect of rationalization has been to prepare informational systems for machine processing and storage.

Rationalization has taken three basic directions. The first has been to develop systems for the encoding of economic information and the classification of industrial products. The second has been to rationalize the extremely diverse and complex systems of documentation. The third has been to develop data banks as a major component of ASU.

The creation of a single system of codes (ESKK) for all technical–economic information used in decision making is clearly necessary for the reduction of its ambiguity and for the machine processing and exchange of information.[120] Work on a single system for the classification of ten million products, begun in the early 1960s, continues under the direction of Gosplan's Chief Computer Center and more than three hundred institutes.[121] The reduction of the massively complex and diverse forms of documentation to twelve standard systems has been under the direction of the State Committee on Standards.[122]

The long-term goal in the rationalization of the informational system has been to move to a "paperless" informational system. The core of this conception has been the development of data banks for each of the major systems. The initial goal was to develop a single centralized data bank for the whole system. The storage requirements for a system like ASGS are large, in this case exceeding 500 billion bits of information.[123] Through the 1970s data bank construction, however, was seriously limited even in relatively small systems by low operating memory, weak operating systems software, and incomplete and clumsy systems of data classification.[124] Building data banks is a high-priority task for the 1980s.

An accurate assessment of the processes of design and rationalization of ASU's informational system is extremely difficult because of the decentralized approach to the design of the great majority of systems. Some of the larger and more publicized ASUs undoubtedly have been well designed. On the whole, however, the quality of design has been a major factor contributing to the low utilization and integration of the majority of systems.

The problems of design can be largely traced to the intense pressures of mobilization which resulted in the proliferation of small design groups frequently staffed with poorly trained and inexperienced personnel. By the early 1970s, there were about five hundred autonomous groups which had produced more than three hundred different designs.[125] This condition has had evident consequences for both the utility and compatibility of the ASUs comprising OGAS.

The design organizations adopted a localistic and conservative approach, which led to a design that was usually a simple overlay of the existing formal structure and communication networks.[126] Limited capabilities combined with a lack of consensus on which functions in which sequence should be automated has resulted in incompatible systems. It has also produced a concentration on the simplest and most routine tasks.[127]

The pressure for results forced designers to work rapidly and to introduce the systems without sufficient testing. In the process, the competition for competent systems engineers and technicians became acute.[128] However justified the pressure may have been as a lever against institutional inertia, the policy led to excessive costs, low quality, and lengthened construction schedules. In view of the goal of systemic integration in building OGAS, many of the systems built in the first half of the 1970s will have to be redesigned.

The rationalization of the economic informational systems has also had mixed results. By the end of the 1970s, no unified systems for the coding of information, classification of products, or unification of documents had been achieved. Some progress, nonetheless, has been observable. Although Gosplan has not yet completed an all-union classification of planning documentation, a series of dictionaries and a single list of planning indicators for ASPR can become operational.[129]

More generally, by 1975 the Committee on Standards had produced nineteen branch codes and thirteen unified systems of documentation for 1,700 forms of management activity. Some 350 industrial organizations are using the new systems experimentally. Between 1976 and 1980, nine new codes and two new systems of documentation are scheduled for introduction.[130]

The problems of coding and classification, however, are far from resolved. The systems are cumbersome, include only the simpler categories of data, and are not integrated. More importantly, theoretical problems of language and description remain unresolved.[131]

The effective use of technology in decision making clearly requires a qualitative improvement in the amount and reliability of information used in decision making. Informational constraints, for example, have been severe in the construction of economic models. Paradoxically, although massive amounts of unused and irrelevant data circulate in the system, data requirements far exceed the available pool of information. Lapshin has estimated that the amount of information in all ASUs does not exceed 10^6 to 10^7 bits of information. In his view, an adequate data base for the contemporary Soviet economy should be at least one hundred times larger.[132]

The reliability of the information put into the system has continued to generate skepticism concerning the value of computers in decision making. The error rate in the transmission of data is high. In one informed estimate, it averages one error per 10^3–10^4 bits of information transmitted.[133] This type of error is due to operator mistakes, deficient hardware, high static transmission lines, and other routine human and machine problems.[134] The more complex problems of reliability stem from the distortions created by economic and social-psychological interests. The behavioral sources of unreliable information are deeply institutionalized and will be difficult to eradicate.

The technological base of OGAS

Central to the development of ASU has been the evolution of the hardware and software required to operate the system. Until the early 1960s, Soviet interest was generally confined to military and scientific applications. As a result, prior to 1970, the development and production of general purpose computers proceeded in a thoroughly decentralized and uncoordinated fashion. Between 1951 and 1970, Davis and Goodman have estimated the development of sixty different types of computers. Fewer than twenty models, however, had production runs of more than one hundred units.[135]

The major general purpose computer available for processing economic information in the late 1960s and early 1970s was the Minsk-22, a second-generation machine judged "hopelessly deficient" with respect to input–output devices and secondary storage.[136] By 1973, an upgraded model, the Minsk-32, equipped with a disk unit and operating systems software, appeared. It had the advantage of functioning in both multiprogramming and limited remote processing modes.[137]

The demands for an upwardly compatible family of computers increased as the conception of a national, integrated, computer-based decision-making system progressed. As part of the larger policy of economic and technological integration, the Soviet Union pushed in 1968 for the joint development of such a system within CMEA. Using the architecture of the IBM 360 series as the basis, the ES or Ryad series appeared in production relatively rapidly. The first models of Ryad 1020 began production in Minsk in January 1972.[138]

Through the 1970s, research and development of Soviet computer hardware has accelerated. Because of production problems and the operating constraints derived from the 360 hardware, the lower end of Ryad-1 has been replaced by redesigned models, the 1022 and 1033. In 1975 the Minsk series had been taken out of production, replaced by Ryad 1022. By 1977, Ryad 1033 had also gone into production.[139] Technological development will continue into the 1980s with the production of an improved Ryad-2 series based upon IBM 370. There is some public discussion that a Ryad-3 series with new architectural characteristics may be available in the mid-1980s or later in the decade.[140] A third generation of machines (M-6000 and M-7000), classed as minicomputers, has come on line for general purpose computing as well as process control.[141]

The improvement in Soviet computing capacity over the past decade has been striking. From an estimated 2,000 nonmilitary computers in 1968,[142] the computer park had expanded to 15,000 main frames in 1975. Computer production in the mid-1970s was about 3,200 units annually and growing by 20 percent each year. By 1980, installed main frames should reach 40,000 to 42,000 units.[143]

The capability of Soviet hardware has also advanced. With the advent of Ryad, systemic integration through on-line and remote processing has become technologically feasible. The first series produced capabilities for servicing multiple users and supporting a variety of programming languages and had disk memories, card input–output equipment, and communication terminals.[144] Ryad-2 should extend this capability by including "much larger primary memory, semiconductor primary memory, virtual storage capabilities, block multiplexor channels, relocatable storage, improved peripherals, and expanded timing and protection facilities."[145] Enlarged disk capacity (up to 29M bytes) and multiplexor channels are particularly important for interactive, time-sharing, and remote processing.

Despite the technical advances in central processors, peripherals, and transition to disk storage, major problems continue. Computing power is still woefully short. In one estimate, a mature computing system would require ten times the computing power in place in 1976.[146] The shortage of peripherals and high-capacity disk memories has been severe and has slowed the development of time sharing, remote processing, and data banks. A central issue has been overloaded lines of communication. In 1975, about twenty-five thousand leased telegraph lines were in use but were too slow (50 bits/second).[147] Blocked channels have been characteristic not only of the long lines but within a single city.[148]

The effort of Soviet industry to supply its computer system is an interesting example of the problems inherent in employing the resources of a system to rationalize itself. Like other Soviet products, the usefulness of Soviet computers has been troubled by low quality of output. V. M. Glushkov has complained that workmanship is so shoddy that "it is impossible, as a rule, to avoid a thoroughgoing reconstruction of them."[149] There have also been complaints of a shortage of spare parts, unbalanced assortments of central processors and peripherals, and late deliveries of incomplete sets of hardware.[150] Installation and service have been notably unsatisfactory.

The impact of managerial suboptimization on the production of peripherals and other types of hardware is illustrative. The production of peripherals negatively influences the success indicators of the plant. Although they are relatively inexpensive to make, peripherals are technically complex and labor intensive. The enterprise therefore struggles to manufacture the minimum number of items. Both the Ministry of the Radio Industry and Minpribor have been criticized for lowering production targets despite the shortage.[151]

The predominant economic interest of the ministries in maintaining stable and uninterrupted production has also negatively influenced technological innovation. The Ministry of the Radio Industry, for example, has held up the production of Ryad 1050 and 1060 since 1974 for economic as well as technical reasons. The lack of large central processors, in turn, has been a principal stumbling block in the development of time sharing.[152]

The conflict of interests between the producing ministries and the needs of the economy is evident in other respects as well. The Ministry of the Electronics Industry has repeatedly failed to meet the deadline for special purpose computers. The Ministry of the Electrotechnical Industry has not met the delivery schedules for integrated circuits. Minpribor has also delayed the production of minicomputers. To meet their needs, clients have reverted to the traditional practice of *kustarnyi,* or handicraft production. The manufacture of minicomputers in unspecialized facilities by handicraft methods has had the expected effects of producing high-cost and unreliable machinery.[153]

The lack of special facilities for installation and service of ASUs has been a primary source of the long delays before full operation and downtime of Soviet hardware. After a long discussion, a centralized agency for installing and repairing Ryad-based systems, SoiuzEVMkompleks, has been formed.[154] Whether this agency will have the size, facilities, and expertise to cope effectively with the critical problem of maintenance, though, is unclear.

The development of software as the second element of the technological base for OGAS has been equally challenging. In 1970, after an inspection of Soviet computing facilities, Barry Boehm judged the existing software "extremely ragged." Standard utility programs and large, integrated software packages simply did not exist.[155] Davis and Goodman have attributed the crisis in software at the end of the 1960s to the small number of machines in operation, the constraints of limited peripherals and memories, and the self-engineered software which precluded exchange and cooperation among users.[156]

The development of Ryad clearly changed a bleak situation.

The adoption of IBM 360 software provided Soviet computing with almost a billion dollars' worth of software. Detailed examination of Ryad software by Western specialists indicates that its operating systems and assembly language software is the same as 360 software.[157] The small incompatibilities presumably can be ironed out. Although Soviet computing appears to use 360 software for routine data management applications, they have made progress toward developing larger, integrated software packages for remote processing (KAMA) and for data management (OKA).

How far Soviet computing has absorbed Western applications software is not clear. The major high-level languages – ALGOL, COBOL, FORTRAN, PL/I, and others – have been in use for almost two decades. Western programs for linear programming, CPM, numerical routines, and other applications are easily secured.[158] The shortage of applications software, however, remains a basic constraint on ASU development. Most OASUs and ASUPs in the mid-1970s lacked programs for computing either the long-term or annual plans.[159] The lack of software has also been one of the major reasons for the delay in putting computers into operation.[160]

The reasons for the lag in software development through the first half of the 1970s are apparent. The programs are complex; an enterprise program has several hundred thousand commands, and an OASU program several million. Unlike their U.S. counterparts, Soviet computer manufacturers do not supply software for their machinery. Modular and standard programming has not been highly developed; and self-developed software has often been of questionable quality.[161] An important consideration has been the limited value of 360 software, only 8 percent of ASUPs being equipped with Ryad central processors through 1975.[162]

The limitations of Soviet software can undoubtedly be alleviated as more Ryad hardware comes on line. The quality of Soviet applied mathematics, moreover, is high. As Davis and Goodman have pointed out, software development is less constrained by the Soviet material and bureaucratic environment. There may also be some limited aid from Eastern Europe.[163] An important organizational development for Soviet software has been the creation of Tsentroprogrammsistem. In 1976 the new agency had developed seventeen software packages and had contracts with five hundred clients.[164] Packages for supply, sale, planning, labor, and other applications have been made. Of particular importance has been the appearance of two packages (SIOD and SIGMA) for the operational management of basic production in enterprises of the machine-building branches.[165]

On the whole, as the rationalization of Soviet management enters the 1980s, there have been important advances in creating a technological base for OGAS. It is also clear, however, that Soviet software and hardware must make qualitative advances of a very high order to meet the challenges of an integrated, computer-based decision-making system.

The organization and financing of OGAS

In addition to the complex problems of creating the technology for OGAS, the program of construction has shared many of the traditional problems of Soviet project management. Although the intense pressure and decentralized approach stimulated local initiative and rapid, if uneven, growth, the cost in suboptimization and wasted resources has been high. The program of construction has been particularly flawed by the acute shortage of trained personnel of all types and inadequate methods of financing.

The decision to plunge into the mass construction of ASUs in 1971, despite the critical shortage of personnel, has been among the most serious constraints on OGAS's development. The number of personnel engaged in developing and introducing ASUs grew 250 percent between 1971 and 1975, reaching 250,000. During the Tenth Five-Year Plan, the number is slated to double.[166] There are, in addition, relatively large numbers of operating and service personnel in computer centers. According to Lapshin, the ASUP has no fewer than 40 to 50 operating personnel and from 200 to 300 service personnel[167] at the enterprise level alone. This adds at least 500,000 to the number of computer personnel. A total of 900,000 to 1 million is probably a reasonable estimate for the end of 1975. Although the distribution and level of training for these workers have not been published, indirect evidence suggests only a small minority have had formal or even hands-on training.

The size of investment and, particularly, the methods of financing have been an additional obstacle. The full investment required to build OGAS has not been published. Direct invest ment for all ASU during the Ninth Five-Year Plan approached five billion rubles.[168] This does not include investment in additional manufacturing capacity, communications, operating materials, or training. It also clearly excludes at least part of the design and all of the operating and service costs.

The direct costs for building an OASU averaged three to five million for design and an additional five million for equipment. The first stage of ASUP averaged between one and two million rubles.[169] The predominant branch configuration in 1971 was clearly capital intensive. The switch to time sharing, in one esti-mate, will cut the developmental costs by twenty to twenty-five billion rubles and cut operating costs by two-thirds.[170]

One of the most controversial aspects of the construction costs of ASU has been the question of return on direct investments and methods of measuring that return. Advocates of com-puterization like Lapshin have calculated a return on investment of 0.43 for 1971–5 and 0.5 for 1975, that is, a recovery of in-vestment in two years.[171] Precisely what this index means, how-ever, is unclear.

In the past, over thirty distinct methods have been used to determine the economic effectiveness of computer invest-ment.[172] The most widely used method of comparing construc-tion costs with savings from reduced personnel was evidently simplistic.[173] Measurement of return, moreover, has been con-fined to ASUP. The more expensive national and branch sys-tems, like ASPR, are excluded.

In 1972 a new methodology was adopted. Revised in 1975, the current formula measures return as the ratio of direct costs to the improvement of an enterprise's economic indicators. Be-cause factor analysis is seldom used to measure the specific in-fluence of computers on production, critics complain that ASUP may receive credit for improvements in economic indicators for which it is not responsible.[174] A further complaint is that the revised rules fail to measure, on the positive side, such qualita-tive gains in efficiency as savings in time, improved coordina-tion, and increased quality of production.[175]

The methods of financing OGAS, similar to other large-scale

projects, have also contributed to its disorganized development and reduced utilization. Financing has been channeled through both budget and decentralized sources, with different sources contributing to different phases of development. In 1971–5, financing was on an annual basis and unstable.

Only 8 percent of the total allocation came from the central budget; the remaining costs were covered by ministerial and enterprise funds.[176] Frequently the development of ASUP was held up after the budget-financed design stage because enterprise funds ran out and the ministry diverted funds earmarked for computer development into projects of higher priority. This practice has contributed to the traditional pattern of cost overruns, frozen assets, extended construction schedules, and low productivity for the system.[177] Although the program of computerization has been designated as a goal-program for 1976–80, there is no evidence that the methods of financing or supply have been substantially revised.

The industrial use of computers

The contribution of computers to an improvement in industrial decision making can be evaluated from at least two perspectives. In terms of implementing a system of optimal decision making and control, results have been modest. Computer applications for data processing, however, have grown steadily during the 1970s. In 1968, only 9.1 percent of computers processed economic information, 80 percent of it industrial. By 1973, 65 percent of all computers served the economy. Changes in distribution of machine time were in the same direction. Between 1968 and 1972, computer time spent on economic data processing increased from 23.7 to 43 percent.[178]

As the key system in OGAS, Gosplan's ASPR used computers for about one thousand tasks in Gosplan USSR and two thousand tasks at the republican level. About 20 percent was used for model-based decision making, principally for preplan calculations. The remaining time was spent on routine calculations. Limited multibranch optimal calculations were made for the 1976 plan. Computers developed four variants of input-output relationships for eight thousand products in eleven machine-building branches.[179]

The Chief Computer Center of Gosplan processed most of the data. The annual plan absorbed about 55 percent of computer time. Over 60 percent was used by the departments for consolidation where plan computations are very complex.[180] About 50 percent of all plan documentation is printed out, including all the output for the departments of consolidation.

The strategy of the Central Statistical Administration's ASGS was to place the most labor-intensive work on machines. About half of the two billion indicators annually handled by the CSA is machine processed, with savings in time of up to three days for monthly reports and two months for annual reports. In addition, ASGS facilities are used by more than twenty OASUs and thirty ASUPs, including the Ministry of Agriculture.[181]

The principal value of ASU–MTS has also been more efficient data processing, which is clearly important because the centralized administration of supply is a key source of economic control and requires the greatest amount of information. The amount of data processed by Gossnab between 1970 and 1975 increased a massive 65.8 percent. Without computers, Novikov estimates, an additional 62,000 workers would have been required.[182] Operating time on Gossnab's facilities has exceeded the national average by 20 percent and has a planned growth of 250 percent between 1976 and 1980.

Despite the intellectual achievements of Kantorovich and others, however, optimization of supply planning has been ineffective. An investigation by a Gossnab team revealed that optimal supply plans are seldom implemented. They found that managers implemented only four of fifty-seven optimal plans without correction. Corrections, moreover, were so extensive that the adjusted plans had greater losses than if they had been computed manually.[183]

OASU applications

Among branch ASUs, the number and types of tasks performed by computer differ widely. Each system has been designed independently, has had different priorities, and has been created with wide variations of competence. The data for OASU and ASUP applications, moreover, are incomplete and imprecise. Seventy percent of all OASU have been developed since 1971 under conditions of intense pressure. Their quality of construction and level of use has naturally suffered. Branch ASUs, including ASU-Pribor, are used at about 50 percent of their projected rates. On the whole, the number of tasks mechanized has been higher than average in the instrument-building, coal, machine-building, and metal-processing industries. Applications have been fewer in light industry.[184]

ASU-Pribor is the most advanced OASU. One of its chief designers has claimed the system can compute five or six variants of each enterprise's annual plan and twenty variants of the five-year plan. Supply can be calculated centrally, and, as a result, supply planning by the enterprise can be eliminated. The computations of the ministry now go directly to the territorial organs of Gossnab. Within the ministry, *fondy*, or supply allocation certificates, are now distributed automatically with the attachment of suppliers and clients.

ASU-Pribor has also made progress in the use of control models. It has subsystems for the control of research and development and for monitoring execution of the orders of the ministry and higher economic agencies.[185] The system has also reportedly refined the subsystem for cadres to the point that it can forecast vacancies due to illness, a relatively rare use of stochastic models for decision making.[186]

There are other examples of an advanced use of computers in branch decision making. Virtually all electrical energy in the Soviet Union is distributed by computers; 60–65 percent of geophysical data is processed by machine; and computers are widely used in the distribution network of the agricultural supply agency, Soiuzselkhoztekhnika.[187] Such intensive use, however, is exceptional.

Design, hardware, and software constraints have seriously restricted the scale and types of applications. In 1975 a survey of machine-building ministries noted that only 14 percent of machinery in use was Ryad; 77 percent of computing was still done on Minsk-32 and Minsk-22 central processsors. Software, moreover, was substantially underdeveloped. Machine codes, rather than high-level languages, were used in programming, largely because of the lack of translators. Finally, developed subsystems have been largely restricted to those for technical–economic planning, operational planning and supply, bookkeeping, and reporting.[188]

Through 1975, about 72 percent of machine time was spent on data processing, and 24 percent on analysis and reporting. One survey of OASUs, probably indicative of the early 1970s, reported only 6 percent of technical–economic planning tasks had been computerized. However, 37 percent of bookkeeping, 27 percent of operational information, and 9 percent of supply information has been put on machines.[189] A second estimate, presumably taken later, noted a dramatic rise in the machine computation of planning tasks to 34 percent.[190] As stated earlier, though, only 5 percent of these calculations were optimized.

In 1976, no OASU had computerized planning for the plan as a whole or even for a major subdivision of the plan. Computerized planning has been limited to single products or groups of products. A major direction in the development of OASU in its first phase has been the centralization of supply planning. This function is both heavily labor intensive and a source of suboptimization. Dramatic results have been reported in some systems. ASU–Stroimash (Ministry of Construction, Road and Communal Machine Building) reported a cut in labor costs of twelve times. Man-months in compiling supply plans dropped from 600 to 50, and time from 4½ months to 40 days. Personnel was reduced by 5.5 percent.[191]

Applications in the ASUPs

In the mid-1970s, ASUPs have been the most developed systems. In addition to Frezer, Lvov, and other well-designed and equipped systems, many other ASUPs have reported good results. The Moscow Watch Factory, for example, has used its system for loading equipment, operational planning, inventory control, and recordkeeping.[192] The system of the Kazan Heat Control Plant has reported a reduction in management conferences, more effective production scheduling, improved quality control, and reduced managerial involvement in operational decision making.[193]

Like ASUs at higher levels, the bulk of computer time is allocated to data processing. Accounting and reporting tasks were the majority (75–85 percent). Planning tasks (20–25 percent) were a distant second.[194] Few planning tasks, however, were optimized, and most planning applications were confined to the individual shop. In virtually all ASUPs, there has been a concentrated effort to centralize planning of supply in the plant administration. Computers are also used for engineering computations to a limited extent.[195]

As part of the effort to produce fully automated production systems, a longer-term objective for the 1980s will be the integration of ASUPs with ASUTPs (automated systems for the administration of technological processes). Systems of numerical controls are scheduled to triple in the Tenth Five-Year Plan in the metallurgical, chemical, oil, and oil-refining industries. A direct response to the labor shortage and need for increased quality, the automation of production processes has reportedly raised labor productivity three to five times.[196]

Computers and the existing system

The contribution of computers to management effectiveness appears marginal. By 1975, only 5–10 percent of planning and reporting data had been mechanized, although the proportion was rising. Optimization, however, had reached a plateau; and unresolved policy conflicts, technological and modeling problems, and organizational barriers continued to reduce the value of computers for decision making.

Among the most persistent obstacles to application have been the widely reported "psychological barriers" of managers and specialists to the new technology. Managers frequently reshape optimal decisions or refuse to execute them out of self-interest. There are also social and psychological reasons for resistance.[197]

American experience is useful in this respect. Frock has pointed out that introduction of computers may create serious conflicts among managers because of threatened loss of control over information. Where information is centralized, middle and lower management may suffer a loss of status and function. Increased mechanization also leads to intensified demands for more precise coordination and control over management functions. Finally, conflicts between line and staff may be stimulated, and a sharpened sense of vulnerability may grip everyone participating in the system.[198]

Many of these conditions and relationships can be found in the Soviet situation. In confronting computerization, the average manager has been passive rather than actively hostile. The building of a system is evaluated as another run-of-the-mill campaign, and completion is declared when such routine functions as payroll are mechanized. A check-up of the level of completion of ASUPs has also revealed some deception in reporting completion.[199]

The design of the usual ASU by engineers has clearly reduced its value to line officials. Algorithms and programs often do not correspond to actual production conditions.[200] There is criticism that the functional and computational side of ASU has been stressed excessively.[201] Even among planners, economists, and other specialists, however, the new management technology has created ambivalence because it challenges their status and skills as well.

The development of ASPR, for example, has created serious anxieties among planners in Gosplan and the republican planning agencies. Their resistance has been fueled by the fear that their functions will be reduced to inputing data.[202] A similar resistance is evident in the ministries. Kantorovich has suggested that the slow expansion of optimization in the ministries can be traced to the increased responsibilities and constraints placed on officials, problems of receiving timely information, and the need to maintain continuously updated and corrected plans.[203]

The great bulk of human interaction with the computer has been accumulated at the enterprise level. The widespread distrust of ASUP has been attributed to numerous causes. A primary reason is the distrust of the information fed into the machines. The "feticization of technology" which "pushes human problems to the rear," two computer specialists have complained, simply masks the basic problems: "Objective information is not received from inaccurate sources; deviations are not detected from norms which are not present or are inaccurate."[204] More directly, Pokrovskii, the director of a branch computer design institute, indicates that the head of a functional department has little incentive to furnish full or accurate reports to line managment. He may fear loss of a bonus, have "pseudo-intellectual" motives, or may wish to avoid conflict and protect his own status. Those factors which distort information in the existing system naturally continue to function without significant change with computerization.[205]

The doubt and tension that accompany the introduction of computers is reflected in the apparently widespread practice of ignoring printouts, which often lie unused in piles in the shops. This same distrust of machine-processed information has been noted in a three-year study of a Moscow enterprise, which recorded that 62 percent of foremen and 80 percent of shop heads challenged machine recommendations. There was also a sharp increase in psychological stress among line officials. Half of the foremen went back to production.[206] Disorientation among this group was particularly severe because of loss of control over information.

Systematic study of the impact of computers on managerial behavior is still in its infancy. A Ukrainian study of the Lvov Television Plant provides some interesting, if limited, data on the expectations of managers and designers, the advantages of computerization, as well as the sources of psychological resistance.

The older and less well-educated managers agreed with the designers that computers provide more complete information, better feedback, and a basis for more rational decisions. They also agreed that computers do not contribute to personal development. Managers were more pessimistic than designers, however, on the positive role of computers in promoting innovation, increasing control over subordinates, or raising confidence in information. Managers did expect, however, computers to permit staff reductions.[207]

The study also investigated the sources of psychological resistance. The most serious anxieties were those created by threats of increased pressure and reduced status. Although less intense, fear of increased regulation by superiors and resentment of wage inequities were also significant.[208]

On the whole, it seems clear that psychological resistance, largely by middle management, may be a powerful obstacle to effective use of computers in industry. Whether further experience and training will moderate this opposition is an issue for the 1980s.

4

Modernizing the methods of management

Over the past two decades, perhaps the most complex and least successful aspect of the modernization of industrial management has been the effort to change the behavioral patterns of enterprise managers and labor. The basic objectives have been reasonably clear. The most important task has been to find methods of influencing managerial choice in order to achieve greater integration of the macro- and microeconomies. The second need has been to increase labor productivity.

The closely related objectives are distinct. To achieve greater integration by channeling managerial behavior is primarily a problem of regulating pervasive system conflicts of economic and social interests. Motivating a greater degree of cooperation and productivity is rooted, however, not only in industrial organization but also in the larger social and cultural environment. Effective rationalization of the methods of management extends beyond the enterprise, particularly with respect to labor.

The issue in the solution of both problems is how to regulate behavior in complex organizational systems in order to reduce the gap between formal and informal organizations. Theoretically, the issue touches the foundation of the political system. Since the ouster of Khrushchev in 1964, however, the political leadership has rejected either a return to comprehensive administrative controls or a far-reaching adaptation of formal organization to the pressures of the informal system. This has meant a modification rather than a basic overhauling of the classical model of management.

The ability to generate, at best, only the beginning of a modern theory of management in the 1960s and 1970s has meant that the search for more effective methods of regulation has followed decentralized and disciplinary lines. Economists have advanced the principal propositions for integrating vertical and horizontal interests and improving motivation. Sociologists and psychologists, lacking a strong theoretical and organizational basis, have concentrated on the regulation of personal and small group processes. On the macro and micro levels, the attempt to devise more effective behavioral controls has generated serious political and ideological conflict. The overlap of economic and social approaches to the problem of motivating and controlling the work force has also led to a type of interdisciplinary conflict familiar in Western industrial organization.

Economic methods and the 1965 reforms

In the perspective of two decades, the problem of more effective methods of managing industrial organization as a social system has been the most difficult aspect of the modernization of management. The shift to a cybernetic strategy of rationalization raised the possibility that the application of mathematical models and computers could eventually eliminate the need for a market in the coordination and control of economic activity. The theoretical stress by economic cybernetics on the indeterminacy of economic and social processes within very complex systems, however, has largely underscored Oskar Lange's view that a modern industrial economy is too complex to eliminate a market.[1] As the initial experience of building and operating ASUs has demonstrated, computer-based decisions are not self-executing.

The conceptions underlying the 1965 reforms were relatively simple and are familiar. Mathematical as well as more traditional economists such as A. M. Birman and Evsei Liberman proposed to transform the administrative system into a self-regulating one. More self-regulation, with a corresponding increase in system equilibrium, they argued, could be achieved by reducing the scope and frequency of macro management in the processes of micro management. The priority of systemic goals required by central planning could be ensured through a system of indirect economic and financial controls, or "levers," which simultaneously oriented the manager to national economic goals and satisfied the local interests of the enterprise. The expanded use of the contract in a limited market context would replace a large proportion of formalized administrative procedures.[2]

The contribution of cybernetic models to the development of the 1965 reforms was more theoretical and marginal. Nemchinov's model of operational planning and management clearly passed beyond the political and ideological limits of reform. The important thrust of SOFE was to increase the control of central planners over strategic rather than operational planning and management. The priority of strategic concerns in SOFE, however, did not preclude conceptualizing a system of economic and financial levers consistent with a regime of optimal decision making.

Unlike Nemchinov, Fedorenko stayed within the classical model, proposing what he described as a parametric approach to the reform of planning and control. The conception of structure advanced by SOFE, it will be remembered, was a formal hierarchy of functional subsystems operating autonomously within boundaries set by the central planners. Within this structure, the input and output parameters of each subsystem would be set by connecting a global optimum and a derivative system of shadow prices. Central and local economic interests would ultimately become harmonized through iteration. The important role of unformalized methods in SOFE presumably permitted extensive use of the market.

The strategy of optimal decision making shaped the specific proposals of economic and financial measures which should function as levers. SOFE advanced a single, synthetic indicator for measuring economic performance, a full economic evaluation of all resources, including labor, the exhaustive use of financial and credit mechanisms, and a thorough reform of the pricing system. Although there has been an unresolved tension between shadow and market-determined prices, price was assigned the principal role for orienting the interests of the enterprise to the national economic optimum. SOFE clearly required a pricing system sensitive enough to measure and to communicate relative scarcities and demands in order to implement a system of cost–benefit analysis. Minimally, this dictated that a system of prices based upon average branch costs be abolished.

The conceptions of optimal planners clearly played a marginal role in the concrete formulation of the 1965 economic reforms.

Although the measures adopted in 1965 were compatible with a cybernetic approach to systemic regulation, the language and measures of the reform were conventional, looking back, as Lewin has indicated, to the mixed economy of the New Economic Policy.[3] The more immediate source of the measures adopted in 1965 stemmed from the intense debates of the early 1960s, which arose as a counterresponse to Khrushchev's policy of administrative reform and stress on a rise of Communist Party ideological and organizational influence.[4]

The measures which emerged in 1965 after a year's debate in the Central Committee and Presidium of the Central Committee were a conservative set of proposals comprised of conflicting ideological and institutional interests.[5] The technical difficulty of constructing effective economic and financial determinants of behavior in a complex and interdependent economy naturally produced often highly abstruse debates on the details of the reform. The most important discussions, however, centered on issues of the political economy of socialism, particularly the role of the market in a socialist economy.

The use of a market as the principal institution for regulating the production and exchange of goods and services and stimulating, through competition, the behavior of industrial management was rejected. The pluralist views of Lisichkin, Buzdalov, and Bader, who argued that the market should play the role of chief regulator, were declared incompatible with socialism.[6] Even more decisively rejected was the position of A. M. Birman, who argued that a concept of socialist bankruptcy was required for effective stimulation and control. In a controversial article, he argued that without drastic economic sanctions, such as bankruptcy, economic levers would be less than effective. The socialization of the means of production reduces risk and thus "fosters irresponsibility and sluggishness among economists."[7]

Constraints on the role of the market as an instrument for promoting economic and organizational equilibrium proved decisive in maintaining the traditional hegemony of administrative and political methods of influencing managerial choice. The role of the market was highly restricted. Socialist production property, land, and natural resources could not be considered a commodity except under closely defined conditions. The market could not be used to allocate investment or to set prices. The market also could not regulate an enterprise's final output or product mix; nor could an enterprise select on a competitive basis its suppliers and customers. Until May 1970, when Minpribor was placed on *khozraschet,* or economic accountability, as an experiment, commercial principles were confined to horizontal relationships among enterprises and to the supply system.[8] The narrowly drawn role of the market naturally conditioned the choice and evolution of the economic and financial controls legislated by the reform. More importantly for the objective of modifying managerial behavior, the conservative thrust of the reform failed to change their perceptions of how the system worked.

The strategy of the reform

The measures which emerged at the September 1965 Plenum of the Central Committee, nonetheless, introduced a broad range of limited structural and functional changes in the management system. These included a return to a branch system of industrial management, an initial deconcentration of authority (signaled primarily by a cut of obligatory indicators from thirty-five or forty to nine), and a pledge to dismantle gradually the centralized system of supply. The reform also legislated new planning procedures based upon expansion of direct contracts among enterprises, new indicators for evaluating enterprise performance, a strong emphasis upon the role of interest, credit, and price in decision making, and a new incentive system designed to increase managerial interest in an efficient allocation and use of resources.[9]

The structural effect of the reform was to divide industrial management hierarchically into two decision-making blocks: a macroeconomic sector dominated by administrative methods and assigned functions of strategic planning and control; and a microeconomic sector under new rules. The complexity and interdependence of the industrial economy, however, ruled out any simple division of function between plan and market. Relatively quickly, the initial struggle of the enterprise to establish an autonomous functional sphere gave way to the traditional system of microadministrative controls. The complex of economic and financial levers began to serve as "transmission belts" linking the two blocks.[10]

As Robert Campbell has pointed out, the aggregate of measures adopted in 1965 failed to form a coherent system.[11] The impact of the economic and financial levers was additionally vitiated by the conservative form in which they were adopted.

Two of the nine obligatory planning indicators were singled out for evaluating the success of the enterprise in achieving planned goals and for forming bonus funds. The new indicators were designed to relate the enterprise more rationally to other organizations in the system and to stimulate an interest in efficiency. Both indicators were considered synthetic, measuring as well as creating a stake in the final results of the enterprises' activity.[12]

Realizatsiia, or amount of products sold, was the indicator that oriented the enterprise to its organizational and economic environment. This indicator had the dual objective of creating a stake in physical growth and in the output of goods which met the needs of consumers. The desire to correct the historic imbalance between suppliers and consumers introduced a limited application of the market. This was contained in the provision requiring the formal acceptance and payment for a consignment by the consumer before production could be counted toward plan fulfillment and the formation of bonuses.[13]

The second bonus-forming indicator, *rentabelnost,* or profitability, was adopted to stimulate and measure the efficiency of production. Profitability was calculated as the relation between income and the costs of production. Within centrally established limits, the larger the profits, the larger the incentive fund. Because the ratio of deductions from profits were to be higher for planned than for above-plan profits, the manager's interest in assuming high planned tasks and reduced inputs of capital and labor presumably would be strengthened. Bonuses were tied to the Soviet equivalent of net profit, the amount remaining after payment for resources and the demands of the budget.[14]

The active use of economic methods required a thorough overhaul of the financial, credit, and pricing mechanisms of the existing system. For the purposes of comparative monetary evaluation of enterprise performance as well as stimulating in the manager an interest in economic factors, a series of financial levers were adopted. The most important were: a capital charge; fixed and rent payments; the use of credit and interest rates for financing investment and working capital; and, most important, a basic reform of industrial wholesale prices.

A formal charge for production capital represented a sharp turning away from traditional Soviet practice. Deductions from profits for capital were set at 3 to 9 percent of capital, depending upon the profitability of the enterprise and the normative value of the enterprise's fixed and working capital. By placing an economic value on the acquisition and use of production capital, it was assumed, the traditional strategy of the enterprise in the maximal acquisition of investment and supply would be discouraged because the larger the size of capital stock, the larger the charge and the smaller the deductions from profits. By the same reasoning, the payment for resources provided an incentive for selling unneeded equipment and acquiring the most productive equipment and least expensive raw materials and components.[15]

The use of fixed and rent payments as economic levers had roughly similar purposes. Fixed payments were designed to reduce enterprise income received as the result of accidental factors, such as the production of highly profitable goods which were unrelated to the efficiency of the production process. Rent payments, however, had the task of stimulating the efficient use of natural resources and land. Directed primarily to the extractive and light industries, rent payments also had the function of equalizing the income of enterprises operating in diverse natural conditions.[16]

The reform also proposed a transition from budget financing to the use of credit for investment and working capital. The introduction of long-term credit for capital construction had the goal of creating an economic interest in the most rapid completion of construction and introduction of new capacity. Together with the other economic levers, the use of credit should also have stimulated an economic analysis of investment projects, reduced the intense bureaucratic competition for resources, and stimulated a more effective use of new capacity.[17]

A credit system for working capital, charged against profit rather than cost under the reform, was primarily intended to stimulate a reduction of above-plan inventories and indifference to waste. Shortages of normed working capital were to be covered by bank loans at varying rates of interest, and a charge placed against above-plan material resources. In the latter case, if the enterprise did not liquidate reserves, the bank had the authority to raise credit costs and, in extreme cases, reduce the reserves through forced sale.[18]

The most important and politically sensitive aspect of the reform involved the activization of price as a lever for regulating decision making. It had become increasingly evident in the decade prior to the reform that the traditional system of rigid prices, serving primarily as accounting devices and instruments of social and political policy, produced serious misallocations of resources.[19] Over the past two and a half decades the debate on the role of value in a centrally planned economy has continued. Under contemporary Soviet conditions, Volkonskii has argued, directive plans in physical terms cannot reflect sharp changes in product complexity, quality, or changes in manufacturing costs – or, he might have added, relative demand and scarcities. In his view, the observed longing for a centrally set administrative plan expressed in physical and technical indexes is a continuing manifestation of the conservative illusion that the national economy can be managed "as though it were one large factory."[20]

The objectives of the price reforms in 1966 and 1967 were complex. The conditions of the reform created a need to change the price system in such a way that each "normally operating" enterprise received the income necessary to cover costs and earn a planned profit. Prices were also expected to play a key role in harmonizing social interests through balancing supply and demand. They were to reflect more sensitively actual production costs as a means of comparative evaluation of enterprise economic performance. Prices were also expected to communicate information on demand and to stimulate an interest in efficient resource utilization, improved quality, and technological innovation. Finally, prices would continue to play a central role in the planned distribution of the social product.[21]

In the simplest and most abstract terms, the central issue was how a reformed pricing system could achieve these multiple, complex, and potentially conflicting objectives. The initially severe political and ideological constraints on the market as a primary instrument for setting prices inevitably focused the search within the framework of the classical normative and deductive approach to price setting. This search has taken two basic directions. The first has been to develop model-based prices derived from optimal planning. The second and more intensive search has been to revise the traditional methodologies and procedures of administrative price setting.

One of the initial and strongest attractions of optimal planning has been the conviction expressed by a leading group of economists within CEMI that a system of optimal planning can theoretically produce through shadow prices a fully normative price system, which eliminates the necessity for a market.[22] This ability derives from the fact that the solution of a linear programming problem assigns values (shadow prices) to the limiting factors of production. Linear programming can also solve the problem of optimal pricing directly and thus produce a solution to optimal allocation. The use of shadow prices as a substitute for the market, however, has been controversial. The outlines of the debate have been reflected in the conflicting views of L. V. Kantorovich and V. V. Novozhilov.

Kantorovich has become publicly associated over the years with the concept of "objectively conditioned" (constrained) prices, which are directly derived from the optimal plan. Although his views and those of V. V. Novozhilov are assumed to be very close, Manevich points out that Kantorovich views the optimal plan and shadow prices as directive and formed independently of the market.[23] For Novozhilov, on the other hand, the programmed solution is the starting point for subsequent corrections (iterations), which incorporate social demand. As Manevich notes: "For L. V. Kantorovich the optimal plan is the most rational distribution of resources and concrete tasks for the fulfillment of an earlier constructed plan. For V. V. Novozhilov the optimal plan is a plan of social production which corresponds to the largest degree to social demand."[24] Kantorovich has judged price formation as a well-structured problem subject to a determinate solution. For Novozhilov, optimal price formation is an ill-structured problem. SOFE has clearly chosen Novozhilov's position, which is consistent with a parametric price approach.

The search for a model-based pricing system that narrowly limits the role of the market has been a primary reason for the development of ASOItsen, discussed in Chapter 3. Within ASOItsen, the most important function is the eventual automation of the process of constructing and correcting the industrial price lists formed in the State Committee of Prices. An expanded use of computers in price setting, however, requires solution of some complex methodological problems, which include building an adequate data base and necessary algorithms and programs for computing the price lists. More important are such unresolved questions as the best methodology for calculating prices and what price-forming parameters can best measure differentiated expenditures and consumer utilities.[25] Model-based pricing is still experimental.[26]

The second and dominant thrust of the reform of price-setting procedures was to revise the traditionally normative approach. Within this framework, the price reforms of 1966 and 1967, the first major reform of industrial wholesale prices since 1955, were required to iron out the widely varying rates of profitability among branches and to reduce the irrational system of subsidies which had developed in such industries as ferrous metallurgy and coal.[27] Without some initial rationalization of the existing system of prices, comparative economic analysis was virtually impossible. Price reform was also required to cover increased costs created by the economic levers.

The price reforms continued the traditional formula of cost-plus pricing. The strategy of the reform, however, required some degree of price flexibility. The reform introduced a new principle in the formula for pricing according to average branch costs. The new formula calculated prices as the sum of production costs plus a profit markup computed as a ratio of assets. The general normative or standard rate was set at 15 percent for industry, but exceptions were made for political and economic reasons. Fifteen percent, for example, tended to be too high in capital-intensive industries and too low in less capital-intensive industries and therefore required adjustment.[28]

The new formula had the consequence of complicating the methodology for calculating wholesale prices. It became impossible to apply branch normatives of profitability directly to the pricing of individual products because of the impossibility of direct measurement of the amount of assets used to produce any single product under widely varying conditions. To align enterprise profits with standard branch profitability rates, a complex methodology developed. The methodology consists of finding a standard branch rate of profit in relation to production costs for a given product for the branch as a whole. This ratio is then applied to the planned ruble costs of the product, and the price is adjusted to conform to branch profitability norms. This price

may be further adjusted administratively to achieve such purposes as the encouragement or reduction of the production of
specific products.[29]

In many respects, the setting of current wholesale prices has
been overshadowed by the role of price as a lever for technical
innovation, a key ingredient in the intensive strategy of growth
stressed in the 1970s. Price has been used to stimulate an interest
in higher-quality products by establishing a direct relation between price and product quality.[30] The development of a pricing
methodology for stimulating technical innovation, however, has
been an extremely complex task. The stimulating force of industrial wholesale prices should be high enough to interest producers to make new products but low enough to interest consumers
in using them. The effort to balance these conflicting interests
and tendencies was the goal of a complex methodology adopted
in 1969 and revised in 1974.[31]

The principal techniques for reconciling the interest of the
enterprise in highly profitable products and the social interest in
low-priced, high-quality goods have been temporary and
stepped prices. Both techniques attempt to provide a consciously
controlled dynamic for price change which creates an interest in
product innovation.

Although temporary prices were a usual practice in prereform
pricing policy, primarily as exceptions to standard prices, the
present use of temporary price for new products is designed to
establish at the start of production a price which is high enough
to cover start-up costs plus a normal profit. When initial costs are
recovered, a second, lower, permanent price is set for the product in line with the profit levels of the branch's normal output.[32]
Stepped prices offer another alternative for a system of dated
prices. Over a stated period of time, the price of a new product
changes at preset time intervals from an initially high and advantageous price to a lower, less profitable price. The use of price in
implementing a policy of planned obsolescence, however, particularly for stepped prices, has been plagued by serious methodological difficulties.[33]

The third aspect of the application of economic methods to
enterprise management was the effort to link incentives with
efficient enterprise performance. Three enterprise funds were
created for the purpose of stimulating efficiency: a material in-

centive fund for providing bonuses; a social-cultural fund for the construction of housing, nurseries, kindergartens, and other amenities; and a production development fund, formed from profits, amortization, and the proceeds of sale of equipment and unneeded supply.

The most important of these three funds was the material incentive fund, which was formed in a complicated way. In order to maintain an acceptable ratio between wages and bonuses and to control their size, the bonus fund was fixed as a percentage of the wage fund, which was centrally planned. The formula adopted for deductions from calculated profits into the incentive funds was complex and usually adapted to the circumstances of the individual plant. The formula for the Frezer Machine-Building Plant, for example, was one in which 0.9 percent of the wage fund was deducted into the incentive fund for each 1 percent growth in the amount of products sold over the preceding year and 0.2 percent of the wage fund for each 1 percent of profitability.[34] Because there was a continuous tendency of individual plant totals to diverge relative to branch norms, administrative intervention by the ministry became frequent.

The impact of the reform

An event of the magnitude of the 1965 reforms clearly may have long-term, latent consequences which cannot be fully evaluated. Over the shorter term, however, there is little surprise that its economic and organizational impact appears marginal. Under the reform, economic growth rates were lower than expected; return on capital improved slowly; and technical innovation and labor productivity continued to lag.[35] Suboptimization, adjusted to the new conditions, also remained the dominant pattern of managerial behavior. As an instrument for harmonizing conflicting social and economic interests, the reform clearly failed to close the traditional gap between global and local interests or between formal and informal organization.[36]

The decision to abandon the 1965 economic reforms as the principal strategy of rationalization, announced by Brezhnev in December 1969, clearly involved more than a failure to stimulate efficiency. The shift in strategies, noted in the previous chapter, appears as part of the conservative reaction to the ideological, political, and administrative pluralization which surfaced in Soviet society coincidentally with the reform.[37] Confronted in 1968 with a choice of expanding a market-based strategy of reform, which he appears to have opposed, Brezhnev appears to have turned to a potentially less divisive solution.[38]

The reduced importance of economic and financial levers in the strategy of rationalization in the 1970s remains of interest, however, because it is clear that a technical approach does not resolve the issues of managing industrial organization as a social system. In view of the increasing complexity of the environment and urgent needs for greater efficiency, the problem of developing effective institutional modes for influencing managerial behavior will be as acute in the 1980s as it was in the 1960s. A relatively close look at the consequences of the specific measures adopted in 1965 for decision making may be useful.

As a historical event, the compromised and conservative form in which the reform was legislated and implemented was a primary factor in reducing its impact. The retention of the basic framework of the command economy virtually assured the continuation of the functional characteristics associated with it. The conditions largely responsible for the traditional conflict between formal and informal organization were essentially unmodified, so suboptimization continued as well.

The marginal impact of the reform can also be traced to the lack of coherence of the measures adopted. As a system, the specific measures were complex and contradictory, worked at cross-purposes, and pulled managers in opposing directions. Under these conditions their stimulative influence was insufficient to overcome the force of institutional inertia.

The operational deficiencies of the reform can be traced in the first instance to the technical difficulties of constructing objective and rational general normatives for the planning and control of a complex industrial economy. In conformity with the classical paradigm of organization, the search has been for a universal standard or fixed ratios for regulating economic and organizational relationships, which have been noted previously in this chapter. This issue is found at the center of every aspect of the rationalization of industrial organization. It is at the core of such questions as building mathematical models and designing ASUs as well as developing pricing methodologies or constructing standard, industrywide normatives for forming incentive funds.[39] The combination of conservative conceptualization and implementation and technical deficiencies of the reform may perhaps explain the "psychological barriers" which the managers raised to blunt the operation of economic methods of management. Their failure to adapt, however, may have had other, more subjective sources. The managers approached the reform situationally, reacting to specific measures in a variety of ways. Generally, however, the managers reacted to the reform with a noticeable lack of enthusiasm.[40] Age, training, and experience have given the average industrial manager little taste or skill for dealing effectively with the specific uncertainties created by a market. His traditional uncertainties and skills are of a different order.

The failure of the new success indicators to exercise the expected leverage on managerial behavior was a major blow to the credibility of the reform. The concept of making bonuses directly dependent upon efficient performance should have encouraged managers to undertake tight plans, reduce demands for excessive resources, and stimulate an interest in a more efficient utilization of the factors of production and meeting consumer demand. That they did not can be attributed to their design and implementation.[41]

The indicator of profits sold retained many of the flaws of the traditional quantitative indicators it replaced.[42] The new indicator, however, was not uniformly applied. Many key products in the extractive and machine-building industries continued to be planned in physical terms. In addition, particularly in large urban areas, the labor shortage, constraints on capital, and lack of space objectively limited the expansion of production of many plants. Finally, the traditional practice of planning from achieved levels was retained. The retention of the ratchet principle under the new system naturally worked as a powerful anti-stimulus to taut plans and reduced inventories.[43]

The provision that only products accepted and paid for by the consumer were part of plan fulfillment failed to improve either the assortment or quality of production. The division of the product mix into "advantageous" and "disadvantageous" products continued; the indicator stimulated material intensity by encouraging the use of expensive raw materials and components as a means of inflating a product's price.[44] Under these conditions, the expected feedback from the market dissipated because the enterprise continued to operate in a seller's market and to rely upon an administrative price system.

This provision did, however, add a new complication. Even when the producer fulfilled the plan for deliveries according to contract, delinquent payment by the customer caused plan failure.[45] *Tolkachi,* or "pushers," soon extended their accustomed hunt for inputs to the collections of payment for outputs.

The presence of two bonus-forming indicators naturally encouraged the managers to play games with them. The profitability indicator quickly became the preferred one. Toward the end of the Eighth Five-Year Plan, N. E. Drogichinskii, the chairman of the commission implementing the reform, complained that up to 70 percent of the inventive fund was formed from profitability and only 30 percent from products sold.[46]

Profitability was the more ambiguous indicator and opened up to the managers numerous options for acquiring an adequate level of deductions from profits should the plant's rate of growth decline. The principal difficulty with profitability from the central planner's perspective was its negative impact on technical innovation. Profits for bonus-forming purposes were based upon income after payments, so the manager was reluctant to add to assessed value of capital. This, in turn, discouraged investment by the more profitable enterprises but stimulated it in the presumably less efficient. It also encouraged delaying technical innovation until the end of the planning year in order to maintain stable capital assessments.[47]

The second major set of measures embodied in the reform was initially designed to reinforce the stimulation of the new success indicators. Payment for resources, rent, the replacement of budget financing with interest-bearing credit, together with the new principles of price formation were also to improve resource allocation. In the overall conception of the reform, these measures would modify the manager's behavior by influencing levels of profit and profitability. The manager, primarily interested in increasing the total level of profits from which bonuses were formed, would logically have an interest in acquiring the most productive technologies and most efficient use of resources. The basic objective of reorienting the manager toward the intensive use of resources, however, succeeded only marginally. The cardinal issue of level of profit went to the heart of the reform. The maximum or unlimited pursuit of profit by a ministry or enterprise clearly violated the basic principles of a planned socialist economy. The use of a planned or fixed level of profit need not, but actually did, serve as an antistimulus to a more efficient allocation of resources. Under the normative for planned profits, set generally at 15 percent, the enterprise was permitted to retain only a portion of income as profit. The problem arose from the divergence of planned and actual profits during the reform. Between 1965 and 1973, actual profits grew 2.6 times, but planned rates only doubled.[48] The difference was the "free remainder" of profits, which were automatically deducted into the budget at the end of the year. In 1975 the free remainder of profits was about 35 percent of all industrial profits.

The presence of a limit on profits and a free remainder naturally exercised a strong counterinfluence on the stimulating effect of these measures. As long as the enterprise met the planned rate of profit, by whatever means, any lack of efficiency went unpenalized. The presence of above-plan profits also weakened decisively the impact of payment for resources, rent, interest, and other measures because these could be absorbed as costs without influencing bonuses. Under such circumstances, the connection between profits and incentives became tenuous. A survey of twenty-three thousand industrial enterprises in 1969 indicated that, if 39 percent of the enterprises failed to achieve the 15 percent rate on assets, 61 percent exceeded it. Thirty percent had a profitability rate of 40 percent or over.[49]

The impact of the charge for assets was weakened by factors other than the free remainder of profits. The charge for assets was kept deliberately low at 6 percent (3 percent for the coal industry), which was calculated to be only half of the normative required for measuring the effectiveness of capital investment. Moreover, not all assets were subject to a capital charge. Gertrude Schroeder has estimated that as much as 30 percent of the fixed and 50 percent of the working capital were exempted from evaluation, a condition which further reduced its value as an instrument of economic evaluation.[50]

In addition, the full costs for labor were excluded from evaluation. Of greater importance, the level of norms remained fixed and lagged behind the growth of profits. The result was that in the most profitable industries – petrochemicals and oil refining, metallurgy and metalworking, and light industry – the normative payment for assets had virtually no impact. Such practices as the use of obsolescent equipment and above-plan reserves of uninstalled equipment, including computers, remained untouched.[51]

The provision for fixed payments and rent also had little operational influence. Fixed payments were too small, were given a low priority by the ministry, and presented formidable methodological difficulties. Approximately 90 percent of rent payments were made by oil, gas, and light industries. The coal industry, however, was exempted. In addition, rent charges were too low and were based upon the tonnage of products sold rather than extracted. The result was that no payment was made for the value of resources lost, an important consideration under conditions of deteriorating resources.[52]

The use of credit as a lever also had a relatively weak influence on managerial decision making. The original expectation was that long-term credit would fund a high proportion of new construction and reduce the amount of budget financing and bureaucratic competition for resources.[53] The decline of budgetary financing of investment since the reform has been small. For projects financed by Stroibank, the share of the budget fell from 58 percent in 1966 to 48 percent in 1975.

The share of credit in funding capital investment, however, has remained a low 3 percent of the total. An investigation of long-term credit between 1970 and 1973 of twenty-three industrial ministries indicated that the budget financed about 35 percent of investment, and 58 to 60 percent was generated from other sources. The resort to bank loans varied widely, however, among ministries. Whereas loans financed up to 40.6 percent of the investment of the Ministry of Chemical Machine Building, they financed only 13.6 percent of the needs of the Ministry of the Electrotechnical Industry.[54]

The ministries' avoidance of long-term financing through

loans, despite the initially low interest rate of 0.5 percent, can be attributed to numerous factors. The period of the loan was limited to five years, and most major Soviet construction projects required eight to ten years to complete. Secondly, the ministries have been less than eager for increased bank control. Finally, there has been an alternative source of financing. Capital investment could be internally financed from high profits created by high prices, from excessively low payments for assets, and from the free remainder of profits. Internal financing was also aided through the internal redistribution of enterprise resources.[55]

An increased use of short-term credit for working capital has also been modest; the banks financed 42.6 percent of working capital in 1965, and 44.5 percent in 1972.[56] The banks have not engaged in highly restrictive credit practices with respect to deficits of working capital for payments for goods and services or for wages. Currently about 75 percent of all transfer payments are credited by Gosbank, and an estimated 18 percent of all loans have been made for crediting excessive expenditures and inventories.[57] In large part, the weak stimulating impact of short-term credit can be traced to the extremely low (2 percent) interest rate and to the fact that they have averaged only 2.8 percent of enterprise profits.[58] Even this small sum can be absorbed by the free remainder of profits.

Finally, the activization of price as a lever for stimulating efficiency or technical innovation has been extremely modest. Between 1966 and 1974, in the assessment of Morris Bornstein, enterprise wholesale prices rose 9 percent and branch prices 8 percent and thus were highly stable. The largest increases instituted by the 1967 price reform were in heavy industry, particularly in coal, ferrous metallurgy, petroleum, and electric power. The light and food industries remained stable, and some reductions occurred in the machine-building, metalworking, and chemical industries. One positive result has been to improve the relation of price to cost.[59]

The allocative and stimulative influence of the price reform has been marginal. The economy continued to form "cost-plus-nonscarcity prices, which inadequately reflect and often ignore demand and which frequently conflict with enterprise input and output plans, requiring plan directives and administrative rationing to 'override' the 'signals' provided by prices."[60] As with other aspects of the reform, it has become increasingly clear that current methodologies for forming prices have failed to address the conflicting demands and interests which have accompanied Soviet socioeconomic development. The failure to incorporate consumer utilities or to reconcile the demand for stability and flexibility have been among the most significant limitations of the reform.

The marginally positive or antistimulative role of price is not easily disengaged from the factors with which price is in continuous interaction. The relatively low stimulative effect of the price reform is clearly attributable only in part to methodological difficulties. As the plan–market debate of the 1960s illustrated, price and the other economic levers serve the political and administrative needs of the regime, rather than the reverse. Although the activization of price assumed that it would play an energizing and coordinative function, the tight administrative boundaries placed on the functioning of price ensured that its traditional control functions would retain priority. The use of price as an instrument for controlling profitability helped to promote a chain of secondary reactions which conflicted with some of the primary goals of the reform.[61]

A primary instance of the limited role of price in stimulating efficient allocation of resources is the use of settlement prices in the extractive industries. Settlement prices are formed in a dual price system designed to equalize the profitability of enterprises operating in highly diverse natural conditions. The product is priced for the enterprise according to its individual costs of production but sold according to average branch prices. The dual system, however, separates price from cost and serves frequently to subsidize high-cost and inefficient operations in industries of increasingly scarce resources.[62]

The use of cost-plus as a control over profitability had an equally limited effect in resolving the inherent conflict between the interests of the central planners in low prices and maximum output and the manager's interest in increasing profitability and reduced output. The manager found it an advantage to choose the less labor-intensive production strategy and to increase the costs of materials and components, undeterred by the influence of the payment for assets and interest rates on loans. The division of products into "advantageous" and "nonadvantageous" products, as noted earlier in this chapter, continued without serious change.[63] The managers found it equally useful to avoid excessive commitments to either high-quality output or technical innovation. Such innovations in price formation as the use of stepped prices for new technology have had modest success. Methodological problems of forecasting technical and economic change within a formally controlled price structure, however, have been serious. More important, perhaps, has been the ease with which temporary prices could be manipulated without undertaking the arduous and risky task of innovation.[64]

Under conditions in which price levels became critical to forming income, the managers quickly developed a series of illegal and marginal practices which led to a reform of the State Price Committee in 1970. To raise prices, the managers frequently affirmed prices legally within the authority of the price committee. They padded costs, and the ministries used temporary prices for long periods of time without submitting them to the price committee. More rarely, the ministry put into effect prices which the State Price Committee had refused to confirm.[65]

As the third major innovation introduced in 1965 to restructure managerial patterns of behavior, the new incentive system was designed to interact positively and reciprocally with the new success indicators and economic and financial levers. The marginal impact of these measures naturally reduced the stimulating effects of the incentive system. The new incentive system also had its own particular flaws. Its impact on managerial decision making was therefore complex and, in certain respects, contradictory. It stimulated little interest in the efficient use of resources.

The original conception of making bonuses directly dependent upon profits was initially weakened by the decision to stabilize the size of the fund by linking it with the planned wage fund rather than as a ratio of a variable indicator such as profits. The stimulus of the incentive fund was further reduced by wide differences in formation and distribution within industry. The ministry frequently manipulated the funds, independently of the efficiency of the plant's operation, to bring enterprise funds into line with branch norms.[66] The actual policy of incentive distribution, moreover, has been contradictory. The policy had been to minimize the stimulative role of incentives formed from profits on the production worker but to maximize its impact on the managerial staff.

Throughout the Ninth Five-Year Plan, the incentive fund has averaged 9 to 10 percent of the wage fund. As a portion of the worker's income, incentives have risen from 8.7 percent in 1965 to 16.3 percent in 1973. In the interest of income stability and the prevention of labor turnover, only about half (8.1 percent), however, was formed from the incentive fund. The other half was formed from the wage fund.[67] The trade-off between stimulation and stability is also indicated in the distribution of premiums to the production worker. Approximately 50 percent of the fund has been paid for the results of the year, the so-called thirteenth-month wage. Only 38 percent of the incentives have been paid for current premiums, which are the principal instrument for stimulating efficiency. The force of current premiums has been further reduced through the practice of disbursing it for numerous purposes, including the increase of labor productivity and quality of output. The impact of these latter incentives, however, has been negligible, averaging only 1.4 percent of the average industrial worker's wage.[68]

In contrast to the indifferent impact of the incentive system on the interests of the industrial worker, the influence of the reform's incentive system on the managerial staff has been significant. Under conditions of the reform, all premiums for ITR have been formed from the incentive fund and have constituted between 20 and 30 percent of income and frequently more.[69] In addition, up to 1971, current premiums were the sole form of distribution. The direct dependence of a sizable portion of the income of plant managers and engineering personnel upon the success indicators has been buffered to a degree by the system of special bonuses, but often with negative consequences. Special bonus systems for the delivery of wastes and scrap metal, for example, pay higher amounts than those incentive systems for saving metal.[70]

The provision carried over from the prereform period of depriving the manager of all bonuses for the slightest underfulfillment of the plan pushed the managers in the direction of caution. This was particularly evident with respect to decisions

on labor productivity and the observance of contracts for deliveries.
To some extent, the interests of the enterprise director were split by the provisions of the reform. The indicator for the amount of products sold actually tended to reduce labor intensity and to stress material intensity. The countervailing pressure of the fear of a labor shortage and the rule tying the incentive fund to the size of the wage, however, proved to be the stronger. The manager continued to hoard labor, overstate requests for the wage fund, and search for the lowest possible indicator (under 3 percent, if possible) for labor productivity.[71] In conflict with the goal of the central planners to raise labor productivity in conditions of a growing labor shortage, the managers had a disincentive for the introduction of NOT and, with other reasons, for promoting labor-saving technologies.[72]

The role of economic sanctions, noted in Chapter 1, continued to have a relatively minor impact on the control of managerial behavior. As in the prereform period, fines and other financial sanctions were confined to the enterprise, were too small (1.6 percent of profits), and could, with good management, be charged against the free remainder of profits or included in production costs. Economic sanctions continued to be weakened by the practice of "balancing" fines paid by fines received. For all practical purposes, industrial managers remained without personal liability. Finally, enterprises retained their reluctance to apply for economic sanctions for fear of jeopardizing future relationships.[73] The perception of managerial indifference to economic sanctions led to A. M. Birman's suggestion that some form of drastic sanction such as bankruptcy was required to make economic incentives and sanctions work.

In the 1970s the basic conceptions of the reform have been quietly abandoned. With the shift to a new strategy of rationalization, the dominant thrust in behavioral control in industry has continued to be conservative. The use of indirect economic controls and enterprise self-management has been downplayed with the reinvigoration of direct political and administrative controls. The number of obligatory planning indicators has expanded; methods for forming incentive funds changed; and the role of political mobilization and Party leadership strongly reasserted.

In an evident effort to control the new as well as the older forms of suboptimization, additional obligatory planning indicators were added in June 1971 for labor productivity, the production of the most important types of products in physical terms, and specification of the ratio of new products in the enterprise's total output.[74] Since 1975, in an attempt to eliminate the traditional distinction between "advantageous" and "nonadvantageous" production, the fulfillment of economic contracts became an additional obligatory condition for plan fulfillment.[75] The return to a multiplicity of physical planning indicators to evaluate the performance of the enterprise has, in effect, returned the system of planning to its prereform condition.

The return to physical indicators as well as the desire of the central planners to exert more control over income and labor productivity has also resulted in changing the methods for forming incentive funds. The relationship between profitability and the size of the bonus fund was eliminated. Bonuses as well as wages and salaries are now fixed at the beginning of the five-year plan and adjusted for each of the annual plans. Greater centralized control has also been established over the formation of the social–cultural fund. Since 1972, this fund is formed as a percentage of the bonus fund, and 60 percent must be spent on plant housing and other social needs. In an effort to extend the horizons of managerial decision making, managers are now paid bonuses for the results of the year as well as for current plan fulfillment.[76]

Changes in other provisions of the reform have been minor. There has been no change in the charge for assets, although debts to the bank as well as obligations to the budget must be met before deductions into the incentive funds are made. In August 1973, short-term interest rates were doubled; the length of the period of maturity extended; and the level of formal bank control increased.[77] In June 1976, the control of the State Bank was also extended over the wage fund to control its chronic overexpenditure.[78]

To compensate for the marginal impact of the reform on efficiency, traditional techniques of political mobilization, including a primary emphasis upon socialist competition, were strengthened in 1971. Undoubtedly, Brezhnev touched a deep nerve in December 1969 when he argued that effective organization of labor was "unthinkable without appropriate organization, ensuring strict discipline, correct evaluation of labor of each worker and different collectives, uniting the strength of millions and millions of workers in a single and purposeful force."[79]

An important dimension of the campaign headed by the Communist Party apparatus has been the introduction of *vstrechnoe* (counter) planning. In the process of planning, the local Party committee imposes higher planning targets on the enterprise than those assigned by the ministry during the regular planning process. By 1975, more than seventeen thousand plants and production associations had assumed counterplans. The formalization of what has been an important informal control function of the Party *apparat*, however, contributes to the microimbalance of the economy. Counterplans are not usually accompanied by increases in supply.[80]

The return to conservative methods of mobilization and control which have accompanied Brezhnev's rise to political dominance is clearly not a satisfactory long-term solution to the problems of coordination and control of the industrial economy. By the mid-1970s, the problem of developing effective economic methods of management had reached an impasse. In summarizing the problems of industrial management, Academician Khachaturov observed that, for a problem such as effective planning indicators, no ideal solution was apparent. Each of the local indicators had advantages and disadvantages with respect to economic efficiency.[81] Similar judgments can be made about other economic measures or indicators designed to integrate formal and informal organization and to raise economic efficiency. The turn in the 1970s to scientific methods of management, computers, and organizations of scale does not obviate the need for cooperative human relationships within Soviet industry but rather strengthens the need as it complicates its solution.

The human side of management

It is evident that traditional administrative and economic methods of management have retained their dominance through the 1970s. The role of behavioral sciences and methodologies has remained secondary. On balance, their contribution appears less in the achievement of specific results than in a redefinition of the problems of industry from the perspectives of social integration and psychological motivation. The contribution of the empirical social sciences to the larger problems of socioeconomic development has been limited, despite the emphasis upon global socioeconomic planning. As a general strategy, a purely functional approach based upon social systems theory has been beyond the pale of political legitimacy. The introduction of Parsons into Soviet sociology generated a severe conflict between the traditional ideologists and proponents of functional analysis. Its climax occurred in November 1969 at a conference of the Academy of Social Sciences of the CPSU. The defenders of historical materialism severely attacked Iurii Levada, a leading Moscow University sociologist, for his apoliticism and Parsonian thought.[82]

The complexity and urgency of the problems confronting Soviet society, however, have been such that the exclusive role of the ideologists in defining social development has not been fully restored; to accommodate the conflicting claims of historical materialism and the social sciences, a series of complex and probably unstable compromises have emerged.

Marxist ideological categories have been firmly clamped upon the social sciences. To reduce the gap between conventional sociopolitical categories and concrete social and political processes, the social sciences have assumed the role of a "third layer," mediating the relationship between ideology and social policy.[83] This role appears characteristic of all the middle-range social disciplines, including management science.

In conformity with the basic thrust evident in the reform of economic management, the dominant methodological approach to the analysis of social problems generally has been cybernetics. For example, by 1974, Peter Juviler has noted, legal cybernetics had become the most rapidly expanding subdiscipline within legal science for developing programs to control criminal behavior. The utility of mathematical models and computers for developing large-scale programs of social control is potentially very great. The experience of the 1970s of constructing social models, discussed later in this chapter, however, tends to confirm Juviler's skepticism as to the ultimate value of cybernetic methods in contributing to the control of criminal behavior.[84]

The most basic issue to arise in addressing problems of the

human side of management has been the relative roles of mechanistic and organic approaches to the issues of industrial organization. The conflict between technical and social approaches continues in modified form the extended controversies of NEP. To counter the biases of Taylorism, the NOT movement in the 1920s carried a sociological dimension.[85]

The blending of mechanistic and organic approaches into an effective strategy is clearly no easier under present conditions than it was during NEP. For practical purposes, there have been two distinct conceptions and methodologies for reconciling conflicting social interests and for raising labor productivity. Social planning has been the principal instrument for blending them into a coherent strategy of rationalization. Examined in isolation, neither approach has been particularly effective.

The restricted impact of NOT on labor productivity is partially a result of the low status it retains from the Stalinist period. More importantly, NOT is in conflict with the vital economic interests of the managers in maintaining a labor reserve. NOT has also been hampered by a lack of qualified specialists and training facilities. Departments of NOT are usually small and poorly equipped, and an estimated 40 percent of their time is spent on other tasks. The low status of NOT is indicated by the practice of firing NOT specialists first during any staff cut.[86]

The application of behavioral methods has been constrained even more severely by organizational problems, low status, and inadequately trained specialists. In addition, behavioral science still lacks full legitimacy and a defined policy role.

The lack of trained professional industrial sociologists and psychologists is directly related to the ideological conflicts accompanying the rise of the behavioral sciences. Conservative ideologists, fearing the secularizing effects and competition from the expansion of empirical sociology, have successfully prevented establishment of specialized institutions for training sociologists. As a result, virtually all factory sociologists have been trained in part-time classes or by correspondence.[87] The training of industrial psychologists is only marginally better. Only Yaroslavl University has a program for training this specialty.[88] The problem of competence is compounded by elitist attitudes. Only 1 percent of sociologists with higher education work in the enterprise. They prefer better-paying and more prestigious work in research.

One of the core issues underlying the ideological conflicts of the late 1960s was the question of whether the role of the behavioral scientist was that of social critic or social engineer. In the aftermath of the reorganization in 1972 of the Institute of Concrete Social Research, the role of sociology as an instrument of the goals and policies of the Communist Party was strongly reasserted. M. N. Rutkevich, the institute's new director, declared sociology to be a Party science and the sociologist an ideologically committed observer. His role was not that "of a physician whose function is supposedly the cure of the illnesses of society" but of a specialist who supplies scientific data for decision making.[89]

Throughout the 1970s, Soviet behavioral scientists have undoubtedly been coopted into support of the formal organization. They have, nonetheless, played an ameliorative role, arguing for the humanization of labor. Their self-defined role has been to overcome what they conceive as the narrow technical and economic approaches of the engineer and economist to human relations in the enterprise.[90] They have naturally emerged as critics of Taylorism and the mechanistic approach to improving motivation and social control. Citing U.S. data, for example, Klimov has argued that Taylorism is exhausted; future gains in labor productivity will come from social factors.[91]

Soviet behavioral scientists have also been critical of the heavy stress placed upon formal organization and procedures in the classical NOT approach to the reform of management structures. Kosenko, an organizational psychologist, has expressed an interest in the "federative approach" of American organizational scientists to balancing planned and spontaneous behavior. Citing with approval Gouldner's and Selznick's criticism of the capacity of formal organization to control human behavior comprehensively, he also notes the views of McGregor and Argyris on the importance of informal norms and spontaneity in the execution of organizational tasks.[92]

The criticism of NOT as a strategy of rationalization has concentrated primarily on leadership in small groups, which is discussed in Chapter 5. The treatment of the traditional organizational culture and managerial behavior by behavioral scientists has been strikingly ameliorative. They have argued that the extreme emphasis upon formal authority creates an inherent tendency toward "technocracy," or the elimination of the human factor in management, a reduction in initiative among subordinates, and a growth in suboptimization.[93]

In the interaction of the mechanistic and organic approaches to rationalizing the methods of management, there has naturally been overlap and interpenetration. Plans of NOT are organized separately and implemented individually. In the 1970s, however, they have also become a component in the broader movement for social planning, which also may include the results of social research. Initiatives and implementation of both types of plans have been decentralized. Their impact, therefore, has been extremely uneven.

The movement for NOT

In the 1970s the movement for NOT has been specifically directed toward increasing labor productivity as a means of relieving the labor shortage. NOT clearly has been subordinate to technological innovation as a means of increasing labor productivity. The role of NOT in meeting the shortfall of labor is, nonetheless, important. In the Tenth Five-Year Plan, NOT is targeted to eliminate 1,600,000 jobs. Through 1978, 1,123,000 jobs reportedly have been eliminated.[94]

Over the past dozen years, the movement for NOT has developed in three principal directions. The first has been setting technical output norms and wage rates and organization of labor, principally through time and motion studies. A second important direction which has become particularly significant in the 1970s has been experimentation with various forms of the collective organization of labor. The third and most publicized of the NOT initiatives has been the effort to reduce traditional overmanning through the Shchekino experiment.

The policy of substantially increasing wages during the Ninth Five-Year Plan assumed a corresponding tightening of traditionally loose labor norms. This pressure was generated not only to raise labor productivity but also to bring labor norms closer to technological potential and to control overexpenditures of the wage fund. By 1978, technical norms had been set for almost 80 percent of the industrial workers and about 58 percent of technical and administrative workers.[95]

The actual increase in tension of industrial labor norms in the

1970s has largely depended upon the policy of the individual ministry and the intensity with which the territorial Party apparatus has pressed the issue. There has undoubtedly been marginal to moderate success in raising labor norms. In the machine-building industries, a principal target, average overfulfillment of norms has reportedly been cut from 135 to 118 percent. Forty percent of these workers continued, however, to overfulfill the norms by 120 percent or more, and only 6.9 percent failed to make the new norms.[96] The traditional complaint remains that much of technical norming is a formality and that labor norms continue to be seriously understated.[97]

An increase in labor productivity through expansion of the scope of technical norming has experienced serious problems for familiar reasons. Technical norming is decentralized and conducted by too few poorly trained and paid personnel. Technical norming, relatively simple in plants using mass or continuous technologies, is a difficult project in conditions employing more complex production technologies. Most important, of course, has been the expected resistance of the ministries and enterprises to any reduction in the labor reserve, particularly in view of the labor shortage. Without fundamental change in the system of planning and supply, increased labor norms threaten higher plans, a reduced wage fund, and a possible increase in labor turnover.

The second major thrust of NOT, the brigade organization of labor, has a sociological as well as mobilizational thrust. Still in an experimental stage, brigade organization has three basic features. Jobs become interchangeable; jobs are also enlarged and combined; and, finally, bonuses depend upon the production results of the brigade as a whole.

The intensification of interdependence within the brigade has social as well as economic objectives. The first is to expand social control over young workers and to reduce turnover. The second is to reduce the monotony of the assembly line as well as actually to increase labor norms. The provision for collective bonuses will presumably intensify social pressure within the brigade for higher productivity.[98] That increased social pressure may also strengthen the capacity to enforce restrictive informal norms appears to have been overlooked.

The model for the brigade organization of labor has been the

Volga Automobile Plant (VAZ). Through 1978, the VAZ system has been adopted in twenty-six plants and is in the process of adoption of fifty-two more. Integrated brigades have reported 15 to 20 percent higher labor productivity and 7 to 8 percent higher wages than traditional brigades.[99]

Conceptually, the VAZ system is simple. All workers in the plant are placed in production brigades of one hundred to three hundred men or in brigades of thirty-five to forty auxiliary workers. No worker is assigned to a permanent job or machine. As the result of job enlargement and combination, high norms of output are assigned. The wage system has eliminated both time and piece rates. Production workers are paid according to permanent and temporary rates. Sixty percent of total income is paid according to the individual worker's qualifications and skills, and 40 percent on the collective results of the brigade's work.[100] The VAZ system clearly places a premium on highly productive technology, and for this as well as other reasons its expansion has met stiff opposition from the ministries.

The most publicized and established of the NOT directions to raise labor productivity has been the Shchekino experiment. The experiment was adopted in 1967 at the Shchekino Nitrogen Association in the Ministry of the Chemical Industry. The objective of the experiment has been to provide the enterprise or association with economic incentives to reduce personnel and to encourage job enlargement and combination.

Expanding the Shchekino method has been a special project of the Central Committee. It originated in Tula, whose provincial Party committee placed the majority of plants in the province under the experiment and took direct charge of the redistribution of workers among different ministries. Where local Party committees have been less active, the reform has spread more slowly. In 1977 an estimated one thousand plants were operating on some variation of the original scheme.[101]

Conceived in terms of the 1965 reforms, the conception underlying Shchekino has been to provide sufficient economic stimulation to overcome the resistance of managers to a reduction of their labor reserve. In its original provisions, a cut in the work force would not result in a reduction of the wage fund; all savings were to remain in the enterprise or association; and half of the savings of the wage fund were to be passed on to the shop heads for distribution to workers whose jobs were combined or enlarged. These conditions have not been fully observed. Over the past decade, however, the Shchekino Association reported a rise of labor productivity of 15 to 20 percent, a rise in workers' income of 10 to 20 percent, and a net reduction of forty-three thousand workers. It has been no accident, however, that the largest reductions (20 to 50 percent) have been in service and technical rather than production personnel.[102]

The Shchekino experiment has met with varying degrees of ministerial resistance. In the early years of the reform, Shchekino spread relatively easily in industries with continuous production technologies. It has been opposed more vigorously in the metalworking, machine-building, and other industries with more labor-intensive production technologies.[103]

The reasons for managerial opposition have been general as well as specific to the reform. Undoubtedly, as Brezhnev complained, managerial opposition to this as to other reforms has been rooted in the "stagnating force of inertia" (*kosnaia sila inertsii*).[104] This inertia, however, stemmed from conditions which economic incentives could not overcome. In addition to the general reluctance to cut the labor force, the reform created its own difficulties in implementation.

The reform penalized the most efficient plants because they had less slack. The planning organs created additional obstacles by retaining the ratchet principle of planning and depriving enterprises of the right to continue to transfer savings to the wage fund. The experiment placed a new burden on the managers insofar as released workers had to be retrained. There was also a genuine fear that job enlargement would increase labor turnover. The most serious problem, however, was that plants adopting Shchekino became more dependent upon technical innovation to meet output targets.[105]

This latter condition clearly has been at the heart of the new intensive strategy of growth. Soviet managers' traditional aversion to the risks of technological innovation, however, appears to have been justified in the experience of the Shchekino Nitrogen Association itself.

The association accepted a phenomenal growth target of 62.7 percent in labor productivity for the Ninth Five-Year Plan. The plan was based upon an assumption of the most rapid introduction of highly productive technologies. The plan for new technology, however, could not be implemented, and the production plan became disrupted. By June 1973, the Ministry of the Chemical Industry began to subsidize the association. Bonuses were cut from one-third to one-half. The result was a rapid increase in labor turnover.[106]

In conjunction with a drive to expand the Shchekino method, new rules were announced in April 1978 for going over to the system. Each shop is now given a fixed number of workers. The normative is calculated on the basis of actual levels of manpower in the shop in January 1978. Each worker is given a 20 to 25 percent wage boost. Economies from previous labor cuts can be included in current savings.[107]

The new measures address none of the basic problems which have generated managerial opposition to Shchekino, and there is some reason to doubt whether they will seriously alter managerial perceptions of the value of the method or of their own interests.

Social planning and development

The relatively narrow and direct approach of NOT to the threat of reduced economic growth created by the labor shortage clearly has only limited value in resolving the cumulative social and cultural problems of socioeconomic development. Soviet social research on labor turnover and dissatisfaction does suggest, in the present stage of industrial development, that technological innovation, improved incentive systems, and better organization of labor should improve labor productivity. Dissatisfaction with industrial conditions and unsatisfied social demand constitute serious obstacles to improved labor productivity. The sources and solutions to social dissatisfaction, however, go beyond NOT.

The determination to develop a comprehensive approach to the more complex problems of human behavior in industry has resulted in a rapid development in the 1970s of social planning. Social planning, still in an initial stage, is developing on both macro and micro levels.

On the macro social plane, social planning is an integral element of the concept of long-term plan discussed previously. Social planning, however, is also used in the narrower and more technical sense of "social programming." In this usage, social planning is shorter termed and problem-oriented. It has the specific task of constructing plans or goal-programs of social development for an enterprise, city, or region.[108] Social plans should be based upon social research and should be incorporated into the economic planning system.

Social planning on the macro level clearly involved the most basic issues of social development and of economic, social, and cultural policy. Substantive issues of social policy are evidently studded with difficult choices for which there are no cost-free solutions. The stimulation of the birth rate probably cannot be achieved without a reduction of living standards. The expansion of vocational education may entail a further slowdown in social mobility and a loss in the future of important intellectual or scientific resources. Any serious development of social infrastructure threatens existing patterns of resource allocation. One of the most serious issues raised in the SOFE debate, it will be recalled, was the issue of whether social welfare could stand as the criterion of optimality.

The confrontation of the empirical social scientists and the ideologists of the Communist Party in the late 1960s and early 1970s assumes some importance in this respect. The victory of the ideologists has meant that the definition of goals and strategies of social development has remained firmly in the Party's hands. Their approach, however, has not been simplistic or retrogressive. The use of empirical social science has rather resulted in a blend of traditional and innovative objectives and methods.

This blend becomes evident in an article on the social and cultural goals of development by Iurii Volkov, a politically influential sociologist. In his view these goals can be resolved into three specific objectives. The first is to increase the amount and quality of consumer goods and services needed to meet social demand. The second is to promote the socialist model of life, which involves a struggle against a "consumer's psychology" and expansion of mass culture. The third is that social policy should regulate social development in the direction of social equality.[109]

Since the mid-1960s, social programming has focused on the enterprise. The targets are primarily those which social research has revealed to be sources of dissatisfaction within the work force. The goals of social programming are to uncover the "social reserves" of production, which means stimulating the worker to improve the amount of production and improve its quality.[110]

The typical enterprise social plan, according to authoritative instructions, should be constructed in four sections. The first section should include measures for the elimination of heavy labor, principally through mechanization and automation. Second, social plans should improve the plant's sanitary, hygienic, safety, and aesthetic conditions through the use of color, functional music, attractive clothing, proper lighting, and other measures. Third, social plans should include effective wage and bonus systems, such as increasing the amount of housing, clubs, kindergartens, and other services. The fourth section is a strategy for improving motivation. The measures propose to tighten labor discipline, stimulate ideological conviction, and improve the ideological climate. Traditional methods include an effort to increase the level of political mobilization, a policy intensified in the early 1970s after the brief stress on material incentives during the economic reform. Socialist competition, increasing the role of the Party and other social organizations over labor discipline and turnover, and better agitation and propaganda are among the recommended measures.[111]

Numerous measures are suggested to improve the psychological climate and reduce social conflict. A principal recommendation is to improve the procedures for selecting, evaluating, and training first-line supervisors. To increase social integration, emphasis has been on increasing the influence of official norms, more effective social communication, and use of collective forms of socialist competition and material incentives. Off-the-job social relationships are encouraged by such mechanisms as group vacations and the elimination of such common practices as favoritism in distributing work assignments and bonuses. Personnel departments are encouraged to group workers with similar interests.[112]

The central social policy toward youth has been to deflect their career goals away from professional occupations. This policy has received sustained support from the media and the schools. The long-term measure for reorienting social aspirations has been to convert general secondary into polytechnical education. A decree of June 20, 1972, ordered the expansion of polytechnical education in conjunction with the transition to universal secondary education.[113] As part of an organized effort to improve vocational guidance, some city and provincial *soviets* have set up commissions to conduct lectures and arrange visits by students to factories, construction projects, and other production units. This is frequently combined with work–study projects for the purpose of introducing the young person to various kinds of factory jobs and skills. A special form of vocational guidance was instituted in 1970 in Moscow. Special training plants – the UPKs – established and managed by the local *soviet* but staffed by industry have been set up as work–study units.[114] A decree of the Council of Ministers of August 23, 1974, has ordered the expansion of this particular form of vocational guidance.[115]

In some of the larger plants, orientation programs for new workers have been instituted. Testing and interviewing have also been introduced on a limited scale. In a few plants, programs have been developed for the training and advancement of unskilled young workers; and, to ease the integration of young workers into the production group, ceremonies honoring the first pay of the new worker, for example, have been introduced.[116] A decree of September 6, 1974, ordered the ministries to improve the cafeterias and social services in the dormitories attached to industrial plants.[117]

The most widespread form of adaptation used in Soviet industry is *nastavnichestvo*, a system of apprenticeship and counseling of a new worker by an experienced one. Conceptually, the assignment of new workers to "tutors" reflects the still strong paternalistic influence which exists in Soviet industry. In a relationship similar to the traditional *sheftsvo*, the older worker ideally serves as a role model and assumes responsibility for the young worker's personal as well as professional growth and behavior.[118]

Planning for the social development of married women with children has received considerably less attention, despite its importance for long-term growth. The proposals for improving the situation for women, in addition to improving social services and the conditions of labor, include such measures as reducing the amount of night work, removing women from heavy or harmful work, calisthenics programs, longer luncheon periods, and more frequent work breaks to relieve monotony and fatigue.[119] The reduction of working hours for women, however, is not included in the methodological instructions for constructing an enterprise plan.

The methods for dealing with alcoholism and other forms of social disorganization are considerably more complex. The problem of alcoholism and drunkenness has received sustained official attention. A decree of the Council of Ministers of May 16, 1972, enacted a series of measures designed to reduce the consumption of hard liquor, cut the sale of vodka and reduce its alcoholic content, and increase medical facilities for the treatment of alcoholism.[120] In November 1974, the Young Communist League and the Ministry of Internal Affairs issued a decree for dealing with the special problems of alcoholism among youth.

The national campaign against alcoholism instituted by Brezhnev in the early 1970s has included some unusual and progressive approaches to the treatment of alcoholism. The Dorokhova Glass Plant set up a clinic for alcoholics using psychotherapy, including group therapy, for the treatment of alcoholism.[121] One of the interesting experiments in therapy reported in the press is the course of treatment set up at twelve hospitals in Moscow Oblast. Patients work at a cooperating plant but live in a special dormitory where they can be medically treated. The patient works in a shop under the observation of a doctor and is paid by the medical facility for a period of up to two years. The rate of recidivism is reported to be half of other programs. The number of patients, however, is small (only one hundred can be treated at a time). It is also expensive and has not spread very rapidly.[122]

Social programming in practice

The scope of social planning over the past decade has become quite extensive. At the end of 1975, about twenty thousand plans had been formulated for industrial plants, construction sites, and other production facilities. Throughout the Soviet Union, about 35 percent of the total number of industrial plants and production unions had developed social plans. In the industrially developed areas, the Baltic republics, Moscow, and Leningrad, all industrial facilities had social plans.[123] Social planning in the other republics, however, has been problematical. Because social planning is voluntary, decentralized, and dependent upon local initiative and resources, the results are uneven and difficult to evaluate.

In those plants where the labor shortage is tight and dissatisfaction is high, where the local Party and *soviet* agencies strongly support social planning, and where the plant management takes an active interest in social development, the results of social planning are positive and ameliorative. The number of plants in which this occurs, however, appears to be relatively small.

There are numerous specific instances reported in the literature where the application of social science research has improved the work environment as well as labor productivity. V. G. Loos, for example, has noted the work of a Latvian artist, Monrid Karklinsh, who conceived a plan for the aesthetic transformation of a small plant. Karklinsh painted eight metalcutting machines in different shades of green and designed the plant's work clothes in complementary colors. In one shop, the artist painted the door bright red, one wall black and a second wall in light violet. In response to such a resplendent use of color, labor productivity in the plant rose a reported 10.4 percent, and costs were lowered by 14 percent.[124]

Successful use of social psychological research is also evident. On one production line of the Svetlana Association, women complained of boredom, fatigue, and job dissatisfaction. An investigation by social psychologists revealed that women were working in a single line and had restricted social contact. The assembly tables were rearranged so that the women faced each other, thus broadening their social contact. Labor productivity of this group increased by 10 percent.[125] Other experiments based upon compatibility in job placement have also reported good results.[126]

More systematic efforts to implement social plans have also been discussed. One of the most publicized has been undertaken at the Perm Telephone Plant. Since 1967, this plant has been active in mechanizing and automating production, providing education to raise the rank and wages of workers, improving sanitary conditions, building new housing, clinics, and sports facilities, and providing space for food stores and other services within the plant. One of the distinguishing features in the application of human factor research in this plant has been the use of functional music. The experiment was begun in 1963 and has proven to be very popular. In 1974 the experiment was extended to all shops in the plant. The influence of these measures in promoting labor satisfaction, however, has been mixed. Although labor turnover has been cut to 11.7 percent, only 59 percent of the workers were satisfied with the plant's organization, 68 percent with wages, and 76 percent with the conditions of labor. In this as in other cases, the rise in expectations is more rapid than the ability or willingness to meet demand.[127]

The relatively minor role of social planning in the overall strategy of management rationalization can be attributed to a variety of factors. An active implementation of social planning clearly requires fundamental changes in the allocation of resources as well as a basic reorientation of management values away from production. It is also evident that those aspects of social planning which require technical innovation, improved production organization, and material incentives are dependent upon the rationalization of the economic mechanism. There are also, however, numerous specific intellectual and methodological problems with respect to social planning which are as yet unresolved.

The intellectual problems of social planning are rooted initially in the difficulties of isolating the influence of social and psychological factors in the management or production process. There is not a fully clarified concept, as Rutkevich has complained, of what role the social factor plays in the rise of labor productivity because it cannot be measured against other factors of production. The lack of an explanatory social theory has meant that the causal relationships between the conditions of labor and the dissatisfaction of youth, for example, have not been worked out.[128]

There is no sure sense of what types of changes should be adopted to reform the occupational prestige structure or what the optimal relationship between labor and leisure would be. The result for social planning is that there is little agreement on the social plan's priorities or structure.[129] The ideologists argue for the high priority of questions of social structure and social control; the social scientists, for the development of the individual; and the managers, for production needs.[130]

The inability to develop a common conception as to what a distinctive socialist life style entails clearly limits planners' ability to translate social priorities and preferences into quantitative social indicators.[131] Methodologically, as Kerimov and Pashkov have noted, social planning lacks principles; and those methods which have been tried are ineffective, unsubstantiated, and actually in conflict with each other.[132]

The methodological difficulties become particularly apparent on a global scale because of the ideological overlay. As an international UNESCO conference held in Moscow in the summer of 1976 indicated, Soviet sociologists have formally rejected either structural functionalism or mathematical modeling as the sole methodologies for social planning. In response to the presentation of Karl Keutsch, A. G. Zdravomyslov argued against what he considered to be Deutsch's effort to substitute "deideologized" mathematical concepts for Marxism.[133]

It is part of the dilemma produced by the use of scientific management methods in planning that social plans using empirical social indicators cannot be conducted without the use of social models. The construction of social models, as in the similar cases of economic and organizational modeling, however, has been hampered by the complexity and dynamism of Soviet social processes and by the primacy of normative methods in the definition of social change. Presently, Soviet social planners are using about one hundred parameters, and that number is increasing.[134] In this respect a primary obstacle to the construction of social planning models lies in the dearth of social information. The social statistics collected by the Central Statistical Administration are inadequate for this type of detailed planning.[135]

Data requirements for social planning models are dependent upon the goals and priorities of the plan, which are as yet undefined. What information to collect, how to measure it, and how to present it in a form suitable for directive planning are also unresolved questions. The highly imprecise and inconsistent form in which social indicators are presented are, in V. G. Podmarkov's view, a result of the lack of understanding of the underlying social process.[136] In any case, it has been too difficult analytically to develop social indicators by region and social group.

Perhaps the major methodological question with respect to social planning is not whether a social optimum can be calculated or the economic consequences of social planning measured but whether a normative approach to social planning can be used at all. The social and psychological determinants of human behavior have not been isolated, and therefore directive planning methods are essentially trial-and-error attempts at solving social problems. In the view of one leading social planner, a cybernetic or engineering approach is simply inadequate. Not only are there numerous aspects of the social process which cannot be directly controlled, but the plans themselves become too abstract, even at the enterprise level, to cope effectively with the diversity met in everyday social life in the plant.[137] Empirical and problem-oriented planning lends itself more easily to a situational rather than normative approach.

Within the enterprise, the formidable methodological obstacles to effective social planning have been largely overshadowed by more practical problems of implementation. Among the most important of these factors are the quality of the enterprise plan, the "psychological barriers" of the managers, the uncertain role of the behavioral scientists, the limited resources available for the implementation of social plans, and the limited influence of social plans in shaping the larger social and cultural environment.

One of the basic complaints against enterprise social plans is their generally low quality. This is, initially, a direct result of the lack of trained sociologists and psychologists in the plant. Many social plans are drawn up without any social research, and as a result many social indicators in the social plan are either arbitrary or simple linear extrapolations from existing conditions. This appears to be one of the reasons for the view among Soviet managers that the data received from sociological surveys are untrustworthy and that the solutions offered for such problems as labor turnover or the dissatisfaction of youth are simplistic.[138]

Low expectations for the results of social planning is, however, only one aspect of the "psychological barrier" erected by Soviet plant managers to the proposals of the behavioral scientists. The psychological resistance to change is due, in part, to the inability of many managers to grasp either the nature or consequences of the social factor.[139] Their strong technological and production orientation is a deeply rooted bias against a recognition of the human factor. This bias is reinforced by the traditional division of labor, which has relegated social issues to the social organizations in the enterprise. It is also due to the lack of material interest in social planning. The plans are not yet obligatory, are not connected with the production plan, and have no direct influence on the incentive system. As one Soviet specialist has complained, social plans are useful in making speeches and reports or as a basis for making increased demands in the allocation of resources. The recommendations themselves, however, are given low priority and little implementation. This attitude, in turn, strengthens the impression that the methods themselves have very little validity.[140]

The status and role of the plant sociologist or psychologist is unquestionably low in the average enterprise. Although this position reflects the evaluation of the social scientist's contribution to the solution of problems of interest to the manager, it is also due to the novelty of the social scientist's functional role in decision making. In practice, the director frequently does not know how or where to employ him, and the sociologist or psychologist just as frequently does not know what he can do. The lack of organizational definition is increased by the usual practice of subordinating the sociological or psychological service to the department of economics, NOT, or design office rather than a separate department. As a consequence, he is frequently assigned to jobs that have little to do with his role.[141]

One of the most evident and difficult impediments to the implementation of the enterprise's social plan is that many aspects of it are beyond its resources and control. Eliminating two of the most frequently cited sources of labor dissatisfaction, the organization of production and working conditions, requires fundamental organizational measures in the improvement of planning and supply. Secondly, insofar as the social plan becomes a social program, its financing and material support is heavily dependent upon the ministry. This support is frequently difficult to secure because of the generally low priority assigned to social planning by most ministries.[142]

The obstacles to a strong implementation of social planning are also partially attributable to the unanticipated consequences of its success. The most common example is the situation where the application of technology to heavy physical labor may increase the amount of monotonous work and thereby increase the turnover among the better-educated workers.[143] In addition, social need is so extensive in Soviet industry that the resolution of one set of problems simply stimulates a rise in expectations and more dissatisfaction. The experience of Lentekstil with social planning illustrates the problem.

Lentekstil is a large textile *kombinat,* or multiplant complex, housed in old buildings with poor facilities in Leningrad. The *kombinat* has employed a predominantly female labor force, presumably young, with 70 percent living in communal apartments and dormitories. The principal sources of dissatisfaction in this group of enterprises were social services. The social plan for the *kombinat* appears to have been actively implemented. Cafeteria space and eating facilities, for example, were more than doubled between 1968 and 1972. The dissatisfaction of the women, however, remained acute, and they began to complain about the quality and assortment of food in seven of the *kombinat*'s nine plants. They wanted a diet menu installed, sanitary conditions improved, and bookstores, shops, and other facilities added. Many of the most qualified women continued to leave the plant. In this and other plants, the major impediment to more rapid improvement of facilities was that only 70 percent of the *kombinat*'s social–cultural fund could be used because of the tightness of the supply situation.[144]

Finally, the satisfaction of the material and social needs of the Soviet worker can only be partially satisfied within the plant. This perception has been in large part responsible for the movement in the 1970s to extend social planning beyond the enterprise to include urban and regional social planning. Although urban and regional social planning are considered experimental, beginning in 1969 social plans were developed for the cities of Ufa, Leningrad, and Donetsk. Through 1976, social plans have been constructed for twenty cities, fifty agricultural regions, and many city boroughs in Moscow, Leningrad, and other cities. Social development plans have also been constructed for Leningrad and Sverdlovsk provinces.[145]

Social planning for urban and regional development differs from traditional Soviet city planning, which developed after the destruction of World War II. These plans were primarily constructed by architects for urban construction and linked population growth with the development of housing, schools, transportation, services, and cultural institutions. In the newer conception, social plans include the character of social life. Ideally, urban and regional social development plans should shape and control such aspects of social life as the structure of various neighborhoods according to social group, patterns of social interaction, cultural demands, and use of leisure. A major aspect of the study of the urban or regional environment should be the description and control of crime and other forms of social disorganization.[146]

Comprehensive social planning of this type clearly makes significant demands on the quality of social research as well as design. An early and successful example of social developmental planning has been Akademgorodok, a research center of the Siberian Division of the Academy of Sciences and often conceived as a model for urban development under conditions of the scientific–technical revolution.

Akademgorodok was conceptualized as a large functional–spatial system, which included, as part of its design, problems of social interaction, including social stratification. The social conception was to promote a community through building up patterns of social interaction based upon common interests. The new town, designed to maximize the satisfactions of highly trained scientists and technicians far removed from the amenities and cultural resources of the great metropolitan centers, appears to have been successful. The majority (86 percent) of the inhabitants were reported satisfied with the city. One interesting conclusion of the experiment, however, was that the higher the individual's standard of living rises, the greater the desire for privacy and the less the interest in a communal existence.[147]

The most significant effort to direct the social development of a complex metropolitan center has been Leningrad's experiment in problem-oriented social programming. In December 1971 Brezhnev selected Leningrad as the model city for the construction of an integrated socioeconomic plan. In a decree of

May 6, 1972, Gosplan affirmed the organization of the work and authorized the use of program-goal planning procedures.[148]

In the preplan period, the Leningrad City Soviet undertook the direction and coordination of the research into the most important interbranch and social problems confronting the city. CEMI used a tree of goals for integrating branch, interbranch, and social goals within a three-block system composed of goals, programs, and resources. The territorial division of the plan, however, did not use program-goal methods; and, more importantly, the indicators of the national plan were not integrated with the programs. The most fundamental problem was the opposition of the ministries, which succeeded in reducing the interbranch and social divisions of the plan in favor of the traditional primacy of branch development. The new plan in its final form resembled earlier territorial plans.[149]

It is evident that the basic problems of social programming await solution. Plans for regional development, Aitov has complained, are proceeding on a trial-and-error basis primarily because there is no theory of how a region develops. The improvement of the informational and analytical basis will occur slowly, Gosplan having shown little interest in expanding social research for either urban or regional planning.[150]

Regional developmental planning also raises insistent questions of political authority. A primary issue is the growing lack of coincidence between existing administrative boundaries and patterns of urban development. A second is the pervasive "departmental" thrust of the ministries. The failure of the Leningrad City Soviet to subordinate branch programs to interbranch and social goals indicates that marginal changes in formal planning techniques have little value. To redress the balance requires a fundamental reorganization of authority in economic management.

5

Rationalization of formal structure

The reform of formal structure has been among the most complex and controversial problems confronting the modernization of industrial management. As the preceding chapters have indicated, each of the functional approaches to rationalization has had consequences for the allocation of authority, function, and status within industrial management. Anticipated consequences of functional reform for organizational or personal position have been among the important sources of support or opposition to these reforms.

The rationalization of formal structure has proceeded in two distinct overlapping processes. One process has been the systematic reorganization of the ministerial system, which is discussed in Chapter 6. A second, more complex process has been the extended, largely informal responses of the managers to the implications of functional reform for industrial organization. The processes converge as attempts to reform the classical model of management. At both levels, questions of reform have involved the number of hierarchical levels, degrees of centralization, spans of control, relationships between line and staff organs, departmentalization, and other structural issues. The present chapter examines some of the implications of building ASUs, implementing the 1965 reforms, and applying behavioral research to industrial organization.

In the mid-1970s, the application of the systems approach to the design of formal industrial organization became limited. The experience with this approach, which is still in the experimental stage, is discussed in Chapter 6. The more significant influences on the rationalization of industrial organization have flowed from the presumed logic of structural change required by the specific and largely uncoordinated initiatives associated with functional rationalization. The most direct and powerful have been computerization and the economic reform. The influence of social science applications on management structure is still relatively minor.

Computers and structural rationalization

In the 1970s computerization has replaced the economic reform of the 1960s as the most significant influence for structural change. The potential of a large-scale application of technology for the redistribution of authority and control is evident. If an increasing differentiation of structure leads to a larger number of diverse subunits within an organization and, as a result, to greater problems of decision making, coordination, and control, then an increase in informational processing capacity should lead to a more effective functioning of the organization. Coordination should be improved because feedback is more rapid, and the need for differentiation is reduced because computer programs can replace people, to some degree, in an increasingly complex division of labor. Centralized control may also be enhanced; it creates the technical possibilities for a more rapid and effective allocation of tasks and monitoring of performance, particularly insofar as it increases the capacity of higher officials to evaluate performance by outcome rather than process.[1]

Whether the effect of computerization is to increase the degree of centralization, reduce the role of line officials, or create new patterns of authority through a restructuring of departments or participation is problematical. The number of possible relationships emerging from the application of computers to organization is very large. The employment of computers on the scale currently envisioned in the Soviet Union can lead to a broader and more comprehensive system of direct administrative controls. It can also lead to greater delegation of authority and wider participation. The underlying determinants influencing any redistribution of authority and function concern the limits of technology, the practical feasibility of Soviet concepts, and the political and cultural thrust of ongoing institutional relationships.

The operating assumption here is that, although there have

been serious problems in the design and construction of OGAS and its subsystems, institutional pressures have been strong to adapt computers to the existing structure rather than the contrary. The paradigm of the designers has been technological and mechanistic with a strong stress on centralized control. Despite the persuasive argument for subsystem autonomy, some leading Soviet specialists have pressed for a systemic structure in which all subsystems are closely interrelated and interdependent and which requires precise and strict rules to ensure reliability in the operation of the system.[2] The political intention of creating a man-machine decision-making system with a maximum level of centralized programming and control is evident from numerous trends that have been noted in Chapter 3: the preference for linear programming; the stress on globally optimized decisions; the concentration on a normative approach and the use of analytical models in decision making; the strenuous commitment to informational unity and systemic integration; and, not least, the intention to integrate eventually the separate national systems of the Soviet Union and Eastern Europe into a single global system.[3]

It is evident that the two central systems concepts advanced for the incorporation of computers and scientific management methods have not fully worked out the relationship of functional to structural rationalization.

Structural rationalization in the system of optimal functioning of the economy has been secondary to the rationalization of function, particularly of planning.[4] Fedorenko has also recognized, however, that an effective implementation of SOFE requires a fundamental reorganization of the existing formal organization of planning and management. Although details of the "structurization" of the SOFE concept have not been made, Fedorenko and the Central Economico-Mathematics Institute have advocated a three-level hierarchical structure, consisting of national, branch, and production organizations linked vertically and horizontally.[5] At the national level, industrial organization should include large program-goal complexes, which are interbranch and interregional. Within the ministry, Fedorenko has advocated the formation of large scientific-production organs for technical progress as well as large multiplant production associations at the production level.[6]

The evident preference for increasing the scale of economic organization has been accompanied by a complex approach to the definition of an optimal redistribution of authority and function. Fedorenko has recognized that the construction of a single model of the economy as a whole lacks feasibility. In line with the concept of the economy as a highly complex system, he has argued that each subsystem requires a "degree of freedom" to resolve specific problems that fall within centrally set directives.[7] During the course of the 1965 reforms, Fedorenko was extremely critical of the bureaucratic distortions produced by excessive centralization and advocated decentralization of planning and pricing and a sharp reduction in centralized allocation of supply.[8] Over the past decade, however, these views appear to have been modified in the direction of increased centralization (see Chapter 2).

At the heart of the program of structural rationalization proposed by SOFE is the reorganization of the planning system. In effect, Fedorenko has envisioned the construction of the largest man–machine decision-making system in the world. The global design for the planning system projects two basic subsystems. The first is a formalized block of algorithms, which form the core of the man-machine decision-making system. The second block is to be composed of heuristic planning procedures. In 1974 the planning functions of SOFE, including all goal programs, were synthesized into a structure of seven major functional blocks.[9]

The program-goal approach to planning implies, as Fedorenko has noted, an extensive reorganization of the existing structure of planning organs. The basic programs for resource, branch, or regional development can be organized through interbranch or regional organs or through special project organizations, which are interdepartmental. Authority and control of resources, he has argued, should be concentrated in the hands of the project manager.[10] Program-goal planning also requires a basic change in the departmentalization of Gosplan. Departments should be organized on a goal rather than branch basis, and fundamental changes are required in traditional planning procedures.[11] The problems of introducing a reorganization of the planning system are discussed in Chapter 6.

The technological thrust is more visible in the design of

OGAS. Even here, however, the previously discussed complexity of the task of construction has cast serious doubts on the feasibility of full formalization. S. P. Kozlov, a Minpribor official in charge of the design and construction of ASU, has warned against the persistent technological fantasy of total centralization. In a statement similar to Fedorenko's, he has noted that OGAS

can in no way be described as some sort of electronic octopus with a central panel whose buttons, if pushed, will determine which screw will be tightened. It will be a multistaged and multitiered system; the lower levels will have a certain degree of independence and initially find the most rational solution.[12]

The tension between the generalized thrust toward increased centralization and the technical, economic, and political constraints which limit the concentration of power has been evident in the construction of Gosplan's ASPR, the most important of the functional subsystems of OGAS. As the central link in the planning system, ASPR will form relationships with the automated systems of other functional organs at the national level as well as with the systems of the republican, provincial, and ministerial planning organs and departments. Since 1972, when active construction of ASPR began, priority has been given to its vertical rather than horizontal relationships.[13]

By design, a high level of coordination and compatibility, however, is required of the systems which interact horizontally with ASPR because their outputs provide significant inputs for planning computations. This is particularly true of its interaction with the ASGS of the Central Statistical Administration, which is expected to be the principal source of planning data.[14] The extent to which a centralization and consolidation of the planning system will, in fact, occur is problematical. Although extensive experimentation on the integration of the planning systems of CSA, the Ministry of Finance, and other state committees has been conducted, progress is slow.[15] In addition to conflicts over the control of informational channels and processing, incompatible software systems are being developed in ASPR and ASGS (Automated System of State Statistics).[16]

If the degree of Gosplan's actual control over the other functional agencies is ambiguous at this stage in the construction of OGAS, preliminary plans within the planning system itself suggest a strong emphasis upon the integrative departments and hence upon increased centralization. The development of the interbranch balance as a planning tool and increased computational power initially should increase the role of the departments for plan consolidation at the expense of the branch departments.[17] A second structural change is also designed to increase the role of the middle level of Gosplan's hierarchy: to create within Gosplan permanent multibranch complexes for fuel–energy, machine-building, agriculture, and other functionally interrelated branches in order to improve planning coordination.[18] The use of network methods for compiling the plan and matrix structure for the management of large territorial and multibranch complexes, should they be formed within Gosplan, probably will increase centralized control over the planning system.

The potential for increased control of Gosplan and the other functional agencies over the ministries has been enhanced over such functions as the planning of supply, finances, prices, state standards, and technical policy through computerization. Within Gosplan alone, as noted earlier, ASPR performs one thousand tasks at the national level and two thousand at the republican level.[19]

Although there is a reasonable expectation that computerization will reduce over time the currently high degree of ministerial suboptimization, the obstacles to closer integration remain formidable, and the structures complex. At the beginning of 1977, with the first stage of ASPR completed, there were fifty-one subsystems in Gosplan USSR, forty of which are branch systems.[20] The structure of ASPR suggests that it is a simple overlay of the existing system. Integration has also been slowed by ministerial opposition and the technical, informational, and programmatic incompatibilities of the various subsystems.[21] Like other forms of rationalization, computerization alone fails to deal adequately with the underlying issues of power and interest which pervade industrial organization.

The development of branch automated systems (OASUs) should increase the authority of the ministry's central *apparat* over the intermediate and production organizations of the branch. The general design recommended by CEMI for OASU actually provides for a large degree of enterprise autonomy through the allocation of most operational decision making to the production unit.[22] Experience with the operation of OASU, however, reveals a different pattern.

The tendency has been to concentrate both strategic and operational decision-making authority in the central *apparat,* thus strengthening existing patterns. At the end of 1974, for example, the computer center of the Ministry of the Coal Industry performed some ninety-three specific tasks. Among the more important computations made at the top are the accounting and analyses of the production indicators for each coal mine; the centralized payment of suppliers; the calculation of the wage fund and all premiums; the distribution of capital investment for each mine; and the determination of the production capacity, supply, and other needs of each production unit.[23]

A similar trend toward centralization is apparent in other ministerial systems. In this respect, ASU–Pribor may be the model for the systems of the machine-building branches. With the addition of a central data bank, collection of data from the production associations and enterprises has expanded. At the beginning of 1976, data on 384 indicators for each operating enterprise were collected and stored at the branch level.[24] Both planning and supply have become more centralized as the system has developed. As in other ministries, the power of the enterprise over supply appears to have been sharply reduced, the enterprise having been relieved of the task of compiling supply requests. The supply plan is composed by the Chief Computer Center on the basis of normatives; the *fondy* (supply authorizations) and assignment of producers and clients are distributed by computer.[25]

One of the most significant consequences of the development of ASU–Pribor has been the further centralization of operational management, a result of increased speed in the transmission and processing of information.[26] In ASU–Pribor, some twenty-three tasks of operational management and control are now performed by the computer center in Moscow.[27] The expanded operational capabilities of the ministerial *apparat* are currently expressed in two basic directions in most ministries. Initially, the rapid dissemination of information on production and supply permits the computer center to "anticipate possible deviations" in plan fulfillment. Then, the computer center can monitor the timeliness and degree of fulfillment of ministerial and other commands and orders.[28]

The control system of the Ministry of Industrial Construction may be typical. Each order of the ministry is placed on a disk in the computer center. Periodic reporting on the degree of fulfillment is then demanded of those responsible for that task. Systematic monitoring of specific orders has strengthened the traditionally weak control structures of the ministries; formal compliance with ministerial orders has apparently increased.[29]

If OASU has reduced the relative autonomy of the production association or enterprise, within the enterprise a similar centralization of authority has occurred with the development of ASUP. In Glushkov's phrase, the plant director's office has been turned into a "super dispatcher."[30]

The degree to which computerization has influenced centralization within the enterprise has been conditioned by numerous factors, including design and production technology. Some ASUP built for large and complex production complexes have been planned as decentralized systems and function as unintegrated subsystems at the enterprise or shop level.[31] Technology also influences the level of centralization. In branches using continuous production technologies, such as the electric power, chemical, and oil-drilling and refining industries, computers can coordinate the full production cycle. In branches employing discrete technological processes or producing a wide variety of products, the systems are usually less centralized. Systems installed in continuous processing industries, however, are more technologically demanding; they must have a real time capability and are more vulnerable to breakdown because they are more highly integrated and centralized.[32]

During the early, highly pluralistic approach to the development of ASUP, the computers were integrated into a largely unrationalized formal structure.[33] The structure of informational flows has thus assumed a wheel configuration. Each of the subsystems has been directly connected with the plant computer center, and lateral relationships have been largely ignored. As a result, each subsystem usually functions as a closed system, increasing the level of centralization but maintaining existing patterns of horizontal communications. To the extent that traditional structures have been strengthened, the level of organizational integration has been lower than expected.[34] The clear exception to a moderate level of centralization in overall plant control is in plants using mass production technologies with a high level of routinized functions. The Lvov Television Plant is an example of a plant in which operational planning and control has been sharply centralized as the result of computerization. Virtually all aspects of production scheduling and shop management have been concentrated in the plant computer center. The computer center transmits daily production assignments to each shop, determining in detail what parts are to be made, in what quantity, and with what equipment. The computer center also calculates demand, production of spare parts, inventory control, and expenditures on production and performs a large number of reporting and other functions.[35] Similar reports of a high level of centralization of operational management have been noted for Moscow's Frezer Plant, Likhachev, Minsk Tractor, Kazan Heat Control Equipment, and other specialized machine-building enterprises.[36]

If the impact of computerization on the vertical distribution of authority has been of primary concern, its influence on line-staff relations, the interaction of man and machine, and departmentalization have not been insignificant. Although the level of operation of ASUP in industry as a whole is too diverse for firm generalizations, certain trends appear dominant.

The primary consequence of computerization has been to strengthen the functional aspects of management. Existing systems, in the view of a leading designer of OASU, A. I. Pokrovskii, have been of little value to line management because they are used largely for computational purposes.[37] Moreover, control over and access to information is an important resource for line management, so changes in this relationship have significant political implications. The combination of centralization in decision making and growth in the role of specialists has been one of the principal reasons for the emergence of "psychological barriers" among lower line officials to the use of computers. Whether intensive training of these managers will reduce existing antagonisms is still unclear.

The computer, however, also poses a threat to the role and status of the functional specialist as well because he is principally involved in the man–machine dialog. The key questions at every level of the hierarchy involve both changes in decision-making procedures and the number and types of functions that can be turned over to the machine. In general, responsible Soviet spokesmen like Fedorenko have recognized that full formalization of decision making verges on technological fantasy. Moreover, there is recognition that the higher and more complex the decision, the more significant will be the role of human experience and intuition. Under these conditions, it is clear that the amount of unprogrammed decision making remains high.[38] In practice, the number and types of decisions which can be turned over to the machine depend on the quality of models and algorithms that can be developed.

There is no consensus on what will be the final distribution of authority and function between man and machine. In one study devoted to the rationalization of the Ministry of Wood and Woodworking Industry, a group of Moscow University specialists defined the functions which could be automated. Although the list contains several ambiguities, it is useful. The division of functions between man and machine in constructing the annual plan is presented in Chart 5.1. In this particular design, it is apparent that some of the politically sensitive aspects of the planning process, such as the defense of the plan in Gosplan, remain human functions.

The extent to which management functions within the enterprise can be automated also varies in current estimates. Although the degree of automation, like the degree of centralization, is conditional, some general estimates have been made. Boris Milner, an outstanding Soviet specialist, has concluded that about 50 percent of the planning functions, 50 percent of reporting, 10 percent of technological functions, and 20 percent of supply planning can be automated.[39] A more optimistic projection, however, has suggested that approximately two-thirds of routine management functions (600 of 950) can be put on machines. Data collected on the operation of four large ASUPs, for example, indicate that up to 95 percent of some functions can be automated.[40] With automation, the principal direction of structural change has been to expand the planning department and merge departments such as supply and sale or finance and accounting.

Chart 5.1. *Automation of branch technical–economic planning*

Machine-processed subfunctions	Manually processed subfunctions
Calculation of demand for products	Environmental and ecological protection
Definition of annual enterprise control figures	Affirmation of enterprise plans
Integration of divisions of annual plan	Organization of planning process
Definition of nonplanned production	Development of planning methods
Calculation of most rational relations among enterprises of the branch	Establishment of list of normatives and norms by lower organizations
Control over distribution of plans to enterprises	Defense in Gosplan of the aggregated branch plan
Price formation and control	Working-out of instructions for price formation
Annual planning of products sold	Checking-up of functional administrations and *glavki* on practices of current planning
Annual planning of wage fund	Disseminating of leading experience
Definition of nondirective plan indicators	
Analysis of statistical reports	
Comparative analysis of enterprise performance	
Calculation of technical–economic normatives	

Source: N. G. Kalinin, ed., *Organizatsiia upravleniia v sisteme ministerstva,* Moscow: Izdatelstvo Moskovskogo universiteta, 1974, pp. 259–61.

One of the most complex and controversial issues to arise with ASU has been the role and authority of the computer center. The underlying question has been whether ASU will have an independent decision-making role or will be simply an informational resource. For some managers, ASU's computer center is the new core of the management system; for others, however, it is simply a technology for processing information. To a large degree, these evaluations shape approaches to such specific issues as the formal status of the computer center in management structure, its relationships with other management organs, and the rules, incentives, and sanctions which should govern its performance. Current practice at the branch and enterprise levels varies widely.

In general, virtually all computer centers collect, process, and disseminate information, maintain the system physically, and guide the overall development of the branch's information system.[41] The formal structure of computer centers, however, varies. They tend to be organizationally complex. The Chief Computer Center of the Ministry of Light Industry, for example, has eleven departments. In addition to those directly engaged in data processing, there are departments for internal administration, servicing, and maintaining the computer center and for information channeling and control.[42]

The authority of the computer center in decision making, quite naturally, has been a politically sensitive issue. On the whole, the role of the chief computer center at the branch level has been established "spontaneously." Although each computer center is considered to be part of the ministry's *apparat,* their financial status (the majority are on *khozraschet*) and subordination differ. The chief computer center is generally subordinate to a chief functional administration and thus has a reduced status and role.

There is a consensus that, to be effective, its authority should be raised by making it report directly to the leadership of the ministry. One of the reasons for the restricted role of the ministry's computer center lies in the lack of definition of its authority before it begins to operate.[43] This is initially due to the competition with other departments. It can also be attributed, as A. B. Vengerov points out, to the absence of a theory of how to unify such diverse aspects of the management structure as rationalization of the definition of indicators for evaluation of the performance of management functions and how to define the rules for behavior in conditions of ASU.[44]

The emergence of the computer center as an integral element in the decision-making process has raised new and complex issues at all levels of the hierarchy with respect to the input, processing, output, and storage of data. Particularly significant questions of input and storage concern the accuracy, security, and privacy of information, and these concerns have intensified with the development of central data banks, remote access, and time sharing. On the issue of the output of data, interesting questions have arisen in relation to the juridical force of machine commands and whether the man or machine has primary responsibilities for computing and other errors in data processing.

The problem of the accuracy and reliability of input data is central to the increased confidence and use of ASUs. The technological dimension only marginally affects the underlying economic, social, and psychological causes of the distortion of information. Developing formal controls over machine-processed information has proven to be difficult. Through 1976, no legal norms had been developed to regulate the completeness, accuracy, and timeliness of data.[45] There are also no sanctions for producing low-quality information, although both Minpribor and the Ministry of the Sea Fleet have reportedly lowered the bonuses of officials responsible for transmitting inaccurate or distorted data.[46]

The concentration of information in centralized data banks with remote access capabilities raises potentially critical issues on the maintenance of data security. Given the traditionally intense concern of the Soviet bureaucracy with secrecy and tight control over information, the political implications of control over unauthorized access to data are significant. The design of most ASUs is primarily directed toward a planned and controlled distribution of information. The general dilemma, however, is evident. Although the planned distribution of information maximizes control, the utility of the system may be sharply reduced. Raising the value of the system by increasing access to data may have the effect of opening the system. Whether the development of the ES series and its associated software, based on IBM's 360 series, also means that some variant of the Resource Security System developed by IBM for its Time Sharing System 360 will be adopted is unknown to the author.[47] Indeed, with the development of time sharing as the future mode for information processing, problems of structure and redistribution of authority are entering a new and unexplored stage.

The question of whether machine commands have administrative force raises new and controversial issues in Soviet administrative law. Complex problems of accountability are directly involved in determining, for example, whether information transmitted over a wire or displayed on a terminal has the same obligatory character as a signed document. One specific aspect of the problem is the degree of responsibility which a computer center assumes for its mistakes. The Chief Computer Center of the State Committee for Material–Technical Supply sent out late allocation orders for nonferrous metals. In assessing formal responsibility for the losses which occurred, however, it was the Chief Supply Administration for Nonferrous Metals that was held accountable.[48] Similar types of problems of accountability are involved in establishing the responsibility of analysts, programmers, and other computer specialists for inadequate modeling or other forms of ineffective application of scientific management methods.

On the whole, computerization has had only a moderate influence on industrial organization. The traditional mechanistic paradigm and Taylorist approach to organizational design have helped to create informational systems which are largely overlays of the existing formal structures. Pressures for organizational change are significant, though. The basic thrust favors increased concentration and growth in the role of the functional services. Whether the powerful constraints against change can be overcome is problematical. Moreover, it is clear that the technological variant is not fully congruent with other forms of functional rationalization.

The economic reform and structural rationalization

By the mid-1970s, it became increasingly apparent that the application of the systems approach and new technologies to industrial decision making is incapable of fully integrating the diversity of functions and interests in the contemporary Soviet economic environment. The implications of the economic reform for the rationalization of management structure were close and direct, as the Nemchinov and SOFE models, among others, have pointed out. The primary structural problem was defined as finding an optimal relationship between centralization and decentralization and broadening horizontal relations. Implicit in the reform, in addition, was the establishing of an expanded role for the economist in decision making.[49] Both objectives became deeply controversial.

The search for effective methods of reducing the overload on the central planners and managers without a simultaneous loss of centralized control had been an underlying theme of virtually all debates preceding the reform and during the initial phase of its implementation. The extended discussions on the relative role of the plan and the market, the nature of *khozraschet* and legitimate boundaries of its application, and the operational consequences of the reform for the Communist Party and Soviet state touched the political system's most sensitive nerve. The objective of expanding the operational authority of the enterprise could not be separated from the problems of functional reform.

There is little evidence of an intention on the part of the Soviet leadership to legislate a radical alteration of management structure along the lines advocated by Nemchinov in 1964. The disassembly of the complex microstructure of administrative controls over planning and enterprise management was a proposal which extended beyond the boundaries of legitimacy. The goal of the majority of reformers was more modest, essentially the substitution of direct administrative controls by indirect economic controls operating through a limited application of market principles within the context of a formal bureaucratic structure.

Redistribution of authority within this framework was to be one of selective delegation. Typical in this respect were the parametric views of Fedorenko, who advocated a "creative adaptation" of the traditional principle of democratic centralism. The central planners maintained strategic control over the key political and economic factors and delegated operational authority to the enterprise within these limits. The criterion for the redistribution of authority and functions vertically would be the availability of information.[50]

The Statute on the Socialist Enterprise enacted as a result of the September 1965 Plenum formally reduced the number of detailed administrative controls. The number of obligatory planning indexes was reduced. The enterprise increased its control over working capital, depreciation allowances, and the wage fund. It also gained the right to affirm its own managerial staff and budget within centrally set guidelines. The enterprises were empowered to sell surplus, unused or obsolescent raw materials, and equipment and were allowed greater freedom over social and cultural development and technological innovation. Delegation was also apparent in the expansion of the authority of the republican councils of ministers. Their control over the siting of new construction and reconstruction of old facilities within their administrative boundaries was strengthened; they were also given the right to review all enterprise production plans independently of their ministerial subordination.[51]

A particularly important dimension to the redistribution of authority envisaged by the reform was the proposal to increase the enterprise's control over inputs and outputs through a limited broadening of choice in horizontal relationships. Control over inputs through centralized administrative rationing, as Gregory Grossman has pointed out, has been a primary instrument of administrative control.[52] To reduce the heavy costs in manpower and allocative efficiency and to improve coordination, a policy was adopted of reducing the number of centrally distributed products, establishing wholesale trade in the means of production, and expanding direct and long-term ties between producers and clients through the use of contracts. The decentralization of supply planning and limited introduction of the market had evident advantages in increasing horizontal communication, reducing the single greatest source of information overload, restricting the amount of centralized coordination and operational management, and integrating input and output plans.[53]

The failure of the 1965 reforms to change the functioning of industrial management in significant ways can be attributed in part to the resistance to the proposed reorganization of authority. This was initially expressed in the tight constraints placed on the role of the market in the planned economy. Questions of the nature of *khozraschet* and the boundaries between administrative and economic incentives and controls remained controversial and unresolved. At one end of a continuum were the arguments of Nemchinov, A. M. Birman, and others advocating the wide use of the market and a large measure of enterprise autonomy. The pressure from the other end of the continuum sought to narrow the meaning of *khozraschet* to economic stimulation or to its traditional function as an accounting device. The variety of interpretations of the concept of *khozraschet* were simultaneously arguments for and against an extension of the market and greater enterprise autonomy.[54]

The most controversial and complex of the problems associated with the application of *khozraschet* as a principle of structural rationalization was to vertical relationships. The source of underlying tension was evident. By introducing an element of equivalency and mutual responsibility between hierarchical levels, vertical *khozraschet* could undermine the legal basis of strict administrative subordination. This threat provoked a sharp conflict.

Some legal scholars and economists, like Laptev and Shtenko, supported the application of *khozraschet* from the worker's bench to the central *apparat* of the ministry. Others, like G. Kh. Popov and S. S. Bratus, however, opposed placing the *apparat* of the ministry on *khozraschet,* arguing that they performed adminstrative rather than production functions.[55] Similar although less intense arguments were advanced for preserving the distinction and primacy of administrative authority in the enterprise.

The basic problem of adapting the formal organization of industry to the conditions of the reform, as Novozhilov noted in one of his last essays, was to find effective methods of containing illegal or informal administrative pressure on the formally delegated rights of the enterprise.[56] The failure of containment has many causes, one of the most basic being the lack of precise definition of the formal boundaries between the administrative and economic sectors.

Numerous specific and complex issues of legal definition of authority and procedure were ignored or left unanswered. Among the most important were such questions as the reconciliation of the roles of the ministry as an administrative agency and producer of goods. The issue of how to evaluate economically the losses and gains to the enterprise resulting from the decisions of the *glavki* and functional administrations of the ministry was ignored. No formal solutions were found to such problems as the permissible limits of disagreement between the ministry and enterprise or what agency or agencies should handle conflicts within the ministry.[57] The failure to define explicitly these and other basic issues of authority meant that they were decided informally in the course of the reform's implementation.

The limited and ambiguous structural dimension of the reform was matched by its conservative implementation. During the first three years of the reform, the employment of economic levers in their adopted form failed to reconcile the conflicting interests of the enterprise and the higher management agencies or to provide a visible increase in motivation and control. Despite the contrary assurances of Kosygin,[58] the reestablishment of the branch ministries resulted in the reimposition of most of the pre-1965 (the year the *Sovnarkhoz*, or Council of National Economy, was abolished) patterns of authority and interaction between the ministerial *apparat* and the enterprises. This was due in large part, as Jerry Hough has noted, to the fact that "the new ministers were the very men who had held top posts in the ministries a decade earlier."[59]

At an early stage of the reform, it became apparent that the officials of the ministry were opposed to any basic change in the vertical distribution of authority and actively struggled to control their behavior administratively.[60] This intent was demonstrated with particular force in 1966 in a Central Committee investigation that charged the ministries with an effort to evade the controls of the central functional agencies and, alternatively, with exercising tight control over the enterprise. The ministries' management of the enterprises, the report noted, was characterized by sharp jurisdictional conflicts between different levels of the hierarchy, overloaded channels of information, slow feedback, and extensive problems of coordination.[61]

A major violation of the spirit of the reform and rights of the enterprise was evident in the widespread evasion by the ministries of the distinction between the relatively few obligatory planning indicators and the more numerous nonplanned or "accounting" indicators presumably required for computational purposes.[62] The informal increase in the number of centrally planned indicators was also achieved through the administrative imposition of additional planned tasks, which was accompanied by such familiar practices as the late distribution of plans, frequent changes in the output plans without prior consultation or adjustment in other indicators, failure to deliver authorized amounts and types of supply, manipulation of enterprise resources, and other practices discussed in Chapter 1.[63]

The struggle for control over enterprise resources and behavior was not confined to the ministry. Virtually all of the central functional agencies succeeded to some degree in restricting the autonomy delegated to the enterprise. The Ministry of Finance, for example, set the indicator for the "free remainder" of profit for the enterprise; however, to plan this indicator, a financial official explained, it was necessary to plan other financial indicators which were in the legal competence of the enterprise. Under this procedure, "accounting" indicators were informally transformed into directive indicators in a manner similar to the output plan.[64] Similar complaints of encroachment and "excessive zeal" were voiced in the relationship between the State Bank and the enterprise.[65]

The decentralization of planning and control was intimately linked with modification of the system of centralized administrative allocation. The provisions for reorganization of the supply system, in the judgment of Karl Ryavec, were among the least successfully implemented, largely because of the genuine anxieties over loss of control aroused by the prospects of dismantling the structure of centralized allocation, particularly with respect to the means of production.[66] Although each of the proposed changes in the structure of the supply system has been partially put into practice, their implementation has been slow and ambiguous. Because of the key role of administrative allocation in the control of industrial organization, the execution of the provisions for decentralization in the distribution of supply, for establishing direct ties between enterprises, and for wholesale trade in the means of production will be reviewed in some detail.

From a historical perspective, the secular trend in supply planning has been a deconcentration in the distribution of products. Between 1953 and 1971, the number of material balances and plans of distribution worked out by Gosplan and approved by the Council of Ministers had declined from 2,390 to 277.[67] During the first two years of the reform, there was a significant deconcentration in the planned distribution of inputs. In 1968 Gosplan constructed a total of 1,969 balances and distributional plans. The State Committee for Material–Technical Supply planned another 103 balances, only marginally lowered from previous levels.

The major shift downward occurred in the number of products distributed by the chief supply administrations and the new territorial supply agencies of Gossnab. In 1965 the former planned about 12,000 products or product groups. By 1968, they planned 3,198 balances, and the territorial supply agencies 9,228. The role of the ministries in supply planning sharply increased. They composed 1,814 plans for general distribution and another 26,000 for internal branch distribution.[68] Since 1970, the distribution of authority over resource allocation has remained relatively stable.[69]

The degree to which this deconcentration represents a genuine decentralization in the supply system, however, is questionable. As the result of the reorganization of the 1960s, Gosplan directly controls only 20 percent of the total number of oil products produced in Soviet industry. This 20 percent, however, is 95 percent of total production. The balances and plans of distribution of seven types of oil products having critical industrial and military importance (among them, gasoline and aviation fuel) are confirmed by the Council of Ministers and are 87 percent of the total volume. The fifty oil products planned solely by Gosplan are only 8 percent of the total. The remaining 5 percent is distributed by Gossnab and its agencies. Gosplan exercises a similar level of control over other key industrial products: iron and steel (99 percent), lumber (97 percent), fuel (100 percent), and chemicals (90 percent).[70] The tight control by Gosplan over primary industrial resources remains a crude but effective control mechanism over the whole of the industry economy.

The expansion of the market principle in relieving the stresses of the system of administrative allocation has also proceeded ambiguously and unevenly. The broadening of horizontal relationships through establishing direct and long-term relationships between producers and clients has aroused the fear that the market relationship would expand to the point where the enterprise would select its partners, producing a situation equated by some conservatives with the end of the central planning system.[71] Despite this resistance, however, more than 6,000 producers and 25,000 clients have some proportion of their supply delivered according to direct contract.[72]

The implementation of direct ties, nonetheless, has been constrained. In heavy industry it is restricted to large-scale deliveries of a limited range of homogeneous products and to enterprises using serial or mass production technologies.[73] In 1976 turnover through this channel amounted to 37 billion rubles. It included 80 percent of the ball bearings and cement as well as sizable proportions of the ferrous metallurgy, chemicals, rubber, and construction materials produced by Soviet industry.[74] It should be noted that the development of direct ties between light industry and Soviet wholesale and retail organizations has been more extensive.

The second mode of expanding the use of market, through wholesale trade in the means of production and the derationing of some industrial products, has proceeded more slowly. Designed to reduce the heavy load on the supply system of small quantities or unusual assortments of production materials, the unrationed sale of such products through the 752 stores set up for this purpose amounted to only 6 billion rubles in 1974. Moreover, there has been a common complaint that these stores carry a poor assortment of goods and are unevenly stocked.[75]

In the early phase of the reform, there were a few experiments with the derationing of products, which aroused significant interest. The unrationed distribution of oil was tested in eight provinces of the Russian Republic, Minsk Province, and Estonia. There has also been an experiment in the free sale of 875 groups of chemicals and construction materials in Cheliabinsk, Orenburg, and Kurgan provinces in the Russian Republic.[76] As with other experiments with the market, these early and tentative steps have not been extended. In the 1970s, as the interest of the Soviet leadership in the economic reform receded, reliance on indirect economic methods related to the market also receded.

One of the major organizational expectations created by the 1965 reforms was a growth in the role of the economic services in enterprise decision making. Traditionally dominated by an engineering and production orientation, the reform's stress on economic factors in the evaluation and control of the enterprise assumed greater influence by the economist on planning the choice of technologies, the more efficient use of resources, and supply and sale.[77]

Although the role of the economist in decision making has varied, the growth of his influence has been less than expected in many respects, the consequence of the more general fate of the reform. More specifically, however, the redress of the traditional imbalance between technical and production services and the economists proved difficult to achieve in practice, as became particularly evident in the initial phase of the reform in the effort to establish the post of chief economist or deputy director for economic questions in the enterprise. In 1967 the Ministry of Nonferrous Metallurgy, for example, classified the chief economist as a consultant, with no administrative authority over either the technical or economic departments.[78] In those ministries in which the chief economist was charged with coordinating the economic services, sharp clashes of jurisdiction were frequent, particularly with the chief bookkeeper. Few ministries formally defined the rights and responsibilities of the chief economist, thus further fueling jurisdictional conflicts within enterprise management.[79]

The reduced role of the economist can also be traced to the sudden and heavy load of new and complex functions on the average plant's economic services. Emerging from a long period of neglect, the economic services lacked the capacity for developing long-range policies, forecasting demand, or computing effective economic strategies for supply and sale, technical development, and other enterprise functions.[80] This inability was largely due to the low status and inadequate training of personnel in the economic services. Drogichinskii estimated in 1968 that only 15 percent of the largest and best-equipped enterprises going over to the reform had economic cadres capable of making the computations required by the new conditions.[81] The introduction of economic models and computers in industrial decision making not only has sharpened the need for new and more highly trained economists in the enterprise but also will probably change the nature of the function and the authority associated with it.

In retrospect, it is clear that the redistribution of authority and function within the enterprise could not be divorced from the deeper dynamics of the reform as a whole. The failure of the measures in the form in which they were adopted in 1965 to influence significantly either the functions or structures of industrial management was a complex event.

The turn to alternative strategies and policies of structural rationalization in the late 1960s reflected disillusionment with the results of the reform. The pressures for reconcentration of authority were clearly those which more generally led Brezhnev to abandon the reform in favor of another strategy. These included such previously noted factors as the increase in the size and complexity of the formal structure, the ambiguous and skeptical attitude of the managers to the reform, and the growth of administrative pluralism and suboptimization. Political factors involving ideological conflict, the rise of political dissent, and a threatened loss of organizational function created additional pressures for the reimposition of centralized political and administrative controls.

The decisions of the Twenty-fourth Congress were designed to counter these tendencies toward diffusion of authority in industrial organization. The development of OGAS, on balance, has been a strong step toward the vertical concentration of authority. The effect of dismantling the major measures of the economic reform has been in a similar direction. Severing the linkage between profitability and the incentive fund has strengthened the centralized administration of the formation and distribution of incentive funds. The multiplication of success indicators has also reversed the trend toward deconcentration. The return to traditional forms of political and ideological mobilization of resources represented a dramatic effort to reassert the direct role of the Party.

As part of expanding direct controls by the Party apparatus over the economic and other functional bureaucracies, Party rules were modified in 1971. They granted the primary Party organs of economic, medical, educational, and research institutions increased rights of administrative control.[82] How active the primary Party organs of Gosplan, Gossnab, and the other functional agencies have become is unclear. The policy of expanding the participation of Party organs in industrial decision making and control appears to have been principally directed toward the industrial ministries, where the problems of suboptimization have been acute.

As a means of increasing the responsiveness of the central *apparat*s of the ministries to centrally established objectives and priorities, the Party organs of the chief functional administrations and other departments attempted to influence the selection of enterprise managers. They assumed enlarged responsibilities for the enforcement of national priorities in coordinating the work of the central *apparat* and for controlling their execution of superior Party and state orders.[83]

In research and academic institutions, primary Party organs were encouraged to promote applied industrial research and to use socialist competition as a means of producing more intense plans. Socialist competition was even extended to the major institutes of the Academy of Sciences.[84] In institutions of higher learning, such as Moscow's prestigious Bauman Institute, primary Party organs intervened in virtually every phase of the educational process from admissions to curriculum. Special concern was devoted to the selection of teaching personnel.[85] This tightening of political controls over research and educational institutions appears to have been part of the campaign to stamp out political dissidence,[86] particularly among scientific and technical personnel, and the growth of Western cultural influences.

There is little evidence to suggest that the emphasis upon political mobilization has been any more successful than in the past in promoting industrial efficiency or organizational cohesion. Socialist obligations imposed through counterplanning have usually been made *"na glazok,"* or arbitrarily.[87]

Generally, the sources of socialist obligations have not been clear, economically or technically based, or fulfilled under close supervision. Moreover, they have had the expected negative effect on informal bargaining relationships. Because higher plan obligations are not coordinated with proportionate increases in supply, the traditional imbalances between production and supply plans have usually been increased. To compensate for the expected rise in production targets, the managers simply discount them during the initial phase of planning and so are pressed even further in the direction of lower plans and higher inventories.[88]

The new policy of active control over the upper levels of the ministerial bureaucracy also appears to have been only marginally effective. The reaction of managers of Soviet institutions has, not unexpectedly, been one of strong resistance. There have been heated debates on the precise limits of authority of the primary Party organs with respect to the traditional prerogatives of Soviet line and functional officials. Open conflict broke out in opposition to what many officials conceived to be an attack on professional competence and their own authority.[89] There was also a developed sense of *déjà vu* in this as in other forms of the redistribution of authority and control. The policy of curbing the autonomy of the ministerial *apparat* was viewed as another campaign which would have little long-term effect on the inertia and ingrained habits of the bureaucracy.[90]

The policy of structural rationalization which began in the spring of 1970 was only secondarily influenced by the legislation adopted in 1965. The program of reorganization of industry which became official in March 1973 envisioned a thoroughgoing rationalization of the ministry. Soviet developmental theory has always exhibited a marked preference for economies of scale. The demands of the technological thrust as well as the objective of greater concentration and specialization of production intensified the underlying preference for large-scale organization.[91] Although the formal goal of structural rationalization in the 1970s has been the optimization of authority relationships, the actual result appears to have been to strengthen the movement toward increased centralization.

The behavioral impact on industrial structure

The overall impact of the social and psychological approaches on the rationalization of management structure must be judged marginal, although the problem of human relations is clearly – in view of the labor shortage – among the most important in industrial management. The social dimension of management is intimately involved with core issues of the goal culture, particularly with questions of industrial democracy, social mobility and equality, and human development and satisfaction. It is also a major aspect of the promotion of social order and of labor productivity. Although the social and psychological approaches to management rationalization cannot be reduced to questions of structure, issues related to the redistribution of authority through changes in patterns of participation and in the modes by which authority is allocated are evidently significant.

Although the scientific–technical revolution has been ritually affirmed as compatible with the eventual development of full social equality, empirical social theory is more ambiguous. To those Soviet behavioral scientists for whom the problem of social control is primary, such as the social cyberneticists and sociologists like Popova, the search is for social mechanisms or levers that direct behavior in socially and politically approved channels. This approach clearly supports a hierarchical system of unequal statuses.

Other sociologists and social psychologists, whose intellectual origins are rooted in organic premises, stress the significance of personal and social autonomy in human motivation and development. They have been critical of Taylorism and the classical, mechanistic approach to organizational design, the primary reliance on material incentives, and, more recently, the social consequences of computerization. G. S. Iakolev of the Institute of Social Research, for example, has declared that the introduction of computers does not remove the necessity for decentralization because the social and psychological costs of overcentralization remain.[92]

The structural conflict between technology and social consciousness is basic because an insistent question of socioeconomic development has been the role of social opinion in restructuring authority relationships in industry. During the 1970s, the policy of the Soviet political leadership has been to repress political dissidence and to strengthen traditional forms of mobilization and administrative controls.

It is evident that a cautious experimentation with industrial democracy does not constitute a major trend in the reform of formal structure. There has been, however, an interest in delegating authority to the mass social organizations in the plant on issues of direct personal interest to the worker or to the primary production collective. Authority over such problems as labor safety, labor discipline, and incentives may be shared by management with the trade unions or other production groups. Complex financial or economic decisions, however, are assumed to be beyond the competence of the bench worker.

The differentiated approach to delegating authority in order to increase the level of worker satisfaction is seen in the plan of rationalization adopted by G. Kh. Popov and the Moscow State University group for the production association Voskhod. In a study of the relationship between the level of satisfaction and participation, only a small proportion of the 190 administrative workers expressed total dissatisfaction. Lesser degrees of dissatisfaction, however, were widespread.[93] The primary sources of dissatisfaction with the distribution of authority centered on issues of personal concern: the distribution of premiums, and procedures for the evaluation and promotion of management personnel. This group believed that decentralized control over bonuses was required to make them effective. There was also a unanimous view that promotions should be from inside and that evaluation of personnel performance should be through certification.[94]

How far deconcentration of authority on issues of social and psychological importance to management workers has developed in Soviet industry is unclear. Through the 1970s, however, the practice appears to have been highly restricted.

Recruitment and evaluation of managers

In many respects, the central issue in the rationalization of management authority has been the most effective methods for the selection, promotion, and evaluation of management personnel. The issue is basic not only for increasing management efficiency but also relieving some of the social frustration created by a decline in opportunities for upward social mobility. There is in the 1970s some doubt whether every worker carries a baton in his knapsack.[95] The issue is basic as well insofar as it throws into relief the conflicting values of the utopian and existing political cultures.

From the narrower perspectives of organizational rationalization, the objective of refashioning the methods of evaluating and promoting management personnel is to reduce the gap between formal and informal management structures. This is clearly an extremely complex problem because it initially involves adjusting the historic conflict between formal bureaucratic methods of appointment and control and ascriptive and personalized methods characteristic of the informal structure.

Over the past fifteen years, two distinct approaches have arisen as modes for rationalizing this aspect of industrial organization. The application of democratic and scientific methods clearly have different political and ideological significance and radically different consequences for the distribution of authority. If the election of industrial management officials appears to be the more certain way of identifying formal and informal organization, it also is a radical departure from existing practice. The use of scientific methods, on the other hand, is not only congruent with the bureaucratic model but also designed to strengthen it. It is part of the complexity of the existing situation, however, that the application of either democratic or meritocratic principles to industrial organization has evoked strong political and bureaucratic opposition.

Since the mid-1960s, there has been a tentative and cautious experimentation with the election of managerial staff at the enterprise level. Election may take several institutional forms. In the Soviet context, *vybornost* is generally understood as the selection of "leading" (usually line) officials through majority vote.[96] Although there are indications of broad grass-roots support for election of managers up to the post of director, the adoption of this procedure by Popov and Dzhavadov has been rejected as "premature." In their view, the average worker still lacks the competence to judge the suitability of a candidate for a director's post, or even for the head of a large shop.[97] The election of first-line supervisors, however, is less controversial. Election of brigade leaders and foremen is justified less as a matter of ideological principle than as a means of reducing the conflict between formal and informal leaderships and improving the psychological climate.[98]

The support for even this limited form of democratization, however, is not complete. A survey of nine hundred workers, engineering personnel, and line managers printed in 1977 reveals that basic approval came largely from workers on the bench and technicians. But 25 percent of the foremen, 33 percent of the shop heads, and 50 percent of the plant managers were opposed. In this respect, it is significant that only 50 percent of the mail received by *Literaturnaia gazeta* supported moderate change in existing practice. The letter writers, most of whom presumably were members of the intelligentsia, were in strong opposition to any radical change in the appointive system.[99]

The ambivalent and divided opinion on the desirability of the election of even first-line managers undoubtedly reflects the values derived from the social and cultural stratification of Soviet society. It also reveals, however, the pervasive fear of increased organizational pluralism, which has influenced so many facets of structural rationalization. The election of brigade leaders or foremen is viewed as the opening wedge leading to the election of all industrial managers. In addition, elections would shift the primary loyalties of the foreman from his supervisors to his worker-constituents.[100]

Despite these anxieties, experimental programs for the election of foremen have been initiated in Krasnoiarsk, Baku, and Estonia. Shock construction brigades in Bratsk have also reportedly begun to elect brigade leaders and foremen.[101] Whether such elections conform to Western electoral procedures, however, may be questionable. Electoral procedures for which there is detailed information appear to be highly conditioned. In the well-publicized experiment in Riga's Kommutator Production Union, nomination to each post is confined to a single candidate. Multiple candidacies and open competition or campaigning is barred to preserve collective solidarity and prevent complicating job relationships. To be elected, a candidate must receive 75 percent of the vote with 80 percent participating. Any position may be filled by appointment, although a subsequent election is required.[102] There is no clear indication, however, that election is tantamount to appointment to the post.

If there has been extreme caution in the revision of bureaucratic methods of appointment and evaluation, there is nevertheless a recognition that the traditional system of recruitment and evaluation has serious deficiencies under contemporary conditions. The older system advanced as the basic formal criterion for assessing the success of the manager in meeting the plan is itself a highly relative indicator. Informal assessment, which has received little systematic research, has normally included personal evaluations by superiors based on information on the *kharakteristika,* or personnel report, and information secured through informal networks. Evaluation and certification of political reliability have been the responsibility of the interested Party committee. The use of such trial-and-error methods of recruiting and evaluating industrial managers, however, has proved costly. Moreover, the removal of incompetent industrial executives has frequently been a difficult and sensitive matter.[103]

The application of new methods in selecting and evaluating management personnel has been paradoxical. The interest in Western and Eastern European research and practice has remained strong. Implementation, however, has been limited and experimental. The use of new approaches has been confined to the enterprise. Moreover, Soviet scientists have been cautious about the value of such specific techniques, such as testing, for evaluating managerial potential.[104] The basic methods in current use are formal competition (*konkurs*) and various forms of certification (*attestatsiia*).

There are clear indications that distinctive approaches are developing for the recruitment and evaluation of different types of managers. The use of formal competition for the selection of managers for professional institutions has been most widespread and firmly established, presumably in deference to the high level of skills which must be coordinated and controlled. *Konkurs* was established in 1953, shortly after Stalin's death, when appointment to teaching and research posts in higher education was made subject to open examination. In 1957 competition was extended to the selection of scientific personnel; in 1970 it was applied to creative personnel in the theater and other performing arts.[105] Meritocracy in the form of open competition has not been extended to other sectors of the state bureaucracy, but there is very frequently a high degree of informal competition for desirable administrative positions.[106] The underlying question with respect to *konkurs* is clearly the degree to which such procedures bind the Party and state officials responsible for the operation of the institution.

The question of the finality of the procedure arose in connection with the far more limited application of open competition for posts in industry. In 1966 the principle was extended experimentally to the selection of shop heads in selected industries. Vacancies were advertised in the press, and candidates were publicly interviewed by a special plant commission, which then selected the most suitable candidate. The choice of the commission, however, was not obligatory on the plant administration and, as with other experiments, has not been extended.[107]

Over the past decade, the major innovation in personnel practice has been the development of certification, which focuses on managerial evaluation and is designed to assess competence and productivity. The procedure may include a variety of techniques, including testing and the use of games. The usual type of certification, however, is usually through expert evaluation by means of certification commissions. Data are systematically collected on the personal qualities and performance of managers and then compared against a set of prescribed limits. The formalized review is then used for salary administration, promotion, transfer, demotion, and termination.[108] As with similar systems in the West, the process is a method of personnel control. A wide variety of forms of certification have been applied in Soviet industry over the past decade. Specific variants have been developed by the Gorkii City Party Committee, the Krasnoiarsk Aluminum Plant, and many other enterprises throughout the country. Some systems have adapted the Saratov zero defects system to personnel evaluation; others have constructed such new methods as Pulsar. Certification is usually applied to lower- and middle-level line personnel and to functional specialists within the enterprise. In some programs, however, particularly in such lagging sectors as the light and food industries, certification has been extended to managers and chief engineers.[109]

The various systems are clearly shaped for specific purposes. The Gorkii and Krasnoiarsk procedures are designed to evaluate line officials and therefore have a prominent political content. The approach to the certification of technical and economic specialists, in contrast, stresses knowledge and skills. Both zero defects and Pulsar are distinguished by their effort to influence motivation.

The Gorkii system is designed to evaluate shop line personnel. The Gorkii City Party Committee and the sociological laboratory of Gorkii State University developed the materials and set the criteria for certification. In this procedure the certification commission is the Bureau of the City Committee, which discusses the results of the review with the manager's superiors. Both the secretary of the shop Party organ and the trade union representative play prominent roles in the process of evaluation.[110]

The political dimension has a dominant function in the Krasnoiarsk approach as well, although the Party *apparat* is less directly involved. With the help of the sociological laboratory of the local university, a questionnaire was developed to secure data on education, experience, positions held, and Party membership. Certification commissions within the plant include both Party and trade union representatives. Each commission concentrates on the manager's organizing abilities, knowledge of the work, effort to improve his qualifications, and relationships with the Party and other social organizations in the plant. The results of the investigation have been used for promotion, demotion, and salary purposes. In each case, plans were worked out for improvement in areas judged to be deficient.[111]

The application of the Saratov zero defects and Pulsar has been directed toward both evaluation and stimulation of functional specialists. The Saratov system, adapted from the system of quality control developed in the 1950s, has been in limited use since the early 1960s. This procedure evaluates the work of the specialist according to the percentage of total production accepted upon first presentation. Because of the ambiguities surrounding the process of evaluation, this method has been controversial and has had limited application. It is principally used in the Berdianski Cable Plant and a few enterprises in Riga.[112]

The most widely publicized system of evaluation has been Pulsar, a program of evaluation and stimulation explicitly conceived as an antidote to routinization and stagnation of functional specialists.[113] Designed by two Lvov economists, the concept has been to inject "pulsation" into the work of a technical, design, or other department by introducing compulsory competition tied to a system of rewards and sanctions among its members. The system was introduced in April 1971 into the department of the chief technologist of the Lvov production union "Elektron." The procedure, which has remained experimental, has also been introduced in the Ninth Construction Trust of the Moscow Oblast Construction Administration.[114]

The method used in Pulsar is simple and direct and has gone through several modifications. Initially the specialists were categorized into five hierarchical groups. Once a month each engineer's work was evaluated by two specialists, and the results published. During the first three months, the effect of Pulsar was to stimulate the intensity of work; then its effects began to wear off. To correct this situation, the rules of the game were changed by linking this evaluation to bonuses, promotions, and demotions. The top 20 percent of the department received additional premiums, and the bottom 20 percent lost part of their bonus. Later, the procedure was revised to include a mandatory rise in salary or position for the upper 10 percent and a similar reduction of the lowest 10 percent.[115] The system, which runs counter to human relations theory, has been bitterly controversial and probably will not be widely adopted.

The process of certification was adopted as national policy after the Twenty-fourth Congress. The direct supervision of certification by the ministry appears to have originated in the Estonian Ministry of Light Industry. In 1971 several ministries formed certification commissions, usually headed by deputy ministers, which set the criteria and guidelines for enterprise commissions. Although the certification commissions have the potential for purging enterprise management, published information on the results of certification suggests that moderation has been the dominant theme. Between 1972 and 1975, the Ministry of Construction Materials investigated more than 130,000 line managers and specialists. In this ministry, about 2,000, or 1.5 percent, failed to receive a positive evaluation. However, 300 directors and 600 chief engineers or first deputies were replaced, and 8,000 put on the promotion reserve list.[116]

The results of certification in the Ukrainian Ministry of Light Industry were less decisive, particularly with respect to enterprise managers and chief engineers. Between 1972 and 1974, 20,000 specialists, 390 directors and 25 chief engineers were certified. Fourteen directors were placed on probation; and 10 managers and 6 chief engineers were removed. Among the specialists, 98.5 percent were positively evaluated. One thousand were raised in rank, and 150 lowered.[117]

The overall impact of innovational personnel practice on the general distribution of authority over the past decade has been marginal. Policy has been cautious. An extensive rationalization of personnel practices in industry requires the development of a large pool of trained specialists, an area which has been neglected in the post-Stalin as well as the earlier period.[118] Moreover, methodological problems have arisen around the newer approaches to certification of competence and performance. A basic criticism has been that present procedures focus excessively on psychological qualities rather than performance of the leader.[119] Controversy has been extensive on the nature and types of criteria and coefficients to be used and applied. The Pulsar experiment, for example, has stimulated charges of biased evaluations and efforts to control the structure and composition of committees.[120] Equally important have been the barriers created by traditional and highly institutionalized methods of selection and evaluation.[121]

Educating the managers

Perhaps the most challenging aspect of the effort to improve the quality of management has been the extensive program of management education undertaken since 1965. The reasons for the serious concern for improving the general quality of management are evident. Under conditions of increasing dynamism and complexity characteristic of the scientific-technical revolution, managers who have the knowledge and skills to apply modern methods of management and sensitivity to human relationships are a vital necessity.[122] Indeed, without an extensive program of reorientation, the programs of the 1960s and 1970s to modernize management would prove abortive.

The task is a dual one. The most pressing is to create a corps of professional managers. The second is to expand the knowledge of modern management among all specialists.[123] Although the issue of the professionalization of management has been ideologically sensitive, a network of centers for management education developed rapidly between 1965 and 1975.

In the first decade, the primary emphasis in management education was on retraining or executive development. The development of management as an undergraduate speciality has been extremely slow, undoubtedly reflecting an underlying ideological tension. It also is a result of an unresolved debate about the nature of management education and whether it should be a graduate or undergraduate specialty. Several higher educational institutions, notably the Ordzhonikidze Institute of Management in Moscow, have created a management "minor." A series of core courses in management are combined with a student's major specialty. Demand for the sixty students graduated as engineer-managers in 1978 from the Ordzhonikidze Institute appears to have been very high.[124]

Success in expanding the amount of management training in the average engineering or economics curriculum, however, has been less evident. Although a new course on the scientific foundations of management has been made part of the curriculum of all institutes of higher education, the proportion of instruction in management remained 3 percent after a decade.[125]

The network for retraining managers has proceeded in a decentralized fashion. The vision of Popov and others of a network combining research with consultation and education has yet to develop except in a few cases.[126] Management education also has not followed the model of the American graduate school of business, which Soviet specialists have examined assiduously. As a means of concentrating time and resources, management education has stressed short, intensive courses on a full- or part-time basis.

Management development since 1965 has proceeded in an essentially decentralized fashion. Methodological and policy controls have been parceled out to the Ministry of Higher and Specialized Secondary Education, the State Committee for Science and Technology, and the State Committee of Labor and Social Questions.[127] The operation and financing of management education, however, has been the obligation of the industrial ministries and republican councils of ministers. One major result of this loosely coordinated and overlapping structure has been the creation of diverse programs of uneven quality.

Since 1971, the centerpiece of the system for management retraining has been the Institute for the Management of the National Economy. The institute trains top-level line managers of the ministries and state committees as well as officials from CMEA. The basic program in the institute is a three-month, full-time course of almost five hundred hours. The stress is on general management functions and modern methods of management. The use of mathematical models and computers in decision making and the role of sociological and psychological methods in management appear as the core of the curriculum. The institute has been distinguished by its faculty, which includes Kantorovich, Glushkov, Milner, and Fedorenko.[128]

The original model for training enterprise officials, still considered the most desirable, uses departments for training line officials and planners set up under the Ministry of Higher and Specialized Secondary Education. Initially, four faculties were created in the Moscow (Ordzhonikidze), Leningrad, and Kharkov Engineering–Economics Institutes and the Uralsk Polytechnical Institute. In 1970 the Plekhanov Institute in Moscow added a faculty for planning industrial production. In 1972 an additional six faculties were set up in other institutes. Their expansion to the proposed 150 to 200 faculties, however, has been stopped.[129]

The few programs offering courses for "organizers of production" are relatively selective. They have been designed for potential managers under age forty. They must have a higher education and at least five years' experience. The courses are full time and planned on a curriculum of six hundred to eight hundred hours over six months.[130] The numbers trained in these schools, however, are small. Over the first ten years, about five thousand were retrained. The numbers, however, have increased. About two thousand were enrolled in the 1976–7 school year.[131]

The quality of these programs is considered high. The curriculum places some stress on the interbranch and theoretical aspects of management. The courses are intensive and focus on the use of mathematical models and ASU in planning and management, NOT, sociological and psychological aspects of management, and the economies of production. In addition to lectures, methods of instruction include seminars, workshops, internships, and business games. The emphasis upon theory appears to vary. The curriculum of the Plekhanov Institute's program, set up for planners and supply workers, includes a thirty-two-hour course on systems analysis in management.[132] In other institutes, this material is probably covered in courses on modeling and ASU.

The overwhelming majority of managers who have undergone management training have passed through the facilities operated by the ministries, state committees, and republican council of ministers. The scale of the operation is large. During the Ninth Five-Year Plan, 5.4 million line officials and specialists moved through the system. In 1975 the total reached approximately 1.5 million.[133]

The network of branch training is highly diverse and complex. In addition to the 11 faculties for training organizers and planners in institutions of higher education, the ministries and state committees have established more than 50 institutes for executive training, which in turn have created 82 affiliated subbranches throughout the country. The ministries have also sponsored 102 specialized departments in local and regional higher educational institutions. The ministries operate, in addition, about 800 management courses in the enterprises. Enterprise officials also are enrolled for programs in the six republican institutes which began in 1969. There is, finally, a wide range of courses offered by technical and other institutes in methods of network planning, specialized computer applications and other phases of management.[134]

The quality of executive training offered by the ministries in the first decade has varied widely. Curricula, forms of instruction, facilities, and purposes are very uneven. Some advanced training institutes, such as those of the Ministry of the Electrotechnical Industry and the Estonian Republican Ministry of Light Industry, are well equipped and staffed model institutes,[135] but few other institutes approach their standards.

The programs are relatively short: two months for full-time and six months for part-time students. Their curricula largely duplicate those offered by the eleven faculties. They include courses on the use of models, ASU, NOT, and economic and behavioral methods. The curricula of the branch institutes differ, however, in their narrow, branch focus and narrow, applied character.

The development of a uniformly high-quality executive training program in slightly more than ten years has naturally proved difficult. Growing pains, particularly within the branch system, have been pervasive. The full-time programs of the Institute of Management of the National Economy, the eleven faculties, and the model institutes appear well conceived and staffed. The great majority of programs, in contrast, has been judged too short to be effective and to suffer from an excessively narrow concentration.[136]

The sources of some of the major problems of executive training are familiar and perhaps to be expected. However persuasive the need in the abstract for a thorough intellectual reorientation of the managers, the production bias of the majority of managers appears high. As V. Zhigalin, the minister of heavy and transport machinery, has noted, "However effective theoretical training may be, the fact remains that an executive's main qualities are formed in his day-to-day activity."[137] This production orientation, in turn, has generated serious conflict between the ministries and the Ministry of Higher and Specialized Secondary Education (in the first instance) on the nature and direction of executive training.

The contest, quite clearly, has been unevenly matched. As a department head of the Ministry of Light Industry has noted, the ministry lacks the staff, resources, and authority to influence seriously the substance of branch programs. The result has been that "contrary to the center's recommendations, the departments in charge of the various institutes are cutting the number of study hours given to the reorganization of work and management and continue to emphasize strictly engineering, technological knowledge."[138] He concludes, "Fragmentation, an almost complete lack of guidance, and hence duplication are major shortcomings of the present system of advanced training."[139]

A principal deficiency of the branch system has been staffing. There are no graduate programs for training researchers and teachers in management, a condition rooted in the failure to create an autonomous management science. During the 1970s, about 1,100 teachers staff these institutions, more than half of whom have scholarly degrees. Most are characterized as narrow technical and economic specialists.[140] The problem of recruiting trained staff is compounded by low pay, inferior status, and heavy teaching loads associated with teaching in a branch institute.[141]

The quality of branch executive training programs has also been reduced by ambiguous ministerial support. Investment in human capital, in this as in other projects, has had relatively low priority. Funding has been inadequate and facilities minimal. The ministries have been particularly reluctant to release managers for full-time or interbranch training.[142]

For the same reasons that promising managers were kept off reserve promotion lists, they are kept within the branch and trained part time. The ministry frequently sends off for full-time training young, unmarried men with higher education, men about to retire, or personnel who are *personae non gratae.* Occasionally, quotas go unfilled.[143] This situation is often compounded by the lack of motivation of students who fail to see a connection between advanced training and career advancement.[144]

The long-term importance of management education in the 1970s cannot be fairly assessed on the basis of its initial experience. Over the past decade, the value and effectiveness of executive training have been reduced by a large number of factors, including the traditional production orientation and organizational culture over industrial management itself. Through the latter half of the 1970s, the movement toward a general theoretical and interbranch approach to management training was stagnant and may have retrogressed to some degree. The power of the ministries and enterprises in reducing the impact of this as well as other aspects of the modernization of management was impressive.

There is, nonetheless, a broad recognition that the competence of the managers must be raised. The scope of the initial effort suggests strongly that, despite institutional inertia, executive training will be a major issue in the 1980s.

6

Toward a new ministerial structure

Over the past decade, the reform of the formal structure of industrial management has been an important element in the general strategy of rationalization. From the perspective of systemic control, the central issue is clearly interbranch management structure. Without a fundamental reorganization of the central *apparat* of industrial management, such projects for the functional rationalization of management cannot be effectively incorporated into the management system.

Despite their evident importance, however, issues of interbranch and large-scale regional management structure are in a stage of early formulation, bitterly controversial, and fraught with major unresolved political and technical issues. Structural reform at this level is a central issue for the 1980s. In the 1970s, principal concentration was on the reform of the ministerial system.

Through the decade, two problems appear to have been particularly important in rationalizing the formal organization of the ministries. The first was to reverse the trend toward more complex organizational structures and increasing administrative costs. The second, closely related issue, was to prevent informal diffusion of power as well as to overcome the costs of excessive centralization. Within this framework, the core issue has been the relative roles which classical and cybernetic approaches should play in reorganization.

The model for the comprehensive rationalization of the internal organization of the ministries announced in March 1973 incorporates both approaches. Although a few ministries have taken a distinctly systems approach to organizational design, the

214

great majority have routinely followed the classical bureaucratic model. The strong Soviet bias for organizations of scale has continued with only minimum modification. The conservative results of the reform are therefore not unexpected. Like the constraints placed upon the introduction of mathematical models, ASU, and the reform of management methods, the complexity of the problems as well as institutional inertia have limited the depth of change. The ministries, in effect, have been in charge of their own reorganization. Nonetheless, there has been some experimentation with large-scale organization which may indicate the future shape of industrial organization in the next several decades.

The 1973 ministerial reform

The general reform of the ministries legislated in March 1973 represents in some respects the culmination of the initiatives taken by Brezhnev at the December 1969 Plenum of the Central Committee. The new direction of structural rationalization became immediately evident in the results of an unpublicized meeting of the Central Committee on the experience of the Leningrad Oblast Party Committee in the creation of production associations.[1] In addition to the policy of more intensive promotion of multiplant organization, the outlines of a broader policy of branch rationalization appeared in the spring of 1970. This latter direction seems to have been formally initiated in August 1969 in a decree ordering the reorganization of the Ministry of the Wood and Woodworking Industry as well as a decree in October 1969 ordering a sharp reduction in administrative costs.[2]

These individual initiatives were consolidated into a distinctive policy in two stages in the first half of 1970. The first phase was a decision by the Council of Ministers that appeared to mark an extension of the principles of the 1965 economic reform when the Ministry of Instruments, Means of Automation, and Systems of Administration was placed on *khozraschet*.[3] A second, more conservative approach to structural rationalization, however, was legislated in May 1970 in decrees ordering a reorganization of the ministries for the chemical industry, oil industry, and coal industry.[4] The model for the 1973 general reform of the ministerial system followed the provisions of the May rather than the March approach to the rationalization of the branch. The methods and concepts used in the program of rationalization begun in 1969 mixed traditional with the new functional and systems approaches. One aspect of reorganization was the simplification and standardization of the formal structure of the ministry, the redistribution of authority, and the reduction of costs and personnel at all levels of the hierarchy. The functional dimension of the program became evident in the policy of extending *khozraschet* to the upper levels of the ministry and the conscious effort to link the formal structure with the development of OASU and the use of mathematical methods of decision making.[5]

From the initial stages of the economic reform, Minpribor has occupied a special position. In contrast to other ministries, virtually all of its plants were transferred to the new system in 1966. A major innovative step was taken in 1968 when all of the chief production administrations were placed on *khozraschet*. Finally, in March 1970, the ministry underwent extensive reorganization with the certification of the first stage of ASU–Pribor. The hierarchy was cut to three levels; the chief production administrations were abolished and replaced by industrial associations on *khozraschet;* and the production association or large enterprise was declared the basic form of organization for production.[6]

The system of authority was also adjusted. All of the industrial associations were placed under the direct control of a deputy minister, thus preserving their character as line agencies. The industrial association as an organizational form represented a projection of the structure and authority of the production union to the intermediate level of management. As in the *glavk,* which it replaced, the head of the industrial union was placed on *edinonachalie.* In contrast to the chief production union, however, both branch and territorial councils of enterprise directors were formed as constituent elements of the decision-making system.[7]

The distinctive and highly controversial feature of the rationalization of Minpribor was placing it on *khozraschet*. The concept of full *khozraschet* in this application included the self-financing of the ministry as a whole and the use of the five-year rather than the annual plan as the instrument for operational planning. Decision making by the ministry was to be guided primarily by long-term economic normatives. The authority of the ministry was to be increased by a cut in centrally planned indicators and increased control over the internal allocation of resources. The ministry, in turn, guaranteed all obligations and payments to the budget from profits. Finally, the incentive system for personnel in the ministry's *apparat* was made dependent upon the profits of the enterprises and production unions.[8]

The legislation of May 28, 1970, ordering the rationalization of the organization of the chemical, oil, and coal industries followed the model of Minpribor except for the controversial measure of placing the whole ministry on *khozraschet*. *Khozraschet* was confined to the intermediate levels of the ministries' structure.

The reform ordered cuts of 15 to 20 percent in the operating costs of the upper and intermediate levels of the three ministries. The number of hierarchical levels was to be cut to three. As in the Minpribor model, the key structural change was the replacement of the *glavk* with a thoroughly revamped intermediate agency of line management, the all-union or republican industrial association. Placed upon *khozraschet,* the industrial union was projected as the chief agency for operational decision making within the ministry.

The redefinition of the role of intermediate line management implied a complex redistribution of vertical authority. The reform proposed an extensive reallocation of authority between the chief functional administrations of the ministry and the new industrial unions. Operational authority over the definition of demand, supply and sale, technical progress, and financial and credit transactions were to be delegated, along with the necessary resources, to the industrial unions. The reform also proposed to centralize many of the functions earlier delegated to the enterprise under the 1965 legislation.[9] The accelerated movement toward the creation of multiplant production associations, which coincided with the reorganization of the three ministries, effectively ended the organizational aspect of the economic reform.

The strategy of rationalization that emerged in 1970 addressed the specific problems of rationalization with varying degrees of relevance. The objective of cutting administrative costs and personnel through a reduction of the intermediate levels of management structure, concentration and specialization of authority, and elimination of small and expensive production facilities have been traditional in the rationalization of management structure. Similarly, the search for economies of operation through standardization of management structure and expansion of its scale has also been used as an antidote to counter the process of organizational differentiation.

Whether such typical measures of structural rationalization serve as adequate responses to the complex environmental and functional demands of Soviet industrial development is more questionable. The reduction of hierarchical levels is a case in point. This measure has been considered necessary initially as a means of simplifying informational flows in the building OASUs. It is also designed to provide the maximum amount of flexibility and economy and the shortest lines of communication. This increased flexibility and feedback is secured, however, at the cost of an enlarged span of control and, most probably, an increased role for functional management.

The dilemmas involved in the imposition of a trilevel ministerial structure become most acute in those four-, five-, and even six-level structures in the extractive and Group B ministries, which manage a large number of small, geographically dispersed facilities producing a great diversity of products with a variety of technologies. In the light, food, meat, and dairy industries the problem is further complicated by the necessity of meeting the widely differing needs of diverse social and cultural groups.[10] How far authority can be concentrated and formal structure standardized in this group of ministries without losing flexibility or control remains unclear. The difficulty of the problem was reflected in the decision in May 1970 to transform the oil and chemical industries into all-union ministries. The Ministry of the Coal Industry, however, continued as a union-republican ministry.[11]

The issue of the optimal number of hierarchical levels in the ministry has been closely correlated with the question of the structure and authority of the industrial union; the fewer number of levels, the greater the degree of formal and informal delegation. The political sensitivity of the issue of placing the upper levels of the ministry's *apparat* on *khozraschet* reflects the implication of this change for the distribution of authority. In this context, two differing conceptions of the mode for defining the role of the industrial union have arisen.

The more conservative variant advocated placing the *glavki* on *khozraschet* with little change in their traditional administrative role. The more innovative alternative, designed to meet to some degree the demands of the new strategy of growth, proposed transforming the chief production administration into a separate organizational system equipped with enlarged organizational capabilities and greater control over resources.[12] This alternative appears to have been inspired by the models of the Svetlana and Likhachev production unions which, among others, functioned as large, multiplant complexes directly subordinate to the ministry and exercising the legal rights of a chief production administration.[13]

The decision to create *khozraschet* industrial unions did not, in itself, resolve the perennial problems of the allocation of authority within the ministry. If the basic thrust of the reform was to redress the traditional imbalance between line and functional agencies at the ministerial level and thus improve coordination and control, the application of mathematical methods and OASU appear to have the effect of strengthening the functional side of management. Under such conditions, reformulation of authority relationships among the ministers, chief functional administrations, and industrial unions is the complex problem of defining meaningful boundaries between strategic and operational, line and functional authority. Similar, if less complex questions have naturally arisen with respect to the reallocation of authority and function within the production union and its constituent enterprises.

The model adopted for the rationalization of the ministry also does not directly address one of the most complex of the issues of rationalization: the relationship between branch and territorial principles of industrial organization. The return to the ministerial system in 1965 was closely linked with a policy of centralized control over technical innovation. In the heavy industrial ministries, the industrial union formed on a branch basis is clearly appropriate for a policy of centralization on a national scale. This concept, however, has only limited applicability in the extractive and consumer goods industries. The need to retain a predominantly territorial form of organization was reflected in the decision to retain the vertically integrated *kombinat* as the intermediate line agency in the Ministry of the Coal Industry.[14] The method for integrating these two principles on this level, however, has remained essentially unresolved.

The reorganization of the 1970s has also raised complex issues of departmentalization, including the abolition of old and creation of new departments at the upper levels of the hierarchy. Specific problems have clearly emerged with the projected application of matrix structure and the use of product management at the ministerial level. The growth of larger-scale organization promoted by the reorganization has also rendered the familiar problems of internal coordination and control more intense.

The decrees of March 2, 1973, reflected the problems and compromises which developed with the initial implementation of the May 1970 decrees.[15] The March 1973 decree legislated a variety of possible structures. The predominant forms of ministerial structure were to be two- and three-level structures. In the two-level hierarchy, the production union or large enterprise became directly subordinate to the ministry. The three-level system formed an industrial union or *kombinat* at the intermediate level. The four-level system consisted of a hierarchy of union ministry–union republic ministry–republican industrial union and a production union or large enterprise as the basic production unit.[16]

In the 1973 legislation, the all-union and republican industrial unions were defined as "a single organizational complex" which carried full responsibility for the amount and quality of production and for technical development. As in the earlier approach, each industrial union was placed in direct subordination to the ministry. The principle guiding the allocation of authority was the traditional identification of the legal authority of the union with that of its director. The collegial principle, following the example of the ministry, was added with the formation of a council of directors and advisory technical–economic council. Enterprises or production unions entering the industrial union retained their juridical independence. Both the intermediate and lower levels of the ministry operated on *khozraschet*.[17]

Although there was no formal specification of the relationships of authority between the ministerial *apparat* and the industrial union, the relationships between the industrial union and production units were more clearly defined. The 1973 statutes formally superseded the 1965 Statute on the Socialist Enterprise by delegating full or partial control to the union over a whole range of production activities formerly under the jurisdiction of the enterprise. To guard against arbitrary and incompetent decisions, the industrial union became explicitly liable for errors in planning and operational decision making.[18] But, not unexpectedly, no institutional mechanisms were set up to implement this provision. The ministry retained control over the process of rationalization.

The second major piece of legislation forming the framework for rationalizing the ministerial system was a long-awaited decree of the Council of Ministers of March 27, 1974, on the production unions.[19] The objective of the decree was to reduce the extremely diverse and ambiguous structural relationships which have characterized the development of the production association. The decree, with some exceptions, followed established patterns of organization, incorporating existing practice, and aspects of the 1965 statute on the enterprise and the 1973 decree on the industrial union.

The principles for forming a production union remained territorial proximity, similarity of technologies and types of output, as well as previous patterns of cooperative relationships among plants entering the union. To strengthen specialization and centralization within the union, the decree eliminated independent juridical status for enterprises entering the union, a sharp departure from existing practice. An enterprise, however, could continue to conclude contracts and, under certain conditions, maintain current accounts in the local office of the State Bank.[20]

The internal distribution of authority and function within the production union also largely conformed to existing practice. The *apparat* of the chief enterprise was designated as the normal form of management structure, although the formation of a special *apparat* was not excluded in exceptional cases.

The authority of the general director was strengthened under the 1974 statute. The production union functioned on the principle of *edinonachalie.* The collegial principle was embodied in a council of the union, which was authorized to discuss a broad range of questions. When a conflict developed between the general director and the council, however, the general director's orders were to be executed. The general director also received the important right to appoint and remove the heads of subordinate enterprises. The deputy general director, the union's chief bookkeeper, the head of the legal department, and the head of the quality control department were to be appointed and removed by the ministry.[21] This last provision clearly struck at the traditional "family circle."

Approaches to organizational design

The degree to which the problems of the environment and of structure have been taken into account in the construction of plans of rationalization for individual ministries appears to vary. V. G. Vishniakov has complained that a basic obstacle to an effective reform of the ministries' structure lies in the lack of consensus among organizational specialists on which factors most influence structure; thus, a plurality of approaches to the resolution of organizational problems has developed.[22] The still underdeveloped state of theory is compounded by a shortage of specialists in organizational design and the complexity of the problems to be resolved. It is also evident that the process of developing a design for the rationalization of the ministry is as political as its implementation.

The experience of the Ministry of the Wood and Woodworking Industry in developing a scheme of rationalization throws some light on this process. In 1969 the ministry contracted with Moscow University's Center for Problems of Management of Social Production to develop a plan for rationalization.[23] The project was obviously a difficult one. The ministry had a five-level hierarchy producing more than a thousand products, and it employed about a million men in adverse conditions.

After systematic study of the ministry's structure and functions, the problem group proposed three alternative methods of reforming the structure. The first was to regroup the small enterprises into production unions and transform the *glavki* into *khozraschet* industrial unions. The second alternative was to create production unions and reorganize the *apparat* of the *glavki* according to the principles of product management. The third proposal was to strengthen the planning role of the *glavki* and transfer operational management to the production administrations of the ministry. This last variant assumed an extensive exchange of functions and personnel between the central apparat of the ministry and the *glavki*.[24]

Developing a final structure proved difficult because the plan of rationalization was the result of extensive bargaining and compromise. The plan proposed to create three hierarchical levels, abolish the *glavki*, strengthen the chief functional administrations, and use *khozraschet* unions as the operational management structure. The basic plan, however, was modified by Gosplan, the Ministry of Finance, the Committee of People's Control, and the State Committee for Labor and Wages. The final draft authorized a formal structure based upon product management and contained a detailed distribution of authority and functions between the chief functional administrations and the new industrial unions. Formal centralization remained high. With the exception of direct production management and the introduction of new technology, operational authority remained with the ministry.[25]

The functional approach has been dominant in the plan to rationalize the coal industry. The chief functional administrations of the Ministry of the Coal Industry have been reorganized into eight functional groups (supply, construction, and others). Operational authority is concentrated in all-union industrial unions, and each union's structure has six functional directorates. Each directorate controls a group of departments, which are formed according to informational flows. Because the directorate is headed by a line official, it has been categorized as a "functional-line" structure.[26]

The general director of the union and his deputies coordinate the functional directorates, and authority is highly centralized. The structure has been designed to give the management information system a central role. Each industrial union's computer center sends daily reports to the Chief Computer Center in Moscow. These are used primarily for operational control.[27]

Important innovations in organizational design have developed in the construction of new and large-scale production complexes such as the Volga Automobile Plant (VAZ) and the

Kama Truck Plant (KamAZ). In these designs the systems and classical approaches have been combined to distinguish strategic from operational decision making, to separate line and staff authority, and to provide more effective mechanisms for horizontal coordination, including project management.

The design of VAZ modifies line–staff structure extensively. The hierarchy is divided vertically into two levels for strategic and operational decision making. Coordinated by the general direction, the top level focuses on strategic decisions and management of external relationships, and the lower level concentrates on operational decision making within the plant.[28]

The VAZ design showed a marked shift to functionalism at the shop level. Under this system, "the management of the whole system of preparation and control of production is concentrated and centralized" under the general director. Each plant department has full responsibility for a set of production indicators; line personnel in the shop are restricted to direct control over production. The problem with this design is increased difficulties of coordination and control created by forming two distinct levels at the top and introducing functionalism in the shop.[29]

The design for the Kama Truck Plant presents a systems approach to the development of a very large installation. The Kama complex, located in the Tatar Republic, will cover forty square miles and will produce when completed 150,000 three-axle trucks and 150,000 diesel engines a year. Composed of six installations, the plant will eventually employ one hundred thousand workers. It will be three times larger than VAZ, be vertically integrated, and use the most modern production technologies.[30]

The design group for KamAZ was headed by Boris Milner. In evaluating the challenge of the project, Milner has pointed out its unique scale and complexity. There are no analogies for the amount of information and the number of information channels operating in the plant. The project's principal advantage is that the plant can be designed from scratch, free of crippling institutional inertia.

The formal goals of the design are to incorporate the most advanced technological techniques and methods into industrial management. Proceeding from a tree of goals, the designers have separated strategic, coordinational, and operational functions. They have integrated matrix structure with line-staff, used committees extensively, and separated line and functional authority at the intermediate level.

The hierarchy of KamAZ has three levels for strategic, production-economic, and direct production decision making. As a functional system the plant is designed as four blocks or subsystems for technical, economic, social, and production questions. General policy issues will be decided by a coordinating council. Four special committees will handle substantive questions within each decision-making block. Coordinating the interaction of the primary functional blocks will be an executive director, and the directors of the six production facilities will report directly to him.[31]

The management structure of each plant follows essentially the same model. The traditional line-staff structure is preserved. The plant's administrative structure is divided into four decision-making blocks headed by a deputy director. A production committee will coordinate the interaction of the blocks. Operational control will be in a new position, the head of production, with functions similar to those of a chief engineer.[32]

A special feature of KamAZ's design is a conscious effort to improve horizontal coordination through project management. KamAZ will have a variety of technical, economic, social, and other developmental programs, including one for ASU.[33] The project manager will be a middle manager reporting directly to the general director. His staff will follow the Western practice of dual subordination to a project leader and his permanent department head.[34] As a general rule, project managers will have differing amounts of control over financial resources and incentives.[35]

This arrangement differs from the system introduced by Milner into the Urals Heavy Electrical Machinery Plant. In this plant, the project manager has full authority over the entire research and development cycle. He has his own incentive fund and can influence the centralized distribution of premiums. A special department coordinates and controls the various projects.[36]

Whether a production complex of the scale of KamAZ can be managed as a single, integrated organization has yet to be tested.

The structure is extremely complex, and the turn to functional authority may produce problems familiar in Soviet experience. The design, however, does recognize purposes beyond production. The practical value of the design, as Arbatov has noted, depends upon how the managers implement it.[37]

Dimensions of structural change

Developing and implementing concrete plans for the reorganization of the ministries ordered in 1973 has proved, not unexpectedly, to be difficult, as has been indicated by the extension of its completion from 1975 to 1980. Through 1978, twenty-seven general plans were approved by the Council of Ministers and were being implemented. In five years, about 60 percent of Soviet enterprises had become integrated into production unions; ninety-two thousand administrative personnel had been cut, with claimed savings of 17 billion rubles.[38] Actual savings may be more modest. Drogichinskii, on the basis of a cut of eighty-three thousand, estimated savings of only 1.5 billion.[39] In view of the highly honed skills of the Soviet managers in evading administrative cuts, the latter estimate is probably more realistic.[40] Indeed, as Kashirina noted in 1979, many of the claimed savings from rationalization were derived from wholly different sources.[41]

The plans of rationalization have varied in the quality of design and the extent to which they have been implemented. The more successful schemes have been in the specialized and centralized machine-building industries employing mass production technologies. More problematic have been ministries using small-batch technologies and ministries in the extractive and consumer goods industries with complex structures. Initially a variety of principles for structural specialization have been applied. Machine-building ministries have followed a traditional specialization by product. The coal, light, and other consumer goods ministries specialize by product and territory. The Ministry of Nonferrous Metallurgy has used technology as the basis for organization.[42]

Among the more specialized schemes in heavy machine building has been that of the Minsitry of Tractor and Agricultural Machine Building. This ministry, which has figured prominently in Brezhnev's plans for the industrialization of agriculture, was one of the first industrial ministries to have its general plan affirmed by the Council of Ministers.[43] The ministry adopted a two- and three-level system. In 1976, it had nine all-union industrial unions, twenty-seven production unions, and six scientific-production unions (NPO). A reported 3,700 administrative workers have been cut.[44] In this ministry the number of enterprises directly managed from Moscow has been cut in half.

Developing new formal structures for extractive and Group B industries has been more complex. Two examples are the plans for the Ministry of the Coal Industry and Ministry of Light Industry.

The Ministry of the Coal Industry operated under a four- and five-level hierarchy. In 1970, it became a three- and four-level structure. The number of intermediate organs (trusts and *kombinats*) was cut from 56 to 7, and the number of coal mines reduced through merger from 814 to 695.[45] In addition to the all-union industrial unions, 47 production and scientific-production unions were formed. These were large, averaging about 24 enterprises or mines and 55 service organizations. The rationalization reportedly reduced administrative personnel by twenty thousand and saved 130 million rubles.[46]

The Ministry of Light Industry has been an even more complex problem. It contained thirty subbranches and over three thousand enterprises. Ninety-five percent of the ministry's total output was subordinate to a union-republican ministry.

The formal structure of this ministry after reform remains cumbersome. The ministry will have a mixture of two, three, and four levels. There will be 17 union-republican ministries and 1 chief administration subordinate to Moscow. The intermediate level will have 3 all-union and 85 republican industrial unions. The number of independent enterprises was cut by one-third; the remaining will eventually be integrated into 504 production unions. The reorganization presumably will save 85 million rubles.[47]

In her examination of eight union-republican ministries, Kashirina reported projected cuts at the union level from 1,407 intermediate organs to 514, and at the republican level from 361 to 92. All-union and republican industrial unions would constitute 81.5 percent of these units, and management personnel would drop from 39,500 to 20,000.[48]

The replacement of the *glavki* by industrial unions has been a basic element in ministerial reform. These remain large-scale organizations; in 1974, the average all-union industrial union (VPO) managed forty organizations.[49] Many industrial unions are simply old *glavki* renamed; in others, however, the scale of management has been significantly enlarged.

In the Ministry of Tractor and Agricultural Machine Building, the industrial union managing the tractor industry (Soiuztraktorprom) is composed of the four largest tractor-building complexes in the Soviet Union, twenty-one enterprises, and one large research unit.[50] Similarly, Soiuzmetallurgprom of the Ministry of Ferrous Metallurgy manages the production of a large proportion of Soviet steel. It has incorporated a large scientific institute as well as twenty-one *kombinats* and enterprises. Among them, however, are Magnitogorsk, Nizhnii Tagil, Kuznetsk, and the Western Siberian Metallurgical Plant, which are among the largest industrial installations in the Soviet Union.[51]

A dramatic change in industrial organization has been the growth of production unions or associations. Originally approved in September 1965, their early development was frustrated by the *glavki*, managers of merged enterprises, and local Party and Soviet organs, which lost revenue and control over enterprises. Between 1965 and 1970, the number of production unions actually declined.[52] By 1977, production unions were manufacturing 45 percent of production and included about 20 percent of all Soviet enterprises.[53]

The structures of production unions vary widely. In the machine-building industries, the production unions average five or six enterprises. In light industry, the average is nine. *Kombinats* in the chemical, coal, and other extractive industries, however, usually incorporate twenty-five or more enterprises. Size, in turn, influences the number of workers. In production unions of the machine-building industries, the average work force is 5,370, but in light industry it is only 770.[54] The size and complexity of the scientific-production union present special problems because it incorporates such diverse organizations as research institutes, design bureaus, and experimental and production facilities.

One of the most complex issues defining the structure and actual distribution of authority within the ministry has been the legal status of the enterprises entering the production union. In one estimate, 45 percent of the enterprises in production unions were juridically independent. The practical effect is to add another level to the hierarchy.[55]

Legal relationships, however, differ widely by branch. Over 90 percent of the mines entering production unions lost their legal independence, as did 59 percent of enterprises in light industry. At the other end of the scale were over 90 percent of the enterprises of Minpribor and the Ministry of the Meat and Dairy Industry.[56] A large number of contingent factors, including political ones, influence the legal status of an enterprise entering a production union. The principal condition appears to be the distance of the plant from the union's headquarters. In a study of thirty-two ministries, the State Committee for Science and Technology found that only 25 percent of enterprises located in the same city as the union's management retained their independence, in contrast to 44.1 percent of the enterprises outside the cities' boundaries.[57]

Adapting the ministries' internal structure

An important focus of the 1973 reorganization has been the reform of the functional departments of the ministries to accommodate the more complex tasks of management. The general direction of change, on balance, appears to have increased the weight of these departments in decision making at both the central and intermediate levels. In the Ministry of the Gas Industry, for example, the policy has been to strengthen the planning–economic, capital construction, supply, and finance administrations. New divisions have also been created for the standardization and quality of production, norming of material resources, and communications.[58]

Similar types of structural change are evident in the development of industrial unions and large production associations. New functional departments for specialization and concentration of production, design and technological services, NOT, pollution, and other services have been formed.[59] Few of these new departments, however, have been large, as a typical VPO in the

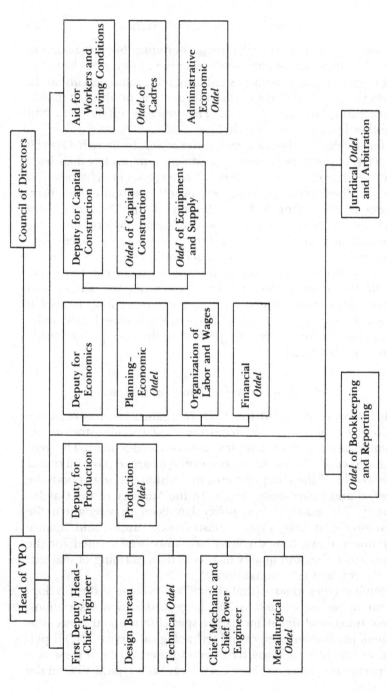

Chart 6.1. Structure of VPO in Ministry of Tractor and Agricultural Machine Building. (Source: N. G. Kalinin, ed., *Sovershenstvovanie organizatsionnoi struktury upravleniia proizvodstvom*, Moscow: Ekonomika, 1974, p. 25.)

Ministry of Tractor and Machine Building indicates. (See Chart 6.1.)

Shifts in personnel size are not, of course, certain indicators of basic shifts of power within the ministry, although they are strongly suggestive. A comprehensive survey of personnel shifts in fifteen ministries between 1969 and 1973 confirms the impression gained from other sources of the increased role of the chief functional administrations. Personnel in these administrations increased sharply in thirteen ministries. In those ministries which abolished the *glavk* in 1970, the shift toward functionalism was particularly marked. The proportion of personnel in the functional administrations in the Ministry of the Chemical Industry increased from 36 to 68.1 percent of the central *apparat* and from 50.8 to 68.4 percent in the Ministry of the Oil Industry.[60]

Through 1976, about four hundred of the approximately six hundred *glavki* had been abolished, and the five hundred unions now contain the majority of personnel at the intermediate level.[61] The addition of new functions and a more complex structure than the *glavk* have increased the size of this unit. This increase, however, has varied. Whereas the Ministry of Construction and Road Machine Building has increased an average of 103 workers, the unions of the Ministry of Tractor and Agricultural Machine Building have grown by 237. The Ministry of Light Industry's average unit size has jumped by 253 management workers.[62]

Initial investigation of the impact of the formation of production unions on the complexity and size of industrial organization at this level has also revealed mixed results. In a 1974 study of structural change in a sample of unions, significant simplification of structure was achieved in only 19 percent of the unions, with the best results observed in about 50 percent of *kombinat*s formed in the coal, chemical, and a few other ministries. Structural complexity, however, actually increased in 26 percent of the unions. In the majority of unions (55 percent) there was no change in either structure or staff. This latter group included not only such large, technically advanced unions as Avtozil and Sigma but also the majority of unions in light industry. Among the unions included in this study, management personnel were reduced in 53 percent of the cases, and administrative costs cut in 73 percent. Management personnel, however, had increased in 43 percent of the sample.[63]

It is clear that changes in structure at both the intermediate and production levels have not been significant. In the majority of industrial ministries, computer centers have not been installed in the all-union industrial unions. The *apparat* of the union is usually in the same city as the ministry. In such cases, the chief computer center of the ministry usually processes the data for the industrial union as well as the functional administrations.[64] In the 1974 study, only 7.5 percent of the unions investigated had their own computer centers; moreover, in those unions which had developed ASUs, the system operated only in the chief enterprise in the great majority of cases.[65]

Authority relationships under the new structure

In many respects the core issue in the reform of formal structure has been the question of the redistribution of authority. Through the 1970s, it is clear that the pattern of structural change in the ministries was mixed, and the cumulative impact on the distribution of authority quite diverse. It should be noted that such diversity is not in itself irrational because optimization of authority relationships may require increased delegation and in other ministries a greater degree of centralization.

On the whole, the formal objectives of the plans have been to distinguish strategic from operational decision making through deconcentration of authority. The matrix describing the redistribution of functions in the coal industry is probably typical for industry as a whole. As Table 6.1 indicates, the policy has been to concentrate authority over technological innovation, production, and financial and economic management at the intermediate level.

The policy of strengthening the role of the chief functional administrations and of deconcentrating authority to large industrial unions clearly raised threats of functionalism from the *apparat*, suboptimization from the industrial unions, and increased conflict between them. To increase the integrating role of the ministers and their deputies, the functional administrations and industrial unions have been regrouped under deputy ministers.[66] The coordinating role of the planning-economic adminis-

Table 6.1. *Matrix of ministry of the coal industry*

	Number of administrative functions					
	Existing system			New structure		
Groups of functions	Ministry	Kombinat	Enterprise	Ministry	Production union	Production unit
Organization of administration	62	62	49	62	64	31
Technical progress	101	108	105	83	145	42
Production	90	133	90	75	140	37
Economic activity	179	87	57	72	93	11
Capital construction	41	50	39	39	54	11
Material–technical supply	41	45	26	38	47	15
Cadres and services	72	71	55	67	72	22
Total	486	566	421	436	615	173

Source: A. A. Timme, *Struktura, protsess upravleniia narodnym khoziaistvom*, Moscow: Znanie, 1975, p. 31.

tration has been strengthened for the same purpose. Neither structural change has been particularly successful. The State Bank and the Ministry of Finance have opposed any effort to delegate authority to deputy ministers because of their fear of weakening *edinonachalie.*[67]

Through the 1970s there has been little visible change in the formal relationships between the functional departments and new industrial unions. To avoid some of the consequences of functionalism, the industrial unions remain directly subordinate to the ministry. But, to avoid blockage, the principle of restricted functionalism - the right of a functional department to issue binding orders on a line agency - has also been retained.[68]

An increase in the autonomy of the intermediate level, one of the major objectives of the reorganization (by reducing the scope and frequency of intervention of the central *apparat*) presumably would also cut the incidence and costs of functionalism in the management of the ministry. On the whole, the implementation of the provisions for increased delegation to the industrial unions of functions formerly concentrated in the ministry has been marginal. There is the judgment among Soviet specialists that the development of the role of the industrial union has been slow and that it differs insignificantly from the *glavk* in both authority and control over resources.[69] Change in this, as in other aspects of the reform, has been stymied by such factors as the technical, economic, and geographical structure of the branch, complexity of management relationships, commitment of the ministry's leadership to the reform, level of institutional inertia, amount of uncommitted resources, and pervasive conflicts of social and economic interests among organizational units. Under such conditions, implementation of a program of either centralization or decentralization becomes a high-risk enterprise.

Delegation of authority from the central to intermediate level appears to have followed the general prescription of the reorganization insofar as the central *apparat* has retained tight control over key areas of authority and resources. In effect, formal delegation has been largely confined to secondary issues with respect to both the industrial unions and the union-republican ministries. Numerous examples of this tendency can be found in Soviet literature.

Among the formal rights delegated to the production unions of the Ministry of the Coal Industry, for example, are the authority to increase the wage fund of underaged workers, to conduct work on housing and communal services, and to ensure construction sites with additional land.[70] Regarding capital construction, the Ministry of the Oil Industry has delegated the intermediate-level organizations the right to form title lists of projects of estimated costs of 0.5 to 2.5 million rubles.[71] In the Ministry of the Wood and Woodworking Industry, the unions were delegated control over capital repair and the construction of housing. Many smaller functions, however, have not been delegated, in large part because of opposition by such agencies as the Ministry of Finance.[72] As a means of controlling administrative costs, all business trips require the approval of a deputy minister, a procedure which has not only been ineffective but has generated a mass of paper.

A similar pattern is apparent in the process of delegation to the union-republican ministries. It is clear that the basic thrust since the late 1960s has been to reduce the autonomy of these ministries. This was signaled in 1970 by the transformation of the Ministry of the Chemical Industry and the Ministry of the Oil Industry into all-union ministries. The standard argument that technical development requires centralization has also resulted in the formerly republican ministries for communal economy, everyday services, and autotransport becoming union-republican ministries.[73]

The contrary process of delegating formal authority over limited and secondary matters, however, has also been in evidence. The Ukrainian Ministry of the Coal Industry, for example, may raise the plan of a subordinate production union for the production and sale of coal up to 1 percent of the plan affirmed by the union ministry. It can independently conduct open and closed competition for the best research and development work. In limited circumstances, the ministry can make payments for equipment, estimates of which have not been included in the plan affirmed in Moscow. The ministry also enjoys a few other rights of comparable scope.[74]

The limited delegation of formal authority within the ministry is not, to be sure, identical with its actual distribution, which is variable and highly conditioned, even within the same ministry.

Underlying the inevitable contingencies, however, deeply rooted patterns of conflict and cooperation associated with the command economy continue to dominate vertical relationships within the ministry. The continuity in the institutional framework has been evident in a variety of ways.

The struggle of the ministries to curb the autonomy of the industrial unions has been aided by the retention of the management apparatus of the industrial union in the same city as the ministry's *apparat*. The effectiveness of their efforts, however, has also been constrained by a series of factors, which include the still uneven application of technology to decision making and control as well as the failure to develop the management methods necessary for control of those endemic conflicts of interest that exist among organizational units.

More specifically, the resistance of the ministries to transfer authority and functions to the industrial unions is exhibited in their slow development of a precise division of authority between the functional departments and unions. In the Ministry of Ferrous Metallurgy, for example, only 102 of 183 structural subdivisions of the central *apparat* and industrial unions had formal regulations. In this ministry as well as in others in which general regulations have been worked out, the rights of the union over supply, technical policy, and preparation of cadres have been defined so vaguely that the traditional rights and practices of the central *apparat* remain untouched.[75]

The ministries have been as reluctant to delegate control over resources as they have been over authority. Participation of the industrial unions in decisions over the planning of supply appears to vary with conditions. The most significant factor limiting the control of the ministry has traditionally been information. On the whole, the influence of computers on planning procedures has been minimal. The state of development of computerization of supply, however, has been critical in the degree of centralization with respect to this function. In the instruments, chemical, automobile, road construction, and oil industries, the normative modeling of supply requirements has progressed to such a state that supply needs are calculated directly within the ministries' chief supply administrations with the aid of computers. In other ministries, among them heavy machine building, electrotechnical, and light – all traditionally

more decentralized – the system remains as before. The industrial unions continue to collect supply requests from subordinate
units, and supply plans are composed through the usual
methods of incremental bargaining.[76]

A central technique of the ministry in reducing the autonomy
of the industrial union has been to fail to create or even reduce
the financial and technical resources available to the industrial
union. The possession of such resources has been considered
vital to raising the role of the middle level.

As the Gosplan investigation of the implementation of the
March 1973 decrees has observed, a large number of industrial
unions lack the necessary financial reserves for independently
aiding the production unions and enterprises under their jurisdiction.[77] The strategy of the ministries has been to delay the
formation, cut, or restrict the use of several of the specific funds
which the industrial unions have been legally authorized to set
up. This appears to be particularly true with respect to the special funds for mastering new technology, scientific research, the
reserve fund for offering temporary financial aid to the enterprise or union, and the reserve fund for amortization.[78] In specific cases, the ministry has failed to form a fund at the request
of the Ministry of Finance.

The failure of the ministries to implement fully the financial
provisions of the reorganization has also been extended to the
development of the research and development facilities at the
intermediate level. As in other aspects of structural reform, initial results have been mixed. In the ministries for the lumbering
industry, fish, coal, gas, and agricultural machine building, significant resources have been assigned to the industrial or production unions for this purpose. The dominant thrust in implementing this provision, however, has been the contrary one. In
several machine-building branches, the all-union industrial
unions actually possessed 50 percent fewer facilities than the
abolished *glavki*. The research facilities of the Ministry of Ferrous Metallurgy had also been cut in half.[79]

The continuity in the roles of the *glavk* and industrial union
can be attributed to other factors than ministerial opposition.
There is little evidence that a wholesale change in management
personnel at this level has been achieved. Moreover, competition
and conflict among the VPO for resources is a potent instrument

for informal ministerial control. An article in *Pravda* in January 1978 illustrates the point as well as highlighting the vagaries and contingencies involved in the actual process of rationalization. The competition of the industrial unions for control over enterprises has been a marked feature of this as well as previous reorganizations. In the Ministry of the Electrotechnical Industry, which went over to the new structure in 1976, two plants of the same *glavk* with similar technologies and products were assigned to different industrial unions. Through the efforts of the head of the VPO, one of the plants was reassigned. The chief engineer of the second VPO, however, protested the shift and announced he would not transfer it. The chief of the first VPO then appealed to the production administration of the ministry, which ordered the plant transferred. The chief of the second VPO then appealed to the ministry, which supported, not unexpectedly, the production administration. During a conference of the branch trade union organization, the delegate of the second VPO, however, made a personal appeal to A. K. Antonov, the minister, to reconsider the decision. He did, and through the beginning of 1978 the issue remained unresolved.[80]

The resistance of the ministries to delegate sufficient authority or resources to the intermediate levels of management has clearly influenced authority relationships between the industrial and large production unions and their subordinate enterprises, although this relationship naturally varies widely, conditioned by numerous factors.

Initially, it is evident that the provisions adopted in 1973 for centralizing a large number of functions previously delegated in 1965 to the enterprise have been largely implemented. The number and type of functions which have been centralized, however, differ. Virtually all VPOs have centralized functions and resources for research and development, investment and capital construction, housing funds, and the preparation of cadres. Only some, however, have formally centralized such economic and financial services as supply and sale and centralized payments to the bank and budget.[81] The basic impulse has been to centralize those services with a high political salience. The campaign initiated in the early 1970s to improve product quality, for example, has resulted in a large number of centralized control services (OTK) being established within the industrial union.[82] Moreover, where normative methods of decision making have been developed for such functions as planning labor and wage (or supply), full centralization of function has occurred.[83]

The combination of often intense informal competition between the VPOs and ministerial *apparat* and, as part of that, the reluctance to delegate either authority or resources has naturally influenced the relations of the VPO with the production unions and enterprises within their jurisdiction. The formal centralization of functions within the industrial union sharpens the traditional problem of the gap between authority and responsibility characteristic of the relations between intermediate and lower management with the top of the hierarchy.

The anomalous position of the VPO is expressed by its continued close dependence on the *apparat* of the ministry and the continuing practice of the functional administrations of bypassing the VPO to deal directly with the enterprise.[84] It is also evident in the manipulation of the resources and indicators of the enterprise by the ministry without the prior consultation required by the 1973 law.

The response of the heads of production unions or enterprise directors reinforces this pattern. Sharply opposed to the reduction in their own authority and control over resources and accurately perceiving where the power in the ministry lies, they bypass the VPO and also deal directly with the functional and production administrations of the ministry.[85] The role of the VPO thus becomes what it was for the *glavk*; control over plan fulfillment. There is judgment that, as in the past, the *apparat* of the VPO is deeply involved in resolving a large number of small problems, particularly those concerned with supply. The larger problems such as technical innovation and economic analysis fall by the way.[86]

Authority in the production unions

The larger production unions which are directly subordinate to the ministry in the two-level system have a structure like the VPO but have a legal basis for a greater concentration of authority because enterprises entering them without juridical independence can assume the role of shops in a single enterprise. Where this has occurred, as in the coal industry, where 90 percent of the mines and enterprises entering production associations have lost their independence, centralization is high. They have centralized control over technical education, bookkeeping, inventories, loading and unloading, and supply of utilities to the mines and cities in their jurisdiction. They have also centralized control over special funds, contact with external organizations, and control over such facilities as pioneer and rest camps.[87]

A basic complaint in the relationship between the large production union and the ministry is the former's lack of authority and control over resources. In a position similar to the VPO, they are forced to turn to the ministry's *apparat* for the solution of numerous small questions. As the general director of the Ukrainian automotive production union has complained, a "large part" of current production questions are decided within the walls of the production and other administrations of the Ministry of the Automobile Industry.[88] Presumably the pattern observed in the three-level systems of bypassing the intermediate level is practiced here as well.

The degree to which production unions have implemented a strategy of close operational control over their enterprises has varied. In those production unions, or industrial unions, which have well-developed computer systems or which are territorially compact, centralization of operational management and control is high.[89]

The chief enterprise of Moscow's Zil production union, whose plants are territorially dispersed, for example, has centralized, computer-aided operational planning and control for all of its affiliated plants. Each detail of production for each product is calculated in Moscow, and centralized production reports for all the plants are calculated daily. With the aid of the computer, the Moscow management can calculate the production plan for each shop and sector.[90] A similar type of centralization is observed in the production union Moloko, a territorially concentrated meat and dairy complex in Moscow. The *apparat* of the chief enterprise in this union has concentrated virtually all control over planning, supply, technical reequipment and reconstruction, sales, and financial and material reserves.[91]

The extent to which a full centralization of authority according to the classical model is desirable, or possible, however, is disputed. Broad differences in the approaches of the ministries as well as limiting organizational and production factors have operated as a constraint on full centralization within the union.[92] In the 1974 study of unions previously cited in this chapter, a high degree of decentralization over virtually all management functions was evident, except in the territorially compact unions such as Moloko.[93] Even in schemes of rationalization, as in the coal industry, which anticipate a sharp reduction in the autonomy of the enterprise, such functions as production planning, control over cadres, the technical preparation of production, and the planning of labor and wages have remained decentralized.[94]

A leading student of production unions, V. D. Stundiuk, has noted the significance of territorial proximity and legal status for the formal distribution of authority. Where there is a dispersal of plants, such services as construction and capital repair tend to be decentralized. Centralization of economic and financial relationships usually occurs in production unions with integrated production units but are decentralized in unions with enterprises with independent legal status. Finally, whether such functions as supply and sale are decentralized depends upon a whole range of production factors such as variety and stability of output, complexity of technology, and number of clients.[95]

From the vantage point of the late 1970s, two conflicting trends in the distribution of authority have emerged. There is evidence, on one hand, that the number of enterprises with independent juridical status, while still large, is dropping, thus pointing to increased centralization. A second trend, however, is observable in the movement gathering momentum in the 1970s of major enterprises in metropolitan areas to resolve some of their growth problems through affiliation with other enterprises in distant areas. A study of Zakarpathian Province in the Ukraine noted that plants within this province were associated with chief enterprises in Kiev, Leningrad, Ulianovsk, and even as far as Omsk in Western Siberia. Prevented from expanding in the metropolitan areas because of shortages of land and labor, these enterprises search for plants in areas with a good climate and adequate labor and transportation.[96] Management controls over these plants tend to be weaker because of distances involved.

The scientific–production union

An important direction in the rationalization of the ministry has been experimentation with new organizational forms. Of particular interest in this respect has been the development of scientific-production unions (NPOs). Conceived as a device for speeding up research and development and introducing new technologies into production, the NPO has a formal structure which integrates research, design, experimental, and production facilities into a single organizational complex. At the end of the 1970s, the degree of completeness and level of integration of NPO varies widely. The NPO has produced particularly complex problems in the formal distribution of authority and function.

The results of the creation of scientific–production unions within the ministry appear mixed. An investigation of more than 100 of the 130 NPOs has shown them to be a more effective form of organization for technical innovation than the traditional branch system. The time for research and development is reduced; the technical level of production is raised; and new products and technologies have been more rapidly introduced.[97] An official of the State Committee for Science and Technology has estimated that the average reduction of time in the development and introduction of new products into production has been from 1.5 to 2 years with a rise in quality.[98]

The NPO is also of interest organizationally because it has been the primary institution in the ministry to introduce matrix structure and network planning models into research and development. Project management in the NPO follows Western models closely. The basic organizational unit is the project group (*kompleksnyi brigad*), composed of scientific and technical specialists from various departments. The usual network model uses critical path methods, or CPMs, to establish stages of work, time frames, sequential and parallel work processes, the responsibilities of executors, and resource allocation. Control as well as computation is computer-based.[99]

Project groups are usually headed by a scientist or technologist, although patterns appear to differ. In NPO–Pishcheprom, the authority of the leader is detailed in a code. His responsibilities appear to end, however, with the completion of the design; coordination is assigned to a permanent department for the development and introduction of technology. Other NPO, however, have established the authority of the project manager over the whole cycle from design to introduction into production.[100]

In NPO–Plastpolimer, which has a highly centralized permanent structure, the project manager is responsible for the full project and functions as a line official. A similar authority is vested in the project manager in NPO–Soiuzgaz-Avtomatika, which has a responsibility for developing ASUs for the gas industry. In addition to establishing the network model for the project, the manager can issue the model as a directive instrument of control and maneuver up to 5 percent of the total wage bill for the project and 10 percent of supply and finance. With respect to the sensitive issues of disciplining members of the project, the project manager can remove a member from the project but negotiates the bonus of the project member with the head of his permanent department. On the whole, work in this NPO has been speeded up by two to three times, and there has been a growth in labor productivity of 30 to 50 percent.[101]

The future of project management in the NPO is unclear. The problem of the distribution of authority between the project manager and the head of the permanent department is unresolved, and communication has become more complex. Whether as a solution to this problem or as a manifestation of the basic bureaucratic impulse toward fixed and predictable relationships, the tendency has been to form project groups into permanent departments under a single leadership.[102]

Although the NPO appears superior to traditional Soviet forms of organizing research and development, it is undoubtedly experiencing serious problems of structure and adaptation to the values and demands of the ministry's environment. Similar problems of organizational integration are being experienced in the construction of agroindustrial unions and probably will be found in the development of multinational unions in the Soviet bloc.

Through the middle 1970s it has been clear that there has been no consensus on the NPO's purposes or functions, and thus its role in the ministry has been undefined and its legitimacy questioned. In the view of one Soviet specialist, the whole legal basis for the operation of the NPO is in disorder. Unresolved problems of structure have been one of the principal reasons for a number of NPOs falling apart.[103] One central issue has concerned power in the NPO. Although a scientific research or design institute has normally been placed at its head, other functional groups have been in sharp competition with the scientists for control over the organization. A second major issue has been where to place the NPO in the hierarchy of the ministry. Although the formation of VPOs would appear to have provided a basis for solution, there has been an underlying tug of war between those who want to centralize technical policy and those who want to bring research and development close to production.[104]

Controversy has also been sharp on the degree to which services and functions should be centralized in the union. Practice appears to vary widely. Some NPOs, like Plastolimer and Positron, have fully centralized virtually all functions in the chief institute. Others, like Soiuzteklomash, have not centralized any services. The majority of NPOs, however, have mixed systems in which the basic services and functions are centralized. In these unions, planning, supply, finance, and wages are normally centralized.[105]

Problems of structure are closely related to the underlying difficulty of functional integration. In those unions that have developed project management, computerization has served as an instrument of organizational integration. The majority of unions, however, have experienced serious difficulties in ordering their diverse and complex processes.

The reasons for the difficulty in functional integration lie in differences in the nature of the activities to be harmonized. Soviet specialists, in particular, have pointed to the distinction between the processes of research and production. The products of research are ideas. Its results are difficult to measure, and the risks of achieving useful results are higher. Not least, research procedures and expenditures are long term. In contrast, the products of industrial production are material, specific, determinate, and subject to more predictable programming.[106] These cleavages sharpen the normal problems of planning, evaluation, and development of an effective system of material stimulation.

The lack of coordination in planning has been one of the most troublesome of the issues hampering the operation of the NPO. The ministry normally sets the plans for production, scientific research, and technical progress. The plans, however, are issued at different times by different functional administrations and are not coordinated at the ministerial level. In addition, because some NPOs are constituted of territorially separated units, their plans often need coordination on a territorial level.[107] These deficiencies in planning procedures are closely linked with the application of *khozraschet* in the scientific–production union.

It is clear that the complex problems of pricing new products observed in the traditional economics of technical innovation or of financing research and development have not been fully resolved in the NPO. The most urgent problems of management, however, stem from the issues of finding effective planning and evaluative indicators. The NPO is usually assigned the same success indicators as the industrial enterprise. There is, however, the recognition that the use of success indicators based upon some measurement of input–output is inappropriate because the product is so difficult to measure. In one case, for example, where the NPO received its plan in tons, the new product was, not surprisingly, extremely material-intensive.[108]

There have been, nonetheless, serious conflicts among Soviet economists on the most effective indicators for stimulating cooperation and measuring efficiency. The choice has evolved between an index of profitability based upon savings achieved by the introduction of new technology and some index based upon the savings of time. In an effort to resolve the conflict, the State Committee of Labor and Wages, the State Committee for Science and Technology, and the trade unions agreed upon the index of savings received through the introduction of new technology. Experiments using this indicator as well as *realizatsiia* (amount of products sold) have been instituted in the Ministry of the Electrotechnical Industry.[109] Whether the index of savings from new technology can be used has been doubted, however, because it depends upon agencies other than the NPO for its implementation.

The problem of success indicators is closely related, in turn, to the question of the formation and distribution of premiums to different functional groups in NPOs. Over the past decade, four or five different systems have evolved within the same union.[110] In one large machine-building NPO, Kriogenmash, premiums for scientific and technical personnel have been based upon savings in the wage fund, whereas the industrial component uses the criteria of *realizatsiia* and profitability.[111] The use of different criteria clearly produces inequities. An industrial worker doing the same work as a technician will be paid more. Scientists usually receive 5 to 6 percent of the wage fund, whereas workers will average 20 to 30 percent. This inequity is sharpened by the conflicting motivations of technical and industrial personnel. The technicians have a strong economic interest in the most rapid introduction of new products and processes. Industrial personnel, however, continue to have a strong disincentive against technical innovation.[112]

The fragility of an NPO like Kriogenmash is illustrated by the response of its personnel to a joint decree by Gosplan, the Central Statistical Administration, and the Ministry of Finance issued in March 1976. The decree ordered that scientific-technical personnel of NPOs be included in the number of production personnel for the purposes of calculating labor productivity. The expected reduction of bonuses threatened an exodus of the scientists from this as well as other unions.[113]

The problems of the NPO are also closely intertwined with the policies and interests of the ministry, which remain short term and operational. Many ministries have been resistant to the formation of the NPO; and, as with the VPO, the unions often lack laboratory and experimental facilities as well as other resources.[114] The ministries have also tended to direct the research of NPOs to narrowly defined themes of immediate interest, thereby reducing the applicability of the results. Finally, under pressure for increased current production, the ministry frequently diverts their activity from research and development to serial production. In some NPOs, current production absorbs up to 90 percent of their time and resources.[115] Some part of this diversion is clearly attributable to the use of success indicators appropriate to industrial production.[116]

In its present state of development, the ministerial scientific-production union appears to be less than adequate as the vanguard of the scientific–technical revolution.

Rationalization in perspective

As Soviet management enters the 1980s, it is evident that the problems of industrial organization remain unresolved. Overall, the degree to which the formal structure of the ministry has been simplified and made more efficient has been, at best, modest. The more urgent issues of large-scale interbranch and regional management, moreover, have yet to be addressed. The reasons for the marginal results are undoubtedly as complex as the problems that the reform was designed to solve. Initially, it is evident that only a few of the ministries have had expertly constructed schemes of rationalization. Secondly, the design and implementation of the general schemes have been decentralized, and the ministries have mounted significant opposition to structural change in depth. Finally, the reorganization has proceeded largely in isolation from the rationalization of the functions of management. The reform has therefore failed to reduce the traditional gap between formal and informal organization.

The quality of organizational design has been uneven. In part, this reflects the diverse conditions confronting the individual ministry. Design and implementation have been more successful in heavy industrial ministries with simpler structures using mass or continuous production technologies than in the extractive and Group B industrial ministries.[117] Design problems, however, can also be attributed to the shortage of specialists and tight time frames established in the 1973 decree. The general reorganization followed essentially historical forms, new methodologies being unavailable. Virtually no technical or economic feasibility studies were carried out in preparation for reform. The consequence has been the generation of late, hastily designed, and stereotyped designs and a mechanical merger of enterprises into production associations.[118]

The central problems, however, appear less in the design than in implementation of the reform. Institutional inertia and suboptimization by the ministries have been as pervasive in this as in other aspects of the modernization of industrial management. Drogichinskii, whose Gosplan department has been in charge of implementing the reform, has accused the ministries of attempting to increase the size of their central *apparat*s and preserving the *glavki*. He also charges that they have resisted any realignment of enterprises, maintained the juridical independence of small plants, and displayed indifference to reducing the number of auxiliary production personnel.[119] V. V. Dementsev of the Ministry of Finance has also complained that ministries deviate from approved plans during their implementation and that administrative costs have stabilized or even risen with the reform.[120]

The suboptimizing behavior of ministerial decision making is rooted in a familiar conflict of interests. This conflict has surfaced primarily in a traditional bureaucratic duel with the Ministry of Finance. During the 1969–73 phase of structural rationalization, the Ministry of Finance routinely rejected efforts by the ministries to increase the size of the functional administrations and industrial unions or to increase the salaries of those officials whose work load increased as the result of the reform. The Ministry of Finance also succeeded in blocking the efforts of the ministries to form administrative structures without registering them with the ministry.[121]

The effort of the Ministry of Finance to establish strict controls over the ministries' structures and staffs, however, has stimulated an evasion of the rules. The size of the central departments and the industrial unions has increased, and the ministries have attempted to increase the number of production unions.[122] A check on the implementation of the general plan of the Ministry of the Gas Industry, for example, revealed that the ministry had illegally diverted resources to create unauthorized production unions. This evasion of staff limits led to an increase of personnel in eleven production unions and an expenditure of 762,000 rubles in excess of budget.[123]

In evaluating the response of the ministries to the demand to cut administrative costs and personnel, it should be noted that the ministries have developed a number of accounting and other techniques designed to maintain acceptable levels of manpower and resources. An investigation of the implementation by the industrial ministries of the October 1969 decree on the reduction of administrative costs revealed that the ministries inflate budget requests during the planning process. Some also conceal administrative costs in budget categories for amortization of buildings, inventories, security, equipment, and other operational categories. In the union-republican ministries, a usual device is to complicate accounting procedures in order to make audit more difficult. To avoid presenting a single administrative budget, the ministry delegates to the union-republican ministry the right to form its own budget, which, presumably, is also open to manipulation.[124]

One of the most widely used devices of the ministry to avoid cutting administrative personnel is to allocate the cuts unevenly. The ministry seldom cuts its own apparatus or that of the middle link; it normally passes the reduction on to the production union or enterprise. Within the production unit, the reductions in personnel are usually carried out at the lowest administrative level. From 1971 to 1975 the Ministry of Ferrous Metallurgy absorbed part of the costs of reorganization by reducing the number of foremen by 2,600, or 25 percent. The Ministry of Light Industry cut 2,300 foremen during the same period.[125]

The failure of the ministries to reallocate authority has had its own consequences for the viability of the structures developed since 1973. The combination of increased organizational scale and centralization naturally intensifies the overload on the chief functional administrations of the ministry. Informational processing problems multiply; the span of control increases and feedback is reduced.[126] The direct subordination of production unions to the central *apparat* of the Ministry of the Wood and Woodworking Industry has increased the span of control to sixty subdivisions.[127] A similar increase in the scale of the industrial unions, although smaller than their counterparts in Eastern Europe, is viewed by specialists, like Popov, as too large for efficient management and as leading inevitably to *administrirovanie* or bureaucratism. Some view the reorganization or liquidation of the VPO as inevitable.[128]

The reduced impact of the reorganized ministries is also related to the as yet incomplete and partial implementation of the rationalization of management functions. The development of OASU is still confined in the majority of ministries to a few subsystems, and active use of scientific methods of management is still exceptional. The continued predominance of administrative methods of control appears to have prevented significant change in the perceptions or motivations of Soviet managers at any level of the hierarchy.

The failure of the reform of management methods, chiefly embodied in the 1965 economic reforms, has left untouched the traditional conflict of interests associated with the command economy. The impulses toward suboptimization have thus continued, expressed in 1973 and 1974 in the sharp struggle among and within ministries for control over enterprises.[129] This has been only partially countered by the emphasis upon the political mobilization of resources initiated in 1969 by Brezhnev. A consequence of increased political pressure on resources, in conditions of incomplete functional rationalization, however, is simply to intensify the chronic imbalances of the system of planning and supply.

There is therefore little surprise in the complaints published in the Soviet press over the past several years of continuous intervention by the ministries' central *apparat*s in operational decision making. As in the past, they have been cited for frequent changes of plans, inadequate or incomplete distribution of supply, and frequent manipulation of success indicators in the interest of plan fulfillment.[130] Nor have the problems changed. Analysis of 140 letters and telegrams to the minister and deputy ministers of the Ministry of Tractor and Agricultural Machine Building noted that 45 percent were concerned with problems of supply and 35 percent with speeding up construction, also usually concerned with supply. Decisions by the ministry still required about a month.[131]

The case of the Ministry of the Wood and Woodworking Industry illustrates the limitations of even an expertly designed formal management structure that operates under adverse natural and economic conditions. The ministry has experienced annual losses estimated at 2.5 to 3 billion rubles.[132] In addition, the ministry has been charged with failure to fulfill production plans for lumber, wastage of timber, and indifference to conservation. Among its deficiencies, the ministry has been accused of failure to equip the production units or to meet the cultural, housing, and other needs of workers in the field.[133] In defense, the minister has pointed to the shortage of supplies and materials, frequent changes of production plans, inadequate transportation, and adverse pricing policies.[134]

There is some evidence to support the view that production unions, like NPOs, are more innovative and efficient than the enterprise. In the 1974 study previously cited, a more rapid pace of technological progress was observed in all unions. Quality of output also improved. In 1973, 45 percent of the unions reported at least 60% of their output was of first quality. Between 1971 and 1973, products with the State Seal of Quality grew in the machine-building unions by 19 percent and in light industry by 3.6 percent.[135]

Specialization also increased in this group of production unions. More characteristic, however, has been the growth of the "natural economy," or the growth in the number of auxiliary shops. Even such leading unions as Sigma added an average of 2.5 shops per year, and Avtogaz, an annual average of 7.5 shops. Like the growth in affiliation, the effort to build auxiliary shops is an effort to maintain the closed or autarkic production patterns of the universal plant. The reasons remain the same: the unreliability of spare parts production and supply.[136]

These reasons also partially explain the results of a survey of twenty-two production unions of all branches located in Estonia. Here, there were virtually no differences in performance between the production union and the enterprise, a condition stemming from the employment of traditional management methods. Level of centralization, for example, appears to have made little difference. The relatively decentralized unions of light industry could not use their expanded options because of problems of planning and supply. In addition, the enlarged autonomy of these unions simply led to a greater degree of suboptimization.[137]

On the whole, it seems clear that Soviet managers remain skeptical about the value of new formal structures and management techniques to improve industrial performance. In a conference held in May 1977 in the Volga Automobile Plant in Togliatti, the "practicals" argued that the superior performance by VAZ was attributable not to its organization but to its superior technology and that its performance could not be repeated in other unions or enterprises without a similar development. Whether such "psychological barriers" can be removed is clearly a crucial question for the spread of a systems approach to management.[138]

The general reorganization of the ministries does not directly address the most significant problems of industrial management created by development. These are predominantly the planning, coordination, and control of those long-term, extremely complex interbranch and developmental projects which are considered vital to the maintenance and growth of the system. As the experience with the construction of OGAS and the Siberian projects has demonstrated, the traditional organizational devices for coordination lack the authority and managerial resources for planning and controlling such immense projects.

The major ministry in a project, a joint commission or a council, or a local *soviet* suffers particularly from an incapacity to establish priorities and enforce performance against countervailing ministerial or departmental interests.[139] The normal response to the pervasive problems of coordination and control of high-priority interbranch and regional development projects has been to increase the involvement of Gosplan or the *apparat* of the Council of Ministers in operational management.[140] The territorial Party apparatus has traditionally played a strong role in regional coordination. The intervention of the central functional agencies such as Gosplan in microcoordination, however, is usually ineffective and, additionally, carries heavy opportunity costs.[141]

There have been numerous proposals for the creation of executive agencies for interbranch and regional coordination. Some are directly related with the program-goal methods of management associated with the creation of SOFE and OGAS. These include the creation of special departments for managing large-scale programs in Gosplan and the State Committee for Science and Technology. A second proposal has been to create "super ministries," which would organize into integrated complexes such related branches as fuel and energy, transportation, and the extractive and consumer goods industries. There have also been calls for creating special centralized organizations for managing major territorial projects such as the BAM railroad, the Non–Black Earth Project and the development of Western Siberia.[142]

Progress toward the creation of large-scale coordinating agencies, however, has been slow. The Latvian Republic has been actively experimenting with program-goal methods of management since 1971 but has used a central coordinating commission under the Latvian Council of Ministers.[143] At the national level, however, program planning and control over large interbranch technical projects remains split between the State Committee for Science and Technology and Gosplan. The former is responsible for planning, resource allocation, and control over research and development, and the latter for operationally directing the introduction of new technologies.[144] The serious problems of coordinating a complex technical project such as computerization suggest the limitations of such an approach.

The organizational policies announced by Brezhnev at the Twenty-sixth Congress indicate some initial movement toward the creation of interbranch planning and management structures. After a long delay Gosplan USSR is setting up multibranch divisions for related groups of industries. These in turn may lead eventually to the formation of "super ministries." A potentially important step toward integrated management of regional development is the formation of a special commission reporting to the Council of Ministers for the management of the Western Siberian petroleum and gas complex. Operational management of the complex, however, will be the responsibility of an interdepartmental territorial commission of Gosplan located in Tiumen.[145] Whether these new structures and agencies will have sufficient authority and resources to control pervasive ministerial suboptimization has yet to be determined.

The promotion of interbranch cooperation on a more limited organizational basis may prove to be equally difficult. An interbranch production union set up in Minsk and composed of eight enterprises belonging to six ministries has remained on paper. Rivalry and competition among ministries has prevented even such simple forms of integration as the unification of auxiliary services.[146]

The case of the interbranch scientific–production unions set up in the late 1960s and early 1970s is instructive in this respect. Interbranch NPOs grew out of an attempt by major scientific research institutes to reduce the load of applied research, which had been rapidly increasing under the pressure of Brezhnev's strategy. Serving essentially as management consultant firms on a market basis, the thirteen interbranch NPOs had flexible structures. Using modern management methods and matrix structure, the NPOs appear to have been highly successful. However, such interbranch NPOs as Fakel (Novosibirsk), Poisk (Sverdlovsk), and Temp (Moscow) have folded.[147]

After 1971, as part of the more general policy of tightening up of controls over industrial management, interbranch NPOs came under attack, primarily from the State Bank and the Ministry of Finance. The "lack of confidence of the financial and credit organs" has been cited as the principal reason for their demise.[148] The autonomy and flexibility of the new structures and their operation outside of the institutional controls of the planning and financial systems clearly created that "fear of loss of control" which has been the principal reason for the suppression of this type of organization.[149] The high income of the specialists hired by the NPOs and the lack of experimental facilities of the firms appear to have been contributing, if secondary factors in their decline.[150]

The need for interbranch coordination, however, is continually growing. The creation of effective organs for interbranch and regional management remains a major task for rationalization in the 1980s.

Afterword

As Soviet industrial management enters the 1980s, the search for a viable management system has had ambiguous or marginal results. Initially, the problems addressed by the various strategies of rationalization are complex and deeply rooted. Burdened from its inception with pervasive and chronic problems of operation, the system of centralized administrative controls has served as a powerful instrument for socioeconomic development. There is clearly serious reason for questioning whether the complex of formal and informal organizations which has become highly institutionalized over the past half-century can respond with sufficient coherence and rationality to the challenges accompanying industrial maturation.

An assessment of these changes should be approached circumspectly because the process of rationalization has proceeded in an uneven and contradictory fashion. In many respects, the most interesting and perhaps in the long run most important aspect of the effort to develop more effective systems of decision making and control has been intellectual. Theoretical concerns have played and presumably will continue to play a significant role in redefining the problems of management and prescribing solutions. The search for a systemic, technically effective theory of management, however, has been heavily burdened by ideological and institutional interests and severe complexity. The major contribution of the search for theory appears in its often trenchant criticism of the administrative model and the growth of cybernetics as a general theory of management.

Quite clearly, there is a strong presumption that urban industrial societies are far too complex and dynamic to be captured within a single, integrated empirical theory. The cultural impact

255

of the search for a general theory of management has, nonetheless, been notable. Basic cleavages in methodology and conception have been introduced into Soviet scientific and organizational culture. The sources of cultural shock have been largely rooted in the experience of examining and selectively incorporating foreign management thought and experience into Soviet thinking on industrial organization. Particularly important in this respect has been the impact of American management science and technologies and Western behavioral research.

The impact of an innovative theory of management, however, has been sharply reduced by the failure to reach theoretical consensus. The evolution of management theory has been uneven and fragmented, split into conflicting schools or tendencies by methodology, academic discipline, and institutional and personal rivalries. From this frequently acerbic development, three distinguishable streams of management thought have emerged to give general guidance to management development.

Of these three approaches, the principal claimant to the status of general theory has been systems analysis, or, more precisely, cybernetics. Derived from control engineering and closely associated with Western management science and technologies, cybernetics generated an intense passion among Soviet natural and social scientists during the 1950s and 1960s. Its intellectual appeal lay primarily in its potential as a methodology and technology for management of very complex systems. Undoubtedly, the application of mathematical models and computers to Soviet economic and management problems has produced, as a distinguished Western student of Soviet planning has pointed out, a revolution. It has also produced, as have the other strategies, serious methodological difficulties and strong ideological, bureaucratic, and political opposition.

That political opposition, arising from the fear of the rise of a new elite of political decision makers, reached into the Politburo is evident in the warning of V. V. Shcherbitskii, first secretary of the Ukrainian Communist Party, in 1973. Approving the critical use of Western management theory, Shcherbitskii declared:

At the same time it must be pointed out that in elaborating problems of the theory of management certain Soviet scientists try to create some kind of abstract schemes which are allegedly of a universal nature but which in fact have been borrowed from bourgeois concepts. What is more, one encounters in individual works on management questions the thoroughly bankrupt and groundless thesis of apportioning managerial activities to some special sphere - a privilege of a certain social stratum.[1]

If the basic approach of cybernetics has been to overcome the constraints of the management system by increasing its capabilities, the economic and behavioral approaches have addressed primarily the human and social problems of the organization. Their common objectives have been to reduce the gap between formal and informal organization through developing mechanisms for self-management within the management system. This is to be achieved through the device of changing the context, rules, and motivations that determine the direction and scope of managerial action.

The central question in the search for effective substitutes for direct administrative planning and controls has been how far subsystem autonomy can develop without threatening global economic priorities or central planning controls. Despite serious questions of the viability of a closed bureaucratic model of industrial organization, the classical paradigm of rationality has been deeply imbedded in the culture of the existing management system. In the conflict between administrative planning and the market, the normative approach or the definition of fixed and largely determinate relationships for regulating most economic and organizational relationships has been decisive.

The experience of the 1965 reforms quickly indicated, however, that the deductive logic of the normative approach produced formulas that are too simple to order the complexity and nonlinearity of most concrete decision-making processes. The repeated breakdowns of formally fixed normatives on a wide range of issues under the pressure of diversity should come as no surprise. Even the limited use of the market embodied in the reforms, moreover, aroused the defensive instincts of the Communist Party apparatus, whose ideological and organizational role was threatened by the emphasis upon material incentives and enterprise autonomy.

The constraints on the generation of a behavioral approach to the modernization of management have been equally strong.

Utopian socialist values have had a relatively minor role in the development of this stream of management thought, although it is far from extinguished. Within the existing framework, forming new conceptions of human relations in industry derived from the social sciences has been opposed on two levels. At the macro level, the effort to develop a conception of the social system based upon functionalism was ruthlessly suppressed in the late 1960s. At the micro level, sociology and psychology have competed, rather unsuccessfully, with the classical Taylorist approach of NOT. An important consequence of the frequently intense ideological, political, and academic opposition to the use of behavioral methods of social control has been to impose tight controls over management research and the training of industrial sociologists and psychologists.

Although the combination of complexity and institutional inertia has proved to be a powerful restraint on innovative management conceptions, problems associated with socioeconomic development are too urgent for intellectual innovation to be suppressed entirely. Stagnation is as threatening as uncontrolled change to the political leadership. Even Party ideologists have cautiously supported "free comradely discussions" of a problem-solving nature which address the complex issues of the contemporary Soviet economy.[2] The central issue has not been whether innovation should occur but whether it can be effectively absorbed within the existing system. The effort to filter the technical substance of Western management thought from its cultural foundations is a vivid example of the political complexities involved.

In the final analysis, the search for an effective theory of management should be judged primarily by its specific contribution to an improvement in the overall functioning of industrial organization. One of the core issues to arise in this respect has been how the rationalization of industrial management should proceed. For historical and ideological reasons, there has been a strong bias for an integrated approach. A systematic and coherent strategy of rationalization could not be projected without a general model.

Consensus on a general model of the management system clearly has failed to emerge. Either implicitly or explicitly, however, the actual course of rationalization over the past fifteen years has been guided by a conception of how the system should work. Structurally, the general models forming the various strategies have been hybrids of distinct, not fully compatible submodels. The general model underlying the 1965 economic reforms, for example, blended bureaucratic and market models. Among cybernetic models, the primary stress on the market in Nemchinov's model placed it beyond the limits of political and ideological legitimacy. In the 1970s the most operational general model has been the system of optimal functioning of the economy, SOFE, a relatively conservative blend of cybernetic and economic measures of reform.

Conceptually, SOFE is a sophisticated effort to optimize decision making and to increase control through incorporating mathematical models and computers into a reformed management system. As a logic of management, SOFE sharply separates strategic from operational decision making and control. Assuming that complexity and institutional inertia will dominate decision making in the short run, SOFE has proposed to increase the systemic control of the central planners by stressing the priority of long-term planning for the most important developmental projects. Long-term plans of fifteen or more years, based upon scientific forecasts, presumably would be simpler and more flexible because they would be less burdened by vested interest.

To achieve these goals, SOFE proposed to extend not only the time frame but also the scope of planning to include social, scientific and technical, political, military, and other aspects of the environment. Planning would develop from final rather than intermediate goals to reduce suboptimization and to increase the rationality of resource allocation. To optimize choice among alternative goals and distributions of resources, SOFE proposed to apply cost–benefit analysis. The optimal planners also argued for a thoroughly revamped system of economic indicators and incentives. Critics of the centralized administrative model, they also advocated a decentralization of key economic functions, a simplification of formal structure, and the institution of program-goal methods of planning and management.

It is evident that the general models were seriously deficient in important ways, and these deficiencies had the result of complicating their implementation. None of the general models was simple. Simplicity and coherence were necessarily sacrificed in the task of blending the reforms into the ongoing system. Secondly, and as a corollary of the first condition, none of the models was complete. Important elements of the strategies were vague or had basic unresolved contradictions. These conditions influenced the hybrid nature of the model, which proved over the course of time to be unstable as the relationships among submodels shifted. In each case, of course, it has been the bureaucratic component which has ultimately come to dominate the general model.

The fact that each of the strategies of rationalization was undertaken as an ill-structured problem subject to a range of conflicting definitions and solutions decisively influenced its implementation. Whether the lack of clarity characteristic of the specific approaches to reform has been the cause or result of the bureaucratic politics which have been inherent in their implementation is debatable. That it has contributed to the ambivalence with which the various reforms have been implemented, however, seems sure.

This study has been only incidentally an examination of the politics of innovation. Nonetheless, the generation as well as implementation of the various strategies of reform has been primarily an exercise of the intermediate levels of the research and management structures. Although Kosygin was publicly identified with the 1965 economic reforms and Brezhnev with the reforms of the 1970s, the type of personal commitment which characterized Khrushchev's approach to reform has been conspicuously lacking. This change in political style is partially a simple reaction to the disorganization of the Khrushchev years. It also reflects, however, the changing political vision and interests of the Communist Party leadership that have resulted from socioeconomic development.

If Stalin could stand outside of the existing system and impose drastic solutions at immense human and material costs, his successors have lacked that option. They are squarely at the center of what has been described here as the traditional system, tied to it by a lifetime of interest and commitment to its development. If this assumption is accurate, then political support for the strategies of reform has been conditioned not only by intraelite conflict but also by the complex conditions which constrain the Soviet leadership under existing circumstances.

On one hand, the larger problems of socioeconomic development become more urgent with time, and there have been unmistakable indications of entropy within the traditional system. On the other hand, none of the strategies which have emerged is fully persuasive as a solution to the problems of industrial management, and none has been without a large number of unknowns and potentially adverse latent consequences for political and ideological control. The political process has therefore been deeply contradictory in its tendencies of cautious and conditioning support for the reforms coupled with exaggerated expectations and impatience with the results. The political half-life of the major reforms of the 1960s and 1970s has been far too short to support serious reform.

More directly, the marginal results of the reforms as a whole can be attributed to the processes whereby the different strategies of rationalization have been adopted and implemented. Lacking a single theory, model, strategy, or political conception of how the ideal system should be created, the actual processes of rationalization have proceeded in a segmented and overlapping fashion, have been poorly coordinated and controlled, and have come into conflict at vital points. Although the general objectives of increasing the efficiency and integration of the management system have been shared, each of the major approaches has been introduced at different times, has had distinct operational priorities, and has experienced different levels of political and administrative support and opposition. This diversity has extended to the definition of the core problems of management and to their solutions.

The substantive differences in the concrete processes of rationalization cannot be easily analyzed as a single, common pattern. Each of the approaches has encountered specific conditions and problems unique to the specific strategy. However diverse the specific objectives and processes, though, there are definite indications that the processes of rationalization have been as decisively shaped by the combination of complexity and institutional inertia as by the search for theory. Both conditions have been pervasive and have mutually supported and reinforced each other.

The impact of complexity and institutional inertia on the process of rationalization has, perhaps, been most critical in the struggle of the classical paradigm with other, alternative management models. Most frequently this has been cast in the conflict of mechanistic and organic approaches to organizational development. This issue has been apparent in the effort to blend plan and market during the economic reforms and in the policy of integrating NOT with management methods based upon social science research. It has also been visible in the policy of blending the classical and systems approach to the rationalization of formal structure. The eventual triumph of the classical model of rationality in virtually every case has been principally the result of institutional inertia.

As a process of organizational change, the processes of rationalization have proceeded through common stages. These have included the preparation and enactment of the program, the organization of its implementation, and its introduction into practice. The intensity of the complexity of the problems encountered and the strength of institutional inertia have differed according to stage and program. As part of the more general reaction against the Khrushchev era, the trend over the past fifteen years has been to formalize the process as part of the search for greater institutional control. For practical purposes, the process of rationalization can be divided into two distinct phases. The first has been one of careful and frequently extensive experimentation and testing. The larger and more difficult stage has been the mass introduction of the reform. These stages have tended to blend; and, where the first phase has experienced an intensive phase of development, as in the case of computers, the pattern of the first stage may dominate the second or mass stage.

In many respects the stage of preparation and adoption has been the most important phase of the process of rationalization. This is the period when the technical conceptions and political support for the reform are developed. Both the quality of the technical conception and depth of political support for the reform are revealed in the allocation of resources devoted to research. In the Soviet political system, as in others, research has the dual functions of developing technical solutions for perceived problems and providing credibility and legitimacy for selected policies. In conformity with Soviet traditions and existing political priorities, the amount of resources devoted to the technical and economic approaches has been impressive. In contrast, the resources allocated to behavioral and organizational research have been limited and scattered, a certain index of their secondary status and role in the process of rationalization.

The adoption of concrete programs of rationalization has normally required a relatively lengthy period of incubation, during which a minimal understanding and consensus have developed on a largely informal basis. The development of the cybernetic conception of management and the SOFE proposals, for example, appear as deliberate and successful efforts by Berg, Nemchinov, Fedorenko, and others to build public support for their conceptions. The behavioral scientists did not and perhaps could not develop a public relations effort of similar scope. In any case, it is clear that the adoption of the economic reforms and SOFE was preceded by at least a decade of discussion, debate, and public advocacy prior to adoption and implementation. This lag time is due largely to the rapid increase in the number of active participants in the process of rationalization and the necessity of developing a political climate and support to sustain the process.

An important factor influencing the process of rationalization has been the feasibility of the programs in the form in which they were adopted. Feasibility, in turn, has been closely linked with the degree of complexity of the programs. A primary attraction of proposals for increasing the role of the market or for introducing industrial democracy has been in their potential for a genuine simplification of the system. The rejection of these solutions and the subsequent effort to create precise and determinate solutions created problems of methodology and implementation quite as complex as those they intended to solve.

The most complex of the programs of rationalization undoubtedly has been the effort to construct a single integrated man-machine decision-making system. The project is as grandiose as any conceived under Stalin, and, even before its implementation, basic questions of its feasibility were raised. In the light of almost a decade of effort to construct OGAS, it seems evident that Soviet resources and knowledge were insufficient to build the system in the form in which it was adopted.

The strong institutional emphasis upon determinate models and normative methods combined with the enormous complexity of Soviet planning problems created severe methodological and informational barriers to the construction of a complex of integrated planning models. Despite impressive Soviet skills in building models with a large number of decision variables, no fully optimal model for any level of the economic hierarchy has been built. The massive complexity of the problems, moreover, has created a pessimistic mood, particularly regarding the long-term plan. Volkov notes,

At the end of the 1960s and beginning of the 1970s, attention to them [long-range models] grew powerfully, but the path to success was thorny [*ternistym*], and many scholars, counting upon quick results of a global character and not achieving them, ceased working. Generally, attention to working out the theoretical problems of modeling in recent years has weakened.[3]

These problems are essentially those related to optimization and have been undergoing public discussion in connection with SOFE for fifteen years. They include the methods of forming and determining the amount of socially necessary working time, a concept of social utility, the criterion of the optimality of production, and its quantification at all levels of the economy.[4]

The question of feasibility is perhaps more sharply raised in the decision to construct an integrated management information system. Like the closely related process of economic modeling, the force of the classical paradigm shaped decisively the underlying conceptions of the system's structure. As the continuing policy conflicts between Fedorenko and Glushkov have indicated, numerous basic issues of structure and functions arose during the preparatory stage. In the absence of a resolution of these issues, the system began to develop as a close overlay of the traditional structure, following a technical and mechanistic design which stressed interdependence and standardization, normative regulation, and informational unity. The complexity of the problem defined by such an approach, however, placed the project in jeopardy.

Issues of feasibility generated by the enormous complexity of the problems as these have been defined by the classical rationality have also clearly stalked the economic reform, social planning, and the reform of the ministries. The tenacity of the classical paradigm is intimately related with the political priorities of centralized controls. The logic of the existing system requires a normative approach based upon fixed ratios toward planning, coordination, and control. The complexity and dynamism of the economy, however, have challenged the normative approach in decisive ways. The economy and society are too complex to be managed effectively without the structural equivalent of a market.

Methodological difficulties in developing normatives for the economic reform presented major barriers to its implementation. In order to develop fixed ratios for profitability, prices, rent, and fixed payments and bonuses, extremely complex formulas had to be constructed, which in turn reduced the coherence and intelligibility of the enacted measures. The clarity of the reform became even cloudier with the introduction of decisive elements of the traditional system into the new program. As part of the compromise, planning continued to proceed from achieved levels rather than final output; physical and quantitative indicators were retained; and cost-plus pricing procedures based upon average rather than marginal costs were carried over as well. Bonuses were tied to fixed rather than variable indicators. Many of the provisions for imposing economic and financial levers were either nominal or not applied at all.

The question of whether social and cultural determinants can be consciously applied to the control of human behavior has been perhaps more sharply raised in the adoption of social planning for the control of social development. The search for normative solutions to the social problems of industry has been required initially by the dependence of social upon economic planning. More to the point, a normative approach is more congruent with the direct control of processes which have fundamental implications for ideological direction and control.

There are strong reasons for believing, therefore, that a cybernetic approach to social management will not be pursued for technical as well as ideological reasons. Most of the severe methodological difficulties experienced with respect to social planning for cities and regions have been rooted in the admitted lack of understanding of empirical social processes. The problem of complexity has been decisive in frustrating a determinate approach to social planning.

Consequently, there should be little surprise at the strength of institutional inertia in this phase of rationalization. Despite the challenge to Taylorism mounted by the behavioral scientists, the scientific organization of labor has weighed heavily in the effort to increase the efficiency of industrial and managerial labor. The application of a human relations approach, Marxist or Western, has remained essentially experimental during the past two decades, hobbled by ideological as well as organizational constraints.

The process of rationalization in the post-Khrushchev period has been characterized by a paradox. Formal strategies have addressed, in the first instance, the functions of management. Even SOFE, the most thoroughly articulated conception of reform, has given relatively minor attention to problems of "structurization." In practice, however, functional and structural aspects of rationalization cannot be divorced.

Like the behavioral sciences, development of empirical approaches to organizational design has suffered from suppression or simple neglect. The sheer complexity of the task of constructing concrete formal structures that simultaneously address diverse and ambiguous functional relationships and growing social needs has prevented the emergence of a stable consensus on how to proceed in building effective formal organizations. The models developed using a systems approach remain as demonstration projects and are largely experimental at the end of the 1970s. Under the pressure of inertia, the bureaucratic model has shaped the central conceptions of the ministerial reforms.

The general schemes adopted to rationalize the organization of the ministries, with exceptions, have tended to stress normatively fixed hierarchical relationships of authority, standardized tables of organization, and a strong bias for centralization within very large organizations. The principle of restricted functionalism has remained as the formal mode for the allocation of authority between line and functional agencies, as has the principle of *edinonachalie*. This classical approach to formal organization, in turn, has imposed rigid limits on the application of innovative methods of management.

The questions of technical feasibility and institutional support for the individual strategy of reform clearly influence the succeeding stage of implementation. Where either has been lacking, mass implementation has not occurred. Questions of technical feasibility loom largest with respect to the implementation of SOFE. The development of an optimal long-term plan, for example, has been beyond the existing technical resources of the planning system. The combination of complexity and inertia is particularly evident in the implementation of program-goal planning, which is still in an experimental stage. So little progress has been made because, in addition to methodological and informational difficulties, there has been no consensus among the planners on the premises for constructing a tree of goals or on the role of programs in existing procedures of planning.

The role of political support for the phase of implementation has been critical as well as highly conditional. Virtually every reform arouses conservative anxieties and opposition, and this expression of institutional inertia at the highest levels has been an important factor in limiting the degree of change. The threat to the Party's ideological and organizational role as well as the failure of the reform to increase the efficiency of decision making created the political basis for Brezhnev's ascendancy over Kosygin and the adoption of a technological strategy. The threats of technocracy and ideological erosion with détente, however, created their own anxieties, as the statement of V. V. Shcherbitskii has indicated. The political crest of the scientific-technical revolution and computerization was clearly reached in 1973. The canceling of the Central Committee Plenum on the STR and sharply reduced tempo in the pace of computerization after 1975 have indicated a waning of political support and a contraction of the scope of the reform and resources allocated for its implementation. Any future reform with implications for serious structural change will very probably confront similar conditions and experience the same shift in political support.

Inevitably, the question of how to implement a program of rationalization under conditions of political opposition and institutional inertia has become a central issue. Two distinct approaches to the implementation of the reforms have emerged, each with its strengths and weaknesses. The 1965 reforms employed a gradualist approach, implementing the reforms according to carefully prepared timetables. The rational and incremental approach to the reforms, however, permitted opposition to consolidate against the reform and quickly subvert it.

To overcome institutional inertia, Brezhnev approached the

construction of OGAS as a political problem. Mobilization techniques were used as a breakthrough strategy, and the strategy of intensive mobilization produced a startling upsurge in the number of ASUs and production associations. The costs and waste of a Bolshevik tempo, however, have been very high, and it may be questioned whether a complex and intricate project such as OGAS can be built at all using techniques of crude political pressure and tight administrative deadlines. The majority of general schemes for the reorganization have also proven to be ineffective, in part because they have been adopted and implemented without technical and feasibility studies and have suffered from stereotyped designs hastily thrown together. It appears most probable that many ASUs and ministerial structures will be redesigned.

Implementation of each of the programs of rationalization during the phase of mass introduction has been essentially an exercise in self-reform. The implementation and introduction of ASUs has been something of an exception because much of the work has been concentrated in specialized design organizations. The other programs have been mainly the responsibility of the planning and industrial organizations. This exercise in self-reform has produced some complex patterns of implementation. Selective implementation and suboptimization have tended to prevail. Some provisions have been implemented fully, others partially, and still other provisions have been ignored or evaded.

The role of the Party apparatus and other external control agencies in implementing the individual strategies of reform has not been directly addressed in this study. The role of the Party apparatus in the expansion of the Shchekino experiment and social planning has been prominent. On balance, however, political intervention as a control mechanism in implementing the plans of reform appears as episodic and insufficient to control the pervasive expression of institutional inertia. The policy of tightening Party controls over the ministries and other economic institutions after 1971 aroused open hostility and evasion and seems to have been informally dropped.

More relevantly, the political leadership has failed to respond to repeated calls for agencies with strong and centralized power and effective sanctions to control the process of rationalization. There has been a movement to incorporate the introduction of computers and NOT into the central planning system. In those cases, however, where a specialized agency for operational control has been created, as in the cases of the economic reform and OGAS, its powers were limited in enforcing compliance. This evident unwillingness to establish strong centralized controls is probably attributable to the conditional political support of the top political leadership as well as the strength of the opposition to it.

The reasons for the extensive suboptimization so evident during the stage of implementation are numerous and, to some degree, situational. Certainly some of the institutional inertia can be attributed to the trained incapacity of the managers or to the threat to the status and skills of those displaced by technological or organizational change. The technical and production orientation of the managers, for example, makes the systematic implementation of a behavioral approach to management reform highly improbable. The opposition of middle managers and functional specialists to the use of computers more clearly reflects the conflict of personal and institutional interests. The evidence of institutional inertia, however, should not necessarily be interpreted as blind reaction.

There may be serious, or at least understandable reasons for failing to implement the reform fully. The managers may see the reform as partial or flawed and a short-term campaign. In implementing the economic reforms, for example, it became evident that, without fundamental changes in the centralized allocation of supply and a curbing of ministerial power, the managers remained skeptical about the reform and resisted implementing it. In general, wherever the proposed measures have threatened to disrupt or complicate ongoing operational tasks or lines of authority, implementation became questionable. None of the reforms introduced sufficient organizational slack, time, or resources to increase the possibilities of successful execution. Throughout the period, the implementation of the various programs has been subordinate to operational and production tasks.

A summary judgment of the impact of the various strategies of reform on the efficiency and integration of industrial management is difficult to make in any precise way. On the whole, the essential characteristics of the traditional system have remained intact, and the chronic problems of operational management and organizational integration are unresolved. Undoubtedly, change has occurred, but this appears to be primarily in informal organization, which cannot be easily measured or observed. Probably the most important change over the past fifteen years has been the effort to develop an empirical theory of management. Potentially important alternative models have arisen that may influence future organizational development. The actual achievement in development of an effective theory, though, has been modest. Theory is still in an embryonic state; it is incomplete in basic respects; and, most importantly, the problems have an order of complexity which defy any short-term solution. Whether any theory can be developed for a central planning system of the Soviet type remains in doubt.

The impact of specific programs of rationalization on the problems of management has been uneven but essentially marginal. The most important initiative of the 1970s – the blending of mathematical models and computers into an integrated decision-making network – has had only mixed success in increasing either the efficiency or integration of the management system. Through the 1970s, the central conceptions of SOFE, which was designed to increase the strategic control of the central planners over socioeconomic development, have not been achieved. Planning from final results, development of goal programs, and long-term optimal planning could not be implemented. Greater progress has been made with optimization of five-year plans, but relatively little with operational planning and control. Application of network planning models for increased coordination and control has been confined to comparatively small projects.

Constraints on the development of computer-based management systems have frustrated conservative illusions of a fully centralized and automated decision-making and control system. Major problems in the design, equipment, and use of computers have produced incompatible and incomplete systems which have only marginally influenced management structure. Where ASUs have been introduced, the main thrust has been to concentrate authority and function, particularly in relation to supply. On balance, the overall result has been to strengthen existing management structures.

In retrospect, the greater potential for improving the efficiency and integration of industrial organization has been the effort to introduce greater self-management into the existing system. The rejection of the market as the primary mechanism for regulating the industrial economy ensured that the chronic conflict of global and local interests continued without essential change. The performance of the industrial economy has slowed in the late 1970s and even declined in important respects. Measures designed to deconcentrate authority were successfully undermined by the resistance of the chief functional agencies and the ministries. The traditional gap between formal and informal organization remains as Soviet management enters a new decade.

The dominance of the classical paradigm has dictated an essentially Taylorist approach to improving motivation and control. Defective success indicators and weak and contradictory economic and financial controls have narrowed the impact of material incentives on managerial behavior. Not surprisingly, without consistent ministerial support, NOT has remained largely formal in improving labor productivity. Although the introduction of social science research into industrial relations has been ameliorative, the restricted application of behavioral methods has naturally reduced its impact. At the end of the 1970s, social planning has been essentially an ideological exercise.

Institutional inertia and ministerial suboptimization have also been apparent in confining change resulting from the structural reforms of the 1970s. Although Gosplan began a major reorganization in conformity with SOFE in the late 1970s, other structures associated with the planning reforms of the early 1970s – "super ministries," multibranch and large-scale project management structures – have yet to materialize. Although the 1973 reforms have resulted in a sharp reduction in the number of intermediate-level organizations, the central *apparat* of the ministry has put up strong resistance to any delegation of control. The results of the creation of production associations on the distribution of authority have been more variable but have pointed, as a whole, to increased centralization.

Whether there has been any gain in administrative efficiency over the past fifteen years can be questioned. Although the rapid increase in administrative personnel at the enterprise level during the economic reforms has probably slowed with the creation of production associations, the expected savings from the reforms of the 1970s have been disappointing. Computerization has absorbed perhaps a million men and tens of billions of rubles. Suboptimization has as clearly minimized reduction of administrative costs from the 1973 ministerial reforms.

A more promising effort to increase administrative efficiency has been the extensive development of management retraining through which several million managers have passed over the past fifteen years. The recognition of the inadequate formal training of Soviet managers has been an important step forward for the modernization of the management system. The quality of management retraining, however, has been uneven. The training of high-level executives appears to be good; the policy of creating a mass system of managerial education, however, was premature. The lack of trained instructors, educational facilities, and resources and low ministerial support have reduced the quality of instruction and motivation of the managers. Over the short term, there is doubt that managerial retraining has more than marginally changed either the attitudes or capabilities of Soviet managers. Nevertheless, the system of managerial education may eventually form part of a more comprehensive system of management development.

As Soviet management enters a new decade, it seems evident that the modernization of industrial management has reached an impasse. Further organizational development requires relatively fundamental structural change. The patterns of institutional change over the past fifteen years suggest, however, that such a far-reaching adaptation of industrial organization is highly unlikely to come about under Brezhnev's political leadership. Some evidence of this is contained in the decrees of July 1979, legislating further adjustments in the system for the Eleventh Five-Year Plan.[5]

The reforms indicate a further lowering of optimization and computerization in the strategy of reform and a cautious and gradual swing back to the policies of the 1965 economic reforms. The turn to economic methods, however, is far from complete. The reform of planning continues, with some modifications, the directions established at the beginning of the decade. The fifteen-year plan has been replaced by a set of integrated, twenty-year programs of scientific and technical progress and plans extending over two five-year plans. Program-goal methods of planning will also continue. As in the past, a particular stress has been placed upon the use of the five-year plan as the basic instrument of planning. There is an expressed intention to strengthen social planning by including social plans as a consolidated division of the plan.

The 1979 decrees appear to extend the Minpribor experiment to the industrial ministries as a whole. Multiple planning indicators, including physical indicators, will continue to be used; but an index of "pure product," used experimentally by Gosplan, will be extended gradually. Incentive funds are to be formed normatively according to a broad range of success indicators. Primary indicators will be fulfillment of contractual obligations of supply and relative increase of high-quality output in the total output of a production complex. The incentive system for scientific–production unions will be the summary effect of savings achieved through the introduction of new technology. The reform also continues the priority of NOT and the brigade movement.

Anticipated structural change will also be marginal. There will be some effort to adjust vertical relationships. New procedures for planning "from below," a decentralized form of planning used under Khrushchev, will be instituted. There are also plans for decentralizing control of the distribution of bonuses to the brigade. This trend toward decentralization, however, is balanced by a major emphasis upon socialist competition and counter (*vstrechnoe*) planning and, most of all, by an expanded use of normatives. The continuing strength of the classical paradigm is evident.

The measures of reform adopted for the Eleventh Five-Year Plan are clearly palliatives representing minor adjustments in the management system. None of the measures designed to strengthen *khozraschet* increases the role of the market in the management of heavy industry except for the provision for direct ties. The stress on the political mobilization of resources and tight administrative controls continues despite the clear evidence that these measures have been ineffective in the past.

The basic problems of industrial management thus continue unresolved into the 1980s. The complexity of the decision-making environment is increasing, and the availability of natural resources and labor declining. Major problems involving the massive development of natural resources and satisfaction of social demand have become more urgent over the decade. The pressures to increase the efficiency of production and distribution are building up and presumably will require some fundamental decisions by the successors of the present political leadership.

There is no clear indication of what form these decisions will take. If the conflict between environment and industrial organization reaches a stage that the political leadership in conjunction with other elite groups judges to be critical, then presumably some institutional adaptation will occur. Whether such an adaptation would take the form of intensification of administrative controls and coercion or adaptation in the direction of political and economic pluralism along the lines sketched by the Nemchinov model is, in large part, situational. Within the context of Soviet historical development, both options are evident.

Without the pressures of an intense and probably prolonged institutional crisis, there seems to be little reason for expecting either a radical conservative reaction or movement toward a democratic socialist solution. If there are present tensions in the system, it is still far from certain that pressures generated by socioeconomic development will create such a crisis in the shorter term. Institutional inertia is a powerful force for limiting structural change. It will presumably constrain the successors of Brezhnev and Kosygin as firmly as it has bound them. Under such conditions, the outlook is for maintenance of the traditional system with continuous and incremental attempts at reform.

A slow and limited adaptation of the formal organization of industrial management, however, is not without its costs in terms of reduced economic efficiency. It may, on the other hand, stimulate further a diffusion of authority and loss of function to informal organization, which is a clear sign of entropy. The evidence gathered over the past dozen years, for example, suggests that a "second economy" has developed.[6] The emergence of informal markets, illegal practices, and corruption of the official system suggests, within available evidence, that this process is relatively well developed. Whether this growth in the informal organization produces a silent revolution in Soviet management will probably be decided in the 1980s.

Notes

Chapter 1. The context of management reform

1 See William J. Conyngham, *Industrial Management in the Soviet Union*, Stanford, Cal.: Hoover Institution Press, 1973; and Jerry F. Hough, *The Soviet Prefects: The Local Party Organs in Industrial Decision-Making*, Cambridge, Mass.: Harvard Press, 1969.

2 T. H. Rigby, "Stalinism and Mono-Organizational Society," in Robert C. Tucker, ed., *Stalinism: Essays in Historical Interpretation*, New York: Norton, 1977, p. 53.

3 Victor A. Thompson, *Modern Organizations*, New York: Knopf, 1961, ch. 2.

4 James D. Thompson, *Organizations in Action: Social Science Bases of Administrative Theory*, New York: McGraw-Hill, 1967, ch. 1.

5 G. I. Petrov, *Sovetskoe administrativnoe pravo – chast obshchaia*, Leningrad: Izdatelstvo Leningradskogo universiteta, 1970, pp. 18-20, 175-7.

6 G. Kh. Popov, ed., *Funktsii i struktura organov upravleniia, ikh sovershenstvovanie*, Moscow: Ekonomika, 1973, pp. 45-50.

7 I. Sh. Muksinov, *Sovet ministrov soiuznoi respubliki*, Moscow: Iuridicheskaia literatura, 1969, pp. 179-83.

8 An excellent description of Gosplan's structure is in F. I. Kotov, *Organizatsiia planirovaniia narodnogo khoziaistva SSSR*, Moscow: Ekonomika, 1974, ch. 3.

9 Popov, *Funktsii i struktura*, p. 134.

10 See N. S. Koval, ed., *Planirovanie narodnogo khoziaistva SSSR*, 3rd ed., Moscow: Vysshaia shkola, 1973, pp. 90-1.

11 Popov, *Funktsii i struktura*, p. 125.

12 V. V. Laptev et al., eds., *Pravovye problemy rukovodstva i upravleniia otrasliu promyshlennosti v SSSR*, Moscow: Nauka, 1973, pp. 30-6.

13 V. V. Parfenov and N. Mironov, *Pravda*, December 25, 1969, p. 2.

14 S. E. Kamenitser, *Osnovy upravleniia promyshlennym proizvodstvom*, Moscow: Mysl, 1971, pp. 30-1.

15 Iu. Lapshin, *Planovoe khoziaistvo*, no. 3 (1974): 128.

16 V. I. Golikov, ed., *Effektivnost upravlencheskogo truda*, Kiev: Naukova dumka, 1974, pp. 99-100.

17 A. Levikov, *Literaturnaia gazeta*, December 17, 1975, p. 11. Translated in *Current Digest of the Soviet Press*, vol. 28, no. 30 (1976): 3. Cited hereafter as *CDSP*.

18 M. A. Ivanova and I. A. Samarina, *Tekhnicheskii progress i struktura ITR i sluzhashchikh*, Moscow: Ekonomika, 1970, pp. 112–13.

19 Hough, *Soviet Prefects*, p. 262.

20 David Granick, *Managerial Comparisons of Four Developed Countries: France, Britain, United States and Russia*, Cambridge, Mass.: MIT Press, 1972, pp. 235–45.

21 Cited in D. N. Dobrychev, *Organizatsiia upravleniia razrabotkami novoi tekhniky*, Moscow: Ekonomika, 1971, p. 167.

22 L. N. Denisova, "Sotsializm i novyi tip rukovoditeliia promyshlennogo predpriiatiia," in V. G. Afanasev, ed., *Nauchnoe upravlenie obshchestvom*, vol. 2, Moscow: Mysl, 1968, p. 131.

23 M. A. Ivanova and I. A. Samarina, *Tekhnicheskii progress*, p. 30; also, V. Ozira, "Upravlencheskie kadry. Sovershenstvovanie raboty s kadrami na predpriiatiiakh," in D. M. Gvishiani and S. E. Kamenitser, eds., *Problemy nauchnoi organizatsii upravleniia sotsialisticheskoi promyshlennostiu*, Moscow: Ekonomika, 1974, p. 434.

24 Ivanova and Samarina, *Tekhnicheskii progress*, p. 49.

25 Golikov, *Effektivnost*, p. 51.

26 E. Fainburg, *Literaturnaia gazeta*, no. 29 (1971): 10.

27 *Pravda*, December 12, 1974, p. 2.

28 L. Barashkov, *Literaturnaia gazeta*, July 21, 1976, p. 11; *CDSP*, vol. 28, no. 33 (1976): 15.

29 A. Levikov, *Literaturnaia gazeta*, November 5, 1975, p. 11; *CDSP*, no. 30 (1976): 2.

30 David Granick, "Managerial Incentives in the USSR and in Western Firms: Implications for Behavior," *Journal of Comparative Administration*, vol. 5, no. 2 (1973): 184.

31 Ibid., pp. 184–5.

32 *Zhenshchiny v SSSR*, Moscow: Statistika, 1975, p. 80.

33 Gail W. Lapidus, "The Female Industrial Labor Force: Dilemmas. Reassessments, and Options," in Arcadius Kahan and Blair A. Ruble, eds., *Industrial Labor in the USSR*, New York: Pergamon Press, 1979, pp. 232–79.

34 Denisova, "Sotsializm i novyi tip rukoviditeliia," p. 162.

35 Ozira, "Upravlencheskie kadry," p. 436.

36 See Hough, *Soviet Prefects*, ch. 8.

37 G. Kh. Popov and G. A. Dzhavadov, eds., *Upravlenie i problema kadrov*, Moscow: Ekonomika, 1972, pp. 59–60.

38 Granick, "Managerial Incentives," p. 172.

39 Mervyn Matthews, "Top Incomes in the USSR: Toward a Definition of the Soviet Elite," *Survey*, vol. 21, no. 3 (1975): table 4, p. 9.

40 A. P. Volkov, *Ekonomicheskaia gazeta*, no. 23 (1973): 4.

41 F. Kholodkhov, *Pravda*, December 19, 1975, p. 2.

42 See V. G. Afanasev et al., eds., *Upravlenie sotsialisticheskim proizvodstvom*, Moscow: Ekonomika, 1978, pp. 107–13.

43 See Koval, *Planirovanie*, pp. 106–13.
44 Ibid., pp. 290–304.
45 Laptev, *Pravovye problemy*, pp. 69–74.
46 Iu. M. Kozlov et al., eds., *Metody i formy gosudarstvennogo upravleniia*, Moscow: Iuridicheskaia literature, 1977, pp. 105–6.
47 A. Vlasov, *Sovetskii gosudarstvennyi apparat*, Moscow: Gosudarstvennoe izdatelstvo iuridicheskoi literatury, 1959, p. 162.
48 Kotov, *Organizatsiia planirovanirovniia*, p. 161.
49 V. I. Turovtsev, ed., *Gosudarstvennyi i obsshchestvennyi kontrol v SSSR*, Moscow: Nauka, 1970, chs. 4, 5.
50 See Conyngham, *Industrial Management*, pp. 5–8.
51 T. S. Khachaturov, *Voprosy ekonomiki*, no. 8 (1973): 17–18.
52 Murray Feshbach and Stephen Rapawy, "Soviet Population and Manpower Trends and Policies," in U.S. Congress, Joint Economic Committee, *Soviet Economy in a New Perspective*, Washington, D.C.: Government Printing Office, 1976, p. 133.
53 Abram Bergson, "Toward a New Growth Model," *Problems of Communism*, vol. 22, no. 2 (1973): 1–9, esp. 7–9.
54 V. Peredentsev, *Nash sovremmenik*, vol. 6 (1975): 118–31. Abstracted in *CDSP*, vol. 27, no. 32 (1975): 1–7.
55 V. G. Treml, "Alcohol in the U.S.S.R.: A Fiscal Dilemma," *Soviet Studies*, vol. 27, no. 2 (1975): 164.
56 Popov, *Funktsii i struktura*, p. 52.
57 See N. G. Kalinin, ed., *Organizatsiia upravleniia v sisteme ministersva*, Moscow: Izdatelstvo Moskovskogo universiteta, 1974, p. 77.
58 N. Fedorenko, *Voprosy ekonomiki*, no. 3 (1970): 64.
59 Michael Ellman, *Soviet Planning Today*, Cambridge University Press, 1971, p. 68.
60 E. Z. Maiminas, *Protsessy planirovaniia v ekonomike: informatsionnyi aspekt*, 2nd ed., Moscow: Ekonomika, 1971, pp. 337–8.
61 Ellman, *Soviet Planning*, p. 70–2.
62 Ibid., pp. 71–4.
63 Alec Nove, *The Soviet Economy: An Introduction*, 2nd rev. ed., New York: Praeger, 1969, ch. 6.
64 A. Dorovskikh, *Planovoe khoziaistvo*, no. 8 (1975): 72.
65 Ellman, *Soviet Planning*, pp. 66–70.
66 *Izvestiia*, August 14, 1976, p. 2; *CDSP*, vol. 27, no. 33 (1976): 22.
67 N. Singur and I. Panfilov, *Planovoe khoziaistvo*, no. 5 (1974): 25–31.
68 V. Kolomnikov and I. Freginskii, *Voprosy ekonomiki*, no. 8 (1975): 68.
69 I. Zamoiskii, *Planovoe khoziaistvo*, no. 5 (1974): 54.
70 V. I. Turovtsev, *Narodnyi kontrol v sotsialisticheskom obshchestve*, Moscow: Izdatelstvo politicheskoi literatury, 1974, p. 184.
71 A. Sidorov and S. Voronin, *Literaturnaia gazeta*, no. 4 (1973): 10.
72 *Pravda*, August 4, 1974, p. 2; and *Izvestiia*, January 7, 1973, p. 3.
73 V. M. Manokhin, *Gosudarstvennaia ditsiplina v narodnom khoziaistve*, Moscow: Iuridicheskaia literatura, 1970, p. 71.

278   *Notes to pp. 32–7*

74 V. Kulikov, *Sotsialisticheskaia zakonnost*, no. 5 (1973): 8–13.
75 S. Protserov, *Planovoe khoziaistvo*, no. 5 (1974): 58–60.
76 *Ekonomicheskaia gazeta*, no. 50 (1973): 13.
77 Conyngham, *Industrial Management*, pp. 143–5, 198–202, 244–9.
78 V. Biriukov, *Izvestiia*, January 10, 1974, p. 2.
79 V. Taranov, *Ekonomicheskaia gazeta*, no. 5 (1973): 10.
80 See the classic analysis of Joseph Berliner, *Factory and Manager in the USSR*, Cambridge, Mass.: Harvard University Press, 1957.
81 Nove, *Soviet Economy*, pp. 181–6; see also Joseph S. Berliner, *The Innovational Decision in Soviet Industry*, Cambridge, Mass.: MIT Press, 1976.
82 Feshbach and Rapawy, "Soviet Population," pp. 138–9.
83 Golikov, *Effektivnost*, pp. 105–6.
84 Iu. E. Volkov, *Sotsiologicheskie issledovaniia*, no. 1 (1976): 12–13.
85 L. M. Danilov, ed., *Dvizhenie rabochikh kadrov v promyshlennosti*, Moscow: Statistika, 1973, pp. 15–16.
86 V. S. Nemchenko, ed., *Sotsialno-ekonomicheskie voprosy organizatsii truda*, Moscow: Izdatelstvo Moskovskogo universiteta, 1974, p. 3.
87 Danilov, *Dvizhenie*, p. 133; N. A. Aitov, *Tekhnicheskii progress i dvizhenie rabochykh kadrov*, Moscow: Ekonomika, 1972, pp. 73–5.
88 Aitov, *Tekhnicheskii progress*, p. 50.
89 L. M. Danilov and I. I. Matrozova, eds., *Problemy ispolzovaniia rabochei sily v usloviiakh nauchno-tekhnicheskoi revoliutsii*, Moscow: Ekonomika, 1973, pp. 217–18.
90 D. P. Kaidalov and E. I. Suimenko, *Aktualnye problemy sotsiologii truda*, Moscow: Ekonomika, 1974, pp. 113–14.
91 A. E. Kotliiar and S. Ia. Turchaninova, *Zaniatost zhenshchin v proizvodstve*, Moscow: Statistika, 1975, p. 117.
92 Ibid.
93 A. G. Kharchev and S. I. Golod, *Professionalnaia rabota zhenshchin i semiia*, Leningrad: Nauka, 1971, p. 62.
94 Kotliiar and Turchaninova, *Zaniatost*, pp. 68–9.
95 G. A. Slezanov, "Sotsialno-demograficheskie gruppy v sostave sovetskogo rabochego klassa," in V. Veselovskii and M. N. Rutkevich, eds., *Problemy razvitiia sotsialnoi struktury obshchestva v Sovietskom soiuze i Polshe*, Moscow: Nauka, 1976, p. 19.
96 Aitov, *Tekhnicheskii progress*, pp. 52–3.
97 Iu. L. Sokolnikov, *Sotsiologicheskie issledovaniia*, no. 1 (1976): 94–5.
98 Iu. Sosin, *Ekonomika i organizatsiia promyshlennogo proizvodstva*, no. 5 (1976): 166–74.
99 Aitov, *Tekhnicheskii progress*, p. 62.
100 E. V. Magnitskaia and L. I. Shishkina, "Effektivnost ditsiplinarnogo vozdeistviia na narushitelei trudovoi ditsipliny," in A. S. Pashkov et al., eds., *Chelovek i obshchestvo*, 15 vols., Leningrad: Izdatelstvo Leningradskogo universiteta, 1966–76, 7: 84.
101 See K. A. Moraleva, "Sotsialnyi kontrol za trudovoi ditsiplinoi v proizvodstvennom kollektive," in Plashkov, ed., *Chelovek i obshchestvo*, 12: 176–7.

102 G. Popov, *Pravda*, February 8, 1970, p. 2.
103 F. Burlatskii, *Novyi mir*, no. 7 (1972): 147.
104 A. Butenko, *Kommunist*, no. 6 (1972): 54–6.
105 See Julian Cooper, "The Scientific and Technical Revolution in Soviet Theory," in Frederick J. Fleron, Jr., ed., *Technology and Communist Culture: The Sociocultural Impact of Technology Under Socialism*, New York: Praeger, 1977, pp. 154–62.
106 I. A. Zhukovskii, "Nauka – proizvoditelnaia sila sotsialisticheskogo obshchestva," in A. I. Mogilev, ed., *Nauchno-tekhnicheskaia revoliutsiia i sotsialnyi progress*, Moscow: Politizdat, 1972, pp. 120–9.
107 B. M. Kedrov, ed., *Nauchno-tekhnicheskaia revoliutsiia i sotsializm*, Moscow: Politizdat, 1973, pp. 165–9.
108 See Roundtable, *Voprosy filosofii*, no. 1 (1973): 48–60; E. I. Fainburg, *Voprosy filosofii*, no. 10 (1971): 33; A. G. Kharchev, *Voprosy filosofii*, no. 12 (1975): 63.
109 Kedrov, *Nauchno-tekhnicheskaia revoliutsiia*, p. 307.
110 P. N. Fedoseev, *Kommunist*, no. 5 (1975): 33.
111 T. V. Kerimov, *Voprosy filosofii*, no. 1 (1972): 51–2.
112 Kedrov, *Nauchno-tekhnicheskaia revoliutsiia*, p. 286.
113 V. Glushkov, *Literaturnaia gazeta*, no. 17 (1971): 12.
114 Burlatskii, *Novyi mir*, no. 7 (1972): 147.
115 G. Kh. Popov, *Problemy teorii upravleniia*, 2nd ed., Moscow: Ekonomika, 1974, pp. 23.
116 V. Kelle, *Kommunist*, no. 8 (1974): 54–64. Reprinted in *Joint Publications Research Services*, 62297 (1974): 72. Cited hereafter as *JPRS*.
117 For studies of the development of demography and mathematical economics, see Helen Desfosses, "Demography, Ideology and Politics in the USSR," *Soviet Studies*, vol. 28, no. 2 (1976): 248–50; and Richard W. Judy, "The Economists," in H. Gordon Skilling and Franklyn Griffiths, eds., *Interest Groups in Soviet Politics*, Princeton, N.J.: Princeton University Press, 1971, pp. 232–40.
118 K. Karlamov, *Kommunist*, no. 1 (1975): 123.
119 O. A. Deineko, *Metodologicheskie problemy nauki upravleniia proizvodstvom*, Moscow: Nauka, 1970, pp. 118–19.
120 Robert W. Campbell, "Management Spillovers from Soviet Space and Military Programmes," *Soviet Studies*, vol. 23, no. 4 (1972): 586–90.
121 A. I. Berg, "Introduction," in A. I. Berg et al., eds., *Organizatsiia upravleniia*, Moscow: Nauka, 1968, pp. 5–6.
122 S. V. Utechin, *Russian Political Thought*, New York: Praeger, 1963, p. 212; Robert F. Miller, "The New Science of Administration in the U.S.S.R.," *Administrative Science Quarterly*, vol. 16, no. 3 (1971): 249–50.
123 Stephen F. Cohen, *Bukharin and the Bolshevik Revolution: A Political Biography, 1888–1938*, New York: Knopf, 1973, pp. 97, 118–19.
124 D. M. Gvishiani, *Organizatsiia i upravlenie*, 2nd enl. ed., Moscow: Nauka, 1972, esp. chs. 7, 8.
125 See B. Z. Milner, ed., *SShA: organizatsionnye formy i metody upra-

vleniia promyshlenymi korporatsiiami, Moscow: Nauka, 1972, pp. 235, 241-3. See also L. E. Evenko, *SShA,* no. 7 (1972): 15-28.

126   B. Z. Milner, *Problemy upravleniia v sovremmenoi Amerike,* Moscow: Znanie, 1974, pp. 21-9.

127   Milner, *SSha: organizatsionnye formy,* pp. 80-101.

128   See V. N. Churmanteeva, *SShA: podgotovka rukovodiashchego personela promyshlennykh korporatsii,* Moscow: Nauka, 1975.

129   D. M. Gvishiani, *Kommunist,* no. 12 (1970): 115-18.

130   V. M. Shepel, in A. M. Omarev, ed., *Voprosy upravleniia ekonomikoi,* Moscow: Izdalelstvo politicheskoi literatury, 1974, pp. 253-4.

131   *Pravda,* March 2, 1974, p. 2.

132   D. Gvishiani, *Kommunist,* no. 11 (1978): 96-8.

133   See G. Kh. Popov, *Izvestiia Akademii nauk: seriia ekonomicheskaia,* no. 1 (1971): 58-71.

134   D. Pravdin, *Voprosy ekonomiki,* no. 1 (1978): 64.

135   Popov, *Problemy,* p. 212.

136   Deineko, *Metodologicheskie problemy,* pp. 100-1.

137   Gvishiani, *Problemy nauchnoi organizatsiia,* p. 534.

138   Ibid.

139   D. M. Gvishiani, *Ekonomicheskaia gazeta,* no. 24 (1966): 6.

140   D. M. Gvishiani, *Sotsialisticheskii trud,* no. 10 (1972): 20-8.

141   Pravdin, *Voprosy ekonomiki,* no. 1 (1978): 60.

142   O. A. Deineko, ed., *Problemy nauchnoi organizatsii upravleniia sotsialisticheskoi promyshlennostiu,* Moscow: Ekonomika, 1968, pp. 602-3.

143   Popov, *Problemy,* p. 44.

144   *Pravda,* June 2, 1978, p. 3.

145   See *Kommunist,* no. 14 (1972): 86-102.

146   An excellent example is the criticism of B. V. Biriukov and O. K. Tikhomirov of a Polish scholar's book on the pyschological basis of decision making. Iu. Kozeletskii, *Psikhologicheskaia teoriia reshenii,* Moscow: Progress, 1979, pp. 464-500.

Chapter 2. The systems approach to management reform

1   Loren R. Graham, *Science and Philosophy in the Soviet Union,* New York: Knopf, 1972, p. 324.

2   Simon Kassel, "Cybernetics and Science Policy in the Academy of Sciences - 1970," *Soviet Cybernetics Review* (September 1970): 3.

3   N. Stefanov, N. Iakhiel and S. Kachaunov, *Upravlenie, modelirovanie, prognozirovanie,* Moscow: Ekonomika, 1972, p. 7.

4   V. V. Agudov and B. V. Plesskii, *Filosofskie nauki,* no. 3 (1972): 54.

5   V. A. Lektorskii and V. S. Shvyrov, *Voprosy filosofii,* no. 1 (1971): 146-47.

6   I. V. Blauberg, V. N. Sadovskii and B. G. Iudin, *Voprosy filosofii,* no. 8 (1978): 41.

7   N. G. Gaaze-Rapoport, "Kibernetika i teoriia sistem," in I. V.

Blauberg et al., *Sistemnye issledovaniia ezhegodnik,* Moscow: Nauka, 1973, p. 65.
8 Ibid., pp. 66–75.
9 "Cybernetics," in C. D. Herring, ed., *Marxism, Communism and Western Society: A Comparative Encyclopedia,* 8 vols., New York: Herder and Herder, 1972–3, 2: 288–90.
10 E. Z. Maiminas, *Protsessy planirovaniia v ekonomike: informatsionnyi aspekt,* 2nd ed., Moscow: Ekonomika, 1971, p. 9.
11 B. V. Biriukov, *Kibernetika i metodologiia nauki,* Moscow: Nauka, 1974.
12 Ibid., p. 74.
13 Soviet literature on information theory is enormous. See, for example, V. G. Afanasev, *Sotsialnaia informatsiia i upravlenie ob-shchestvom,* Moscow: Politizdat, 1975, ch. 1; I. I. Grishkin, *Poniatie informatsii,* Moscow: Nauka, 1973; and Iu. I Cherniak, *Informatsiia i upravlenie,* Moscow: Nauka, 1974.
14 Afanasev, *Sotsialnaia informatsiia,* pp. 10–12.
15 V. P. Bogolepov, *Ekonomicheskaia gazeta,* no. 15 (1967): 19.
16 A. I. Berg, *Cybernetics: The Science of Optimal Control,* Washington, D.C.: Joint Publications Research Service, 1968, pp. 14–15.
17 V. Glushkov, *Kommunist,* no. 18 (1970): 72.
18 V. G. Afanasev, *Kommunist,* no. 17 (1974): 46.
19 Lektorskii and Shvyrov, *Voprosy filosofii,* no. 1 (1971): 148–9.
20 See the article of E. Z. Maiminas, "Economic Cybernetics," in *Great Soviet Encyclopedia,* 3rd ed., vol. 12, New York: Macmillan, 1973, pp. 346–7.
21 A. M. Birman, *Nekotorye problemy nauki ob upravlenii narodnym khoziaistvom,* Moscow: Ekonomika, 1965, pp. 42–5.
22 Piotr Sztempka, *System and Function: Toward a Theory of Society,* New York: Academic Press, 1974, pp. 169–70.
23 Alexander Vucinich, "Marx and Parsons in Soviet Sociology," *Russian Review,* vol. 33, no. 1 (1974): 3–5.
24 David Silverman, *The Theory of Organizations: A Sociological Framework,* New York: Basic Books, 1971, pp. 54.
25 For slightly differing views of Parsons, see G. P. Davidiuk, *Vvedenie v prikladnuiu sotsiologiiu,* Minsk: Vyssheishaia shkola, 1975, pp. 159–63; A. A. Ruchka, *Sotsialnye tsennosti i normy,* Kiev: Naukova dumka, 1976, pp. 70–1; I. M. Popova, ed., *Problemy sotsialnogo regulirovaniia na promyshlennykh predpriiatiiakh,* Kiev: Naukova dumka, 1973.
26 Popova, *Problemy,* p. 9.; also, Ruchka, *Sotsialnye tsennosti,* pp. 20–30.
27 Popova, *Problemy,* pp. 6–8.
28 S. G. Moskvichev, *Problemy motivatsii v psikhologicheskikh issledovaniiakh,* Kiev: Naukova dumka, 1975, pp. 112–23. See also Gvishiani, *Organizatsiia i upravlenie,* 2nd enl. ed., Moscow: Nauka, 1972, p. 316.
29 Iu. I. Cherniak, *Prostota slozhnogo,* Moscow: Znanie, 1975, pp. 118–23.

30 Iu. M. Kozlov, *Upravlenie narodnym khoziaistvom SSSR*, 2 vols., Moscow: Izdatelstvo Moskovskogo universiteta, 1971, 2: 4-18.

31 L. Leontiev, *Ekonomicheskie problemy razvitogo sotsializma*, Moscow: Nauka, 1972, p. 125.

32 V. M. Glushkov, *Pravda*, June 10, 1972, p. 3. The model of a technologically determined decision-making system is not assumed here to exhaust Glushkov's personal views on the nature of the Soviet economic system. As a leading publicist and advocate of the need to incorporate technology in economic management, however, Glushkov has continued to view the technological dimension as primary. For a recent view which incorporates the series of decisions taken in 1971 and later, see his *Makroekonomicheskie modeli i printsipy postroeniia OGAS*, Moscow: Statistika, 1975.

33 N. Ia. Petrakov, *Upravlenie khoziaistvennymi sistemani*, Moscow: Znanie, 1975, p. 5.

34 Ibid., pp. 6-8.

35 N. Ia. Petrakov, *Novyi mir*, no. 8 (1970): 178. A more extensive statement of his views on plan and market is contained in his *Khoziaistvennaia reforma: plan i ekonomicheskaia samostoiatelnost*, Moscow: Mysl, 1971, ch. 2.

36 V. Nemchinov, *Kommunist*, no. 5 (1964): 74-87. A full translation is in *Current Digest of the Soviet Press*, vol. 16, no. 18 (1964): 3-8. Cited hereafter as *CDSP*.

37 Ibid., p. 3.

38 Stanley H. Cohn, *Economic Development in the Soviet Union*, Lexington, Mass.: Heath, 1970, p. 88.

39 Nemchinov, in *CDSP*, vol. 16, no. 18 (1964): 4-8.

40 V. G. Afanasev, *The Scientific Management of Society*, trans. L. Ilyitskaya, Moscow: Progress, 1971, p. 7.

41 Ibid., p. 117.

42 Ibid.

43 Two excellent articles on the approach of V. G. Afanasev can be found in Donald V. Schwartz, "Decision-making, Administrative Decentralization, and Feedback Mechanisms: Comparisons of Soviet and Western Models," *Studies in Comparative Communism*, vol. 7, nos. 1, 2 (1974): 146-83; and Schwartz, "Recent Soviet Adaptations of Systems Theory to Administrative Theory," *Journal of Comparative Administration*, vol. 5, no. 2 (1973): 233-64.

44 Afanasev, *Scientific Management*, esp. ch. 7. See also V. G. Afanasev, *The Scientific and Technological Revolution; Its Impact on Management and Education*, trans. Robert Daglish, Moscow: Progress, 1975, esp. ch. 7.

45 A. I. Prigozhin, *Sotsiologicheskie aspekty upravelniia*, Moscow: Znanie, 1974, pp. 15-31.

46 Ibid.

47 N. A. Fedorenko, *Optimal Functioning System for a Socialist Economy*, trans. Iurii Sdobnikov, Moscow: Progress, 1974, pp. 179-82.

48 For a clear analysis of the SOFE conception, see the works of the

Cambridge economist, Michael Ellman: *Soviet Planning Today: Proposals for an Optimally Functioning System,* Cambridge University Press, 1971; and *Planning Problems in the USSR: The Contribution of Mathematical Economics to Their Solution,* Cambridge University Press, 1973. The interest group aspect of the discussion has been thoroughly examined by Richard W. Judy, "The Economists," in H. Gordon Skilling and Franklyn Griffiths, eds., *Interest Groups in Soviet Politics,* Princeton, N.J.: University Press, 1971, pp. 209–52.

49 The development of SOFE as a working design for the rationalization of the system of planning and management is the work of a brilliant group of economists and management specialists associated with CEMI as well as other research institutes. As the basic paradigm for the policy of rationalization, however, Fedorenko has emerged as its principal spokesman. The rise of political specialists like Fedorenko and Glushkov who mediate the relationships of the political and technical spheres appears as an important aspect of Soviet political development.

50 N. Fedorenko, ed., *Optimalnoe planirovanie i sovershenstvovanie upravleniia narodnym khoziaistvom,* Moscow: Nauka, 1969, p. 19.

51 Fedorenko, *Optimal Functioning,* p. 22.

52 N. P. Fedorenko and E. Maiminas, *Voprosy ekonomiki,* no. 3 (1971): 15–16.

53 N. Fedorenko, *Kommunist,* no. 5 (1972): 61–2.

54 Fedorenko, *Optimal Functioning,* pp. 25–6. What constitutes the precise boundaries between the social and technical systems, however, is unclear.

55 Ibid., p. 24.

56 The assumptions of SOFE are well stated in N. Fedorenko and S. Shatalin, *Vorposy ekonomiki,* no. 6 (1969): 98–9.

57 The concept of metaplanning is developed in N. P. Fedorenko, ed., *Kompleksnoe narodno-khoziaistvennoe planirovanie,* Moscow: Ekonomika, 1974, p. 24.

58 Ibid., p. 25.

59 Ibid., p. 26.

60 The most comprehensive statement on SKP is in Fedorenko, *Kompleksnoe planirovanie,* ch. 10. An extensive statement in English is in N. P. Fedorenko, ed., *Economic Development and Perspective Planning,* trans. Jenny Warren, Moscow: Progress, 1975.

61 The system of forecasting envisaged by SOFE is described by Fedorenko in *Ekonomika i organizatsiia promyshlennogo proizvodstva,* no. 1 (1973): 65–6.

62 Ibid., pp. 67–72.

63 *Ekonomicheskaia gazeta,* no. 2 (1974): 14; N. Fedorenko, *Voprosy ekonomiki,* no. 5 (1975): 48–9. See also the collection of articles in N. P. Fedorenko, ed., *Sistema modelei optimalnogo planirovaniia,* Moscow: Nauka, 1975.

64 Ellman, *Planning Problems,* pp. 64–5.

65 N. P. Fedorenko, *Voprosy ekonomiki,* no. 6 (1972): 99.

66 N. Fedorenko, "Economico-Mathematical Model in Soviet Economic Planning," in UNESCO, *The Social Sciences: Problems and Orientations*, The Hague: Mouton, 1968, pp. 348–51.

67 Fedorenko, *Voprosy ekonomiki*, no. 6 (1972): 98.

68 Fedorenko, *Kommunist*, no. 5 (1972): 64–5; Fedorenko, *Ekonomika i organizatsiia promyshlennogo proizvodstva*, no. 1 (1973): 68; and Fedorenko, *Ekonomicheskaia gazeta*, no. 2 (1974): 14.

69 In 1967, on the crest of the wave for decentralization, Fedorenko stressed the basic role of the state in the planning and coordination of the economy as well as the necessity for some decentralization. See Fedorenko, *Planovoe khoziaistvo*, no. 4 (1967): 8–10.

70 V. F. Pugachev, *Ekonomika i matematicheskie metody*, II, no. 5 (1966): 657.

71 Fedorenko, *Voprosy ekonomiki*, no. 6 (1972): 102.

72 Fedorenko, *Optimalnoe planirovanie*, p. 22; see also Fedorenko, *Sotsialisticheskie printsipy*, p. 46.

73 See, for example, A. I. Katsenelinboigen and E. Iu. Faerman, *Ekonomika i matematicheskie metody*, vol. 3, no. 3 (1967): 331–46; the excellent article of A. I. Katsenelinboigen, I. L. Lakhman and Iu. V. Ovsienko, in *Ekonomika i matematicheskie metody*, vol. 5, no. 4 (1969): 510–25. Also, N. P. Fedorenko, *O razrabotke sistemy optimalnogo funktsionirovaniia ekonomiki*, Moscow: Nauka, 1968, p. 205.

74 N. P. Fedorenko, in G. A. Dzhavadov, ed., *Organizatsiia upravleniia*, Moscow: Ekonomika, 1971, p. 83.

75 N. P. Fedorenko, *Kompleksnoe planirovanie*, p. 158; Fedorenko, *Ekonomika i matematicheskie metody*, vol. 12, no. 2 (1976): 236.

76 For a strong defense of the role of optimal prices and their compatibility with commodity–monetary relations, see A. Lure, *Voprosy ekonomiki*, no. 7 (1966): 61–4; V. Volkonskii, *Voprosy ekonomiki*, no. 3 (1967): 50–1.

77 N. P. Fedorenko, *Planovoe khoziaistvo*, no. 4 (1967): 11.

78 Fedorenko, *Optimalnoe planirovanie*, p. 22.

79 Fedorenko, *Voprosy ekonomiki*, no. 6 (1972): 104.

80 Fedorenko, *Optimalnoe planirovanie*, p. 19.

81 Fedorenko, in Dzhavadov, *Organizatsiia upravleniia*, pp. 77–8; Fedorenko, *Sotsialisticheskie printsipy*, pp. 52–3.

82 For a critique of the 1965 reform, see Fedorenko, *Planovoe khoziaistvo*, no. 4 (1967): 13–17; and more recently, Fedorenko, *Ekonomika i matematicheskie metody*, vol. 11, no. 1 (1975); 18–25.

83 Fedorenko, in Dzhavadov, *Organizatsiia upravleniia*, p. 71; Fedorenko, *Voprosy ekonomiki*, no. 6 (1972): 106.

84 Fedorenko, *Voprosy ekonomiki*, no. 3 (1970): 58–60.

85 Fedorenko, in Dzhavadov, *Organizatsiia upravleniia*, p. 81.

86 Fedorenko, *Sotsialisticheskie printsipy*, pp. 51–2.

87 Fedorenko, *Voprosy ekonomiki*, no. 6 (1972): 104.

88 I. A. Vatel and N. N. Moiseev, *Ekonomika i matematicheskie metody*, vol. 13, no. 1 (1977): 17.

89 Ibid.

90 Robert W. Campbell, *The Soviet-Type Economies: Performance and Evolution*, 3rd ed., Boston: Houghton Mifflin, 1974, p. 199.

91 For an excellent article analyzing the disputes among Soviet economists on the use of mathematical methods, see V. S. Dunaev, in I. I. Kuzminov and S. V. Rogachev, eds., *Politicheskaia ekonomika sotsializma: nauchnaia osnova rukovodstva narodnym khoziaistvom*, Moscow: Mysl, 1975, pp. 131-40.

92 E. Z. Maiminas, in N. P. Fedorenko, ed., *Problemy planirovaniia i prognozirovaniia*, Moscow: Nauka, 1974, pp. 15-16.

93 Ibid., pp. 26-31.

94 See Ellman, *Soviet Planning Today*, pp. 4-11.

95 On the role of the Communist Party in setting the goals of development, see Fedorenko and Maiminas, *Voprosy ekonomiki*, no. 3 (1971): 27.

96 Fedorenko, in Dzhavadov, *Organizatsiia upravleniia*, p. 65.

97 Ibid.

98 See Fedorenko, *O razrabotke*, p. 193.

99 Fedorenko, *Planovoe khoziaistvo*, no. 8 (1968): 18; Fedorenko, *Sistema modelei*, pp. 7-10.

100 Fedorenko, *Optimalnoe planirovanie*, p. 18.

101 Fedorenko, *Voprosy ekonomiki*, no. 6 (1972): 96-7.

102 See, for example, V. Maevskii, *Planovoe khoziaistvo*, no. 1 (1969): 21-3.

103 N. P. Fedorenko, in John T. Dunlop and N. P. Fedorenko, eds., *Planning and Markets: Modern Trends in Various Economic Systems*, New York: McGraw-Hill, 1969, p. 61.

104 See N. Ia. Petrakov, *Kiberneticheskie problemy upravleniia ekonomikoi*, Moscow: Nauka, 1974, pp. 32-7.

105 Maevskii, *Planovoe khoziaistvo*, no. 1 (1969): 23.

106 For an extensive critique of the problems of creating a working mechanism, see O. Iun, *Voprosy ekonomiki*, no. 11 (1973): 102-3. As Iun notes, the mathematical difficulties of optimization have been of such an order that optimization models which have been developed give only a partial description of the economy and virtually exclude noneconomic factors.

107 Petrakov, *Kiberneticheskie problemy*, p. 37.

108 V. Cherniavskii, *Voprosy ekonomiki*, no. 6 (1976): 50.

109 Ia. Kronrod, *Planovoe khoziaistvo*, no. 10 (1975): 92-3.

110 For a savage attack on marginal theory and linear programming as a vulgarized adaptation of the Western theory of the firm, see the first of three articles of A. Kats, *Planovoe khoziaistvo*, no. 7 (1972): 92-103. Fedorenko's reply is in Fedorenko, *Problemy planirovaniia*, pp. 35-70.

111 N. Fedorenko, *Kommunist*, no. 5 (1972): 63-4.

112 Campbell, *Soviet-Type Economies*, p. 195.

113 For an account of a recent debate on the concept of social utility, see the report of V. Dunaeva, *Voprosy ekonomiki*, no. 7 (1975): 69-78.

114 A. Eremin and L. Nikoforov, *Voprosy ekonomiki*, no. 6 (1969): 112.
115 Ibid., p. 113. For an analysis of this particular debate, see Ellman, *Soviet Planning Today*, pp. 9-11.
116 *Ekonomicheskaia gazeta*, no. 42 (1976): 6.
117 N. P. Fedorenko, *Ekonomika i matematicheskie metody*, vol. 10, no. 3 (1974): 419-22.
118 Ia. Kronrod, *Planovoe khoziaistvo*, no. 5 (1973): 85.
119 See Eremin and Nikoforov, *Voprosy ekonomiki*, no. 6 (1969): 117-18. For a defense of the objective nature of SOFE's prescriptions, see V. G. Grebennikov, O. S. Pchelintsev and S. S. Shatalin, *Ekonomika i matematicheskie metody*, vol. 10, no. 6 (1974): 1079-81.
120 S. Strumilin, *Voprosy ekonomiki*, no. 4 (1968): 121-2.
121 Eremin and Nikoforov, *Voprosy ekonomiki*, no. 6 (1969): 124.
122 Kronrod, *Planovoe khoziaistvo*, no. 5 (1973): 85-7.
123 N. Fedorenko, *Ekonomicheskaia gazeta*, no. 28 (1974): 10.
124 S. Strumilin, *Voprosy ekonomiki*, no. 1 (1967): 146-9.
125 S. Strumilin, *Voprosy ekonomiki*, no. 4 (1968): 115-22.
126 *Ekonomika i matematicheskie metody*, vol. 9, no. 2 (1973): 366-8.
127 *Planovoe khoziaistvo*, no. 10 (1973): 152-7. The conference is translated in *CDSP*, vol. 25, no. 47 (1973): 1-4.
128 Ibid.
129 *Planovoe khoziaistvo*, no. 9 (1975): 152.

Chapter 3. Developing a technology of management

1 L. I. Brezhnev, *Ob osnovnykh voprosakh ekonomicheskoi politiki KPSS na sovremennom etape*, 2 vols., Moscow: Politizdat, 1975, 1: 438.
2 Ibid., 1: 436.
3 Paul Cocks, "The Policy Process and Bureaucratic Politics," in Paul Cocks, Robert V. Daniels and Nancy Whittier Heer, eds., *The Dynamics of Soviet Politics*, Cambridge, Mass.: Harvard University Press, 1976, pp. 165-6.
4 Brezhnev, *Ob osnovnykh voprosakh*, p. 374.
5 *Pravda*, March 31, 1971, pp. 2-10. A full translation is in *Current Digest of the Soviet Press*, vol. 23, no. 13 (1971): 5, 11. Cited hereafter as *CDSP*.
6 Ibid., 13-14. See also editorial, *Kommunist*, no. 3 (1971): 11-12.
7 S. Shatalin, *Voprosy ekonomiki*, no. 7 (1971): 15-18. The program of the Twenty-fifth Congress is in *XXV Sezd Kommunisticheskoi partii Sovetskogo soiuza. Stenograficheskii otchet*, 3 vols., Moscow: Politizdat, 1976, 1: 84-7.
8 B. Karpenko, *Planovoe khoziaistvo*, no. 12 (1975): 110-118.
9 Iu. N. Bronnikov, comp. *Upravlenie sotsialisticheskoi ekonomikoi*, 2nd ed., Moscow: Moskovskii rabochii, 1975, pp. 436-8.
10 N. P. Fedorenko, ed., *Economic Development and Perspective Planning*, trans. Jenny Warren, Moscow: Progress, 1975, pp. 95-6.
11 L. V. Kantorovich, *Matematicheskie metody v organizatsii i planirovanii proizvodstva*, Leningrad: Izdatelstvo Leningradskogo universiteta, 1939.

12 Alfred Zauberman, *The Mathematical Revolution in Soviet Economics*, New York: Oxford University Press, 1975, p. 30.

13 A. Bachurin, *Planovoe khoziaistvo*, no. 6 (1972): 18–20.

14 L. V. Kantorovich et al., in L. V. Kantorovich, *Essays in Optimal Planning*, intro. Leon Smolinski, White Plains, N.Y.: International Arts and Sciences Press, 1976, pp. 228–31.

15 See H. A. Simon, *The Shape of Automation for Men and Management*, New York: Harper & Row, 1965, pp. 46–7.

16 V. Cherniavskii, *Voprosy ekonomiki*, no. 6 (1976): 49.

17 Ibid., pp. 50–1.

18 Ibid., p. 51.

19 Ibid., pp. 52–3.

20 See William J. Conyngham, *Industrial Management in the Soviet Union*, Stanford, Cal.: Hoover Institution Press, 1973, p. 72.

21 For a list of the most important long-term forecasting problems, see A. I. Klinskii, *Planirovanie ekonomicheskogo i sotsialnogo razvitiia*, Moscow: Mysl, 1974, pp. 23–4.

22 N. F. Fedorenko, *Ekonomika i matematicheskie metody*, vol. 9, no. 2 (1973): 195–203.

23 See S. A. Sarkisian and L. V. Golovanov, *Prognozirovanie razvitiia bolshchikh sistem*, Moscow: Statistika, 1975, p. 73 and *passim*.

24 Iu. I. Cherniak, *Sistemnyi analiz v upravlenii ekonomikoi*, Moscow: Ekonomika, 1975, pp. 72–6.

25 A. Levin, *Voprosy ekonomiki*, no. 1 (1976): 56–7. The argument against a behavioral approach is made by B. Davidovich, *Planovoe khoziaistvo*, no. 5 (1976): 115.

26 Levin, *Voprosy ekonomiki*, no. 1 (1976): 50, 57–8.

27 *Voprosy ekonomiki*, no. 8 (1976): 151–2.

28 Zauberman, *Mathematical Revolution*, p. 7.

29 Vladimir G. Treml et al., *The Structure of the Soviet Economy: Analysis and Reconstruction of the 1966 Input–Output Table*, New York: Praeger, 1972, pp. 11–26. A discussion of the 1972 ex post model is developed in V. G. Treml et al., "The Soviet 1966 and 1972 Input–Output Tables," in U.S., Congress, Joint Economic Committee, *Soviet Economy in a New Perspective*, Washington, D.C.: Government Printing Office, 1976, pp. 332–76.

30 Treml et al., *Structure*, ch. 2.

31 A. Efimov, *Voprosy ekonomiki*, no. 11 (1976): 35, 43.

32 V. Vorobev, *Planovoe khoziaistvo*, no. 7 (1973): 55.

33 Efimov, *Voprosy ekonomiki*, no. 11 (1976): 35.

34 A. Efimov, in N. F. Fedorenko, ed., *Optimalnoe planirovanie i sovershenstvovanie upravleniia narodnym khoziaistvom*, Moscow: Nauka, 1969, pp. 141–55. An authoritative description of the methodology is in V. V. Kossov, *Mezhotraslevye modelie*, Moscow: Ekonomika, 1973.

35 U.S., Congress, *Soviet Economy in New Perspective*, pp. 333–5.

36 Albina Tretyakova and Igor Birman, "Input–Output Analysis in the U.S.S.R.," *Soviet Studies*, vol. 28, no. 2 (1976): 181–6.

37 Vorobev, *Planovoe khoziaistvo*, no. 7 (1973): 55.

38 Ibid., pp. 56-7.
39 A. Efimov, *Voprosy ekonomiki*, no. 11 (1976): 44.
40 Cherniavskii, *Voprosy ekonomiki*, no. 6 (1976): 49-50.
41 *XXV Sezd*, p. 64.
42 G. Popov, *Voprosy ekonomiki*, no. 2 (1977): 57-8.
43 R. Kozlov and V. Safronov, *Voprosy ekonomiki*, no. 1 (1977): 117-18.
44 Ibid., pp. 120-1.
45 N. Fedorenko, *Ekonomika i matematicheskie metody*, vol. 14, no. 4 (1978): 636.
46 Ibid., p. 633.
47 G. M. Dobrov et al., *Programmno-tselevoi metod upravleniia v nauka*, Moscow: Central Scientific Research Institute "Elektronika," 1974, pp. 42-52.
48 R. Tsvylev, *Voprosy ekonomiki*, no. 7 (1971): 80-2.
49 V. Ilin, *Voprosy ekonomiki*, no. 1 (1976): 7.
50 V. Krasovskii, *Voprosy ekonomiki*, no. 12 (1976): 39-49.
51 R. Raman, *Ekonomika i matematicheskie metody*, no. 2 (1978): 379.
52 Iu. Kormnov, *Voprosy ekonomiki*, no. 1 (1977): 86-94.
53 Krasovskii, *Voprosy ekonomiki*, no. 12 (1976): 40.
54 Fedorenko, *Ekonomika i matematicheskie metody*, vol. 14, no. 4 (1978): 636.
55 Cherniak, *Sistemnyi analiz*, pp. 72-6.
56 V. I. Pavliuchenko, *Ekonomicheskie problemy upravleniia nauchnotekhnicheskim proizvodstvom*, Moscow: Nauka, 1973, p. 88.
57 A. Efimov, *Voprosy ekonomiki*, no. 12 (1978): 24-5.
58 G. Popov, *Kommunist*, no. 18 (1976): 78.
59 N. Fedorenko, *Kommunist*, no. 16 (1978): 37-8.
60 Cherniavskii, *Voprosy ekonomiki*, no. 6 (1976): 54.
61 Fedorenko, *Kommunist*, no. 16 (1978): 38.
62 A. G. Aganbegian, K. A. Bagrinovskii and A. G. Granberg. *Sistema modelei narodno-khoziaistvennogo planirovaniia*, Moscow: Mysl, 1972, pp. 255-6.
63 The methodology for building optimal TKP is in A. G. Aganbegian and D. M. Kazakevich, eds., *Optimalnoe territorialnoproizvodstvennoe planirovanie*, Novosibirsk: Siberian Division, Nauka, 1969, ch. 5.
64 A description of the TKP of Moscow and Moscow Oblast is in M. Goxberg, *Planovoe khoziaistvo*, no. 1 (1976): 51-62.
65 V. Mozhina and V. Savelev, *Planovoe khoziaistvo*, no. 8 (1976): 24-32.
66 M. K. Bandman, ed., *Modelirovanie formirovaniia territorialnoproizvodstvennykh kompleksov*, Novosibirsk: Siberian Division, Nauka, 1976, p. 120.
67 Ibid., p. 15.
68 Bronnikov, *Upravlenie*, p. 447.
69 Cherniavskii, *Voprosy ekonomiki*, no. 6 (1976): 54.
70 L. V. Kantorovich et al., *Ekonomika i matematicheskie metody*, vol. 14, no. 5 (1978): 826.

71 I. Romanov, *Planovoe khoziaistvo*, no. 10 (1978): 53.
72 A. Bliusin and L. Dudkin, *Voprosy ekonomiki*, no. 7 (1976): 82.
73 M. V. Lagutin, in D. G. Zhimerin and A. P. Vladislavlev, eds., *Avtomatizirovannye sistemy upravleniia*, Moscow: Ekonomika, 1976, p. 43.
74 Kantorovich et al., *Ekonomika i matematicheskie metody*, vol. 14, no. 5 (1978): 824.
75 Iu. P. Lapshin, *Razvitie avtomatizirovannykh sistem upravleniia v promyshlennosti*, Moscow: Ekonomika, 1977, pp. 196.
76 Ibid.
77 Kantorovich et al., *Ekonomika i matematicheskie metody*, vol. 14, no. 5 (1978).
78 V. O. Cherniavskii, *Effektivnost proizvodstva i optimalnost planirovaniia*, Moscow: Ekonomika, 1973, p. 180.
79 L. V. Kantorovich, *Ekonomika i organizatsiia promyshlennogo proizvodstva*, no. 3 (1976): 130–2.
80 A. A. Modin et al., *Ekonomika i matematicheskie metody*, vol. 11, no. 4 (1975): 624.
81 A. M. Omarev, ed., *Voprosy upravleniia ekonomikoi*, Moscow: Politizdat, 1974, pp. 178–9.
82 Modin et al., *Ekonomika i matematicheskie metody*, vol. 11, no. 4 (1975): 623.
83 D. G. Zhimerin, *Obshchegosudarstvennaia avtomatizirovannaia sistema upravleniia*, Moscow: Znanie, 1975.
84 Iu. Lapshin, *Planovoe khoziaistvo*, no. 11 (1973): 122.
85 Zhimerin, *Obshchegosudarstvennaia*, pp. 41–2.
86 B. A. Volchkov, *Avtomatizirovaniia sistema planovykh rashchetov*, Moscow: Ekonomika, 1970, pp. 6–7, 14–15.
87 V. M. Lagutin, ed., *Ekonomiko-matematicheskie metody v snabzhenie*, Moscow: Ekonomika, 1971, p. 35; a detailed description of ASU–MTS is given by its designer, V. Korotchenko, *Materialno-tekhnicheskie snabzhenie*, no. 6 (1974): 3–24.
88 T. Levtrinskii and N. Kalita, *Ekonomicheskaia gazeta*, no. 2 (1975): 14.
89 N. P. Fedorenko, ed., *Otraslevye avtomatizirovannye sistemy upravleniia*, Moscow: Nauka, 1973, pp. 28–32.
90 The designers have described ASU–Pribor in V. S. Siniak and L. V. Klimenko, *Otraslevaia avtomatizovannaia sistema upravleniia priborstroitelnoi promyshlennostiiu – ASU–Pribor*, Moscow: Znanie, 1974.
91 V. I. Loskutov, *Avtomatizirovannye sistemy upravleniia*, Moscow: Statistika, 1972, pp. 76–9.
92 I. M. Bobko, in Zhimerin and Vladislavlev, *Avtomatizirovannye sistemy*, pp. 164–70.
93 Loskutov, *Avtomatizirovannye sistemy*, pp. 156–8; see also S. O. Petrovskii and G. M. Pyzhik, *Nauchnaia organizatsiia proizvodstva*, Moscow: Ekonomika, 1971, pp. 135–52.
94 An extended discussion is in William J. Conyngham, "Technology

and Decision Making: Some Aspects of the Development of OGAS," *Slavic Review*, vol. 39, no. 3 (1980): 436–41.

95 For their agreement on fundamentals, see their joint article in *Voprosy ekonomiki*, no. 7 (1964): 87–92.

96 See N. P. Fedorenko, ed., *Kompleksnoe narodno-khoziaistvennoe planirovanie*, Moscow: Ekonomika, 1974, ch. 9.

97 V. M. Glushkov, *Makroekonomicheskie modeli i printsipi postroeniia OGAS*, Moscow: Statistika, 1975, pp. 146–59.

98 V. G. Afanasev, *Sotsialnaia informatsii i upravleniia obshchestvom*, Moscow: Politizdat, 1975, pp. 300–2.

99 Kathryn M. Bartol, "Soviet Computer Centers: Network or Tangle?" *Soviet Studies*, vol. 23, no. 4 (1972): 608–18.

100 *Pravda*, January 21, 1971, p. 3.

101 *Materialy XXIV Sezda KPSS*, Moscow: Politizdat, 1971, pp. 256, 295–8.

102 Wade B. Holland, "A Tsar for Soviet Computing," *Soviet Cybernetic Review*, vol. 2, no. 2 (1972): 7–10.

103 Ibid.

104 *Literaturnaia gazeta*, no. 9 (1972): 10.

105 Holland, "Tsar."

106 Glushkov, *Trud*, October 15, 1976.

107 Glushkov, *Izvestiia*, March 8, 1974, p. 2.

108 See V. A. Miasnikov, *Ekonomika i organizatsiia promyshlennogo proizvodstva*, no. 6 (1974): 87–96. Translated in *CDSP*, vol. 27, no. 30 (1975): 13–14; G. Semborskii and V. Simchera, *Voprosy ekonomiki*, no. 7 (1974): 82–4, 86–7.

109 N. Kononov, *Vestnik statistiki*, no. 4 (1975): 52–3.

110 Zhimerin, *Pravda*, February 17, 1976, p. 3.

111 Iu. Lapshin and V. Korovkin, *Planovoe khoziaistvo*, no. 4 (1976): 103.

112 S. Sazonov, *Ekonomicheskaia gazeta*, no. 3 (1976): 17; Semborskii and Simchera, *Voprosy ekonomiki*, no. 7 (1974): 82.

113 *XXV Sezd*, 1: 84–7.

114 E. Z. Maiminas, *Protsessy planirovaniia v ekonomike: informatsionnyi aspekt*, 2nd ed., Moscow: Ekonomika, 1971, pp. 228–9.

115 Afanasev, *Sotsialnaia informatsiia*, p. 188.

116 See Iu. Cherniak, in N. F. Fedorenko, ed., *Issledovanie potokov ekonomicheskoi informatsii*, Moscow: Nauka, 1968, pp. 17–22.

117 V. M. Glushkov, *Ekonomika i organizatsiia promyshlennogo proizvodstva*, no. 2 (1979): 35.

118 Fedorenko, *Otraslevye*, pp. 38–9.

119 N. Zenchenko, *Ekonomika i organizatsiia promyshlennogo proizvodstva*, no. 1 (1976): 30–1.

120 Sh. Kamaletdinetdinov, *Voprosy ekonomiki*, no. 1 (1974): 121.

121 N. Cheshenko, *Ekonomicheskaia gazeta*, no. 47 (1973): 10.

122 V. V. Boitsov, *Ekonomicheskaia gazeta*, no. 11 (1972): 8.

123 V. P. Klimenko, A. I. Lutsenko and L. A. Savchenko, *Avtomatizirovannaia sistema gosudarstvennoi statistiki*, Moscow: Znanie, 1976, p. 24.

124 M. A. Appak, *Pribory i sistemy upravleniia*, no. 6 (1978): 7-8.
125 V. V. Solomatin, in G. A. Dzhavadov, ed., *Organizatsiia upravleniia*, Moscow: Ekonomika, 1972, p. 77.
126 Glushkov, *Izvestiia*, March 8, 1974, p. 2.
127 K. Karpich, *Voprosy ekonomiki*, no. 10 (1973): 50-1.
128 Iu. Lapshin, *Planovoe khoziaistvo*, no. 11 (1973): 122.
129 N. Lebedinskii, *Planovoe khoziaistvo*, no. 5 (1977): 11; and editorial, *Planovoe khoziaistvo*, no. 5 (1977): 6.
130 I. A. Almazov, *Pribory i sistemy upravleniia*, no. 3 (1978): 10.
131 E. G. Iasin, *Ekonomika i matematicheskie metody*, vol. 13, no. 5 (1977): 1075.
132 Lapshin, *Razvitie*, p. 113.
133 Lapshin, *Planovoe khoziaistvo*, no. 11 (1973): 129-30.
134 A. N. Sukhov, *Kontrol i obespechenie dostovernosti informatsii v ASU*, Moscow: Znanie, 1977, pp. 10-12.
135 N. S. Davis and S. E. Goodman, "The Soviet Bloc's Unified System of Computers," *Computing Surveys*, vol. 1, no. 2 (1978): 95. See also Martin Cave, "Computer Technology," in Ronald Amann, Julian Cooper and R. W. Davies, eds., *The Technological Level of Soviet Industry*, New Haven: Yale University Press, 1977, pp. 377-403.
136 Davis and Goodman, "Soviet Bloc's Unified System," p. 95.
137 Ibid., p. 96.
138 Ibid., pp. 100-2.
139 V. Miasnikov, I. Korostelin and Iu. Krasov, *Vestnik statistiki*, no. 2 (1979): 40.
140 P. S. Pleshakov, *Ekonomicheskaia gazeta*, no. 31 (1978): 15.
141 Lapshin, *Razvitie*, p. 247.
142 Richard W. Judy, "The Case of Computer Technology," in Stanislaw Wasowski, ed., *East-West Trade and the Technology Gap*, Praeger, 1970, pp. 61-4.
143 R. Turn and A. E. Nimitz, *Computers and Strategic Advantage: I. Computer Technology in the United States and the Soviet Union*, R-1642-PR, Santa Monica, Cal.: Rand, 1975, p. 10.
144 Ibid.
145 Davis and Goodman, "Soviet Bloc's Unified System," p. 109.
146 Iu. Lapshin and V. Korovkin, *Planovoe khoziaistvo*, no. 4 (1976): 103.
147 Afanasev, *Sotsialnaia informatsiia*, pp. 296-7.
148 V. Novopavlovskii, *Sotsialisticheskii trud*, no. 1 (1973): 67.
149 Quoted in Robert C. Toth, *Washington Post*, December 29, 1975, p. B-8.
150 R. Khairetdinov, *Voprosy ekonomiki*, no. 1 (1975): 51.
151 M. Rakovskii, *Pravda*, March 2, 1977, p. 2.
152 Ibid.
153 Ibid.
154 Miasnikov et al., *Vestnik statistiki*, no. 2 (1979): 49.
155 Barry Boehm, "Extensive Tour Yields Report on Current Soviet Computing," *Soviet Cybernetics Review*, vol. 1, no. 1 (1971): 4.
156 Davis and Goodman, "Soviet Bloc's Unified System," p. 112.

157 Ibid., p. 113; see also A. M. Larionov, ed., *Sistema matematicheskogo obespecheniia ES EVM*, Moscow: Statistika, 1974.
158 Davis and Goodman, "Soviet Bloc's Unified System," p. 114.
159 Zhimerin, *Pravda*, June 9, 1974, p. 2.
160 Khairetdinov, *Voprosy ekonomiki*, no. 1 (1975): 52-3; V. Semenikhin, *Izvestiia*, September 18, 1974, p. 3.
161 Rakovskii, *Pravda*, March 2, 1977, p. 2.
162 B. V. Karpov and V. V. Solomatin, *Pribory i sistemy upravleniia*, no. 2 (1978): 3.
163 Davis and Goodman, "Soviet Bloc's Unified System," pp. 114-15.
164 D. G. Zhimerin, *Ekonomicheskaia gazeta*, no. 14 (1976): 7.
165 N. I. Cheshenko, *Ekonomika i matematicheskie metody*, vol. 13, no. 5 (1977): 1090.
166 Lapshin, *Razvitie*, pp. 110, 123.
167 Ibid., p. 215.
168 Ibid., p. 114.
169 S. A. Abdurakhmanov, Iu. P. Lapshin and E. G. Iakobenko, *Avtomatizirovannye sistemy upravleniia narodnym khoziaistvom SSSR*, Moscow: Ekonomika, 1972, pp. 5-6.
170 Semborskii and Simchera, *Voprosy ekonomiki*, no. 7 (1974): 83-7.
171 Lapshin, *Razvitie*, p. 128.
172 Semborskii and Simchera, *Voprosy ekonomiki*, no. 7 (1974): 89.
173 Omarev, *Voprosy*, p. 250.
174 Lapshin, *Razvitie*, pp. 207-8.
175 S. Sazonov, *Ekonomicheskaia gazeta*, no. 3 (1976): 17.
176 Ibid.
177 A. V. Kazanets, *Ekonomicheskaia gazeta*, no. 46 (1973): 6.
178 V. Loskutov and Iu. Lapshin, *Planovoe khoziaistvo*, no. 5 (1976): 49.
179 *Planovoe khoziaistvo*, no. 5 (1977): 4; V. Bezrukov, *Planovoe khoziaistvo*, no. 5 (1976): 51.
180 Bezrukov, *Planovoe khoziaistro*, no. 5 (1976): 51.
181 G. Ovarchenko, *Vestnik statistiki*, no. 1 (1978): 4; V. Miasnikov et al., *Vestnik statistiki*, no. 1 (1979): 42-3; I. Ivanov and V. Zavialov, *Vestnik statistiki*, no. 6 (1978): 51-2.
182 D. Novikov, *Materialno-tekhnicheskie snabzhenie*, no. 12 (1978): 50-1.
183 I. V. Zhezhko, *Ekonomika i organizatsiia promyshlennogo proizvodstva*, no. 3 (1979): 86.
184 Lapshin, *Razvitie*, p. 31.
185 V. S. Siniak, *Pravda*, January 27, 1976, p. 3.
186 D. G. Zhimerin, *Ekonomicheskaia gazeta*, no. 14 (1976): 7.
187 Loskutov and Lapshin, *Planovoe khoziaistvo*, no. 5 (1976): 32-4.
188 V. S. Siniak and V. I. Sakharov, in Zhimerin and Vladislavlev, *Avtomatizirovannye sistemy*, pp. 60, 59.
189 V. A. Miasnikov, *Ekonomika i organizatsiia promyshlennogo proizvodstva*, no. 6 (1974): 91.
190 Lapshin, *Razvitie*, p. 219.
191 N. I. Klimenko, in Zhimerin and Vladislavlev, *Avtomatizirovannye sistemy*, pp. 77-8.

192 Kazanets, *Ekonomicheskaia gazeta*, no. 46 (1973): 6.
193 N. Ivanshin, *Ekonomicheskaia gazeta*, no. 47 (1975): 6.
194 Lapshin, *Razvitie*, p. 219.
195 Karpov and Solomatin, *Pribory i sistemy upravleniia*, no. 2 (1978): 2.
196 Miasnikov et al., *Vestnik statistiki*, no. 2 (1974): 40; Lapshin, *Razvitie*, pp. 211-12.
197 N. Fedorenko, *Kommunist*, no. 16 (1978): 35.
198 L. R. Frock, Jr., "Seven Deadly Dangers in EDP," in Robert N. Anthony, John Dearden and Richard F. Vancil, eds., *Management Control Systems: Cases and Readings*, Homewood, Ill.: Irwin, 1965, pp. 540-1.
199 V. M. Glushkov, *Izvestiia*, May 13, 1975, p. 3.
200 R. Khairetdinov, *Voprosy ekonomiki*, no. 1 (1975): 49.
201 A. I. Pokrovskii, *Ekonomika i organizatsiia promyshlennogo proizvodstva*, no. 2 (1976): 122-36. Translated in *CDSP*, vol. 28, no. 31 (1976): 6-7.
202 M. Dorokhev and A. Vasilev, *Planovoe khoziaistvo*, no. 12 (1975): 127-31.
203 L. Kantorovich, *Ekonomicheskaia gazeta*, no. 26 (1974): 14.
204 V. Kolomnikov and I. Frezinskii, *Voprosy ekonomiki*, no. 8 (1975): 69.
205 Pokrovskii, *Ekonomika i organizatsiia promyshlennogo proizvodstva*, no. 2 (1976).
206 Khairetdinov, *Voprosy ekonomiki*, no. 1 (1975): 50.
207 V. G. Voitsekhovskii et al., in L. V. Sokhan and K. K. Grishchenko, eds., *Sotsialnye problemy ASU*, Kiev: Naukova dumka, 1976, pp. 155, 158.
208 The high technological optimism of the designers is indicated by their belief that labor satisfaction would be improved (78 percent), career growth fostered (55 percent), and the psychological climate improved (47.5 percent). In contrast, only 50 percent of the managers expected improved labor satisfaction; 30 percent career growth; and 40 percent a healthier psychological climate. Ibid., p. 160.

Chapter 4. Modernizing the methods of management

1 Cited in Alfred Zauberman, *The Mathematical Revolution in Soviet Economics*, New York: Oxford University Press, 1975, p. 37.
2 For a clear statement of these notions, see P. G. Bunich, ed., *Nauchnye osnovy i praktika khoziaistvennogo rascheta*, Moscow: Ekonomika, 1974, pp. 85-6.
3 Moshe Lewin, *Political Undercurrents in the Soviet Economic Debates: From Bukharin to the Modern Reformers*, Princeton, N.J.: Princeton University Press, 1974, pp. xvi-xvii, ch. 7.
4 Abraham Katz, *The Politics of Economic Reform in the Soviet Union*, New York: Praeger, 1972, esp. chs. 7-9.

5 A discussion of these debates is in Michel Tatu, *Power in the Kremlin*, trans. Helen Katal, New York: Viking, 1968, pp. 437–60.
6 A. M. Omarev, ed., *Voprosy upravleniia ekonomikoi*, Moscow: Politizdat, 1974, p. 68.
7 A. Birman, *Novyi mir*, no. 1 (1967): 167–9. A condensed version of this remarkable article is in *Current Digest of the Soviet Press*, vol. 19, no. 13 (1967): 16. Cited hereafter as *CDSP*.
8 On the limits of the application of *khozraschet*, see D. A. Allakhverdian, *Finansovo-kreditnyi mekhanizm razvitogo sotsializma*, Moscow: Finansy, 1976, p. 47; see also the remarks of P. G. Bunich in N. Fedorenko et al., *Sotsialisticheskie printsipy khoziaistvovaniia i effektivnost obshchestvennogo proizvodstva*, Moscow: Ekonomika, 1970, pp. 33–42.
9 There has been an extensive literature on the 1965 reforms. Among recent books, see Paul R. Gregory and Robert S. Stuart, *Soviet Economic Structure and Performance*, New York: Harper & Row, 1974; Karl W. Ryavec, *Implementation of the Soviet Economic Reforms: Political, Organizational and Social Processes*, New York: Praeger, 1975; and Joseph Wilczynski, *Soviet Economic Development and Reforms: From Extensive to Intensive Growth Under Central Planning in the USSR, Eastern Europe and Yugoslavia*, London: Macmillan, 1972.
10 Bunich, in Fedorenko et al., *Sotsialisticheskie printsipy*, p. 35.
11 Robert W. Campbell, "Economic Reform in the USSR," *American Economic Review*, vol. 58, no. 2 (1968): 550.
12 For an excellent statement of the purposes of the new success indicators, see S. M. Iampolskaia, ed., *Ekonomicheskaia nauka i khoziaistvennaia reforma*, Kiev: Naukova dumka, 1970, p. 188.
13 N. E. Drogichinskii and V. G. Starodubrovskii, *Osnovy i praktika khoziaistvennoi reformy v SSSR*, Moscow: Ekonomika, 1971, pp. 276–77. A more recent Soviet source is L. A. Pupola, *Sovershentsovanie khozrascheta: put povysheniia ekonomicheskoi effektivnosti proizvodstva*, Riga: Zinatne, 1976, p. 75.
14 Drogichinskii and Starodubrovskii, *Osnovy*, pp. 277–8; Iu. Bronnikov, ed., *Upravlenie sotsialisticheskoi ekonomikoi*, Moscow: Znanie, 1975, p. 113.
15 Drogichinskii and Starodubrovskii, *Osnovy*, pp. 346–56.
16 Ibid., pp. 357–72.
17 M. Atlas and N. Lisitsian, *Voprosy ekonomiki*, no. 7 (1967): 51–60; see also Drogichinskii and Starodubrovskii, *Osnovy*, chs. 10–11.
18 *Ekonomicheskaia gazeta*, no. 42 (1976): 7.
19 A. Rumiantsev and P. Bunich, *Kommunist*, no. 5 (1968): 97–8; V. K. Sitnin, *Ekonomicheskaia gazeta*, no. 21 (1971): 7–8.
20 V. A. Volkonskii, *Ekonomika i organizatsiia promyshlennym proizvodstvom*, no. 1 (1977): 29–39. A translation is provided in *CDSP*, vol. 29, no. 9 (1977): 9.
21 Alec Nove, *The Soviet Economy: An Introduction*, 2nd rev. ed., New

York: Praeger, 1969, pp. 241-2; L. I. Maizenberg, *Problemy tsenoobrazovaniia v razvitom sotsialisticheskom obshchestve*, Moscow: Ekonomika, 1976, pp. 34-5.

22 V. G. Grebennikov, O. S. Pshelintsev and S. S. Shatalin, *Ekonomika i matematicheskie metody*, vol. 11, no. 1 (1975): 4.

23 V. E. Manevich, *Razvitie teorii planovogo tsenoobrazovaniia v sovetskoi ekonomicheskoi literature*, Moscow: Nauka, 1975, p. 102.

24 Ibid. For a summary of the problems of developing and using a system of optimal prices, see E. G. Liberman, *Ekonomicheskie metody povysheniia effektivnosti obshchestvennogo proizvodstva*, Moscow: Ekonomika, 1970, pp. 157-74.

25 I. Neminushchii, V. Chaplanov and M. Sorokina, *Planovoe khoziaistvo*, no. 3 (1976): 104-5; see also M. Kokorev, *Planovoe khoziaistvo*, no. 7 (1976): 108.

26 Kokorev, *Planovoe khoziaistvo*, no. 7 (1976): 109.

27 Nove, *Soviet Economy*, pp. 247-8.

28 Morris Bornstein, "Soviet Price Policy in the 1970's," in U.S. Congress, Joint Economic Committee, *Soviet Economy in a New Perspective*, Washington, D.C.: Government Printing Office, 1976, p. 22.

29 Ibid. The methodology of price formation is also discussed in Maizenberg, *Problemy*, pp. 61-77.

30 Maizenberg, *Problemy*, pp. 117-22.

31 Bornstein, "Soviet Price Policy," p. 27.

32 The pricing policy for new products is discussed in Joseph S. Berliner, "Flexible Pricing and New Products in the USSR," *Soviet Studies*, vol. 27, no. 4 (1975): 525-44; Michael J. Lavelle, S. J., "The Soviet 'New Method' Pricing Formulae," *Soviet Studies*, vol. 26, no. 1 (1974): 81-97; and Bornstein, "Soviet Price Policy," pp. 27-31.

33 Ibid.

34 Drogichinskii and Starodubrovskii, *Osnovy*, p. 279.

35 George W. Feiwel, *The Soviet Quest for Economic Efficiency: Issues, Controversies and Reforms*, 2nd ed., New York: Praeger, 1972, pp. 369-70.

36 L. Volodarskii, *Pravda*, July 8, 1968, p. 3.

37 See Chapter 3.

38 For his essentially conservative approach to the reform and the preservation of the Party's organizational role, see the speech of Brezhnev to the Moscow City Party Conference, *Pravda*, March 30, 1968, pp. 1-2.

39 For an exhaustive account of the problem of establishing normatives for forming incentive funds, see Drogichinskii and Starodubrovskii, *Osnovy*, pp. 281-4.

40 For an extremely interesting discussion by the managers of their attitudes toward the Liberman proposals, see *Ekonomicheskaia gazeta*, no. 1 (1963): 8-13; ibid., no. 2 (1963): 11.

41 Excellent accounts of the implementation of the reform are in, among many accounts, Gregory and Stuart, *Soviet Economic Struc-*

ture, pp. 352–7; Gertrude E. Schroeder, "Soviet Economic Reforms: A Study in Contradictions," *Soviet Studies*, vol. 20, no. 1 (1968–9): 10–13.

42 Feiwel, *Soviet Quest*, pp. 373–7; see also, for an early analysis of the problem, P. Bunich, *Voprosy ekonomiki*, no. 10 (1967): 46–58.

43 Schroeder, "Contradictions," pp. 16–21. G. A. Egiazarian, *Materialnoe stimulirovanie rosta effektivnosti promyshlennogo porizvodstva*, Moscow: Mysl, 1976, pp. 158–9, 257–8.

44 P. Bunich, *Trud*, May 15, 1976, p. 2.

45 N. E. Drogichinskii, ed., *Sovershenstvovanie mekhanizma khoziaistvovaniia v usloviiakh razvitogo sotsializma*, Moscow: Ekonomika, 1975, p. 89.

46 Drogichinskii and Starodubrovskii, *Osnovy*, p. 278.

47 Feiwel, *Soviet Quest*, pp. 374–5.

48 D. Allakhverdian, *Voprosy ekonomiki*, no. 10 (1974): 125.

49 Bornstein, "Soviet Price Policy," p. 24.

50 Gertrude E. Schroeder, "Post-Khrushchev Reforms and Soviet Public Financial Goals," in Zbigniew M. Fallenbuchl, ed., *Economic Development in the Soviet Union and Eastern Europe*, vol. 2, New York: Praeger, 1976, p. 357.

51 Drogichinskii, *Sovershenstvovanie*, p. 231; N. Deviatkova, *Planovoe khoziaistvo*, no. 1 (1974): 86–92.

52 Schroeder, "Post-Khrushchev Reforms," p. 353; John H. Kramer, "Prices in the Conservation of Natural Resources in the Soviet Union," *Soviet Studies*, vol. 24, no. 3 (1972): 371–2; Feiwel, *Soviet Quest*, pp. 380–1.

53 The issue of what proportion of new construction should be financed from the budget is a complex one because self-financing carries with it the loss of centralized control. See M. Atlas and I. Zlobin, *Voprosy ekonomiki*, no. 1 (1975): 123.

54 Allakhverdian, *Mekhanizm*, p. 174.

55 Drogichinskii, *Sovershenstvovantie*, pp. 232–4; Iu. Iarkin, *Kommunist*, no. 4 (1977): 51; P. Podshivalenko, *Voprosy ekonomiki*, no. 5 (1974): 39–47.

56 Schroeder, "Post-Khrushchev Reforms," p. 358.

57 Allakhverdian, *Mekhanizm*, pp. 169–70.

58 Ibid.

59 Bornstein, "Soviet Price Policy," p. 23.

60 Ibid.

61 Gertrude E. Schroeder, "The 1966–67 Soviet Industrial Price Reform: A Study in Complications," *Soviet Studies*, vol. 20, no. 4 (1969): 462–77. See also Jean Marczewskii, "The Role of Prices in a Command Economy," *Soviet Studies*, vol. 23, no. 1 (1971–2): 109–10.

62 Allakhverdian, *Mekhanizm*, pp. 205–6.

63 I. Konnik, *Sotsialisticheskaia industriia*, October 19, 1976, p. 2. See also Liberman, *Ekonomicheskie metody*, pp. 33–6.

64 For a fine-grained examination of the problems of technical innovation, see Joseph S. Berliner, *The Innovational Decision in Soviet Industry*, Cambridge, Mass.: MIT Press, 1976. See also his article, "Prospects for Technological Progress," in U.S., Congress, *Soviet Economy*, pp. 431–46.
65 V. Stepachenko and E. Danilov, *Ekonomicheskaia gazeta*, no. 24 (1969): 9; also Bornstein, "Soviet Price Policy," pp. 32–3.
66 Egiazarian, *Materialnoe stimulirovanie*, p. 151; see also Artemov, p. 41; Schroeder, *Contradictions*, pp. 16 ff.; P. Bunich, *Pravda*, September 17, 1970, p. 2.
67 Iu. Artemov, *Voprosy ekonomiki*, no. 8 (1975): 41.
68 P. G. Bunich, *Trud*, May 15, 1976, p. 2.
69 Artemov, *Voprosy ekonomiki*, no. 8 (1975): 42.
70 *Pravda*, December 19, 1975, p. 3.
71 F. I. Loshchenkov, *Ekonomicheskaia gazeta*, no. 43 (1971): 5.
72 For an excellent article on the approach of the manager to labor productivity and NOT, in particular, see V. Voronkov and G. Roman, *Voprosy ekonomiki*, no. 9 (1974): 49–55; M. Gliantsev, *Sotsialisticheskii trud*, no. 2 (1976): 114–22; V. Volkov, *Sotsialisticheskii trud*, no. 4 (1976): 59–68.
73 F. Rabinovich, *Izvestiia*, April 3, 1969, p. 3. See also the comprehensive article of P. G. Bunich, *Ekonomika i organizatsiia promyshlennogo proizvodstva*, no. 6 (1976): 26–39. A condensed version is in *CDSP*, vol. 29, no. 4 (1977): 20–21.
74 The decree of the Council of Ministers can be found in K. U. Chernenko and M. S. Smirtiukov, comp., *Resheniia partii i pravitelstva po khoziaistvennym voprosam*, 11 vols., Moscow: Politizdat, 1964–77, 8: 508–12. For a discussion of the 1971–2 changes, see Jan Adam, "The Incentive System in the U.S.S.R.: The Above Reform of 1965," *Industrial and Labor Relations Review*, vol. 27, no. 1 (1973): 84–92; Gregory and Stuart, *Soviet Economic Structure*, pp. 357–8; Marie Lavigne, *The Socialist Economies of the Soviet Union and Eastern Europe*, trans. T. G. Waywell, White Plains, N.Y.: International Arts and Sciences Press, 1974, pp. 78–9. The changes are also discussed in detail by Gertrude E. Schroeder, "Recent Developments in Soviet Planning and Incentives," in U.S., Congress, Joint Economic Committee, *Soviet Economic Prospects for the Seventies*, Washington, D.C.: Government Printing Office, 1973, pp. 30–5.
75 Drogichinskii, *Sovershenstvovanie*, p. 89.
76 Chernenko and Smirtiukov, *Resheniia*, 8:509–10; see also Schroeder, "Developments," pp. 34–5.
77 Schroeder, "Developments," pp. 34–5; Schroeder. "Post-Khrushchev Reforms," pp. 358–9.
78 Chernenko and Smirtiukov, *Resheniia*, 11: 346–8.
79 L. I. Brezhnev, *Ob osnovnykh voprosakh ekonomicheskoi politiki KPSS na sovremennom etape*, 2 vols., Moscow: Politizdat, 1975, 1: 419–20.

80 Egiazarian, *Materialnoe stimulirovanie*, pp. 156-7; see also E. Prigozhin, *Planovoe khoziaistvo*, no. 9 (1975): 123-6; P. Grechishnikov, *Planovoe khoziaistvo*, no. 1 (1974): 19-27.
81 T. Khachaturov, *Planovoe khoziaistvo*, no. 6 (1974): 18.
82 See V. E. Koslovskii and Ia. Sychev, *Filosofskie nauki*, no. 3 (1970): 173-85.
83 V. A. Iadov, *Filosofskie nauki*, no. 2 (1968): 70-6.
84 Peter H. Juviler, *Revolutionary Law and Order: Politics and Social Change in the USSR*, New York: Free Press, 1976, pp. 162-6.
85 Samuel Lieberstein, "Technology, Work and Sociology in the USSR: The NOT Movement," *Technology and Culture*, vol. 16, no. 1 (1975): 48-66.
86 A. Golov, *Sotsialisticheskii trud*, no. 1 (1979): 91-9.
87 L. Kogan, *Sovetskaia Rossiia*, November 1, 1974, p. 2.
88 V. Kasakov, *Sotsialisticheskaia industriia*, March 4, 1979, p. 2. Translated in *CDSP*, vol. 31, no. 18 (1979): 15.
89 M. N. Rutkevich, *Pravda*, September 14, 1973, p. 3. An abstract is in *CDSP*, vol. 25, no. 37 (1973): 1, 26.
90 M. T. Iovchuk, A. G. Kharchev and V. A. Iadov, *Filosofskie nauki*, no. 5 (1970): 7, 11.
91 N. Klimov, *Sotsialisticheskii trud*, no. 4 (1972): 13-17.
92 O. I. Kosenko, *Voprosy psikhologii*, no. 4 (1975): 155-61.
93 V. G. Shorin, G. Kh. Popov and G. D. Goriachev, *Stil roboty rukovoditeliia*, Moscow: Znanie, 1976, pp. 12-13.
94 B. Gavrilov, *Sotsialisticheskii trud*, no. 5 (1979): 54.
95 M. Gliantsev, *Sotsialisticheskii trud*, no. 5 (1979): 80.
96 Ibid., p. 81.
97 S. Novoshilov, *Sotsialisticheskii trud*, no. 1 (1979): 111.
98 Gavrilov, *Sotsialisticheskii trud*, no. 5 (1979): 57-8.
99 Golov, *Sotsiologicheskii trud*, no. 1 (1979): 89.
100 A. Osipov, *Sotsialisticheskii trud*, no. 3 (1978): 58-62.
101 A. Mirgaleev, *Voprosy ekonomiki*, no. 10 (1977): 105.
102 K. Cherednichenko and L. Goldin, *Kommunist*, no. 11 (1979): 38, 42.
103 V. Boldyrev, *Pravda*, May 26, 1972, p. 2.
104 Cherednichenko and Goldin, *Kommunist*, no. 11 (1979): 45.
105 V. Parfenov and V. Shevtsov, *Pravda*, March 28, 29, 1977, p. 2. Translated in *CDSP*, vol. 29, no. 13 (1977): 14-17.
106 Ibid.
107 Cherednichenko and Goldin, *Kommunist*, no. 11 (1979): 46.
108 M. N. Rutkevich, in D. A. Kerimov et al., eds., *Planirovanie sotsialnogo razvitiia*, Moscow: Mysl, 1976, pp. 24-30.
109 Iu. E. Volkov, *Sotsiologicheskie issledovaniia*, no. 2 (1976): 10-20.
110 V. G. Podmarkov, *Sotsiologicheskie issledovaniia*, no. 1 (1976): 24-6.
111 D. A. Kerimov et al., eds., *Planirovanie sotsialnogo razvitiia kollektiva predpriiatiia*, 2nd ed., Moscow: Profizdat, 1975, pp. 96-138.
112 Ibid., pp. 139-49.
113 Chernenko and Smirtiukov, *Resheniia*, 9: 129-34.

114 Iu. E. Volkov and Iu. S. Loshkurev, *Trudovoe vospitanie molodezhi,* Moscow: Politizdat, 1976, pp. 46–60.
115 Chernenko and Smirtiukov, *Resheniia,* 10: 261–3.
116 A. T. Ivanov, *Nastavnik – aktivnyi vospitatel molodezhi,* Moscow: Politizdat, 1976.
117 Chernenko and Smirtiukov, *Resheniia,* 10: 263–6.
118 Volkov and Loshkurev, *Trudovoe vospitanie,* pp. 87–8.
119 A. E. Kotliiar and S. A. Turchaninova, *Zaniatost zhenshchin v proizvodstve,* Moscow: Statistika, 1975, pp. 96–103.
120 Chernenko and Smirtiukov, *Resheniia,* 9: 91–4.
121 F. Bassin, V. Rozhnev and M. Rozhnova, *Kommunist,* no. 14 (1974): 60–70. Translated in *CDSP,* vol. 27, no. 3 (1975): 4–5.
122 N. Churakov, *Izvestiia,* July 13, 1975, p. 3.
123 V. G. Podmarkov, *Sotsiologicheskie issledovaniia,* no. 3 (1976): 30.
124 V. G. Loos, *Promyshlennaia psikhologiia,* Kiev: Tekhnika, 1974, pp. 136–7.
125 A. Sventsitskii, *Izvestiia,* March 4, 1972, p. 5.
126 For other examples, see V. Shustikov, *Kommunist,* no. 14 (1976): 102–11.
127 See the special series of articles in *Ekonomika i organizatsiia promyshlennogo proizvodstva,* no. 1 (1974): 88–95.
128 M. N. Rutkevich, *Sotsiologicheskie issledovaniia,* no. 3 (1975). Translated in *Joint Publications Research Service* 66196, November 21, 1975, p. 15. Cited hereafter as *JPRS.*
129 V. G. Podmarkov, *Sotsiologicheskie issledovaniia,* no. 1 (1976): 26.
130 D. A. Kerimov and A. S. Pashkov, *Sotsiologicheskie issledovaniia,* no. 3 (1975). Translated in *JPRS* 66196, November 21, 1975, p. 27.
131 A. Smirnov, *Planovoe khoziaistvo,* no. 1 (1975): 34–46.
132 Kerimov and Pashkov, *JPRS* 66196, p. 23.
133 A report is in *Sotsiologicheskie issledovaniia,* no. 1 (1977): 203.
134 Ibid., pp. 204–5.
135 Kerimov and Pashkov, *JPRS* 66196, p. 32.
136 V. G. Podmarkov, *Sotsiologicheskie issledovaniia,* no. 1 (1976): 28.
137 Ibid., pp. 20–1.
138 V. Shustikov, *Kommunist,* no. 14 (1976): 108.
139 E. M. Andreev and S. F. Frolov, in V. G. Afanasev, ed., *Nauchnoe upravlenie obshchestvom,* 13 vols., Moscow: Mysl, 1976, 10: 105.
140 G. N. Cherkasov and G. G. Zaitsev, *Sotsiologiia i nauchnaia organizatsiia truda,* Leningrad: Lenizdat, 1973, pp. 36–7.
141 Ibid. See also Andreev and Frolov, in Afanasev, *Nauchnoe upravlenie,* p. 106.
142 A. Libkind, *Pravda,* August 5, 1975, p. 3.
143 For the experience of the Perm Telephone Plant, see E. G. Antosenkov, *Ekonomika i organizatsiia promyshlennogo proizvodstva,* no. 1 (1974): 67.
144 I. K. Strelkovskii and N. P. Firsova, in V. P. Polozov, ed., *Chelovek i obshchestvo,* vol. 14, Leningrad: Izdatelstvo Leningradskogo universiteta, 1976, pp. 78–80.

145 N. A. Aitov, *Sotsiologicheskie issledovaniia*, no. 1 (1977): 70.
146 A. V. Dmitriev and M. N. Mezhevich, *Sotsiologicheski issledovaniia*, no. 4 (1976): 51–5.
147 M. V. Timishevskaia, "Some Consequences of a City Building Experiment," in Murray Yanowitch and Wesley A. Fisher, ed. and trans., *Social Stratification and Mobility in the USSR*, White Plains, N.Y.: International Arts and Sciences Press, 1973, pp. 138–51.
148 L. A. Basilevich, in A. S. Pashkov and M. N. Mezhevich, eds., *Problemy sotsialnogo planirovaniia v gorode i regione*, vol. 15, Leningrad: Izdatelstvo Leningradskogo universiteta, 1976, p. 83.
149 Ibid., pp. 83–4.
150 Aitov, *Sotsiologicheskie issledovaniia*, no. 1 (1977): 73–4.

Chapter 5. Rationalization of formal structure

1 For a review of the interaction of technology and organizational authority, see Jeffrey Pfeffer, *Organizational Design*, Arlington Heights, Ill: AHM, 1978, ch. 3.
2 V. V. Laptev et al., eds., *Pravovye problemy rukovodstva i upravleniia otrasliu promyshlennosti v SSSR*, Moscow: Nauka, 1973, p. 506.
3 See A. B. Vengerov, *Uchenye zapiski*, vol. 28, Moscow: Ministerstvo iustitsii, 1973, p. 17.
4 N. P. Fedorenko, *Voprosy ekonomiki*, no. 6 (1972): 102.
5 N. P. Fedorenko, *Kommunist*, no. 5 (1972): 64–5.
6 N. P. Fedorenko, *Voprosy ekonomiki*, no. 6 (1972): 103.
7 Ibid., p. 102.
8 See N. P. Fedorenko, *Ekonomicheskaia gazeta*, no. 2 (1974): 14.
9 An extensive statement of the planning system's structure is in N. P. Fedorenko, ed., *Kompleksnoe narodno-khoziaistvennoe planirovanie*, Moscow: Ekonomika, 1974, pp. 153–5.
10 N. P. Fedorenko, *Ekonomika i organizatsiia promyshlennogo proizvodstva*, no. 1 (1973): 68.
11 Ibid., p. 71.
12 S. P. Kozlov, *Pravda*, July 11, 1973, p. 4.
13 V. Glushkov, *Trud*, October 15, 1976, p. 2.
14 N. Lebedinskii, *Voprosy ekonomiki*, no. 10 (1974) 15–16.
15 V. Bezrukov and V. Shekhovtsov, *Voprosy ekonomiki*, no. 3 (1975): 108.
16 V. Glushkov, *Izvestiia*, March 8, 1974, p. 2.
17 In ASPR, 60 percent of the tasks have been concentrated in the departments for consolidation. Editorial, *Planovoe khoziaistvo*, no. 5 (1977): 4.
18 The structural changes in Gosplan required by ASPR are outlined in V. Budavei, B. Raisberg and O. Iun, *Planovoe khoziaistvo*, no. 11 (1974): 21–2.
19 *Planovoe khoziaistvo*, no. 5 (1977): 3–5.
20 Ibid.
21 V. Bezrukov, *Planovoe khoziaistvo*, no. 5 (1977): 44–7.

22 A. Modin, *Voprosy ekonomiki*, no. 12 (1973): 119.
23 N. Lebedinskii, *Planovoe khoziaistvo*, no. 10 (1974): 19–20.
24 V. Siniak, *Pravda*, January 27, 1976, p. 3.
25 Ibid.
26 V. Glushkov, *Literaturnaia gazeta*, no. 5 (1975): 12.
27 Siniak, *Pravda*, January 27, 1976, p. 3.
28 *Planovoe khoziaistvo*, no. 1 (1976): 115.
29 N. Kumichev and A. Matveev, *Planovoe khoziaistvo*, no. 9 (1973): 136–8.
30 V. Glushkov, *Literaturnaia gazeta*, no. 5 (1975): 12.
31 P. Iurev, *Planovoe khoziaistvo*, no. 2 (1974): 132.
32 V. I. Loskutov, *Avtomatizirovannye sistemy upravleniia*, Moscow: Statistika, 1972, pp. 76–9.
33 A. Aganbegian, *Ekonomicheskaia gazeta*, no. 21 (1973): 8.
34 Loskutov, *Avtomatizirovannye sistemy*, pp. 153–4.
35 S. O. Petrovskii and G. M. Pyzhik, *Nauchnaia organizatsiia proizvodstva*, Moscow: Ekonomika, 1971, pp. 141–5.
36 A. I. Griaznov, *Avtomatizirovannaia podsistema operativno-kalendarnogo planirovaniia predpriiatiia*, Moscow: Znanie, 1974, pp. 4–5.
37 A. I. Pokrovskii, *Ekonomika i organizatsiia promyshlennogo proizvodstva*, no. 2 (1976): 122–36. A condensed version is in *Current Digest of the Soviet Press*, vol. 28 (1976): 6–7.
38 B. Z. Milner, ed., *Organizatsionnye struktury upravleniia proizvodstvom*, Moscow: Ekonomika, 1975, p. 162.
39 Ibid.
40 V. A. Trainov, *Avtomatizatsiia upravleniia (ekonomiko-organizatsionnye voprosy)*, Moscow: Znanie, 1977, p. 33.
41 Vengerov, *Uchenye zapiski*, 29: 14.
42 V. S. Bondarenko and V. V. Tolstosheev, *Glavnyi vychisliternyi tsentr otrasli*, Moscow: Znanie, 1976, p. 37.
43 Laptev, *Pravovye problemy*, pp. 520–1.
44 Vengerov, *Uchenye zapiski*, 29: 10.
45 V. S. Bondarenko, *Sovetskoe gosudarstvo i pravo*, no. 9 (1976): 13.
46 Ibid.
47 A review of the Resource Security System is in Harry Katzen, Jr., *Computer Data Security*, New York: Van Nostrand Reinhold, 1973, pp. 153–72.
48 Bondarenko, *Sovetskoe gosudarstvo i pravo*, no. 9 (1976): 16–17.
49 B. V. Rakitinskii, *Formy khoziaistvennogo proizvodstva predpriiatiiami*, Moscow: Nauka, 1968, p. 17.
50 N. F. Fedorenko et al., eds., *Sotsialisticheskaia printsipy khoziaistrovaniia i effektovnost obshchestvennogo proizvodstva*, Moscow: Ekonomika, 1970, p. 46.
51 See the speech of K. T. Mazurov, *Pravda*, October 2, 1965, pp. 2–8.
52 Gregory Grossman, "Innovation and Information in the Soviet Economy," *American Economic Review, Papers and Proceedings*, vol. 56, no. 2 (1966): 129.

53 Michael Ellman, *Soviet Planning Today: Proposals for an Optimally Functioning System*, Cambridge University Press, 1971, pp. 90–1.
54 See Chapter 4.
55 L. A. Leontiev, *Ekonomicheskie problemy razvitogo sotsializma*, Moscow: Nauka, 1972, pp. 142–3.
56 V. V. Novozhilov, *Voprosy ekonomiki*, no. 10 (1970): 57–8.
57 G. V. Pronskaia, *Pravovye voprosy organizatsii i deiatelnosti promyshlennykh obedinenii*, Kiev: Naukova dumka, 1971, pp. 84–90.
58 A. N. Kosygin, *Izbrannye rechi i statii*, Moscow: Izdatelstvo politicheskoi literatury, 1974, p. 288.
59 Jerry F. Hough, *The Soviet Prefects: The Local Party Organs in Industrial Decision-making*, Cambridge, Mass.: Harvard University Press, 1969, p. 75.
60 M. Odinets and V. Fomin, *Izvestiia*, September 29, 1966, p. 2.
61 *Partiinaia zhizn*, no. 24 (1966): 25–6.
62 See E. G. Liberman, *Ekonomicheskie metody povysheniia effektivnosti obshchestvennogo proizvodstva*, Moscow: Ekonomika, 1970, pp. 32–3.
63 See A. K. Kravtsov and V. I. Eitingon, *Sovetskoe gosudarstvo i pravo*, no. 6 (1968): 86–7.
64 T. M. Ganilov, *Sovetskoe gosudarstvo i pravo*, no. 9 (1972): 76–80.
65 Karl W. Ryavec, *Implementation of the Soviet Economic Reforms: Political, Organizational and Social Processes*, New York: Praeger, 1975, pp. 112–14.
66 Ibid., pp. 225–6.
67 Gertrude E. Schroeder, "The 'Reform' of the Supply System in Soviet Industry," *Soviet Studies*, vol. 24, no. 1 (1972): 98.
68 Ibid.; see also Ellman, *Soviet Planning Today*, p. 91.
69 I. A. Kalinin, *Planovoe khoziaistvo*, no. 7 (1977): 115.
70 A. Sidorov and S. Voronin, *Literaturnaia gazeta*, no. 4 (1973): 10.
71 N. Drogichinskii, *Voprosy ekonomiki*, no. 4 (1974): 27–9.
72 Editorial, *Pravda*, July 7, 1977, p. 1.
73 Ryavec, *Implementation*, pp. 228–30.
74 E. A. Khrutskii, *Sovershenstvovanie upravleniia materialnotekhicheskim snabzheniem*, Moscow: Znanie, 1974, p. 1.
75 Drogichinskii, *Voprosy ekonomiki*, no. 4 (1974): 27–9.
76 Khrutskii, *Sovershenstvovanie*, p. 41.
77 D. Nikitin, *Planovoe khoziaistvo*, no. 5 (1971): 42–4.
78 Ibid., p. 44.
79 A. N. Zavialova, ed., *Upravlenie sotsialisticheskim proizvodstvom*, Moscow: Ekonomika, 1968, pp. 146–7.
80 Rakitinskii, *Formy*, p. 17.
81 N. Drogichinskii, *Voprosy ekonomiki*, no. 3 (1968): 29.
82 *XXIV Sezd Kommunisticheskoi partii Sovetskogo soiuza. Stenograficheskii otchet*, 2 vols., Moscow: Politizdat, 1971, 1: 122.
83 *Pravda*, August 25, 1971, p. 2.
84 V. Konotop, *Partiinaia zhizn*, no. 19 (1973): 16–25.
85 *Pravda*, August 25, 1971, p. 2.
86 See Rudolph L. Tokes, "Varieties of Soviet Dissent: An Overview,"

in Rudolph L. Tokes, ed., *Dissent in the USSR: Politics, Ideology and People*, Baltimore: Johns Hopkins University Press, 1975, p. 12.
87 A. Kovalenko, *Partiinaia zhizn*, no. 20 (1973): 31-2.
88 P. Bunich, *Pravda*, September 17, 1970, p. 2.
89 *Pravda*, February 24, 1972, p. 2.
90 A. Kostiuk, *Pravda*, February 11, 1972, p. 3.
91 E. Fillipov, *Planovoe khoziaistvo*, no. 1 (1975): 94-5.
92 G. S. Iakolev, *Voprosy filosofii*, no. 5 (1971): 36-7.
93 G. Kh. Popov, ed., *Sovershenstvovanie sistemy vnutrifirmennogo upravleniia*, Moscow: Izdatelstvo Moskovskogo gosudarstvennogo universiteta, 1972, p. 187.
94 Ibid., p. 191.
95 A. Levikov, *Literaturnaia gazeta*, no. 5 (1975): 11. Translated in *CDSP*, vol. 28, no. 30 (1976): 1.
96 B. D. Levin and M. N. Perfilev, *Kadry apparata upravleniia v SSSR*, Leningrad: Nauka, 1970, p. 155.
97 G. Kh. Popov and G. A. Dzhavadov, eds., *Upravlenie i problema kadrov*, Moscow: Ekonomika, 1972, pp. 99-100.
98 Ibid.
99 Ia. Kapelius, *Literaturnaia gazeta*, August 31, 1977, p. 11; in *CDSP*, vol. 29, no. 44 (1977): 12.
100 See F. T. Seliukov, *Sovetskoe gosudarstvo i pravo*, no. 4 (1969): 29.
101 G. Kutsev, *Sotsialisticheskaia industriia*, February 12, 1977, p. 2.
102 I. Dizhbit, *Literaturnaia gazeta*, November 3, 1976, p. 11.
103 V. Iakushev and V. Iakhontov, *Literaturnaia gazeta*, no. 36 (1970): 11.
104 V. Ozira, *Voprosy ekonomiki*, no. 9 (1973): 113.
105 V. I. Remnev, *Problemy NOT v apparate upravleniia*, Moscow: Nauka, 1973, pp. 80-1.
106 Ibid.
107 E. E. Vendrov, *Psikhologicheskie problemy upravleniia*, Moscow: Ekonomika, 1969, p. 138.
108 Ozira, *Voprosy ekonomiki*, no. 9 (1973): 113.
109 Remnev, *Problemy NOT*, p. 85.
110 G. Kh. Popov, ed., *Otsenka rabotnikov upravleniia*, Moscow: Moskovskii rabochii, 1976, pp. 49-51.
111 I. Kirianov, *Pravda*, February 1, 1972, p. 2.
112 Popov, *Otsenka*, p. 56.
113 V. Iakushev and V. Iakhontov, *Literaturnaia gazeta*, no. 36 (1971): 11.
114 V. Iakushev, *Literaturnaia gazeta*, no. 21 (1973): 10.
115 *Sotsialisticheskii trud*, no. 10 (1972): 112-13.
116 Popov, *Otsenka*, p. 52.
117 *Ekonomicheskaia gazeta*, no. 29 (1974): 7.
118 V. Matriko, *Literaturnaia gazeta*, January 26, 1977, p. 10. There are still no educational institutions in the Soviet Union to train personnel specialists.
119 Popov, *Otsenka*, p. 52.

120 *Literaturnaia gazeta*, no. 10 (1972): 10.
121 See the debate in *Literaturnaia gazeta*, no. 21 (1971): 10.
122 V. G. Afanasev, *The Scientific and Technical Revolution: Its Impact on Management and Education*, trans. Robert Daglish, Moscow: Progress, 1975, pp. 309–16.
123 Ibid., p. 312.
124 N. Petrov, *Pravda*, June 18, 1978, p. 2.
125 Iu. N. Bronnikov, comp. *Upravlenie sotsialisticheskoi ekonomikoi*, Moscow: Moskovskii rabochii, 1975, p. 481.
126 There are, however, continuing initiatives in this area. In 1979, the Institute of Economics and Organization of Production formed an advanced training institute using the institute's personnel as faculty and the most modern methods of instruction. I. Ognev, *Pravda*, January 15, 1979, p. 3; *CDSP*, vol. 31, no. 2 (1979): 20.
127 L. M. Bodalev, *Sovershenstvovanie podgotovki i povysheniia kvalifikatsii khoziaistvennykh kadrov*, Moscow: Znanie, 1976, p. 14.
128 Ibid., pp. 14–15. The structure and purposes of the new institute is described in *Izvestiia*, February 2, 1971, p. 1.
129 Iu. F. Novgorodskii et al., *Tekhnicheskii progress: sovershenstvovanie podgotovki kadrov*, Moscow: Ekonomika, 1973, pp. 117–23.
130 Bodalev, *Sovershenstvovanie*, pp. 30–1, 34.
131 N. V. Melnikov, *Ekonomicheskaia gazeta*, no. 27 (1970): 10.
132 Bodalev, *Sovershenstvovanie*, p. 33.
133 Melnikov, *Ekonomicheskaia gazeta*, no. 27 (1979): 10.
134 Ibid.
135 The program of the Russian Ministry of Light Industry is discussed by R. Kaera, *Literaturnaia gazeta*, February 23, 1977, p. 11. Translated in *CDSP*, vol. 29, no. 10 (1977): 13–14.
136 A. Zvezdin, *Pravda*, August 1, 1971, p. 2.
137 *Sotsialisticheskaia industriia*, January 29, 1977, p. 2; *CDSP*, vol. 29, no. 10 (1977): 14.
138 A. Belov, *Literaturnaia gazeta*, July 13, 1977, p. 11. Translated in *CDSP*, vol. 29, no. 34 (1977): 13.
139 Ibid.
140 Bodalev, *Sovershenstvovanie*, p. 37.
141 G. A. Brianskii, in G. A. Dzhavadov, ed., *Organizatsiia upravleniia*, Moscow: Ekonomika, 1971, pp. 120–9.
142 Bodalev, *Sovershenstvovanie*, p. 37.
143 V. Bogachov, *Literaturnaia gazeta*, July 13, 1977, p. 11; *CDSP*, vol. 29, no. 34 (1977): 13.
144 A. Levikov, *Literaturnaia gazeta*, no. 13 (1972): 10.

Chapter 6. Toward a new ministerial structure

1 A. Bachurin, in D. Allakhverdian, ed., *Khozraschet i upravlenie*, Moscow: Ekonomika, 1970, pp. 38–9.
2 *Pravda*, October 24, 1969, p. 1.
3 The text of the decree is in K. U. Chernenko and M. S. Smirtiukov,

comp., *Resheniia partii i pravitelstva po khoziaistvennym voprosam*, 11 vols., Moscow: Politizdat, 1964–77, 8: 61–9.

4 Ibid., 8: 131–6.
5 V. Vorotnikov, *Planovoe khoziaistvo*, no. 5 (1971): 32–9.
6 P. G. Bunich, ed., *Nauchnye osnovy i praktika khoziaistvennogo rascheta*, Moscow: Ekonomika, 1974, pp. 128–36.
7 Ibid., pp. 129–30.
8 See N. E. Drogichinskii, ed., *Sovershenstvovanie mekhanizma khoziaistvovaniia v usloviiakh razvitogo sotsializma*, Moscow: Ekonomika, 1975, pp. 126–31; Bunich, *Nauchnye osnovy*, pp. 127–36.
9 Chernenko and Smirtiukov, *Resheniia*, 8: 126–30.
10 Vorotnikov, *Planovoe khoziaistvo*, no. 5 (1971): 35–6.
11 Ibid., p. 38.
12 A. A. Shokin, *Pravovoe polozhenie promyshlennykh obedinenii v SSSR*, Kazan: Izdatelstvo Kazanskogo universiteta, 1972, pp. 30–1.
13 Iu. N. Bronnikov, comp., *Upravlenie sotsialisticheskoi ekonomikoi*, Moscow: Moskovskii rabochii, 1975, pp. 230–3.
14 N. E. Drogichinskii, in D. M. Gvishiani and S. E. Kamenitser, eds., *Problemy nauchnoi organizatsii upravleniia sotsialisticheskoi promyshlennostiu*, Moscow: Ekonomika, 1974, p. 184.
15 The decrees are in Chernenko and Smirtiukov, *Resheniia*, 9: 415–26, 427–59.
16 For an excellent article on the 1973 reform, see Alice C. Gorlin, "Industrial Reorganization: The Associations," in U.S. Congress, Joint Economic Committee, *Soviet Economy in a New Perspective*, Washington, D.C.: Government Printing Office, 1976, pp. 162–88.
17 Chernenko and Smirtiukov, *Resheniia*, 9: 428–32.
18 Ibid., 9: 433–6.
19 Ibid., 10: 136–79.
20 Ibid., 10: 138–40.
21 Ibid., 10: 142–6.
22 V. G. Vishniakov, *Pravovedenie*, no. 4 (1975): 34.
23 The process of plan development is described in N. G. Kalinin, ed., *Organizatsiia upravleniia v sisteme ministerstva*, Moscow: Izdatelstvo Moskovskogo universiteta, 1974, pp. 296–321.
24 Ibid., pp. 301–4.
25 Ibid., pp. 318–21.
26 The reorganized structure of the Ministry of the Coal Industry is described in V. I. Valkovoi et al., *Osnovy ekonomiki i upravleniia ugolnym proizvodstvom*, Moscow: Nedra, 1976, pp. 47–68.
27 A detailed description of a territorial–branch union directly subordinate to a ministry is in V. Radchenko, *Ekonomika Sovetskoi Ukrainy*, no. 1 (1976): 32–7.
28 *Ekonomika i organizatsiia promyshlennogo proizvodstva*, no. 1 (1976): 96–100.
29 Ibid.
30 Herbert E. Meyer, "A Plant That Could Change the Shape of Soviet Industry," *Fortune*, vol. 40 (November 1974): 150–3.

31 B. Z. Milner, ed., *Organizatsionnye struktury upravleniia proizvodstvom,* Moscow: Ekonomika, 1975, pp. 284–305.
32 Ibid., p. 301.
33 Ibid., p. 305.
34 G. Arbatov, *Planovoe khoziaistvo,* no. 5 (1975): 24.
35 Milner, *Organizatsionnye struktury,* pp. 304–5.
36 K. Taksir and M. Krasnokutskii, *Voprosy ekonomiki,* no. 1 (1977): 47.
37 Arbatov, *Planovoe khoziaistvo,* no. 5 (1975): 27.
38 M. Kashirina, *Pravda,* June 10, 1979, p. 2.
39 N. E. Drogichinskii, *Sovershenstvovanie upravleniia proizvodstvom i sozdanie obedinenii,* Moscow: Znanie, 1976, p. 13.
40 See A. Nagovitsin, *Voprosy ekonomiki,* no. 10 (1977): 83–4.
41 Kashirina, *Pravda,* June 10, 1979, p. 2.
42 Nagovitsin, *Voprosy ekonomiki,* no. 10 (1977): 83–4.
43 V. Parfenov, *Pravda,* May 11, 1978, p. 2.
44 V. V. Dementsev, *Razvitie obedinenii i finansy,* Moscow: Finansy, 1976, pp. 37–8. Parfenov, *Pravda,* May 11, 1978, p. 2, however, cites a cut of only 2,140 men.
45 A. A. Timme, *Struktura i protsess upravleniia narodnym khoziaistvom,* Moscow: Znanie, 1976, p. 15; S. Tsimerman, *Sovetskoe gosudarstvo i pravo,* no. 2 (1975): 68–9.
46 Ibid. See also B. F. Bratchenko, *Ekonomicheskaia gazeta,* no. 8 (1974): 5.
47 Dementsev, *Razvitie,* pp. 34–5; see also Gorlin, "Industrial Reorganization," pp. 176–8.
48 M. Kashirina, *Voprosy ekonomiki,* no. 2 (1977): 50–1.
49 V. I. Maksimenko et al., *Ekonomika i organizatsiia promyshlennogo proizvodstva,* no. 2 (1977): 62.
50 Dementsev, *Razvitie,* pp. 39–40.
51 Ibid., p. 31.
52 Alice C. Gorlin, "The Soviet Economic Associations," *Soviet Studies,* vol. 26, no. 1 (1974): 9.
53 Dementsev, *Razvitie,* p. 21; M. Panova and S. Kozlov, *Ekonomicheskaia gazeta,* no. 52 (1977): 7.
54 Maksimenko et al., *Ekonomika i organizatsiia promyshlennogo proizvodstva,* no. 2 (1977): 62.
55 Panova and Kozlov, *Ekonomicheskaia gazeta,* no. 52 (1977): 7.
56 Dementsev, *Razvitie,* p. 25.
57 Maksimenko et al., *Ekonomika i organizatsiia promyshlennogo proizvodstva,* no. 2 (1977): 66.
58 S. A. Ordazhev, *Ekonomicheskaia gazeta,* no. 6 (1974): 7.
59 Drogichinskii, *Sovershenstvovanie,* p. 35.
60 Vishniakov, *Pravovedenie,* no. 4 (1975): 27.
61 M. Kashirina, *Voprosy ekonomiki,* no. 2 (1977): 51.
62 A. Nagovitsin, *Voprosy ekonomiki,* no. 10 (1977): 90.
63 Maksimenko et al., *Ekonomika i organizatsiia promyshlennogo proizvodstva,* no. 2 (1977): 67.

64 Iu. P. Lapshin, *Razvitie avtomatizirovannykh sistem upravleniia v pro-myshlennosti*, Moscow: Ekonomika, 1977, pp. 188–9.
65 Maksimenko et al., *Ekonomika i organizatsiia promyshlennogo proiz-vodstva*, no. 2 (1977).
66 B. Bratchenko, *Planovoe khoziaistvo*, no. 9 (1974): 15.
67 Tsimerman, *Sovetskoe gosudarstvo i pravo*, no. 2 (1975): 75.
68 Vishniakov, *Pravovedenie*, no. 4 (1975): 34.
69 V. Seliunin, *Sotsialisticheskaia industriia*, August 4, 1977, p. 2.
70 L. Rutman, *Sovetskoe gosudarstvo i pravo*, no. 9 (1976): 57–8.
71 Ibid., p. 56.
72 Tsimerman, *Sovetskoe gosudarstvo i pravo*, no. 2 (1975): 20–2.
73 I. O. Bisher, *Sovetskoe gosudarstvo i pravo*, no. 5 (1973): 30.
74 Rutman, *Sovetskoe gosudarstvo i pravo*, no. 9 (1976): 55.
75 M. Kashirina, *Pravda*, June 11, 1977, p. 2.
76 I. Sonin, *Sotsialisticheskaia industriia*, January 16, 1977, p. 2.
77 Kashirina, *Pravda*, June 11, 1977, p. 2.
78 F. Liner, *Sotsialisticheskaia industriia*, July 7, 1977, p. 2.
79 *Sotsialisticheskaia industriia*, April 13, 1977, p. 2.
80 B. Abramov, *Pravda*, January 22, 1978, p. 2.
81 Nagovitsin, *Voprosy ekonomiki*, no. 10 (1977): 85.
82 P. G. Bunich, *Upravlenie, ekonomicheskie rychagi, khozraschet*, Moscow: Nauka, 1976, p. 252.
83 Nagovitsin, *Voprosy ekonomiki*, no. 10 (1977): 91.
84 Kashirina, *Pravda*, June 11, 1977, p. 2.
85 S. P. Makarov and A. Z. Seleznev, *Razvitie obedinenii v promyshlen-nosti*, Moscow: Izdatelstvo Moskovskogo universiteta, 1976, pp. 165–6.
86 Kashirina, *Pravda*, June 11, 1977, p. 2.
87 Tsimerman, *Sovetskoe gosudarstvo i pravo*, no. 2 (1975): 70.
88 M. Pogostinskii, *Sotsialisticheskaia industriia*, August 19, 1977, p. 2.
89 Maksimenko et al., *Ekonomika i organizatsiia promyshlennogo proiz-vodstva*, no. 2 (1977): 66–7.
90 G. Iastrobstov, *Pravda*, December 5, 1976, p. 2.
91 N. I Antonov, in V. Abramov, comp. *Nauchnaia organizatsiia proiz-vodstva, truda i upravleniia*, Moscow: Moskovskii rabochii, 1974, pp. 317–19.
92 On the constraints on centralization within the union, see N. E. Drogichinskii, *Voprosy ekonomiki*, no. 4 (1974): 26–7.
93 Maksimenko et al., *Ekonomika i organizatsiia promyshlennogo proiz-vodstva*, no. 2 (1977).
94 G. Golovanov, *Pravda*, June 30, 1977, p. 3.
95 V. D. Stundiuk, *Obedineniia i upravlenie promyshlennostiu*, Moscow: Nauka, 1976, pp. 61–70.
96 A. Dolgopatov, *Sotsialisticheskaia industriia*, December 14, 1977, p. 2.
97 G. A. Dzhavadov, *Sovetskoe gosudarstvo i pravo*, no. 1 (1975): 27.
98 V. Pokrovskii, *Sotsialisticheskaia industriia*, July 13, 1977, p. 2.

99 K. I. Taksir, *Nauchno-proizvodstvennye obedineniia*, Moscow: Nauka, 1977, pp. 81-95. Cited hereafter as *NPO*.
100 Taksir, *NPO*, pp. 88-9.
101 Ibid., pp. 89-92.
102 Ibid., pp. 82, 93.
103 A. Orlov, *Sotsialisticheskaia industriia*, March 16, 1977, p. 2. See also M. Iudin, *Pravda*, January 5, 1975, p. 2.
104 G. A. Dzhavadov, *Sovetskoe gosudarstvo i pravo*, no. 1 (1975): 41.
105 Ibid., pp. 40-1; Taksir, *NPO*, p. 94.
106 M. Iudin, *Pravda*, January 5, 1975, p. 2; V. Pokrovskii, *Sotsialisticheskaia industriia*, July 13, 1977, p. 2.
107 B. Tabachnikas and M. Skliar, *Voprosy ekonomiki*, no. 12 (1976): 73; Taksir, *NPO*, pp. 96-7.
108 Orlov, *Sotsialisticheskaia industriia*, March 16, 1977, p. 2; Pokrovskii, *Sotsialisticheskaia industriia*, July 13, 1977, p. 2; Taksir, *NPO*, pp. 105-9.
109 Tabachnikas and Skliar, *Voprosy ekonomiki*, no. 12 (1976): 78-9.
110 K. Taksir, *Voprosy ekonomiki*, no. 11 (1972): 50.
111 V. Beliakov, *Ekonomicheskaia gazeta*, no. 52 (1975): 15.
112 M. Iudin, *Pravda*, January 5, 1975, p. 2.
113 G. Shein, *Sotsialisticheskaia industriia*, June 14, 1977, p. 2.
114 Taksir, *Voprosy ekonomiki*, no. 11 (1972): 48, 50.
115 Dzhavadov, *Sovetskoe gosudarstvo i pravo*, no. 1 (1975): 37.
116 An added complaint of the NPO is continuous interference by the ministry in its functions. The deputy general director of Soiuzgazavtomatika has noted that, although the union has formally delegated authority over developing and installing new technology, the technical administration of the ministry is in frequent direct contact with the designers and producers of new equipment. The capital construction administration also becomes directly involved in the supervision of the installation of new technology. This practice, in turn, seriously restricts the role of the union in its functions. V. Eliseev, *Sotsialisticheskaia industriia*, April 13, 1977, p. 2.
117 *Pravda*, March 14, 1977, p. 1.
118 V. G. Vishniakov, *Pravovedenie*, no. 4 (1975): 26; see also Kashirina, *Pravda*, June 10, 1979, p. 2.
119 N. G. Drogichinskii, *Planovoe khoziaistvo*, no. 5 (1975): 9.
120 Dementsev, *Razvitie*, pp. 45-6.
121 Vishniakov, *Pravovedenie*, no. 4 (1975): 34-5.
122 See Drogichinskii, *Planovoe khoziaistvo*, no. 5 (1975): 9; A. Odinets, *Ekonomicheskaia gazeta*, no. 35 (1974): 7; Kashirina, *Pravda*, June 11, 1977, p. 2; *Pravda*, May 23, 1975, p. 1.
123 *Izvestiia*, September 18, 1975, p. 2.
124 V. V. Laptev et al., eds., *Pravovye problemy rukovodstva i upravleniia otrasliu promyshlennosti v SSSR*, Moscow: Nauka, 1973, pp. 172-3.
125 *Ekonomicheskaia gazeta*, no. 22 (1976): 8.

126 Iu. Irasek, N. Oznobin et al., *Planirovanie razvitiia sistem upravleniia sotsialisticheskim proizvodstvom*, Moscow: Progress, 1976, p. 41.
127 N. Bratchenko, *Planovoe khoziaistvo*, no. 9 (1974): 7.
128 Makarov and Seleznev, *Razvitie*, p. 167.
129 Odinets, *Ekonomicheskaia gazeta*, no. 35 (1974): 7.
130 See *Pravda*, January 14, 1977, p. 2; *Sotsialisticheskaia industriia*, March 17, 1977, p. 2; G. Kiperman, *Sotsialisticheskaia industriia*, June 1, 1978, p. 2; N. Kernogo, *Sotsialisticheskaia industriia*, February 4, 1977, p. 2; V. Reva, *Pravda*, November 24, 1976, p. 2; and many others.
131 V. Parfenov, *Pravda*, May 11, 1978, p. 2.
132 N. Medvedev, *Planovoe khoziaistvo*, no. 10 (1976): 87–97. A summary is translated in *CDSP*, vol. 29, no. 1 (1977): 15.
133 *Izvestiia*, July 12, 1975, p. 2.
134 Medvedev, in *CDSP*, vol. 29, no. 1 (1977): 1.
135 Maksimenko et al., *Ekonomika i organizatsiia promyshlennogo proizvodstva*, no. 2 (1977): 67–8.
136 Ibid., pp. 68–70.
137 E. Vitsur, *Kommunist Estonii*, no. 11 (1975): 64–5.
138 M. Panova and S. Kozlov, *Ekonomicheskaia gazeta*, no. 52 (1977): 7.
139 V. V. Vasilev, *Sovetskoe gosudarstvo i pravo*, no. 4 (1977): 12; Tsimerman, *Sovetskoe gosudarstvo i pravo*, no. 2 (1975): 25–6.
140 V. V. Laptev, *Sovetskoe gosudarstvo i pravo*, no. 1 (1977): 30–1.
141 A. E. Lunev, *Sovetskoe gosudarstvo i pravo*, no. 11 (1976): 121–3; Tsimerman, *Sovetskoe gosudarstvo i pravo*, no. 2 (1975): 25–6.
142 G. Popov, *Pravda*, July 6, 1977, p. 3; V. S. Pronina, *Sovetskoe gosudarstvo i pravo*, no. 1 (1977): 30–6. Popov, in particular, stresses the urgent necessity of dealing with the problems of territorial management.
143 For an account of Latvia's experiment, see M. L. Raman, *Ekonomicheskaia gazeta*, no. 49 (1977): 8.
144 V. Disson, *Planovoe khoziaistvo*, no. 7 (1977): 82–3.
145 *Ekonomicheskaia gazeta*, no. 9 (1981): 11.
146 V. Romashkin, *Sotsialisticheskaia industriia*, August 26, 1977, p. 2.
147 K. Taksir and M. Krasnokutskii, *Voprosy ekonomiki*, no. 1 (1977): 49.
148 Ibid.
149 John Lowenhardt, "The Tale of Torch-Scientist Entrepreneurs in the Soviet Union," *Survey*, no. 4 (1974): 113–21.
150 Taksir and Krasnokutskii, *Voprosy ekonomiki*, no. 1 (1977): 49.

Afterword

1 V. V. Shcherbitskii, *Kommunist*, no. 6 (1973): 33.
2 I. I. Kuzminov, in I. I. Kuzminov and S. V. Rogachev, eds., *Politicheskaia ekonomika sotsializma: nauchnaia osnova rukovodstva narodnym khoziaistvom*, Moscow: Mysl, 1975, p. 7.

3 M. Volkov, *Kommunist*, no. 10 (1978): 69.
4 Ibid., pp. 69–70.
5 These measures have been in preparation for several years. They are announced in two decrees in which there are genuine differences of emphasis. The first is in a short decree of the Central Committee. The second decree, from which this description is taken, is contained in a joint Central Committee and Council of Ministers resolution. Both are published in *Kommunist*, no. 12 (1979): 3–4, 5–15.
6 On the "second economy," see Gregory Grossman, "Notes on the Illegal Private Economy and Corruption," in U.S., Congress, Joint Economic Committee, *Soviet Economy in a Time of Change*, 2 vols., Washington, D.C.: Government Printing Office, 1979, 1: 834–55.

Bibliography

Abdurakhmanov, S. A., Iu. P. Lapshin, and E. G. Iakobenko. *Avtomatizirovannye sistemy upravleniia narodnym khoziaistvom SSSR.* Moscow: Ekonomika, 1972.

Afanasev, V. G. *Nauchnoe upravlenie obshchestvom.* Moscow: Politizdat, 1968.

The Scientific and Technical Revolution: Its Impact on Management and Education. Translated by Robert Daglish. Moscow: Progress, 1975.

The Scientific Management of Society, trans. L. Ilyitskaia, Moscow: Progress, 1971.

Sotsialnaia informatsiia i upravlenie obshchestvom. Moscow: Politizdat, 1975.

, ed., *Problemy nauchnogo kommunizma.* 11 vols. Moscow: Mysl, 1966–76.

Afanasev, V. G. et al., eds. *Nauchnoe upravlenie obshchestvom.* 13 vols. Moscow: Mysl, 1967–80.

Upravlenie sotsialisticheskim proizvodstvom. Moscow: Ekonomika, 1978.

Aganbegian, A. G. et al. *Metodicheskie polozheniia optimalnogo otraslevogo planirovaniia v promyshlennosti,* 2nd ed. Novosibirsk: Siberian Division, Nauka, 1969.

Aganbegian, A. G., K. A. Bagrinovskii, and A. G. Granberg. *Sistema modelei narodno-khoziaistvennogo planirovaniia.* Moscow: Mysl, 1972.

Aganbegian, A. G. and D. M. Kazakievich, eds. *Optimalnoe territorialno-proizvodstvennoe planirovanie.* Novosibirsk: Siberian Division, Nauka, 1969.

Aitov, N. A. *Tekhnicheskii progress i dvizhenie rabochykh kadrov.* Moscow: Ekonomika, 1972.

Allakhverdian, D. A. *Finansovo-kreditnyi mekhanizm razvitogo sotsializma.* Moscow: Finansy, 1976.

Anthony, Robert N., John Dearden and Richard F. Vancil, eds. *Management Control Systems: Cases and Readings.* Homewood, Ill.: Irwin, 1965.

Antonsenkov, E. G. and V. D. Kalmyk, eds. *Otnoshenie k trude i tekuchest kadrov.* Novosibirsk: Siberian Division, Nauka, 1970.

Aunapu, F. F. *Metody podbora i podgotovki rukovoditelei proizvodstva.* Moscow: Ekonomika, 1971.

Azrael, Jeremy R. *Managerial Power and Soviet Politics.* Cambridge, Mass.: Harvard University Press, 1966.

Bandman, M. K., ed. *Modelirovanie formirovaniia territorialno-proizvodstvennykh kompleksov.* Novosibirsk: Siberian Division, Nauka, 1976.

Barskii, L. A. et al. *Ispolzovanie ekonomiko-matematicheskikh modelei v upravlenii i planirovanii v tsvetnoi metallurgii.* Moscow: Metallurgiia, 1975.

Bell, Daniel. *The Coming of Post-Industrial Society: A Venture in Social Forecasting.* New York: Basic Books, 1973.

Belousov, R. A. and Gerkhard Shultz, eds., *Teoreticheskie problemy upravleniia sotsialisticheskoi ekonomikoi.* Moscow: Mysl, 1974.

Berg, A. I., ed. *Cybernetics: The Science of Optimal Control.* Washington, D.C.: Joint Publications Research Service, 1968.

———, ed. *Organizatsiia i upravleniia.* Moscow: Nauka, 1968.

Berg, A. I. and Iu. I. Cherniak. *Informatsiia i upravlenie.* Moscow: Ekonomika, 1966.

Berliner, Joseph. *Factory and Manager in the USSR.* Cambridge, Mass.: Harvard University Press, 1957.

The Innovational Decision in Soviet Industry. Cambridge, Mass.: MIT Press, 1976.

Biriukov, B. V. *Kibernetika i metodologiia nauki.* Moscow: Nauka, 1974.

Birman, A. M. *Nekotorye problemy nauki ob upravlenii narodnym khoziaistvom.* Moscow: Ekonomika, 1965.

Birman, I. Ia., ed. *Optimalnyi plan otrasli.* Moscow: Ekonomika, 1970.

Blauberg, I. V. et al. *Sistemnye issledovaniia ezhegodnik.* Moscow: Nauka, 1973.

Bliakhman, L. S., B. G. Sochilin, and O. I. Skaratan. *Podbor i rasstanovka kadrov predpriiatii.* Moscow: Ekonomika, 1968.

Bliakhman, L. S., A. G. Zdravomyslov, and O. I. Skaratan. *Dvizhenie rabochei sily na promyshlennykh predpriiatiiakh.* Moscow: Ekonomika, 1965.

Bobryshev, D. N. *Organizatsiia upravleniia razrabotkami novoi tekhniki.* Moscow: Ekonomika, 1971.

Bondarenko, V. S. and V. V. Tolstosheev. *Glavnyi vychisliternyi tsentr otrasli.* Moscow: Znanie, 1976.

Brezhnev, L. I. *Ob osnovnykh voprosakh ekonomicheskoi politiki KPSS na sovremennom etape.* 2 vols. Moscow: Politizdat, 1975.

Bronnikov, Iu. N., comp. *Upravlenie sotsialisticheskoi ekonomikoi.* 2nd ed. Moscow: Moskovskii rabochii, 1975.

Bunich, P. G., ed. *Nauchnye osnovy i praktika khoziaistvennogo rascheta.* Moscow: Ekonomika, 1974.

Campbell, Robert W. *The Soviet-Type Economies: Performance and Evolution.* 3rd ed. Boston: Houghton Mifflin, 1974.

Central Statistical Administration USSR. *Itogi vsesoiuznoi perepisi naseleniia 1970 goda.* Moscow: Statistika, 1972.

Narodnoe khoziaistvo SSSR za 60 let. Moscow: Statistika, 1977.

Zhenshchiny v SSSR. Moscow: Statistika, 1975.

Chagin, B. A. *Ocherk istorii sotsiologicheskoi mysli v SSSR.* Leningrad: Nauka, 1971.

Cherkasov, G. N. and G. G. Zaitsev, eds. *Sotsiologiia i nauchnaia organizatsiia truda.* Leningrad: Lenizdat, 1973.

Chernenko, K. U. and M. S. Smirtiukov, eds. *Resheniia partii i pravitelstva po khoziaistvennym voprosam.* 11 vols. Moscow: Politizdat, 1964–77.

Cherniak, Iu. I. *Informatsiia i upravlenie.* Moscow: Nauka, 1974. *Prostota slozhnogo.* Moscow: Znanie, 1975.

Sistemnyi analiz i upravlenie ekonomikoi. Moscow: Ekonomika, 1975.

Cherniavskii, V. O. *Effektivnost proizvodstva i optimalnost planirovaniia,* Moscow: Ekonomika, 1973.

Churmanteeva, V. N. *SShA: podgotovka rukovodiashchego personela promyshlennykh korporatsii.* Moscow: Nauka, 1975.

Cocks, Paul, Robert V. Daniels, and Nancy Whittier Heer, eds. *The Dynamics of Soviet Politics.* Cambridge, Mass.: Harvard University Press, 1976.

Cohen, Stephen F. *Bukharin and the Bolshevik Revolution: A Political Biography, 1888–1838.* New York: Knopf, 1973.

Cohn, Stanley H. *Economic Development in the Soviet Union.* Lexington, Mass.: Heath, 1970.

Connor, Walter D. *Deviance in Soviet Society: Crime, Delinquency and Alcoholism.* New York: Columbia University Press, 1972.

Conyngham, William J. *Industrial Management in the Soviet Union.* Stanford, Cal.: Hoover Institution Press, 1973.

Danilov, L. M., ed. *Dvizhenie rabochikh kadrov v promyshlennosti.* Moscow: Statistika, 1973.

Danilov, L. M. and I. I. Matrozova, eds. *Problemy ispolzovaniia rabochei sily v usloviiakh nauchno-tekhnicheskoi revoliutsii.* Moscow: Ekonomika, 1973.

Davidovich, B. Ia. et al., *Metody prognozirovaniia spros.* Moscow: Ekonomika, 1972.

Deineko, O. A. *Kompleksnaia ratsionalizatsiia upravlencheskogo apparata.* Moscow: Ekonomika, 1972.

Metodologicheskie problemy nauki upravleniia proizvodstvom. Moscow: Nauka, 1970.

Deineko, O. A. et al., eds. *Problemy nauchnoi organizatsiia upravleniia sotsialisticheskoi promyshlennostiu* Moscow: Ekonomika, 1968.

Dobrov, G. M. et al. *Programmno-tselevoi metod upravleniia v nauke.* Moscow: Central Scientific Research Institute "Elektronika," 1974.

Drogichinskii, N. E., ed. *Sovershenstvovanie mekhanizma khoziaistvovaniia v usloviiakh razvitogo sotsializma.* Moscow: Ekonomika, 1975.

Drogichinskii, N. G. and V. G. Starodubrovskii, eds. *Osnovy i praktika khoziaistvennoi reformy v SSSR.* Moscow: Ekonomika, 1971.

Dunlop, John T. and N. P. Fedorenko, eds. *Planning and Markets:*

Modern Trends in Various Economic Systems. New York: McGraw-Hill, 1969.

Dzarasov, S. S., ed. *Planomernaia organizatsiia i upravlenie proizvodstvom.* Moscow: Izdatelstvo Moskovskogo universiteta, 1971.

Dzhavadov, G. A., ed. *Organizatsiia upravleniia.* Moscow: Ekonomika, 1971.

Egiazarian, G. A. *Materialnoe stimulirovanie rosta effektivnosti promyshlennogo proizvodstva.* Moscow: Mysl, 1976.

Ellman, Michael. *Planning Problems in the USSR: The Contribution of Mathematical Economics to Their Solution.* Cambridge University Press, 1973.

Soviet Planning Today: Proposals for an Optimally Functioning System. Cambridge University Press, 1971.

Evenko, I. *Sovershenstvovanie upravleniia khoziaistvom i vychislitelnaia tekhnika.* Moscow: Ekonomika, 1967.

Fallenbuchl, Zbigniew M., ed. *Economic Development in the Soviet Union and Eastern Europe.* vol. 2. New York: Praeger, 1976.

Fedorenko, N. P., ed. *Economic Development and Perspective Planning.* Trans. Jenny Warren. Moscow: Progress, 1975.

Issledovanie potokov ekonomicheskoi informatsii. Moscow: Nauka, 1968.

Kompleksnoe narodno-khoziaistvennoe planirovanie. Moscow: Ekonomika, 1974.

Optimal Functioning System for a Socialist Economy. Trans. Iurii Sdobnikov. Moscow: Progress, 1974.

Optimalnoe planirovanie i sovershenstvovanie upravleniia narodnym khoziaistvom. Moscow: Nauka, 1969.

Otraslevye avtomatizirovannye sistemy upravleniia. Moscow: Nauka, 1973.

Problemy planirovaniia i prognozirovaniia. Moscow: Nauka, 1974.

Sotsialisticheskie printsipy khnoziaistvovaniia i effektivnost obshchestvennogo proizvodstva. Moscow: Ekonomika, 1970.

Voprosy proektirovanniia otraslevykh avtomatizirovannykh sistem upravleniia. Moscow: Nauka, 1970.

Feiwel, George R. *The Soviet Quest for Economic Efficiency: Issues, Controversies and Reforms,* 1st and 2nd eds. New York: Praeger, 1967, 1972.

Fleron, Frederick J., Jr., ed. *Technology and Communist Culture: The Sociocultural Impact of Technology Under Socialism.* New York: Praeger, 1977.

Gershchenkron, Alexander. *Economic Backwardness in Historical Perspective.* Cambridge, Mass.: Harvard University Press, 1958.

Glezerman, G. E. and O. Reingold, eds. *Razvitoe sotsialisticheskoe obshchestvo: sushchnost, kriterii zrelosti, kritika revizionistikh kontseptsii.* Moscow: Mysl, 1975.

Glushkov, V. M. *Makroekonomicheskie modeli i printsipy postroeniia OGAS.* Moscow: Statistika, 1975.

Gordon, L. A. and E. V. Klopov. *Chelovek posle raboty.* Moscow: Nauka, 1972.

Graham, Loren R. *Science and Philosophy in the Soviet Union.* New York: Knopf, 1972.

Granick, David. *Managerial Comparisons of Four Developed Countries: France, Britain, United States and Russia.* Cambridge, Mass.: MIT Press, 1972.

Gregory, Paul R. and Robert S. Stuart. *Soviet Economic Structure and Performance.* New York: Harper & Row, 1974.

Grishkin, I. I. *Poniatie informatsii.* Moscow: Nauka, 1973.

Gvishiani, D. M. *Organizatsiia i upravlenie,* 2nd enlarged ed. Moscow: Nauka, 1972.

————,ed. *Organizatsiia upravleniia.* vol. 1. Moscow: VINITI, 1971.

Gvishiani, D. M. and S. E. Kamenitser, eds. *Problemy nauchnoi organizatsii upravleniia sotsialisticheskoi promyshlennostiu.* Moscow: Ekonomika, 1974.

Gvishiani, D. M. et al., eds. *Ocherki teorii upravleniia promyshlennym proizvodstvom.* Moscow: Ekonomika, 1968.

Voprosy teorii i praktiki upravleniia i organizatsii nauki. Moscow: Nauka, 1975.

Hardt, John P. et al., eds. *Mathematics and Computers in Soviet Planning.* New Haven: Yale University Press, 1967.

Herring, C. D., ed. *Marxism, Communism and Western Society: A Comparative Encyclopedia.* 8 vols. New York: Herder and Herder, 1972–3.

Hollander, Paul. *Soviet and American Society: A Comparison.* New York: Oxford University Press, 1973.

Hough, Jerry F. *The Soviet Prefects: The Local Party Organs in Industrial Decision-making.* Cambridge, Mass.: Harvard University Press, 1969.

Hutchings, Raymond. *Soviet Economic Development.* Oxford: Basil Blackwell, 1971.

Iadov, V. A. and V. I. Dobrinin, comps. *Molodezh i trud.* Moscow: Molodaia gvardiia, 1970.

Iampolskaia, S. M., ed. *Ekonomicheskaia nauka i khoziaistvennaia reforma.* Kiev: Naukova dumka, 1970.

Inkov, Iu. I. *SSha: Informatsionnye sistemy v promyshlennykh firmakh.* Moscow: Nauka, 1976.

Irasek, Iu. et al. *Planirovanie razvitiia sistem upravleniia sotsialisticheskim proizvodstvom.* Moscow: Progress, 1976.

Iusupov, V. A. and N. A. Volkov. *Nauchnye osnovy gosudarstvennogo upravleniia v SSSR.* Kazan: Izdatelstvo Kazanskogo universiteta, 1972.

Ivanchenko, V. M. *Metodologiia narodnogo khoziaistvennogo planirovaniia.* Moscow: Ekonomika, 1975.

Ivanov, A. T. *Nastavnik – aktivnyi vospitatel molodezhi.* Moscow: Politizdat, 1976.

Ivanova, M. A. and I. A. Samarina. *Tekhnicheskii progress i struktura ITR i sluzhashchikh.* Moscow: Ekonomika, 1970.

Kahan, Arcadius and Blair A. Ruble, eds. *Industrial Labor in the USSR.* New York: Pergamon Press, 1979.

Kaidalov, D. P. and E. I. Suimenko. *Aktualnye problemy sotsiologii truda.* Moscow: Ekonomika, 1974.

Kalinin, N. G., ed. *Organizatsiia upravleniia v sisteme ministerstva.* Moscow: Izdatelstvo Moskovskogo universiteta, 1974.

Kalita, N. G. and G. I. Mantsurov. *Sotsialisticheskie proizvodstvennye obedineniia.* Moscow: Ekonomika, 1972.

Kamenitser, S. E. *Osnovyi upravleniia promyshlennym proizvodstvom.* Moscow: Mysl, 1971.

Kantorovich, L. V. *Essays in Optimal Planning.* Intro. Leon Smolinski. New York: International Arts and Sciences Press, 1976.

Matematicheskie metody v organizatsii i planirovanii proizvodstvom, Leningrad: Izdatelstvo Leningradskogo universiteta, 1939.

and A. B. Gorstko. *Optimalnye resheniia v ekonomike.* Moscow: Nauka, 1972.

Karpov, P. P. *Raspredelenie sredstv proizvodstva v novykh usloviakh khoziaistvovaniia.* Moscow: Ekonomika, 1972.

Katzen, Harry, Jr. *Computer Data Security.* New York: Van Nostrand Reinhold, 1973.

Kedrov, B. M., ed. *Nauchno-tekhnicheskaia revoliutsiia i sotsializma.* Moscow: Politizdat, 1973.

Kerimov, D. A. et al. *Planirovanie sotsialnogo razvitiia kollektiva predpriiatiia.* 2nd ed. Moscow: Profizdat, 1975.

Planirovanie sotsialnogo razvitiia. Moscow: Mysl, 1976.

Khachaturov, T. S. *Sovetskaia ekonomika na sovremennom etape.* Moscow: Mysl, 1975.

Kharchev, A. G. and S. I. Golod. *Professionalnaia rabota zhenshchin i semiia.* Leningrad: Nauka, 1971.

Khrutskii, E. A. *Sovershenstvovanie upravleniia materialno-tekhnicheskim proizvodstvom.* Moscow: Znanie, 1974.

Kirichenko, V. N. *Dolgosrochnyi plan razvitiia narodnogo khoziaistva SSSR.* Moscow: Ekonomika, 1974.

Klimenko, L. V. *Otraslevaia avtomatizirovannaia sistema upravleniia priborstroitelnoi promyshlennostiu – ASU–Pribor.* Moscow: Znanie, 1974.

Klimenko, V. P., A. I. Lutsenko and L. A. Savchenko. *Avtomatizirovannaia sistema gosudarstvennoi statistiki.* Moscow: Znanie, 1976.

Klinskii, A. I. *Planirovanie ekonomicheskogo i sotsialnogo razvitiia.* Moscow: Mysl, 1974.

Kobrinskii, N. E., E. S. Maiminas and A. D. Smirnov. *Vvedenie v ekonomicheskuiu kibernetiku.* Moscow: Ekonomika, 1975.

Kossov, V. V. *Mezhotraslevye modelie.* Moscow: Ekonomika, 1973.

Kosygin, A. N. *Izbrannye rechi i stati.* Moscow: Politizdat, 1974.

Kotliiar, A. E. and S. Ia. Turchaninova. *Zaniatost zhenshchin v proizvodstve.* Moscow: Statistika, 1975.

Kotov, F. I. *Organizatsiia planirovaniia narodnogo khoziaistva SSSR.* Moscow: Ekonomika, 1974.

Koval, N. S., ed. *Planirovanie narodnogo khoziaistva SSSR.* 3rd ed. Moscow: Vysshaia shkola, 1973.

Kozikov, I. A. *Problemy sootnosheniia nauchnotechnicheskoi i sotsialnoi revoliutsii.* Moscow: Izdatelstvo Moskovskogo universiteta, 1972.

Kozlov, Iu. M. *Upravlenie narodnym khoziaistvom SSSR.* 2 vols. Moscow: Izdatelstvo Moskovskogo universiteta, 1971.

Kutnetsov, K. K. and P. I. Rapoport. *Setevye metody planirovaniia i upravleniia v ugolnoi promyshlennosti.* Moscow: Nedra, 1975.

Kuzmin, E. S. and A. A. Bodalev, eds. *Sotsialnaia psikhologiia i sotsialnoe planirovanie.* Leningrad: Izdatelstvo Leningradskogo universiteta, 1973.

Kuzmin, E. S., I. P. Volkov and Iu. N. Emelianov. *Rukovoditelei i kollektiv.* Leningrad: Lenizdat, 1974.

Kuzminov, I. I. and S. V. Rogachev, eds. *Politicheskaia ekonomika sotsializma: nauchnaia osnova rukovodstva narodnym khoziaistvom.* Moscow: Mysl, 1975.

Lange, Oskar. *Introduction to Econometrics.* 2nd enl. ed. New York: Macmillan, 1963.

Lapshin, Iu. P. *Razvitie avtomatizirovannykh sistem upravleniia v promyshlennosti.* Moscow: Ekonomika, 1977.

Laptev, V. V. et al. *Pravovye problemy rukovodstva i upravleniia otrasliu promyshlennosti v SSSR.* Moscow: Nauka, 1973.

Larionov, A. M., ed. *Sistema matematicheskogo obespecheniia ES EVM.* Moscow: Statistika, 1974.

Lavigne, Marie. *The Socialist Economies of the Soviet Union and Eastern Europe.* Trans. T. G. Waywell. White Plains, N.Y.: International Arts and Sciences Press, 1974.

Lenin, V. I. *Collected Works.* 4th ed. 45 vols. Moscow: Foreign Languages Publishing House, 1960–70.

Selected Works. New York: International, 1971.

Leontiev, L. A. *Ekonomicheskie problemy razvitogo sotsializma.* Moscow: Nauka, 1972.

Levin, B. D. and M. N. Perfilov. *Kadry apparata upravleniia v SSSR.* Leningrad: Nauka, 1970.

Lewin, Moshe. *Political Undercurrents in Soviet Economic Debates: From Bukharin to the Modern Reformers.* Princeton, N.J.: Princeton University Press, 1974.

Liberman, E. G. *Ekonomicheskie metody povysheniia effektivnosti obshchestvennogo proizvodstva.* Moscow: Ekonomika, 1970.

Livshits, Ia. Z. *Dokumentatsionnoe obespechenie upravleniia.* Moscow: Znanie, 1975.

Loos, V. G. *Promyshlennaia psikhologiia.* Kiev. Tekhnika, 1974.

Loskutov, V. I. *Avtomatizirovannye sistemy upravleniia.* Moscow: Statistika, 1972.

Lunev, A. E., ed. *Organizatsiia raboty ministerstv v usloviiakh ekonomicheskoi reformy.* Moscow: Nauka, 1972.

Lunev, A. E., M. I. Piskotin and Ts. A. Iampolskaia, eds. *Nauchnye osnovy gosudarstvennogo upravleniia v SSSR.* Moscow: Nauka, 1968.

Maiminas, E. Z. *Protsessy planirovaniia v ekonomike: informatsionnyi aspekt.* 2nd ed. Moscow: Ekonomika, 1971.

318   Bibliography

Maizenberg, L. I. *Problemy tsenoobrazovaniia v razvitom sotsialisticheskom obshchestve.* Moscow: Ekonomika, 1976.

Maksimov, A. L. *Premirovanie rabochikh SSSR v usloviiakh khoziaistvennoi reformy.* Moscow: Nauka, 1971.

Mamutov, I. S. *Inzhener: sotsiologo-ekonomicheskii ocherk.* Moscow: Sovetskaia Rossiia, 1973.

Manevich, V. E. *Razvitie teorii planovogo tsenoobrazovaniia v sovetskoi ekonomicheskoi literature.* Moscow: Nauka, 1975.

Mangutov, I. S. and L. I. Umanskii. *Organizator i organizatorskaia deiatelnost.* Leningrad: Lenizdat, 1975.

Manokhin, V. M. *Gosudarstvennaia ditsiplina v narodnom khoziaistve.* Moscow: Iuridicheskaia literatura, 1970.

Marczewski, Jan. *Crisis in Soviet Planning: Eastern Europe and the USSR.* New York: Praeger, 1974.

Matthews, Mervyn. *Class and Society in Soviet Russia.* New York: Walker, 1972.

McGregor, Douglas. *The Human Side of Enterprise.* New York: McGraw–Hill, 1960.

Melkumov, L. G. et al., eds. *Avtomatizirovannye sistemy planirovaniia i upravleniia v ugolnoi promyshlennosti.* Moscow: Nedra, 1971.

Meyer, Monique. *L'Entreprise industrielle d'état en Union sovietique.* Paris: Cujas, 1967.

Midtsev, V. V. et al., eds. *Sovremennyi pravyi revizionizm.* Moscow: Mysl, 1973.

Mikhaliuk, V. B. *Ispolzovanie zhenskogo truda v narodnom khoziaistve.* Moscow: Ekonomika, 1970.

Milner, B. Z. *Problemy upravleniia v sovremennoi Amerike.* Moscow: Znanie, 1974.

———, ed. *Organizatsionnye struktury upravleniia proizvodstvom.* Moscow: Ekonomika, 1975.

SShA: organizatsionnye formy i metody upravleniia promyshlennymi korporatsiiami. Moscow: Nauka, 1972.

SShA: sovremennye metody upravleniia. Moscow: Nauka, 1971.

Mitrofanov, V. *Kontrol i reviziia khoziaistvennoi deiatelnosti promyshlennykh predpriiatii.* Moscow: Finansy, 1965.

Mogilev, A. I., ed. *Nauchno-tekhnicheskaia revoliutsiia i sotsialnyi progress.* Moscow: Politizdat, 1972.

Moiseev, A. V. et al. *Sotsialno-ekonomicheskie problemy truda molodezhi.* Moscow: Higher Komsomol School, 1974.

Mordzhinskaia, E. D. and Ts. A. Stepanian. *Budushchee cheloveskogo obshchestva.* Moscow: Mysl, 1971.

Moskvichev, S. G. *Problemy motivatsii v psikhologicheskikh issledovaniiakh.* Kiev: Naukova dumka, 1975.

Muksinov, I. Sh. *Sovet ministrov soiuznoi respubliki.* Moscow: Iuridicheskaia literatura, 1969.

Nemchenko, V. S. et al. *Professionalnaia adaptatsiia molodezhi.* Moscow: Izdatelstvo Moskovskogo universiteta, 1974.

Nove, Alec. *An Economic History of the U.S.S.R.* London: Penguin Press (Allen Lane), 1969.

The Soviet Economy: An Introduction. 2nd ed. rev. New York: Praeger, 1969.

Novgorodskii, Iu. F. et al. *Tekhnicheskii progress: sovershentsvovanie podgotovki kadrov.* Moscow: Ekonomika, 1973.

Omarev, A. M., ed. *Nauchnye osnovy upravleniia sotsialisticheskoi ekonomikoi.* Moscow: Nauka, 1972.

Voprosy upravleniia ekonomikoi. Moscow: Izdatelstvo politicheskoi literatury, 1974.

Paniukov, V. S. *Ustoichnost kadrov v promyshlennosti.* Kiev: Naukova dumka, 1976.

Parygin, B. D. *Osnovy sotsialno-psikhologicheskoi teorii.* Moscow: Mysl, 1971.

Pashkov, A. S. et al., eds. *Chelovek i obshchestvo.* 15 vols. Leningrad: Izdatelstvo Leningradskogo universiteta, 1966-76.

Pashkov, A. S. and M. N. Mezhevich, eds. *Problemy sotsialnogo planirovaniia v gorode i regione.* Leningrad: Izdatelstvo Leningradskogo universiteta, 1976.

Pavliuchenko, V. I. *Ekonomicheskie problemy upravleniia nauchnotekhnicheskim progressom.* Moscow: Nauka, 1973.

Petrakov, N. Ia. *Khoziaistvennaia reforma: plan i ekonomicheskaia samostoiatelnost.* Moscow: Mysl, 1971.

Kiberneticheskie problemy upravleniia ekonomikoi. Moscow: Nauka, 1974.

Petrov, G. I. *Sovetskoe administrativnoe pravo - chast obshchaia.* Leningrad: Izdatelstvo Leningradskogo universiteta, 1970.

Petrovskii, S. O. and G. M. Pyzhik. *Nauchnaia organizatsiia proizvodstva.* Moscow: Ekonomika, 1971.

Pfeffer, Jeffrey. *Organizational Design.* Arlington Hts., Ill.: AHM, 1978.

Podmarkov, V. G. *Vvedenie v promyshlennuiu sotsiologiiu.* Moscow: Mysl, 1973.

Popov, G. Kh. *Tekhnika lichnoi raboty.* 3rd ed. Moscow: Moskovskii rabochii, 1971.

, ed. *Funktsii i struktura organov upravleniia, ikh sovershenstvovanie.* Moscow: Ekonomika, 1973.

Metody upravleniia sotsialisticheskim proizvodstvom. Moscow: Ekonomika, 1971.

Otsenka rabotnikov upravleniia. Moscow: Moskovskii rabochii, 1976.

Problemy teorii upravleniia. 1st and 2nd eds. Moscow: Ekonomika, 1970, 1974.

Sovershenstvovanie sistemy vnutrifirmennogo upravleniia. Moscow: Izdatelstvo Moskovskogo gosudarstvennogo universiteta, 1972.

Popov, G. Kh. and G. A. Dzhavadov, eds. *Upravlenie i problema kadrov.* Moscow: Ekonomika, 1972.

Popova, I. M., ed. *Problemy sotsialnogo regulirovaniia na promyshlennykh predpriiatiiakh.* Kiev: Naukova dumka, 1973.

Prigozhin, A. I. *Sotsiologicheskie aspekty upravleniia.* Moscow: Znanie, 1974.

Prokurov, V. S. *Informatsiia v ASPR.* Moscow: Ekonomika, 1975.

Pronin, I. I. *Rukovodiashchie kadry: podbor i vospitanie.* Moscow: Mysl, 1971.

320   *Bibliography*

Pupola, L. A. *Sovershenstvovanie khozrascheta: put povysheniia ekonomiche-skoi effektivnosti proizvodstva.* Riga: Zinatne, 1976.

Rakitinskii, B. V. *Formy khoziaistvennogo rukovodstva predpriiatiiami.* Moscow: Nauka, 1968.

Remnek, Richard B., ed. *Social Scientists and Policy Making in the USSR.* New York: Praeger, 1977.

Remnev, V. I. *Problemy NOT v apparate upravleniia.* Moscow: Nauka, 1973.

Richman, Barry. *Management Development and Education in the Soviet Union.* East Lansing: Michigan State University Press, 1967.

Soviet Management. Englewood Cliffs, N.J.: Prentice-Hall, 1965.

Rubin, A. M. *Organizatsiia upravleniia promyshlennostiu v SSSR, 1917-1967.* Moscow: Ekonomika, 1969.

Ruchka, A. A. *Sotsialnye tsennosti i normy.* Kiev: Naukova dumka, 1976.

Rutkevich, M. N. and F. R. Fillipov. *Sotsialnye peremeshcheniia.* Moscow: Mysl, 1970.

Ryavec, Karl W. *Implementation of the Soviet Economic Reforms: Political, Organizational and Social Processes.* New York: Praeger, 1975.

Selisheva, L. A. et al., eds. *Nauchnye osnovy i praktika khoziaistvennogo rascheta.* Moscow: Ekonomika, 1974.

Semenov, A. K. *Metody sistemnogo analiza struktury narodnogo khoziaistva.* Moscow: Ekonomika, 1974.

XXIV Sezd Kommunisticheskoi partii Sovetskogo soiuza. Stenograficheskii otchet. 2 vols. Moscow: Politizdat, 1971.

XXV Sezd Kommunisticheskoi partii Sovetskogo soiuza. Stenograficheskii otchet. 3 vols. Moscow: Politizdat, 1976.

Shokin, A. A. *Pravovoe polozhenie promyshlennykh obedinenii v SSSR.* Kazan: Izdatelstvo Kazanskogo universiteta, 1972.

Shorin, V. G., G. Kh. Popov and G. D. Goriachev. *Stil raboty rukovoditelia.* Moscow: Znanie, 1976.

Shorokhova, E. V. and M. I. Bobneva, eds. *Psikhologicheskie problemy sotsialnoi reguliatsii povedeniia.* Moscow: Nauka, 1976.

Silberston, Aubrey and Francis Seton, eds. *Industrial Management: East and West.* New York: Praeger, 1973.

Silverman, David. *The Theory of Organizations: A Sociological Framework.* New York: Basic Books, 1971.

Simon, H. A. *The Shape of Automation for Men and Management.* New York: Harper & Row, 1965.

Skilling, H. Gordon and Franklyn Griffiths, eds. *Interest Groups in Soviet Politics.* Princeton, N.J.: Princeton University Press, 1971.

Sokhan, L. V. and K. K. Grishchenko, eds. *Sotsialnye problemy ASU.* Kiev: Naukova dumka, 1976.

Sokhan, L. V. and V. A. Tikhonovich. *Nauchno-tekhnicheskaia revoliutsiia: lichnost, deiatelnost, kollektiv.* Kiev: Naukova dumka, 1975.

Stefanov, N., N. Iakhiel and S. Kauchaunov, *Upravlenie, modelirovanie, prognozirovanie.* Moscow: Ekonomika, 1972.

Sukhov, A. N. *Kontrol i obespechenie dostovernosti informatsii v ASU.* Moscow: Znanie, 1977.

Syroezhin, I. M. *Ocherki teorii proizvodstvennykh organizatsii.* Moscow: Ekonomika, 1970.

Sztempka, Piotr. *System and Function: Toward a Theory of Society.* New York: Academic Press, 1974.

Thompson, James D. *Organizations in Action: Social Science Bases of Administrative Theory.* New York: McGraw–Hill, 1967.

Thompson, Victor A. *Modern Organizations.* New York: Knopf, 1961.

Tikhomirov, Iu. *Vlast i upravlenie v sotsialisticheskom obshchestve.* Moscow: Iuridicheskaia literatura, 1968.

Tikhomirov, Iu. A., ed. *Problemy effektivnosti raboty upravlencheskikh organov.* Moscow: Nauka, 1973.

Tikhomirov, Iu. A. and V. P. Kazimirchuk, eds. *Pravo i sotsiologiia.* Moscow: Nauka, 1973.

Tikhomirov, O. K., ed. *Chelovek i EVM.* Moscow: Ekonomika, 1973.

Timme, A. A. *Struktura i protsess upravleniia narodnym khoziaistvom.* Moscow: Znanie, 1975.

Tokes, Rudolf L., ed. *Dissent in the USSR: Politics, Ideology and People.* Baltimore: Johns Hopkins University Press, 1975.

Trainov, V. A. *Avtomatizatsiia upravleniia (ekonomiko-organizatsionnye voprosy).* Moscow: Znanie, 1977.

Treml, Vladimir G. *Input–Output Analysis and the Soviet Economy: An Annotated Bibliography.* New York: Praeger, 1975.

et al. *The Structure of the Soviet Economy: Analysis and Reconstruction of the 1966 Input–Output Table.* New York: Praeger, 1972.

Treml, Vladimir G. and John P. Hardt, eds. *Soviet Economic Statistics.* Durham, N.C.: Duke University Press, 1972.

Turn, R. and A. E. Nimitz. *Computers and Strategic Advantage: I. Computer Technology in the United States and the Soviet Union.* R-1642-PR. Santa Monica, Cal.: Rand, 1975.

Turovtsev, V. I., ed., *Gosudarstvennyi i obshchestvennyi kontrol v SSSR.* Moscow: Nauka, 1970.

Narodnyi kontrol v sotsialisticheskom obshchestve. Moscow: Izdatelstvo politicheskoi literatury, 1974.

UNESCO. *The Social Sciences: Problems and Orientations.* The Hague: Mouton, 1968.

U.S. Congress. Joint Economic Committee. *Soviet Economic Prospects for the Seventies.* Washington, D.C.: Government Printing Office, 1973.

Soviet Economy in a New Perspective. Washington, D.C.: Government Printing Office, 1976.

Soviet Economy in a Time of Change. 2 vols. Washington, D.C.: Government Printing Office, 1979.

Ursul, A. D. *Informatsiia.* Moscow: Nauka, 1971.

Utechin, S. V. *Russian Political Thought.* New York: Praeger, 1963.

Valentei, D. I., ed. *Narodnaseleniia.* Moscow: Statistika, 1973.

Vasileva, E. K. *The Young People of Leningrad: School and Work, Options and Attitudes.* Intro. Richard B. Dobson. White Plains, N.Y.: International Arts and Sciences Press, 1976.

Veduta,N. I. *Ekonomicheskaia kibernetika.* Minsk: Nauka i tekhnika,1971.

322   Bibliography

Vendrov, E. E. *Psikhologicheskie problemy upravleniia*. Moscow: Ekonomika, 1969.
Vishniakov, V. G. *Dvoinoe podchinenie organov upravleniia narodnym khoziaistvom*. Moscow: Iuridicheskaia literatura, 1967.
Vlasov, V. A. *Sovetskii gosudarstvennyi apparat*. Moscow: Gosudarstvennoe izdatelstvo iuridicheskoi literatury, 1959.
Volchkov, B. A. *Avtomatizirovannaia sistema planovykh raschetov*. Moscow: Ekonomika, 1970.
Volkov, Iu. E. and Iu. S. Loshkurov. *Trudovoe vospitanie molodezhi*. Moscow: Politizdat, 1976.
Volkov, N. A. *Vysshie i tsentralnye organy gosudarstvennogo upravleniia v SSSR*. Kazan: Izdatelstvo Kazanskogo universiteta, 1971.
Vselovskii, V. and M. N. Rutkevich, eds. *Problemy razvitiia sotsialnoi struktury obshchestva v Sovetskom soiuze i Polshe*. Moscow: Nauka, 1976.
Wilczynski, Josef. *Soviet Economic Development and Reforms: From Extensive to Intensive Growth Under Central Planning in the USSR, Eastern Europe and Yugoslavia*. London: Macmillan, 1972.
Yanowitch, Murray and Wesley A. Fisher, eds. and trans. *Social Stratification and Mobility in the USSR*. White Plains, N.Y.: International Arts and Sciences Press, 1973.
Zaitsev, N. G. *Matematicheskoe obespechenie avtomatizirovannykh sistem upravleniia*. Moscow: Znanie, 1974.
Zaleski, Eugene. *Planning Reforms in the Soviet Union, 1962-1966*. Trans. Marie-Christine McAndrew and Warren Nutter. Chapel Hill: University of North Carolina Press, 1967.
Zauberman, Alfred. *Differential Games and Other Game Theoretic Topics in Soviet Literature: A Survey*. New York: New York University Press, 1975.
———. *The Mathematical Revolution in Soviet Economics*. New York: Oxford University Press, 1975.
Zavialova, A. N., ed. *Upravlenie sotsialisticheskim proizvodstvom*. Moscow: Ekonomika, 1968.
Zdravomyslov, A. G., V. P. Rozhin and V. A. Iadov. *Man and His Work*. Trans. Stephen P. Dunn. White Plains, N.Y.: International Arts and Sciences Press, 1970.
Zhimerin, D. G. *Obshchegosudarstvennaia avtomatizirovannaia sistema upravleniia*. Moscow: Znanie, 1975.
Zhimerin, D. G. and A. P. Vladislavlev, eds. *Avtomatizirovannye sistemy upravleniia*. Moscow: Ekonomika, 1976.
Zvorykin, A. A. and A. M. Geliuta. *Sotsialnye problemy truda i proizvodstva*. Moscow: Mysl, 1969. Trans. Michael Vale. In *Soviet Review*, no. 4 (1974-5).

Index

Academy of the National Economy, 50

Academy of Sciences, 49, 198
see individual institutes

administrative methods of management
see behavioral methods of management, classical models of management, cybernetics, management theory

Afanasev, V. G.
and cybernetic model of management, 64–5

All-Union Institute of Cybernetics, 50

All-State System for Collection and Processing of Information for Reporting, Planning and Management of the National Economy
see OGAS

Arbatov, G., 246

ASGS (Automated System of State Statistics), 125, 179
see also ASU, OGAS, Central Statistical Administration

Ashby, W. Ross, 53, 59

ASOItsen (Automated System for Processing Price Information), 132
and model-based pricing, 139
structure and functions of, 106
see also ASU, economic models, economic reforms, OGAS, SOFE, State Price Committee

ASPR (Automated System for Plan Calculations), 71, 82, 105, 179, 180
applications in planning, 124–5, 180
and centralization, 180
integration with other ASUs, 179
and multibranch projects, 180
"psychological barriers" toward, 128–9
structure of, 106
see also ASU, CEMI, Fedorenko, OGAS, SOFE, State Planning Committee

ASU (Automated Systems of Management), 132, 175, 211
assessment of designs of, 116–7
and centralization, 177–9, 181, 185–6, 188
and computer centers, 185–6
defined, 103–4
as man–machine decision-making system, 103–4, 184–5
problems of installation and service, 120
"psychological barriers" to use of, 128–9, 183
rationalization of information in, 115, 187
see also CEMI, computers, cybernetics, economic models, Fedorenko, Glushkov, OGAS, SOFE, STR

ASU-MTS (Automated Systems for Management of Material-Technical Supply)

323